CRISIS AMID PLENTY

A RAND CORPORATION RESEARCH STUDY

CRISIS AMID PLENTY

THE POLITICS OF SOVIET ENERGY UNDER BREZHNEV AND GORBACHEV

THANE GUSTAFSON

PRINCETON UNIVERSITY PRESS
PRINCETON, NEW JERSEY

Published by Princeton University Press, 41 William Street,
Princeton, New Jersey 08540
In the United Kingdom: Princeton University Press,
Oxford

Library of Congress Cataloging-in-Publication Data

Gustafson, Thane.
Crisis among plenty : the politics of Soviet energy under
Brezhnev and Gorbachev / Thane Gustafson.
p. cm.—(A Rand Corporation research study)
Includes index.
ISBN 0-691-07835-1 (alk. paper)
1. Energy policy—Soviet Union. 2. Petroleum industry and trade—
Government policy—Soviet Union. 3. Gas industry—Government
policy—Soviet Union. I. Title. II. Series.
HD9502.S652G87 1989
333.79'15'094709048—dc20 89-31519
ISBN 0-691-07835-1

This book has been composed in Linotron Galliard

Clothbound editions of Princeton University Press books are
printed on acid-free paper, and binding materials are chosen for
strength and durability. Paperbacks,
although satisfactory for personal collections,
are not usually suitable for library rebinding

Printed in the United States of America by
Princeton University Press
Princeton, New Jersey

This book is dedicated to
Carolyn *and* Nil
with love

CONTENTS

MAPS AND FIGURES

Maps

Figures

TABLES

PREFACE

There are still remarkably few case studies of Soviet policymaking in the Western literature. It is certainly not for lack of information. Since the 1960s Western sovietologists have been increasingly flooded with information about Soviet policy issues, debates, and disputes, and the advent of *glasnost'* in the mid-1980s is now generating a tidal wave. Moreover, political scientists can draw on the excellent work of Western economists, demographers, and geographers, who have led the way in exploring many a topic of political interest.

The political scientist's attention naturally focuses first on the core of the Soviet system of power—the KGB, the Soviet General Staff, and the Politburo—and in these areas, despite some improvements, *glasnost'* has yet to penetrate very far. Most books on Soviet politics under Gorbachev are based on essentially the same methods employed thirty-five years ago: close analysis of leaders' speeches, exegesis of official and semiofficial texts, and tracking of personnel movements—all with one ear to the Moscow grapevine. When we study the Kremlin, we will always have to use kremlinology.

But outside these walled topics is a world of politics and policymaking which is much more open. That is the world of economic and social policy, and studying it will repay the political analyst handsomely. In the Soviet-style command economy, in which politicians are responsible in principle for every sparrow that falls, it is economic and social policy that takes most of the leaders' time and energy. These subjects reveal as much of the leaders' fundamental aims and strategies, and their political culture and resources, as the veiled topics of conventional "high" politics, perhaps even more so. (Indeed, if we had paid more attention to Soviet debates on social and economic policy during the decade before Gorbachev's accession, we would have been less surprised by *perestroika* and better able to follow its evolution.) For social and economic policy, there is a wealth of information available about how decisions are made, the roles of institutions and specialists, the ways political agendas are formed, the place of conflict and learning, the formation and use of power and influence—in short, all the classic themes of politics. Some may argue that in the more secret realms of politics things somehow work differently; but the more we learn about Soviet politics at every level, the more we see its essential unity.

The greater abundance of information available about social and economic policy makes it possible to distinguish between rhetoric and reality, which kremlinology cannot. Speeches and decrees are necessarily mixed messages, part strategy and part tactics, half program and half wish-list. It is essential to get beneath this level to the genesis, implementation, and outcomes of policy, in order to determine who actually wins and loses, who "gets what, when, and how." Indeed, as *glasnost'* brings us more Soviet statistics, more case material, and more sophisticated analysis from the Soviets themselves, we will be under a growing challenge to raise our own standards of analysis. Kremlinology was always a creaky second-best technique; in the future, as the closed topics become more open and the open topics become more important, it will hardly suffice at all.

This book is not offered, however, with the pretension of being an example. *Glasnost'* has yet to transform the study of energy policy, at least where statistical information is concerned. As Joseph Berliner once observed, sovietologists have traditionally been obliged to expend so much effort in the "intelligence" function of piecing together the story that they frequently have had little strength left to weigh its meaning, and I am all too conscious that this book is a case in point.

BECAUSE investment patterns are emphasized throughout the book, a note of explanation will be helpful. There is no faster road to the bottle than the study of Soviet investment statistics. Different organizations use different definitions and different price bases at different times. The reader will soon find that I have been forced to use several sorts of series, and they are not consistent. There are three main ones.

First, in analyzing the overall burden of energy investment versus industrial investment in Chapter 2, I have used the series published in the annual Soviet statistical handbook, *Narodnoe khoziaistvo SSSR*, under the section "kapital'noe stroitel'stvo" (capital construction). This series excludes investment in energy transmission and a portion of exploration, and therefore it substantially understates the actual burden of energy investment. (For further details, see table 2.1 and the accompanying note.)

Second, in discussing oil and gas investment individually, I have attempted to use series that do include transmission and exploration, but these raise two serious problems. The greatest single difficulty is that in 1982 a new price base was adopted, and since about 1984 oil and gas investment has been reported in post-1982 prices. But, since the best investment data for earlier years, particularly for gas, are available only in pre-1982 prices, I have decided to stick to pre-1982 prices throughout and have used a rough deflator to bring later figures to the same approximate base as the earlier ones.[1] The second difficulty is that the Ministry of the Gas Industry uses its own conventions for reporting investment; consequently, the gas numbers reported in, say, table 5.3 are not comparable with those used for table 2.1. There are similar conundrums for reconstructing the numbers on exploration investment discussed in Chapter 3.

Finally, in 1986 and after, *Narodnoe khoziaistvo SSSR* stopped reporting oil and gas separately and began lumping all energy investment into a single new category called the "energy and fuel complex." This quantity is not simply the sum of the previous subsectors; it is evident, therefore, that the statisticians are now defining the energy sector differently. The latest development is the appearance of a new statistical handbook on capital construction, which groups oil and gas investment in a single number.[2] I have not attempted to use the post-1985 numbers, except to track the reported growth rate of energy investment in comparison to the machinery sector.

Debates in the Soviet Union over policy have grown steadily more open over the last twenty years. But compared to a decade ago, when Robert Campbell wrote his classic studies on the economics of Soviet oil and gas, the quality of the available statistics—never very good to begin with—has deteriorated, reaching a low point in the first half of the 1980s. On the whole, *glasnost'* has brought only partial improvements.[3] Particularly where the technical characteristics of oil and gas exploration and development are concerned—drilling efficiency, well depths, and so on—time series must be laboriously built up from scattered references in the Soviet press and specialized journals; consequently, they are not reliable or consistent. The reader is advised to treat the tables and numbers used throughout this book as indicators of trends; for all other purposes they are best considered approximations and used with caution.

[1] With apologies to the economists, I have derived deflators for oil and gas investment by comparing various editions of *Narodnoe khoziaistvo* for the most recent cases in which the same years were reported in old and new prices; I then used the ratio of the two as a deflator. This method probably understates the differences between the two price bases, since the gap appears to widen over time.

[2] Gosudarstvennyi komitet po statistike, *Kapital'noe stroitel'stvo SSSR* (Moscow: Finansy i Statistika, 1988), p. 53.

[3] A welcome recent improvement, hopefully a harbinger, is V. A. Dinkov, *Neft' SSSR, 1917–1987* (Moscow: Nedra, 1987).

ACKNOWLEDGMENTS

It is a pleasant task to thank the many people who have helped in the making of this book. As will be only too apparent, I have trespassed across many different fields, and I am grateful to those who have tried to teach me the landscape and have tolerated my mistakes.

I particularly wish to thank the economists and the geographers, and first of all Robert Campbell and Ed Hewett, who sparked my interest in the subject of Soviet energy and whose own works are models for all scholars. They have patiently read and criticized many an early chapter, and their support and friendship have been the best part of writing this book. For the genesis of the project I am indebted to Abe Becker, whose kindness and example have been invaluable at every point. For their generous patience in reading the manuscript and making valuable suggestions, I am grateful to Joseph Berliner and Holland Hunter.

Among the geographers, I owe a special debt to the late Theodore Shabad, who helped me as he did all his colleagues, with unfailing patience and generosity. Likewise, warm thanks to Leslie Dienes, whose advice, criticism, and extraordinary research greatly benefited me at every stage, and to Matthew J. Sagers of the U.S. Census Bureau, whose own work and patient stewardship of Theodore Shabad's legacy have put the whole field in his debt.

Among the geologists and petroleum engineers, I would like to express particular appreciation to James W. Clarke of the U.S. Geological Survey, Charles L. Adams of *Oil and Gas Journal*, and Caron Cooper of the University of California at Berkeley. Finally, my cordial thanks to Daniel Yergin and his partners at Cambridge Energy Research Associates, Jan Vanous at PlanEcon, Inc., and to the research staff of the Center for International Research, Bureau of the Census.

Among my fellow political scientists, I am grateful to Peter Hauslohner for his insightful criticism and to Grey Hodnett, whose work on energy decisionmaking a decade ago was an early inspiration. At key points I benefited from the kind counsel of David Laitin and Timothy Colton.

Over the eight years since this book began, I have enjoyed the support of many institutions. The Rand Corporation has nurtured the project from the beginning, and I would especially like to thank Constance Greaser, head of the Rand Publications Department, for her unfailing support and encouragement, as well as Richard Solomon and

Barbara Woodfill. Columbia University's Harriman Institute and Research Institute on International Change were happy places for scholarship, and I am grateful to Marshall Shulman and Seweryn Bialer for their hospitality. Georgetown University and the Center for Strategic and International Affairs have provided a stimulating home, and I thank Amos Jordan and Bruce Douglass for their help. Lastly, the list would not be complete without mention of a small corner of paradise, the Stiftung Wissenschaft und Politik in Ebenhausen, where I was fortunate to be a guest, thanks to Klaus Ritter and Friedemann Müller.

Sources of financial support for the book, in addition to the Rand Corporation and Columbia University, included the Ford Foundation and the National Council for Soviet and East European Studies, whose help is gratefully acknowledged.

This is also a welcome opportunity to thank the many friends and colleagues who have provided advice, friendship, and moral support. They include Helge Ole Bergesen, Albert and Frederique Bressand, Eric Jones, Arild Moe, John van Oudenaren, Angela Stent, Albina Tretyakova, and Victor Winston. Finally, I would like to pay affectionate tribute to the memory of Jean and Christophe Riboud.

As always, I thank the Gildersleeve Wood Foundation and its director, C. Silver, for unstinting support over the years.

Several chapters of this book appeared in earlier versions in other places. Initial portions of Chapter 2 were published in U.S. Congress, Joint Economic Committee, *The Soviet Economy in the 1980s* (Washington, D.C.: USGPO, December 1982), vol. 1, pp. 431–456; in Seweryn Bialer and Thane Gustafson, eds., *Russia at the Crossroads: The 26th Congress of the CPSU* (London: George Allen and Unwin, 1982), pp. 121–139; and in Rodger Swearingen, ed., *Siberia and the Soviet Far East: Strategic Dimensions in Multinational Perspective* (Stanford, Calif.: Hoover Institution Press, 1986), pp. 74–99. Parts of Chapters 3 and 4 were previously published in "The Origins of the Soviet Oil Crisis, 1970–1985," *Soviet Economy* 1, no. 2 (Spring 1985), pp. 103–135. An earlier and somewhat longer version of Chapter 5, together with parts of Chapter 9, appeared as *The Soviet Gas Campaign: Politics and Policy in Soviet Decision-Making*, R-3036-AF (Santa Monica, Calif.: Rand Corporation, June 1983). A sketch of Chapter 6 appeared as "Soviet Adaptation to Technological Pressures," in Philip Joseph, ed., *Soviet Adaptation to Technological Pressures*, Proceedings of the 1985 NATO Colloquium on the Soviet Economy (Brussels: NATO Economics Directorate, 1986), pp. 151–198. The section on Soviet compressor development in Chapter 6 appeared in an early form in "The Soviet Response to the American Embargo of 1981–82: The Case of Compressors for the Export Gas Pipeline," in Gordon B. Smith, ed., *The Politics of East-West Trade* (Boulder, Colo.: Westview Press, 1984), pp. 129–143. Portions of Chapter 8 formed part of a longer case study, published as *Soviet Negotiating Strategy: The East-West Gas Pipeline Deal, 1980–1984*, R-3220-FF (Santa Monica, Calif.: Rand Corporation, February 1985). I am grateful to the publishers for permission to draw from them.

In every case the earlier material has been updated and extensively rewritten. In particular, all calculations and estimates have been redone and a number of earlier mistakes corrected. I am grateful to Zell Stanley and Connie Moreno for their patient help in keying in early drafts, as well as to Kathleen Luzzo for her invaluable assistance in troubleshooting the final computer files.

Charlottesville, Virginia
June 1989

ABBREVIATIONS AND ACRONYMS

Arktikneftegazflot	Arctic offshore fleet of MGP, transferred to MNP in 1988
Bashneft'	Bashkir Oil Association
CMEA	Council for Mutual Economic Assistance (also COMECON)
CPSU	Communist Party of the Soviet Union
Eksimgaz	Gas Trade Organization, subordinate to Soiuzgazeksport
FBIS	Foreign Broadcast Information Service (U.S.)
five-year plan	Seventh Plan: 1961–1965 Eighth Plan: 1966–1970 Ninth Plan: 1971–1975 Tenth Plan: 1976–1980 Eleventh Plan: 1981–1985 Twelfth Plan: 1986–1990 Thirteenth Plan: 1991–1995
GKNT	State Committee for Science and Technology
Glavneftemash	Industrial Association for Petroleum Machine Building, subordinate to Minkhimmash
Glavsibtruboprovodstroi	Siberian Pipe-laying Administration, subordinate to Minneftegazstroi
Glavtiumenneftegaz	MNP's agency for Tiumen'
Glavtiumengeologiia	Branch of Mingeo responsible for oil and gas exploration in Tiumen'
Glavyamburgneftegazstroi	Yamburg Gas Construction Agency
gorkom	city committee of the Communist Party apparatus
Gosekspertiza	Project Review Commission of Gosplan
Goskomstat	State Committee for Statistics (replaces Central Statistical Administration [TsSU])
Gosplan	State Planning Committee
Kaspmorneftegaz	Caspian fleet of MGP, transferred to MNP in 1988
LNG	liquid natural gas
Mashinoimport	Foreign Trade Association for Machinery Imports
mbd	millions of barrels per day
Minchermet	Ministry of Ferrous Metallurgy
Minenergo	Ministry of Power and Electrification
Minenergomash	Minstry of Power-generating Machinery

Mingeo	Ministry of Geology
Minkhimmash	Ministry of Chemical and Petroleum Machine-building
Minmontazhspetsstroi	Ministry of Installation and Special Construction Work
Minneftekhimprom	Ministry of Petroleum Refining and the Petro-chemical Industry
Minoboronprom	Ministry of Defense Industry
Minpribor	Ministry of Instrument-making, Automation Equipment, and Control Systems
Mintiazhmash	Ministry of Heavy and Transport Machine-building
Mintransstroi	Ministry of Transportation Construction
MGP	Ministry of the Gas Industry, Gas Ministry
MNGS	Ministry for Construction of Oil and Gas Enter-prises, or Minneftegazstroi
MNP	Ministry of the Oil Industry, Oil Ministry
mtst	millions of tons of standard fuel = mtce (millions of tons of coal equivalent) = 7,000 kilocalo-ries/ton
Narodnoe khoziaistvo SSSR (*Narkhoz SSSR*)	Statistical annual on the Soviet economy
NGL	natural gas liquids
obkom	province committee of the Communist Party ap-paratus
RSFSR	Russian Soviet Federation of Socialist Republics
SMR	construction and assembly work (*stroitel'no-montazhnaia rabota*)
SOAN	Siberian division of the USSR Academy of Sci-ences
SODECO	Sakhalin Oil Development Company
Soiuzgazeksport	the Soviet gas export trading organization, subor-dinated to the Ministry of Foreign Economic Relations. Merged in 1988 with Soiuznefteck-sport, the oil export trading organization
Soiuzmorgeo	offshore exploration agency of MGP, transferred to MNP in 1988
SOPS	Council for the Evaluation of Productive Re-sources, an office of Gosplan
TASS	Telegraph Agency of the Soviet Union, the offi-cial Soviet news wire service
Tatneft'	Tatar Oil Association
TatNIINeftemash	Enhanced Recovery Research Institute
Tiumengazdobycha	Tiumen' Gas Production Association, a subsidi-ary of Tiumengazprom
Tiumengazprom	Tiumen' Gas Association, subordinated to MGP

Uralmash	Ural Machine-building, the leading producer of drilling rigs, subordinate to Mintiazhmash
Vneshtorgbank	Bank for Foreign Trade, Foreign Trade Bank
VNIIEgazprom	All-Union Scientific Research Institute for the Economics of the Gas Industry
VZBT	Volgograd Drilling Technology Plant
Yamburggazdobycha	Yamburg gas development and production agency

CRISIS AMID PLENTY

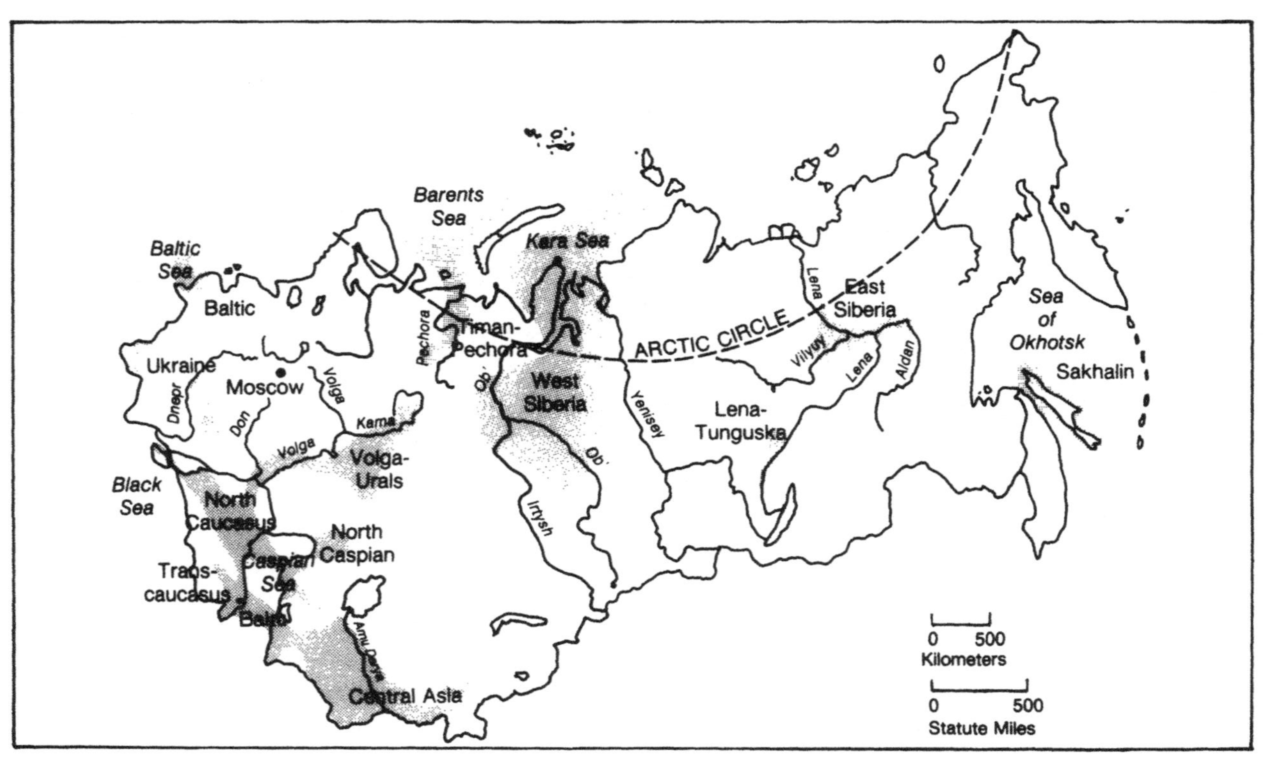

MAP 1. Oil and Gas Regions of the USSR. Source: CIA, *USSR Energy Atlas*, January 1985.

ONE

THE SOVIET ENERGY CRISIS AND THE PROBLEM OF REFORM

The Soviet economy will not be reformed soon. The experience of such command economies as Hungary and China shows how difficult and drawn-out an undertaking reform is, and there are as yet no conclusive successes to point to.[1] It is already clear that the same long road of trial and error awaits Gorbachev and the Soviet reformers.[2] This has produced two sorts of pessimism among Western observers. For the economist, Gorbachev's reforms have not yet gone far enough, because they do not yet go to the heart of the command economy. For the political scientist, they have already gone too far, arousing opposition and unleashing forces the reformers cannot control.

If both of these pessimists are right, then the task of reform in the Soviet Union is not merely herculean but impossible. Yet, is there no gradual middle course that can be both economically and politically viable? That is, after all, the crucial question of any reform, since what makes reform different from revolution is that it attempts to salvage the essence of the established system by adapting it, not overturning it. Between the opposite dangers of excess and inaction, upheaval and paralysis, can an able Soviet leader thread a way?

That depends on just what is wrong in the first place. One of the most important events of the last half-century has been the rise and fall of the Soviet model of economic development. As late as 1960, the Soviet economy appeared to be the most dynamic on the face of the earth. Soviet technology had put the first man-made satellite in space and rivaled the United States in advanced weapons development. So-

[1] On reform in Hungary, see especially Janos Kornai, "The Hungarian Reform Process: Visions, Hopes, and Reality," *Journal of Economic Literature* 24 (December 1986), pp. 1687–1737. On China, see Harry Harding, *China's Second Revolution: Reform after Mao* (Washington, D.C.: Brookings Institution, 1987).

[2] Ed A. Hewett, *Reforming the Soviet Economy* (Washington, D.C.: Brookings Institution, 1988). See also Gertrude E. Schroeder, "Anatomy of Gorbachev's Economic Reform," *Soviet Economy* 3, no. 3 (July-September 1987), pp. 219–241, and the accompanying commmentary by Herbert S. Levine, ibid., pp. 242–245.

viet industry, after successfully repairing the damage done by World War II, had grown at awesome speed throughout the 1950s. But by 1985 the contrast could not have been more complete.

What caused the long slowdown that began in the 1960s, culminating in the crisis of the latter half of Brezhnev's reign, which brought the Soviet economy to a standstill and launched Mikhail Gorbachev on his extraordinary career? Most Western observers—and on this point the political scientists are at one with the economists—take it as an axiom that the secular slide of the Soviet economy since the 1960s is "systemic," that is, rooted in the politico-economic structure of the system.[3] The gist of their case is that the Stalinist strategy of development is exhausted, and along with it the politico-economic structure that serves it. To be sure, there is life in the body yet: degenerative diseases do not conquer the patient overnight, especially so rugged a one as Stalin's progeny. Thus Seweryn Bialer a decade ago distinguished between the "crisis of effectiveness" that loomed before the Soviet Union then and the "crisis of survival" that might threaten it tomorrow.[4]

But for understanding the reformers' predicament, strategy, and prospects, this level of explanation is too broad. A more precise interpretation of the decade is necessary. Just what caused the accumulated ills and dysfunctions of the command system to come together in a simultaneous crisis of industry, agriculture, society, and politics? And why just at the end of the Brezhnev era?

Here is an instance of the most difficult problem in historical explanation and political analysis: to weigh the roles of "structure" and "event" and to understand the place of individuals within them. "Systems," after all, do not allocate resources, design programs, give advice, or make decisions. If the command system creates distorted signals and incentives, it is still the responses of the leaders that will either aggravate the consequences or offset them, delay a crisis or precipitate one. The Soviet slide under Brezhnev is a case in point. Its timing, course, and consequences cannot be understood without examining the part played by leadership and policy, and specifically by Brezhnev himself. The implications for the reformer are obvious: if specific errors of

[3] Among the political scientists, see Seweryn Bialer, *The Soviet Paradox: External Expansion, Internal Decline* (New York: Knopf, 1986); Timothy J. Colton, *The Dilemma of Reform in the Soviet Union*, 2d ed. (New York: Council on Foreign Relations, 1986); Peter Hauslohner, "Gorbachev's Social Contract," *Soviet Economy* 3, no. 1 (January-March 1987), pp. 54–89. Among the economists, in addition to the works by Hewett and Schroeder cited in note 2, see Gur Ofer, "Soviet Economic Growth: 1928–1985," *Journal of Economic Literature* 25 (December 1987), pp. 1767–1833.

[4] Seweryn Bialer, *Stalin's Successors: Leadership, Stability, and Change in the Soviet Union* (Cambridge: Cambridge University Press, 1980).

leadership were a major factor in precipitating a crisis, then correcting those first will buy the reformer precious time and room.

It follows that we will not have a clear picture of the sources of the crisis of the last decade, or of the roots of the present reform movement, or of its prospects until we get down to cases. That is already happening, as economists and political scientists begin to take a closer look at the biggest trouble spots of the decade: agriculture,[5] military-industrial affairs,[6] manpower,[7] and transportation.[8] The subject of the present book is the special trouble spot of energy.

At the book's core is the story of a paradox. Energy is the essential foundation of any industrial economy, and in its abundance of energy the Soviet Union is the mightiest of superpowers. It is the world's largest producer of oil and gas and the third largest producer of coal. Inside its borders are the most plentiful energy reserves of any country. Yet for the last decade the Soviets have been in the throes of an energy crisis. It is not a crisis of penury (in particular, the Soviets are not about to run out of oil) but one of runaway costs, abysmal inefficiency, and repeated shocks and surprises. Moscow's struggles to deal with it have been so demanding and so expensive that energy policy has been the single most disruptive factor in Soviet industry since the mid-1970s and one of the leading proximate causes of the downturn and stagnation of Soviet economic growth.[9] Yet, despite a decade as the Kremlin's most

[5] D. Gale Johnson and Karen McConnell Brooks, *Prospects for Soviet Agriculture in the 1980s* (Bloomington: Indiana University Press, 1983).

[6] See in particular Abraham S. Becker, *Ogarkov's Complaint and Gorbachev's Dilemma: The Soviet Defense Budget and Party-Military Conflict*, R-3541-AF (Santa Monica, Calif.: Rand Corporation, 1987); Jeremy R. Azrael, *The Soviet Civilian Leadership and the Military High Command, 1976–1986*, R-3521-AF (Santa Monica, Calif.: Rand Corporation, 1987); and Timothy J. Colton and Thane Gustafson, eds., *Soviet Soldiers and the State: Civil-Military Relations from Brezhnev to Gorbachev* (forthcoming, 1990).

[7] Peter A. Hauslohner, "Managing the Soviet Labor Market: Politics and Policymaking under Brezhnev" (Ph.D. diss., University of Michigan, 1984).

[8] For the late 1970s and early 1980s, see Holland Hunter and Deborah A. Kaple, "Transport in Trouble," *Soviet Economy in the 1980's* (Washington, D.C.: USGPO, 1982), vol. 1, pp. 216–241; Holland Hunter and Peggy Dunn, "The Soviet Transport Situation," Wharton Econometric Forecasting Associates, Soviet Transportation Research Project, Executive Summary (Washington, D.C.: October 1984).

[9] For discussions of the impact of energy problems on Soviet industrial performance, see Gertrude E. Schroeder, "The Slowdown in Soviet Industry," *Soviet Economy* 1, no. 1 (January-March 1985), pp. 58–60, 70; Leslie Dienes, "The Energy System and Economic Imbalances in the USSR," *Soviet Economy* 1, no. 4 (October-December 1985), pp. 340–372; Boris Rumer, "Structural Imbalance in the Soviet Economy," *Problems of Communism* 33, no. 4 (July-August 1984), pp. 26–28; and Rumer, "Unresolved Problems in Soviet Investment Policy," *Problems of Communism* 31, no. 5 (September-October 1982), pp. 53–68.

urgent industrial problem, the Soviet energy crisis is far from resolved. For the reformers under Mikhail Gorbachev no other issue of economic policy is so great an obstacle to their plans.

How much of the energy crisis of the last decade is due to systemic diseases and how much to the mistakes of a deficient political leadership? Gorbachev blames both. The Soviet economy, he argues, has outgrown the system that created it; but the resulting difficulties were made worse by blind leaders. As he told the Central Committee of the Communist Party of the Soviet Union (CPSU) in January 1987: "The main cause—and the Politburo considers it necessary to say so with utmost frankness at the plenary meeting—was that the CPSU Central Committee and the leadership of the country failed, primarily for subjective reasons, to see in time and in full the need for change and the danger of intensification of crisis phenomena [*krizisnye iavleniia*] in society and to formulate a clear policy for overcoming them."[10] In Gorbachev's list of mistakes energy figures especially prominently: "The striving to restrain the fall of growth rates led to making inordinate expenditures to expand the fuels-and-energy sector, to bringing new natural resources into production at forced rates, and to using them irrationally."[11] Capital productivity in the extractive sector plummeted, and the previous leadership made up for it by pouring in scarce labor. One of the worst "irrational uses," Gorbachev continued, was excessive energy exports; the hard currency bought with them was wasted on "current tasks" rather than on modernizing the economy. In plain speech, what turned a systemic decline into a crisis was Brezhnev.

Is Gorbachev right? Or rather, to what extent is he right? What part of the energy crisis might reasonably have been avoided by a Brezhnev leadership that, while staying "in character," operating within the circumstances, perceptions, and political consensus of its time, and using the instruments available to it, might have used them better, more wisely, more consistently, or with greater foresight? In other words, did it make avoidable mistakes? Or was it defeated by forces it did not understand and could not respond to, dragged down, in addition, by the contradictions and inertia of a physical structure built up over the previous two generations? The question is obviously crucial for Gor-

[10] Mikhail Gorbachev, "O perestroike i kadrovoi politike Partii," *Pravda*, 28 Jan. 1987, p. 1. His predecessor, Konstantin Chernenko, had used the term *crisis* even before Brezhnev's death, but only to refer to the *danger* of crisis if the leadership did not improve its social policies. See "Leninskaia strategiia rukovodstva," *Kommunist*, no. 13 (September 1981), pp. 10–11.

[11] M. S. Gorbachev, "O zadachakh Partii po korennoi perestroike upravleniia ekonomikoi," *Pravda*, 26 June 1987.

bachev or any would-be reformer because it bears on the cardinal questions we raised at the outset. Can Gorbachev do better? How much time and running room does he have? What balance of improved "within-system" policy and radical reform might work?

This book has two aims. First, I will explain the crisis that struck the energy sector in the mid-1970s and analyze the policies that accompanied it, attempting to disentangle the systemic causes from those traceable to the political leadership. In focusing on the two core industries of the energy sector, oil and gas, and on the gathering troubles facing both, I will ask: Did the leaders not know what was happening? How soon did they find out and how did the news reach them? Was there conflict among them or among groups, factions, or institutions? If so, what was at issue? Did political or institutional conflict inhibit or distort effective action? When there was action, did it have the expected results, and if not, why not? Were the leaders well advised, and did they or their experts show the capacity to learn as time went on?

I will also examine the systemic causes of the energy crisis. What were the consequences of the pricing system for energy? What effects did organizational structure have on policy and its implementation? Why did the central planning process perform as it did? What explains the low level of technological innovation in the oil and gas industries and the wasteful use of manpower? What accounts for the poorly planned and inefficient use of foreign equipment? Finally, I will explore the interaction of system and leadership. How did the leaders attempt to deal with the biases produced by the system? Did they offset them or aggravate them? How did various actors outside the top leadership, such as regional authorities and the Party apparatus, deal with systemic distortions?

The second broad aim of this book is to show the place of the energy sector in the Soviet reform problem. Both as cause and as symbol, the energy sector is one of the most visible and difficult problems the reformers face. For the moment, Gorbachev is having better luck with energy than his predecessors; indeed, at this writing the fuels sector is the only part of the economy that is giving good results, partly because of a tightening up that began in 1985. But it is significant—and ominous—that Gorbachev's approach to energy policy is so far almost indistinguishable from Brezhnev's in its two most dangerous aspects: the rapid rise of energy investment and the failure to curb energy consumption. Why is that? Is reform so difficult in the energy sector? I will show why finding "middle roads" to reform should actually be easier in the energy sector than in much of the rest of the economy, and I will argue that in this particular case middle roads are indeed available, opening ways for the reformers to cope with the energy crisis. But if that is the case, why is Gorbachev not taking them?

The Soviet Energy Crisis in Comparative Perspective

This is a book about Soviet politics and policymaking, not about comparative political economy. In particular, it is not meant as yet another indictment of government ownership or state intervention in the economy. Yet the Western reader is bound to wonder whether Soviet energy policies have been better or worse than those of the West, and therefore it is of interest to put the Soviet energy crisis in comparative perspective.

In some ultimate sense, the Western and the Soviet energy crises shared similar causes. Both stemmed from rising energy costs, and both struck economies grown used to cheap oil. Both were aggravated by the poor foresight of governments and industrial planners. In both the threat of shortage was followed by massive and lasting reallocations of resources.

But there the similarities end. In the West a relatively small constriction of supply twice sent energy prices soaring between 1973 and 1981, engendering a host of consequences. Compared to this market response, changes in government policies came late and, in most cases, had less important effects. In the Soviet Union, the reverse was true: the sudden perception of emergency (though belated) brought first a jolting change in government policy. Price responses came more slowly, trailing behind rapidly rising real costs, and had little effect on policy or behavior.[12]

In the West, the result was broad and rapid adaptation by both producers and consumers; in the Soviet Union the adaptations came mainly on the production side. Western exploration and development boomed in all major energy sources, supported by rapid technological innovation that was quickly diffused worldwide. In the Soviet Union the supply response took the form of massive campaigns to boost hydrocarbons and nuclear power, while coal was neglected. These cam-

[12] For an excellent account of the Soviet energy problem up to the early 1980s, with valuable comparative perspectives, see Ed A. Hewett, *Energy, Economics, and Foreign Policy in the Soviet Union* (Washington, D.C.: Brookings Institution, 1984). On Soviet energy prices and their effects, see Robert W. Campbell, "Energy Prices and Decisions on Energy Use in the USSR," in Padma Desai, ed., *Marxism, Central Planning, and the Soviet Economy: Economic Essays in Honor of Alexander Erlich* (Cambridge, Mass: MIT Press, 1983), pp. 249–274.

paigns were conducted with inadequate attention to industrial support, technological innovation, or long-term strategy. The energy sector, though it provided the Soviet Union with most of its hard-currency earnings, failed in the main to exploit Western equipment and know-how, despite a handful of notable exceptions.

But the greatest differences are on the demand side. In the West, higher prices soon led to large reductions in energy use, effectively severing the once close tie between economic growth and energy consumption. Oil consumption in the developed West dropped sharply, both in absolute volume and as a share of total energy use; and despite lower prices and substantial economic growth in recent years, it has been slow to recover. In the Soviet Union there has been little effective energy-saving response to date and only the slightest decline in oil consumption—a decline that is likely to be reversed if the Gorbachev program of accelerated growth is at all successful. Ironically, the most powerful incentive for the Soviets to conserve energy was not the rise of world energy prices in the 1970s but their decline in the 1980s, which cut Soviet hard-currency income and stimulated them to free more oil for export.

One important structural reason the Soviets have been slow to conserve energy is that heavy industry continues to dominate energy consumption. Some of the most dramatic Western savings occurred because consumers drove their cars less and heated their homes more efficiently. In the Soviet Union such savings have been almost entirely absent. But the greatest shortcoming has been the Soviet failure to curb industrial consumption, where the West also did well.

By the mid-1980s the Soviet energy problem had become virtually the exact opposite of that of the West. The latter, having broadened its sources and cut its consumption, now faces periodic oversupply and erratic prices, though it remains dangerously dependent on the volatile Persian Gulf. The Soviet Union, though it has sharply expanded gas output and has so far avoided a collapse in oil production, and though it remains the only major industrial power fully self-sufficient in energy, is also the only one still threatened with shortages and bottlenecks, which it has prevented only through massive spending. In the West energy consumption has become much more efficient than before; in the Soviet Union it has not. In the West energy investment and exploration are sharply down; but the Soviets are investing and exploring more and more, as energy continues to drive the leaders' choices. Natural gas, despite its high cost, is being developed as fast as the Soviets can pipe it to consumers, and in the oil fields they are desperately producing every barrel they can. This paradoxical mixture of success within failure and failure within success sets the Soviet version of the energy problem decisively apart.

Explaining the Soviet Energy Crisis

To preview briefly one of this book's main findings: Soviet energy policy over the last decade and a half has been unbalanced, unstable, and ridden with conflict. These features have worked against the leaders' aims and narrowed their options. The central question is: What accounts for these features and why have they endured, right down to the latest decisions of the Gorbachev leadership?

The Impact of the System

There is a large and excellent literature, spanning two generations, on the functions and malfunctions of command economies. Its main implications for policymaking can be summed up under three themes.[13] First, command systems generate false, incomplete, and inappropriate information, and they put it in the wrong hands. The price system yields misleading signals about supply and demand, particularly for new products and services. Interest rates and discount rates do not reflect society's attitudes (and only imperfectly those of the leaders) toward risk or trade-offs between present and future. Information moves vertically but not horizontally. Those who must make decisions lack good data, while those who have the best data are not responsible for decisions. Plans based on faulty information are unrealizable from the start.

Second, command systems generate irrational incentives and conflicting preferences and provide no way to reconcile them other than cumbersome negotiation or administrative pressure. There is either too little incentive to innovate or too much, and the result is alternately technological stagnation or gold plating. Distorted rewards and a lack of hard financial constraints encourage overuse of all inputs, disregard of quality standards and delivery schedules, and inattention to customer wants.

Third, as a consequence, the objectives set by policymakers are severely distorted in execution. Inputs reach the field in neither the mix nor the sequence required, and they are then used in ways that were not intended. Local producers pass the consequences on to their customers and misreport the results to their superiors, thus setting the stage for the next round of defective policymaking.

[13] The reader will recognize here the the influence of the main themes of Hewett, *Reforming the Soviet Economy*.

This is the systemic setting for policy in the Soviet energy sector, but there is one more systemic factor that is not stressed as much as it should be: the accumulated effects of the system as embodied in the physical infrastructure of the country. Western writers sometimes seem to liken the Soviet system to a sailboat straining against an unfavorable wind. Change the wind, we seem to say, and the boat will quickly right itself. But a more appropriate metaphor for the Soviet economy is that of a gnarled tree that has grown up leaning against the north wind of forced-draft industrialization. Its past is written into the composition and location of its capital stock, the patterns of its roads and railroads, the size and type of its plants, the distribution of its manpower, the kinds of fuel it burns and ore it uses. Even a perfect leader and a perfect reform, whatever those might be, could not right in a generation what has taken two generations to form.[14]

As today's General Secretaries meditate strategies for improving the existing structure, they discover it leaves them little leisure to apply remedies because it requires constant propping up. The wasteful factories absorb ever more raw materials from ever-farther places, the machinery requires constant repair, the agricultural system demands massive subsidy, the labor force needs discipline and pressure. Wells run dry, light bulbs dim, and the Kremlin has no choice but to lay aside its plans and rush to attend to them. Beginning with Khrushchev, each new set of leaders has discovered that their inheritance keeps them in a state of perpetual busyness.

And the problem is growing worse, for two reasons. First, today's leaders and planners are forced to spend valuable time and capital filling in yesterday's neglected programs. The Soviet Union offers the unique spectacle of an industrial power that spends between a quarter and a third of its investment budget on agriculture and food industries while simultaneously pursuing high-priority programs to meet elementary consumer needs and to rebuild and modernize its industrial infrastructure.

Second, the flawed infrastructure itself generates recurrent emergencies, tripping up the leaders and forcing them to divert resources from long-term goals to short-term problems. The result is a continuous state of tension, punctuated by economic surprises, political alarms, and abrupt changes of course. In one key sector after another—in energy, transportation, metallurgy, and agriculture—Soviet leaders have been

[14] As far as I know, this theme was first developed by Egon Neuberger, "Central Planning and its Legacies: Implications for Foreign Trade," in Alan A. Brown and Egon Neuberger, eds., *International Trade and Central Planning* (Berkeley: University of California Press, 1968), pp. 349–377.

forced repeatedly to lay aside long-range strategies to rush shock troops to unanticipated breaches. The result has been a pattern of shortened horizons, unstable priorities, improvised decisions, and wasteful economic offensives. The system that prizes predictability and control as its supreme virtues enjoys remarkably little of either.

As a result, much of Brezhnev's economic policy after the mid-1970s consisted of improvisation under pressure. This realization helps to account for one of the period's most distinguishing characteristics: a constant conflict between the requirements of rational long-term policy and the year-to-year urgency of getting by. It also helps to explain why, despite the existence of a great deal of slack in the system, the slack is needed to deal with the emergencies of the moment and is difficult to mobilize for long-term improvements.

These three infrastructural problems—the distortions resulting from the "gnarled tree" economy, the heavy diversions of resources required to attend to the century's unfinished business, and the distracting emergencies repeatedly arising from both—are major obstacles to sustained and rational policy in the Soviet system. They drain the leaders' vigor and their resources; they encourage risk-averse policies and short-horizon, firefighting behavior. They heighten the political delicacy of whatever reforms are finally undertaken while simultaneously masking the benefits these may produce. The result is to weaken the leaders' incentive to attempt long-term changes and their capacity to implement them.

These points apply with special force to the energy sector. The location of mines and oil and gas fields, the technologies used to work them, the layout of pipelines and refineries all embody decisions made over decades. The same is even more true of the consumption side, since any country's map of energy demand is essentially that of its inherited structure of population and economic activity. The geography of Soviet energy today—supply concentrated in the east, demand concentrated in the west—reflects the imbalances built up over two generations, and the country's low energy efficiency is the legacy of sixty years of extensive growth, now incorporated into energy-wasting machinery, leaky plants and railroad cars, apartment buildings without meters to measure gas or electricity, and the like.

The result of these systemic features is a unique burden on Soviet decisionmakers. How have different leaders struggled with or surrendered to, aggravated or alleviated, its effects?

Issues of Leadership

Faced with a complex and changing world, the ideal "rational" decisionmaker plumbs his preferences, charts his options, attaches probabilities to each outcome, weighs expected returns, and serenely sets sail. In reality, of course, information is never so good, preferences never so clear, and decisionmakers never so smart or united. Instead, real people compromise. They simplify their problems by limiting the outcomes they consider, by assigning arbitrary indexes of risk and time preference, and, above all, by devising standard procedures for dealing with the most common situations. In short, in Herbert Simon's famous phrase, they do not optimize, they *satisfice*.[15] Indeed, in most routine situations they do not reanalyze problems at all; instead they monitor key variables and apply standard procedures in a pattern some scholars have called "cybernetic thinking."[16]

In the Soviet case, since the burden of analysis and computation is especially heavy, decisionmakers are all the more prone to satisficing; indeed, they could hardly function otherwise. The compromise techniques traditionally used by Soviet decisionmakers are as old as the command system itself and give it much of its characteristic appearance: they keep goals few and simple and restate their rankings *ex cathedra* at regular intervals; they divide up decisionmaking functions (long-range assessments and short-range planning, in particular, are entrusted to different institutions); they keep most changes small (as expressed in the Soviet formula "planning from the achieved level"); and they concentrate on a handful of key performance indicators, traditionally physical rather than monetary quantities. Decisionmaking has been further simplified, at least until recently, by limits on debate. Under Gorbachev, these longstanding practices account for much of the apparent resistance to *perestroika*.

These techniques worked better when the economy was smaller and simpler; in a complex advanced economy they yield a progressively cruder picture of reality. What happens if the decisionmaker's environment gradually degrades, or takes a sharp and unforeseen lurch, or both? At such points past satisficing conventions become hindrances. The question then is how successfully decisionmakers are able to break free of past patterns, mobilize new information, re-examine the situation, and chart a sound new course. Again, under the conditions of a command economy and one-party authoritarianism we would expect such reappraisals to be especially difficult. But whether they happen at all, and with what effectiveness, depends on three issues, which we will examine throughout this book: the abilities of the leaders themselves as

[15] Herbert A. Simon, *Administrative Behavior* (New York: Macmillan, 1947).

[16] See in particular John D. Steinbruner, *The Cybernetic Theory of Decision: New Dimensions of Political Analysis* (Princeton, N.J.: Princeton University Press, 1974). On patterns of cybernetic behavior within organizations, see Richard M. Cyert and James G. March, *A Behavioral Theory of the Firm* (Englewood Cliffs, N.J.: Prentice-Hall, 1963).

decisionmakers; the extent and severity of conflict among them; and their capacity to seek advice, to mobilize information, and to learn.

THE QUALITY OF DECISIONMAKING

Was Brezhnev an able leader? Brezhnev possessed above all the virtues of the classic machine politician: essentially, his style of politics was to deal with people and problems by buying them off. To the Party apparatus, he offered privileges and stability; to the military-industrial elite, growing budgets and professional autonomy; to non-Russian politicians, affirmative action and a blind eye to corruption; and to the population at large, vast economic subsidies. This style served Brezhnev well nearly all his life. It was also not a bad formula for a country with many economic and political cleavages, previously exacerbated by Khrushchev. In short, especially by contrast with Gorbachev, Brezhnev appears in retrospect to have been an able "equity" politician.

But what about Brezhnev as an "efficiency" politician, that is, his ability as a problem solver, his capacity to think policy problems through, to relate means to ends, to reconcile the near term and the long, and to choose a consistent approach to risk and uncertainty? One of the most characteristic features of Brezhnev as a policymaker is that he picked his priorities early and clung to them tenaciously to the end of his life. Agriculture was his top civilian priority; and from the moment he decided on a program of heavy investment to modernize the countryside, he not only stayed with it through thick and thin but steadily widened it, first from on-farm to off-farm investment and then to the entire food chain. In the military sector, his other top priority, Brezhnev continued the modernization begun by Khrushchev (which Brezhnev had personally overseen during part of Khrushchev's reign); and right up to Brezhnev's death the military-industrial sector received a growing share of resource inputs.[17] Finally, from 1970 on, the Brezhnev leadership, increasingly aware of the importance of consumer welfare for productivity growth, presided over a steady decline in the share of national income devoted to accumulation.

In short, Brezhnev, at least in his domestic policies, displayed all the characteristics of a cybernetic thinker. His approach to agricultural investment and military investment was that of traditional Soviet industrialization: large bureaucracies, large projects, standard solutions uniformly applied. Unlike Kosygin, who was willing (however cautiously) to re-examine some of the Stalinist approaches and to think in terms of

[17] Robert W. Campbell, "Resource Stringency and Civilian-Military Resource Allocation," in Colton and Gustafson, eds., *Soviet Soldiers and the State* (forthcoming).

economic levers, Brezhnev avoided risk or novelty in his policies; indeed, his one real innovation in economic policy—his expansion of Soviet foreign trade—was aimed at providing insurance for his main programs and should thus be seen as another instance of risk aversion.

It is especially interesting, therefore, to know how such a decisionmaker reacted when faced with a violent disruption in his plans, which, as we shall see, occurred in 1977. Was Brezhnev able to adjust to unpleasant facts? Did he take risks? Did he alter his priorities? Did he conduct an analysis of the problem?

It is difficult to imagine a leader more different from Brezhnev than Gorbachev. His willingness to re-examine the foundations of the Soviet economic system, to rethink problems, to re-evaluate objectives, to reconsider risks and horizons all mark him as an instinctively analytic decisionmaker. Yet so far, as this book will show, there is very little difference between his energy policies and Brezhnev's. Has Gorbachev already been defeated by the system? Has he not yet begun to fight? Or does he share enough of Brezhnev's goals and fears that he has been deterred from taking decisive action?

THE INTERPRETATION OF CONFLICT

Western students of Soviet politics have always been fascinated by the play of power in the Kremlin, and consequently they have tended to treat policy issues from the angle of power politics. Indeed, as recently as two decades ago sovietologists frequently wrote as if policy issues were little more than fronts in the power struggle.[18] But this perception reflects a basic truth about the Soviet system: formal powers and terms of office are undefined, and the institutions through which one gains power are the same as those that make policy.

The Soviet energy crisis, on the face of it, should be a classic illustration of this point. It began just as Brezhnev's health started to fail, and it has evolved in the midst of the most complex political succession since the 1920s. The stakes were enormous, and energy touched on some of the most controversial political issues, such as foreign trade, the economic mechanism, and the allocation of resources. Surely, then, energy policy should have been a major factor in the power politics of

[18] The classic formulation is that of Zbigniew Brzezinski and Samuel P. Huntington, *Political Power: USA/USSR* (New York: Macmillan, 1963), pp. 191–192: "In the Soviet system no real distinction exists between the processes of policy-making and those of acquiring power. . . . In the Soviet Union the key policy-making bodies never adjourn and the campaign for office never ends. Policy proposals are forever directly involved in (even if not always motivated by) the struggle for or the consolidation of personal power."

the last decade. Surprisingly enough, however, it was not. We shall see some form of conflict on almost every page of this book, and some of it, indeed, mirrors deep disagreements among top leaders. But energy never became an overt issue in the succession. One suspects, however, that the main reason for this is that successive General Secretaries (with the possible exception of Andropov), prevented the energy issue from arising by playing it safe and continuing to invest heavily in energy supply.

The energy case also seems on first examination to be a classic example of interest-group politics Soviet-style, pitting major institutional and regional interests against one another. Two recent studies of energy politics, in fact, explain the evolution of Soviet energy policy from precisely this perspective.[19] But I will argue that interest groups—whether institutional, regional, or otherwise—have not been primarily concerned to expand resources or turf. Instead, the players' motives and alignments are more complex: conflict is more frequently due to contending views over risk and uncertainty, over the consequences of alternative strategies, over near-term versus long-term approaches, and over the merits of competing technologies. All of these issues engage political interests, to be sure, but they mainly reflect the difficulties of dealing with a shifting and uncertain reality, as well as differences in the information and analysis available. The absence of market yardsticks, of course, turns the process of choice into one of bureaucratic negotiation. For the Western analyst, then, the challenge is to disentangle what is usually not clear to the players themselves: the interaction of concern for turf, precedence, and resource shares, on the one hand, and differing perceptions of fact, opportunity, and risk, on the other.

Next, we need to consider the extent to which energy policy was shaped by the conflicts described. Were decisions delayed, diverted, or paralyzed altogether? Did the desire to avoid conflict prevent the leaders from re-examining their policies? Did competition among leaders stimulate them, on the contrary, to promote new initiatives? In short, to what extent was conflict itself a cause of the energy crisis?

CAPACITY FOR LEARNING AND ADAPTATION AMONG THE SOVIET ELITE

A vital aspect of political leadership is the ability of leaders to seek good information and advice, to surround themselves with able advisers, and

[19] See Han-ku Chung, *Interest Representation in Soviet Policy-Making: A Case Study of a West Siberian Energy Coalition* (Boulder, Colo.: Westview Press, 1987), and Eric Anthony Jones, "The Bureaucratic Politics of Soviet Energy Policy in the Late Brezhnev Period, 1976–1982: Policy Process and the Energy Balance" (Ph.D. diss., University of Michigan, 1988).

to stimulate new thinking about policy. Despite Brezhnev's reputation as an unimaginative conservative, there was more open and detailed discussion of a broad range of policy issues under him than under Khrushchev.[20] Some of this openness evidently reached Central Committee headquarters on Old Square: Brezhnev's speech writers frequently echoed the latest fashionable ideas on management, computers, environment, and many other subjects. Other leaders, especially Andropov, developed the reputation of being open to new ideas and bright people. Throughout the Brezhnev years specialists in many fields (including many previously suppressed ones) gained in status and expanded the scope of their participation in policymaking. The explosion of new thinking under Gorbachev cannot be understood except as the result of a long evolution under Brezhnev.

Yet one should not exaggerate the extent to which this trend armed Brezhnev's successors with finished policy ideas. The new initiatives and proposals of the first years under Andropov and Gorbachev contained more sentiment than substance. (One recalls Andropov's confession to the Central Committee, in November 1982, that he had no "ready prescriptions" for change, and this point has been echoed by other leaders since.[21]) The gradual improvement in the atmosphere for policy debate and advice did not adequately prepare the Soviet system for innovation and reform by supplying it with concrete policy alternatives backed by data and studies.

Under traditional Soviet conditions the rise of new ideas to the public agenda requires much more than a policy of benign neglect. In an earlier work I examined several cases of the growing influence of policy advisers under Khrushchev and Brezhnev, and I concluded that the prerequisite in all of them was the policy needs and active support of the leaders (if not necessarily of the General Secretary himself).[22] The energy case provides additional illustrations of this point. Energy institutes expanded and multiplied even before the Soviet crisis broke, partly under the influence of the world energy crisis that began in 1973 and partly as a result of the more general growth of econometrics, systems analysis, and other techniques that promised to improve central planning. However, the leaders' overwhelming emphasis on energy

[20] Jerry Hough, in particular, called attention to this aspect of the Brezhnev era in the early 1970s in "The Soviet System: Petrification or Pluralism?" republished in Jerry F. Hough, *The Soviet Union and Social Science Theory* (Cambridge, Mass.: Harvard University Press, 1977), pp. 19–48.

[21] Iurii Andropov, speech to the 22 November 1982 plenum of the CPSU Central Committee, in Iu. V. Andropov, *Izbrannye rechi i stat'i*, 2d ed. (Moscow: Politizdat, 1983), p. 212.

[22] Thane Gustafson, *Reform in Soviet Politics: Lessons of Recent Policies on Land and Water* (New York: Cambridge University Press, 1981), pp. 83–96.

supply had an inhibiting effect on the research profile of these institutes and their personnel, denying them, for example, access to data on the energy intensity of major industrial processes (or inhibiting its measurement in the first place). Research on conservation and fuel switching remained underdeveloped until Gorbachev's accession and the beginning of *perestroika*, and even now it is marked by an approach to demand more characteristic of the engineer than of the economist. As in other areas of Soviet expertise, the most vigorous modeling studies of energy demand developed far away from Moscow, while the State Planning Committee's (Gosplan) own energy institute in Moscow focused mainly on energy supply and slighted conservation.

Despite their focus on energy supply over demand, the writings of Soviet energy specialists in the decade before 1985 showed a growing understanding of the effects of their own policies and of the properties and limits of their own system. The question is: How much of that improved understanding was passed on to the leaders and planners? To what extent did good or bad advice, good or bad data, influence the overall course of energy policy? How did leaders act to improve the quality of advice reaching them or, conversely, to ignore or suppress information and views they disliked? In short, how did leadership shape the relations between knowledge and power in the energy sector, and how did those relations affect the overall course of energy policy?

The Place of the Energy Sector in Soviet Reform

The package of reforms that went into effect at the beginning of 1988 represents the most far-reaching attempt by Soviet rulers to date to overcome the classic dysfunctions of the command economy. If fully implemented, what would it imply for the energy sector?

At the center of the Gorbachev reforms is a vision of the enterprise manager in an efficient socialist economy. He works in a centrally planned system, but one that provides him with stable five-year targets, attractive state contracts for his most important output, and guidelines on the most efficient practices. Within this framework the decisions are his, and his main criterion is profit. He buys most of his supplies and sells most of his output on wholesale markets. He hires and fires workers as his needs dictate, and he pays them according to their performance. He finances his investments and his enterprise's welfare programs from his own earnings. He answers equally to the center and to the workers who elected him.

On the whole, this vision has little relevance to the industries that supply energy. They are very large, capital-intensive systems that play a central role in the economy; consequently, they are unlikely to be allowed the leeway to choose their own investments or set their own growth policy. They produce a small range of uniform commodities, so they are unconcerned about consumer fashions, and they always have a market; moreover, their product is too important to the economy for its price or supply to go unregulated. They rely for their equipment on monopolistic suppliers; therefore they are unlikely to benefit from wholesale markets in producers' goods. They work primarily in remote places, and thus their labor practices raise larger social issues that invite government intervention. They have no official private activities and few unofficial ones. In short, whereas the Gorbachev reforms could have substantial and nearly immediate impact in agriculture, light industry, and services, they are unlikely to have any direct effects on the energy-producing sector.

Energy demand, however, could be a very different story. If Soviet enterprise managers begin truly to focus on profit rather than on gross output, then they may seek to economize on inputs for the first time since the beginnings of the command economy sixty years ago. This could produce dramatic reductions not only in energy consumption but also in the use of energy-intensive materials such as metals and cement. The incentive to save would be all the greater if energy prices were raised. In short, the Gorbachev reforms, if implemented vigorously, really could improve the Soviet energy problem dramatically.

But it is far more probable that this will not happen or, at any rate, not happen soon, because it is most unlikely that Soviet managers will be freed from the tyranny of the gross output target or rescued from the seductions of the soft budget constraint, particularly in the sectors of heavy industry where most Soviet energy is consumed.[23] Even if energy prices are raised, managers are more likely to pass the costs on to their customers than to cut back energy consumption themselves. Moreover, conservation on any meaningful scale will require long-term financial and material investment, which in most cases will detract from the near-term output goals of the enterprises and ministries.

In short, there is a strong possibility that Gorbachev's attempts at systemic reform could fail to produce rapid benefits in the energy sector, thus preventing the leadership from freeing itself from the burden of growing energy investment. But there are expedients that would ease the burden while systemic changes are extended and begin to take hold, and we return to those in the final chapter.

[23] On this concept, see Janos Kornai, "The Soft Budget Constraint," *Kyklos* 39 (1986), pp. 3–30.

One last theme of this book is the interaction of domestic and foreign issues in energy policy. No other part of the Soviet economy is so closely linked with the outside world as the energy sector. From 1973 to 1985 about 80 percent of the Soviet Union's hard-currency revenue from the developed West came from energy exports, and the decade-long boom of high energy prices in the 1970s stimulated the greatest expansion of foreign trade of the Soviet period, bringing leaders and planners into closer touch with the world economy than at any time since the 1920s. Yet the energy sector also illustrates how uneven, incomplete, and ambivalent the Soviet adaptation to this change has been.

Western analysts argue, and Gorbachev agrees, that the Soviets' windfall profits from high world energy prices served the Brezhnev leadership, if not quite as a substitute for reform, then at least as an antacid against mounting economic malaise. If true, then one would have expected the Soviets to use a great deal of Western technology in the energy sector. But their use of it turned out to be limited and selective, and in the following chapters I will attempt to unravel the complexity of Soviet motives and actions.

To sum up the propositions and aims of this book: The state of continuous emergency in the Soviet energy sector over the last decade illustrates better than any other case the paradoxes of the Soviet system in its third generation—the combination of stability and instability, of vigor and paralysis, of learning and resistance, of success and failure. The Soviet economy was never so strong as it once appeared; it is not as weak as it appears now. These are the incongruous elements that one must explain if one is to appraise the Soviet system's ability to adapt to the new industrial era and to endure. If the system has remained stable, it is not least because it has been able, even at its weakest, to respond vigorously to emergencies. Yet in the energy case its very responses have added to the system's imbalance and inefficiency, preparing the way for further trouble.

Is the cycle of campaign and crisis a necessary feature of the command economy, or is it in addition a manifestation of bad leadership by a group of leaders—Stalin's successors—who were ill-suited by background and temperament to the job of modern industrial management? Can the cycle be tempered by better leadership, acting within the limits of politically feasible reforms, or will even the most able and determined leadership be destroyed by an inescapable downward spiral that produces, finally, a crisis of survival?

At the center of the action and drama of Soviet energy policy in the last fifteen years are oil and gas, and I have chosen to concentrate on them. As important as coal, electricity, and, especially, nuclear power are, to deal with them adequately would require another volume; consequently, they are discussed only as needed for an understanding of the overall story. Chapter 2 outlines the development of Soviet energy policy from 1970 to the present. The next two chapters discuss the origins of trouble in the Soviet oil industry and the leaders' responses to it. Chapter 5 analyzes the turn to natural gas and examines in particular the costs of the gas bridge. Chapters 6 and 8 explore the interaction of domestic and foreign economic policy, with an analysis of Soviet motives and strategy in energy exports and energy-related technology imports. Chapter 7 deals with the evolution of Soviet policy on energy conservation and fuel switching. Finally, Chapter 9 analyzes the puzzles of Soviet energy policy and sums up the lessons of the energy case for our understanding of the interaction between policy and system, the character of the recent leadership, and the problem of reform.

TWO

THE EVOLUTION OF SOVIET ENERGY POLICY, 1970–1988

Compared to Western industrial countries, the Soviet Union was slow to shift to oil and gas as the basis of its economy. Following World War II Soviet energy policy lagged in developing hydrocarbons; planners were reluctant to risk resources on exploration because they believed that oil and gas were scarce, high-cost fuels and would remain so.[1] As a result, the Soviet economy continued to run primarily on coal, peat, and wood.[2] It was not until the 1950s that Soviet leaders realized what a treasure trove of oil and gas they possessed.[3] But once official policy changed in the late 1950s, the Soviet economy moved rapidly to hydrocarbons, realizing important gains in energy efficiency throughout the 1960s.[4] From its birthplace in the Caucasus, the Soviet petroleum industry moved after World War II to the Volga Basin and then in the 1960s to West Siberia.

Initial Complacency, 1970–1977

One of the most important questions about policy making is how an issue becomes an issue, or, to put it in political-science language, how policy questions reach the public agenda. In the case of Soviet energy policy, awareness of impending energy problems reached the central

[1] Exploration in Siberia was especially resisted in the 1950s by the geological establishment in Moscow. Local geologists in Tiumen' who first began exploring the Ob' Basin were accused of "squandering the people's money." V. N. Tiurin, "Iamal'skii potentsial," *Oktiabr'*, no. 4 (1976), p. 138.

[2] As recently as 1959 solid fuels (coal, shale, peat, and firewood) accounted for 65 percent of Soviet primary fuel consumption. Between 1959 and 1980, however, oil and gas supplied 80 percent of the increment. Robert W. Campbell, "Energy," in Abram Bergson and Herbert S. Levine, eds., *The Soviet Economy: Toward the Year 2000* (London: George Allen and Unwin, 1983), p. 192.

[3] The best study of the long neglect of oil and gas in the Soviet Union is Robert W. Campbell's landmark book, *The Economics of Soviet Oil and Gas* (Baltimore: Johns Hopkins University Press, 1968).

[4] L. A. Melent'ev and A. A. Makarov, *Energeticheskii kompleks SSSR* (Moscow: Ekonomika, 1983), pp. 33–49.

leadership in two forms and via two main channels: first, as a reaction to the first world oil shock of the early 1970s, and second, as a response to bad news from the domestic oil fields.

At the beginning of the 1970s the energy situation as viewed from the Kremlin must have appeared cloud-free. With the development of the major oil and gas fields of the Volga Basin and the Ukraine in the 1950s and the opening of even larger fields in West Siberia in the 1960s, the Soviet Union was enjoying for the first time the luxury of cheap and efficient energy.

If one looks back to Soviet publications of the early 1970s, it is hard to find any public sign of high-level concern over future energy prospects. In his reports to the Party Central Committee in December 1972 and 1973, Brezhnev gave hardly more than a passing reference to the subject; and Kosygin, in his few published speeches on domestic policy during this period, had equally little to say about energy production or conservation.[5] In September 1972 the deputy prime minister for science and technology, V. A. Kirillin, spoke to the USSR Supreme Soviet on "rational utilization of natural resources" without making more than a passing mention of energy waste, except as a source of pollution.[6] The oil industry, as portrayed in the press at that time, was not without its problems, but they were explained as the consequences of rapid growth. At the September 1972 session of the USSR Supreme Soviet, for example, speakers criticized slow construction, particularly of oil and gas pipelines and of compressor stations.[7] But there was no talk of potential energy shortages.

By 1974 and 1975 one can find evidence of somewhat greater attention to energy policy in Moscow, at least among technical experts. In that year the State Planning Committee (Gosplan) established an Institute for the Integrated Study of Fuel and Energy Problems. In November 1974 energy was the major topic on the agenda of the USSR Academy of Sciences' annual meeting.[8] But the source of the speakers' heightened awareness of energy appears to have been the oil

[5] On 30 September 1972 Kosygin spoke to officials of Gosplan and on 6 October to those of the State Committee for Supply. Unfortunately, only excerpts of these speeches are available. A. N. Kosygin, *K velikoi tseli* (Moscow: Politizdat, 1979), vol. 2, pp. 149–160.

[6] V. A. Kirillin, *Pravda*, 16 Sept. 1972. There is equally little mention of the subject in the discussion that follows.

[7] Speeches by Deputy P. A. Rozenko (*Izvestiia*, 20 Dec. 1972) and Gosplan chairman N. K. Baibakov (*Izvestiia*, 19 Dec. 1972).

[8] *Vestnik Akademii Nauk SSSR*, no. 2 (1975), pp. 3–31. This issue carried the speeches of M. V. Keldysh, A. P. Aleksandrov, V. A. Kirillin, and M. A. Styrikovich. Already in Keldysh's introductory address and in Kirillin's article one can find the stress on coal that

crisis that had struck the West the year before. Their words carry no sense of a Soviet problem but rather an air of unhurried positioning for the future. If experts in Moscow did not yet perceive a crisis, political leaders and planners saw even less reason to worry. The most eloquent evidence is that the share of the energy sector in industrial investment fell steadily throughout the early 1970s, to a low of 28 percent in 1975 (table 2.1). At the Twenty-fifth Party Congress in February 1976 Brezhnev gave little more time to energy than he had in earlier speeches.

Nevertheless, the discussions among experts had evidently reached Prime Minister Aleksei Kosygin, whose own speech to the same Party congress outlined a coal-and-nuclear strategy that echoed the long-term views presented by academicians over the previous two years. Oil and gas, Kosygin declared to the congress delegates, should be saved as much as possible for nonfuel uses. Large coal-fired power plants would supply the Volga and Ural regions, and the vast brown coal reserves of Kazakhstan and Siberia would be converted to electricity by mine-mouth plants located nearby, the power flowing to points of demand in the European USSR over the world's longest high-voltage transmission lines. To begin this long-term shift toward coal, the guidelines for the Tenth Five-Year Plan called for an increase in coal output of 14–16 percent by 1980.

It is clear, however, that what Kosygin was describing to the Party congress was less an immediate plan of action and more a long-term program.[9] Significantly, for all their public stress on coal, the leaders failed to back up their words with an expanded flow of money to that sector. The Tenth Plan guidelines projected a continued decline in coal's share in the total energy balance, from 30 percent in 1975 to 26 percent in 1980,[10] and coal's investment share was also scheduled to slide. The leaders' spending plans showed they were aware that energy

---

became the centerpiece of official energy policy at the Twenty-fifth Party Congress in February 1976.

[9] Neither was the stress on coal entirely new, as one can see from an article by the economist Tigran Khachaturov, "Natural Resources and the Planning of the National Economy," in *Current Digest of the Soviet Press* 25, no. 49 (1973), p. 6. Khachaturov observed, "Since petroleum reserves are not as great as coal reserves, their use as fuel must be limited; petroleum should be used increasingly as a raw material for obtaining products of organic synthesis. . . . It will be better to use gas not as a fuel but as a chemical raw material." But it is clear from the context that Khachaturov was writing about what he considered to be a fairly remote future.

[10] See A. M. Nekrasov and M. G. Pervukhin, eds., *Energetika SSSR v 1976–1980 godakh* (Moscow: Energiia, 1977), p. 149.

TABLE 2.1
Investment in Energy Supply as a Share of Total Investment in Industry, 1970–1985 (excluding transmission; pre-1982 prices)

	Industry (billions of rubles)	*Energy (billions of rubles)*	*Energy Share (%)*
1970	28.6	8.2	28.7
Ninth Plan			
1971	30.3	8.9	29.4
1972	32.4	9.4	28.9
1973	34.1	9.8	28.6
1974	36.6	10.4	28.4
1975	39.9	11.2	28.0
Tenth Plan			
1976	40.6	11.4	28.2
1977	42.6	12.0	28.1
1978	45.2	13.4	29.7
1979	45.4	13.8	30.5
1980	47.6	15.1	31.7
Eleventh Plan			
1981	49.5	16.8	33.9
1982	50.9	17.7	34.8
1983	53.7	18.7	34.8
1984	61.9*	22.2*	35.9
1985	65.5*	25.3*	38.6

SOURCE: Figures on energy investment and overall industrial investment are taken from the yearly statistical handbook, *Narodnoe khoziaistvo SSSR*.

NOTE: Energy investment, as defined in *Narodnoe khoziaistvo* through 1985, excluded investment in transportation (notably pipelines) but included most exploration. As investment in gas transmission grew after the mid-1970s, this measure increasingly understated total investment in energy supplies. In the 1984 issue and after, *Narodnoe khoziaistvo* began reporting investment in post-1982 prices (quantities in post-1982 prices are indicated by an asterisk). I have not attempted to derive a standardized series here, since what is of interest is the share. Finally, in 1986 *Narodnoe khoziaistvo* switched to a broader definition of energy investment. Consequently, I have not attempted to calculate investment shares after 1985.

costs were rising; but their energy strategy remained centered on oil, not on gas or coal, and showed no sense of urgency.[11]

What makes this story of leisurely evolution especially striking is that during this same period storm clouds were clearly gathering over the Soviet oil fields. In the first half of the 1970s oil output from the older regions of the country (principally the Volga Basin) declined far more sharply than had been anticipated.[12] The planners reacted by steadily hiking up the output targets for Siberian oil, but professional oil men in Siberia warned that serious problems would result. (This issue is discussed in detail in Chapter 4.) One of the earliest items to appear in the Soviet press with a portent of things to come was a complaint in 1972 from the chief of the Tiumen' oil industry, V. I. Muravlenko, that funding for oil exploration in West Siberia had been frozen at a constant level for several years.[13] The Middle Ob' fields, one technical specialist asserted in 1973, could not provide an adequate base for further expansion of Soviet oil output after 1980.[14]

These views were not buried in obscure local journals; they were published in the central press and were comunicated directly and publicly to major officials at high-level conferences.[15] But evidently the

[11] For background on Soviet coal and on technological innovation in that industry to the end of the 1970s, see the chapter by William Kelly in U.S. Congress, Office of Technology Assessment, *Western Technology and Soviet Energy Availability* (Washington, D.C.: USGPO, October 1981); Central Intelligence Agency, National Foreign Assessment Center, USSR, *Coal Industry Problems and Prospects*, ER 80-10154 (Washington, D.C.: March 1980); same, *Central Siberian Brown Coal as a Potential Source of Power for European Russia*, SW 80-10006 (Washington, D.C.: April 1980); and Robert W. Campbell, *Soviet Energy Technologies: Planning, Policy, Research and Development* (Bloomington: Indiana University Press, 1980), ch. 4.

[12] See Ed A. Hewett, *Energy, Economics and Foreign Policy in the Soviet Union* (Washington, D.C.: Brookings Institution, 1984), table 2-4. The planners had reckoned on a decline in annual output of less than 150 million tons during 1971–1975, but the actual decline came closer to 260 million tons.

[13] *Izvestiia*, 18 July 1972, translated in *Current Digest of the Soviet Press* 24, no. 29 (1972), p. 20. Muravlenko was soon to become known as one of the most pessimistic critics of the oil outlook for Tiumen'. In an article in 1976 he dwelt at length on the daunting infrastructural requirements for meeting the official output targets of the Tenth Plan. *Sotsialisticheskaia industriia*, 1 Jan. 1976.

[14] *Ekonomika neftianoi promyshlennosti*, no. 6 (1973), p. 8.

[15] The fact that there was communication between technical specialists and at least some leaders over this problem can be seen from the fact that a major meeting on oil exploration, held in Tiumen' in late November 1973, was attended by Party Secretary V. I. Dolgikh, Gosplan Deputy Chairman A. M. Lalaiants, and Minister of Oil V. D. Shashin. The Tiumen' obkom First Secretary, then Boris Ie. Shcherbina (he was promoted one month later to the post of minister of oil and gas construction), criticized the geologists for their failure to move north (*Pravda*, 23 Nov. 1973). Oil Minister Shashin voiced the same concern in an article signed at about the same time (*Neftianoe khoziaistvo*, no. 3 [1974], p. 4).

warnings were not taken seriously. One reason is that the specialists in the field had cried wolf too often. Geologists and oil men had been consistently pessimistic about Soviet oil prospects from the start—and just as consistently wrong.

By the mid-1970s, then, energy had finally become an issue in the Kremlin, having reached the leadership in two forms. The first was the long-term view advocated by the scientific establishment and endorsed by Kosygin. This became the basis of the Tenth Five-Year Plan in 1975. The second was a growing stream of warnings about impending trouble in the oil fields, which was effectively disregarded. This tension between long-term and near-term perceptions, held by different groups with different agendas, has been a constant feature of Soviet energy policy ever since.

The Oil Crisis of 1977–1980

Soviet leaders were unprepared for the crisis that broke over their heads in the second half of the 1970s. Coal production in the Don Basin peaked in 1976 and then slid sharply, as did oil output in the older fields of the European USSR.[16] But the worst news came from West Siberia, which had become the mainstay of the Soviet energy economy. For the first time, geologists failed to meet their assigned targets for additions to proven and probable oil reserves. Other alarm signals went off too: the number of new fields identified, the flow rates of new wells, and, most important, the overall growth rate of Siberian oil output all began to drop. Faced with the possibility that oil output might peak at the end of the decade, the leaders realized they had to act.

In late 1977 Brezhnev decided on a crash program to save the West Siberian five-year oil output target, and in a speech to the December 1977 plenum of the Central Committee he stressed the decisive importance of Tiumen' for this purpose.[17] The decision to implement the program was not made all at once, however, nor was it unanimous. The first months of 1978 witnessed a good deal of discussion over the course to take, during which officials with links to Tiumen' lobbied

[16] Something of the impact of this on policymakers is conveyed in A. Aganbegian and Z. M. Ibragimova, *Sibir' na rubezhe vekov* (Moscow: Sovetskaia Rossiia, 1984), pp. 32–33. Aganbegian, a well-known Siberian economist, is now the head of the Economics Section of the USSR Academy of Sciences and an adviser to Gorbachev. Ibragimova is a Siberian journalist who in the mid-1970s was a correspondent for *Literaturnaia gazeta* and *Ekonomika i organizatsiia promyshlennogo proizvodstva* (*EKO*).

[17] Brezhnev's speech has not yet been reprinted in its entirety, but a lengthy extract appears in L. I. Brezhnev, *Ob osnovnykh voprosakh ekonomicheskoi politiki KPSS na sovremennom etape*, 2d ed. (Moscow: Politizdat, 1979), vol. 2, pp. 445–457.

vigorously for investment in Siberian oil.[18] The Moscow rumor mill had it that "the Siberians had gotten to Brezhnev" and that other major officials were opposed. It is a fact, at any rate, that Gosplan Chairman Nikolai K. Baibakov and Prime Minister Kosygin did not immediately echo Brezhnev's line—hardly surprising, since it amounted to dismantling the Tenth Plan in mid-course and reallocating the already meager investment increment to the energy sector.

During the winter and spring of 1978 Brezhnev had the air of a man on the stump, which recalled his efforts to launch his agricultural policy in the late 1960s. The new policy was apparently consolidated following a trip by Brezhnev to Siberia in the spring of 1978,[19] right on the heels of Kosygin, who had made a similar trip a few weeks before. Brezhnev followed up with a strongly worded speech to the Thirteenth Komsomol Congress in April, and in December an "enlarged session" of Gosplan officials was convened to review the practical issues of speeding up energy development in Siberia.[20]

The official investment statistics dovetail neatly with the change in tone of official speeches after 1977. The share of investment in energy, measured as a percentage of total industrial investment, took a sudden jump after 1977 and continued to climb rapidly until Brezhnev's death in 1982 (table 2.1). Oil investment began growing even faster, increasing its share of industrial investment dramatically from an average of 9.1 percent in the first half of the 1970s to nearly 14 percent in 1980.[21] Annual oil investment grew by nearly two-thirds in four years, from 4.1 billion rubles in 1976 to 6.6 billion in 1980.[22]

The suddenness with which the Kremlin changed its course led some Western observers to look for an outside impetus as well. In 1977 the Central Intelligence Agency (CIA) published three reports on prospects for Soviet oil production and trade, which predicted that Soviet oil

[18] See in particular an article by Tiumen' obkom First Secretary G. P. Bogomiakov in *Literaturnaia gazeta* (18 Jan. 1978), in which he states that the December 1977 plenum had determined precisely the place of the Tiumen' complex in satisfying the needs of the country for oil and gas, thus settling what Bogomiakov described as "not just a few contradictory judgments in views on the future."

[19] Brezhnev's 1978 trip to Siberia was treated by Tiumen' "patriots" as a highly symbolic event, as may be seen from the words of G. P. Bogomiakov at the Twenty-sixth Party Congress: "Of fundamental importance have been the instructions of L. I. Brezhnev on the future development of the fuel and power sector, the advice and comments made by him in the course of his trip to the regions of Siberia and the Far East." *Pravda*, 27 Feb. 1981.

[20] The Gosplan meeting was followed in June by a big conference at Academic City in Siberia on the same subject, which produced detailed recommendations.

[21] *Narodnoe khoziaistvo SSSR v 1985g* (Moscow: Finansy i statistika, 1986), p. 368.

[22] *Narodnoe khoziaistvo SSSR*, relevant years.

output would peak in 1980 and decline sharply thereafter, turning the Soviet bloc into net oil importers.[23] The reports received enormous attention worldwide, not least in the Soviet Union; more than a decade later, the Soviet press still mentions them. The interesting question is: Did the CIA's forecasts play a part in jolting Brezhnev into action? It is not implausible. The Soviet leadership in 1977 still clung to the energy strategy adopted two years before, even though it was plainer by the day that a policy based on coal and nuclear power was more a wishful postponement than a realistic program. The trickle of warnings from Siberia had become a flood, yet the leaders undoubtedly dreaded the disruption to their investment plans that a Siberian rescue would cause. In the midst of this apparent paralysis, the CIA reports may have been precisely the catalyst that the pro-Siberians were looking for. It is ironic, of course, that the core of the CIA's analysis was based largely on Soviet publications and merely repeated what Soviet experts had been warning about for years.

At all events, Brezhnev's emergency response saved the 1980 oil output target, as Chapter 3 describes in detail. But the campaign approach by which the job was done worsened the imbalance and inefficiency already characteristic of Soviet oil operations. The cost of Soviet oil skyrocketed during the second half of the 1970s, and by 1980 Soviet leaders faced the urgent question of what to do next. Energy economists told them that to keep the share of oil in the Soviet energy balance at its 1980 level of 44 percent through the first half of the 1980s, oil investment would have to increase between 3.7 and 3.8 times, that is, from 26.4 billion rubles in 1976–1980 to over 97 billion in 1981–1985, more than half again as much as the investment increase planned for all of Soviet industry.[24] Clearly, some other course was required.

The Turn to Gas, 1980–1981

In 1980–1981 Soviet energy policy took another major turn. While continuing an all-out effort to keep oil output growing, the leaders launched a major campaign to increase the role of natural gas. Gas had been the star performer of the previous five-year plan, since it was the only energy source whose output in 1980 actually reached the target set

[23] Central Intelligence Agency, *The International Energy Situation: Outlook to 1985*, ER77-10240 (Washington, D.C.: April 1977), *Prospects for Soviet Oil Production*, ER77-10270 (Washington, D.C.: April 1977), *Prospects for Soviet Oil Production: A Supplemental Analysis* (Washington, D.C.: July 1977).

[24] The cost of this "inertial" option is discussed in Melent'ev and Makarov, *Energeticheskii kompleks SSSR*, p. 165.

for it. The gas industry had been growing rapidly since the mid-1960s, and in the second half of the 1970s it had made a successful start in developing West Siberian gas and shipping it west by pipeline.

The exercise of making five-year plans forces Soviet leaders and planners, at least in principle, to take their bearings and chart a course that attempts to reconcile the needs of the near and long term. By 1980 it was clear to all that in the previous five years there had been a stunning increase in the costs of oil exploration and development.[25] As early as the fall of 1979, Brezhnev began calling for a rapid increase in gas production in the upcoming five-year plan.[26]

But the idea that Siberian gas, shipped over thousands of miles via expensive pipelines, should become the mainstay of the country's energy economy was still controversial. Decisionmakers had not yet adjusted their thinking to the fabulous gas reserves recently discovered in West Siberia (see Chapter 5), and they continued to think of gas as costly. Should they really burn such a high-value commodity in power plants and municipal heating systems? Several officials, including Brezhnev's own Central Committee secretary for heavy industry, V. I. Dolgikh, and the president of the USSR Academy of Sciences, A. P. Aleksandrov, argued no.[27] It was not so long before, after all, that the minister of gas himself had been arguing for a long-term plan to phase out natural gas as a boiler fuel, on the grounds that it was too scarce and expensive to be consumed in nonpremium uses.[28]

[25] For an excellent Western study, see Albina Tretyakova and Meredith Heinemeier, "Cost Estimates for the Soviet Oil Industry, 1970 to 1990," U.S. Bureau of the Census, Center for International Research, CIR Staff Paper no. 20 (Washington, D.C.: June 1986).

[26] Brezhnev speech at the November 1979 plenum of the CPSU Central Committee. *Pravda*, 28 Nov. 1979.

[27] V. I. Dolgikh, "Povyshat' uroven' rukovodstva predpriiatiiami toplivno-energeticheskogo kompleksa," *Partiinaia zhizn'*, no. 1 (1980), pp. 15–23; A. P. Aleksandrov, "Perspektivy energetiki," *Izvestiia*, 11 Apr. 1979. Until 30 September 1988, Dolgikh was the Central Committee official directly in charge of heavy industry and energy affairs. Aleksandrov (who was president of the USSR Academy of Sciences from 1975 to 1986) had chaired since the mid-1970s a commission to develop a long-term plan for electrical power. His commission continued to support coal and nuclear power as the long-term fuels for power generation while arguing that the share of natural gas in the power plant fuel balance should not grow (*Izvestiia*, 21 Feb. 1981). See also A. P. Aleksandrov, "Energoobespechenie strany," *Kommunist*, no. 4 (March 1981), pp. 84–90.

[28] This position greatly annoyed promoters of Siberian gas, who criticized the gas minister by name. Prominent among them was the first secretary of the Tiumen' obkom, G. P. Bogomiakov, who at this writing still occupies the same position. See "Tiumenskii kompleks i ego budushchee," *Ekonomika i organizatsiia promyshlennogo proizvodstva*, no. 5 (1976), p. 9.

What clinched the argument in favor of a "big gas" policy was that coal-based alternatives, whatever their long-term promise, were manifestly not ready and, in any case, threatened to be much more expensive than gas. Internal studies by Gosplan in the late 1970s showed that transmitting coal "by wire" from Siberia to the European USSR (that is, via high-voltage power lines from mine-mouth power plants) would be less efficient than gas transmission by pipeline.[29] There were some charges, however, that the studies had not been fair. Academy president A. P. Aleksandrov, implying that Gosplan officials were biased in favor of gas, openly accused them of blocking the high-voltage DC line planned to connect mine-mouth plants at Ekibastuz to consumers west of the Urals.[30] But in fact, Gosplan itself appears to have been divided, some planners speaking out openly in favor of a big gas policy, others, including chairman Baibakov himself, maintaining relative reserve.[31]

By the summer of 1980 the leaders had evidently made up their minds to go ahead.[32] One factor in the final decision may have been that Prime Minister Kosygin, who remained an advocate of coal and nuclear power right up to his final public appearances, was ailing.[33] In contrast, Brezhnev's old protégé Nikolai Tikhonov, who gradually as-

[29] A. Nekrasov and A. Troitskii, "Ob osnovnykh napravleniiakh razvitiia teplosnabzheniia narodnogo khoziaistva," *Planovoe khoziaistvo*, no. 2 (1980), pp. 45ff; and A. Troitskii, "Elektroenergetika: problemy i perskpektivy," *Planovoe khoziaistvo*, no. 2 (1979), pp. 18–25.

[30] "Vstupitel'noe slovo prezidenta Akademii Nauk SSSR Akademika A. P. Aleksandrova," *Vestnik Akademii Nauk SSSR*, no. 5 (1980), p. 12. See also the follow-up speech by Academician V. M. Tuchkevich on pp. 98–99.

[31] The warmest public advocate of the big gas policy at this time was S. Iatrov, then director of Gosplan's Institute for the Integrated Study of Fuel and Energy Problems, who echoed Brezhnev's call for displacing fuel oil with gas in power plants. See S. Iatrov, "Toplivno-energeticheskii kompleks," *Ekonomicheskaia gazeta*, no. 10 (March 1980), p. 10. On the other hand, the then head of Gosplan's Oil and Gas Department, V. Filanovskii-Zenkov, devoted an entire article to Siberian energy development without giving gas more than a few cursory lines. "Zapadno-Sibirskii neftegazovyi kompleks: rezul'taty i perspektivy," *Planovoe khoziaistvo*, no. 3 (1980), pp. 19–26. Filanovskii-Zenkov, a long-time oil official, has since returned to the Oil Ministry as first deputy minister. His relative discretion about gas may have been motivated by his greater concern about oil.

[32] One indication that the decision had been made was that the Soviet leaders, after months of hesitation, finally committed themselves to the East-West export pipeline in July 1980, on the occasion of West German Chancellor Willy Brandt's visit to Moscow.

[33] Throughout 1978 and 1979 Kosygin had continued to speak out in favor of coal and nuclear power, while stressing the undesirability of burning oil and gas in power plants (*Pravda*, 2 Mar., 24 May 1979). By mid-1980, while still emphasizing nuclear power and oil displacement, Kosygin did not repeat his previous words opposing the use of gas in power plants (*Pravda*, 18 June 1980).

sumed Kosygin's duties in early 1980 before replacing him officially in the fall, was especially critical of the coal industry and, by implication, favorable to gas.[34] Concern about hard-currency exports was another factor. Announcing the Politburo's decision to the Central Committee in the fall of 1980, Brezhnev justified it in part as a means of satisfying the energy requirements of Eastern Europe.[35] (As it turned out, this was a disingenuous argument, since at that very moment the Soviet leaders were negotiating the export pipeline to Western Europe.)

A review of the debate in 1979–1980 makes it clear that an increase in gas output was never in doubt; that was not the issue. Rather, there were two points of contention. The first was a choice between two horizons. To people like Aleksandrov and Kosygin, natural gas seemed too valuable and expensive to be more than a short-term bridge. Their continued stress on coal and nuclear power, even in the midst of the hydrocarbon emergency, reflected a concern that in the rush to provide for the near term the necessary preparation for a balanced longer range would be sacrificed. The second major concern was that the gas targets would be set so high that the result would be a fresh case of Bolshevik storming, with all the waste and disruption that implied. As preliminary target figures began to circulate in 1980, energy experts associated with Aleksandrov and the Academy of Sciences warned that the necessary industrial support could not be mobilized so fast.[36]

When Brezhnev announced the targets of the gas campaign at the Twenty-sixth Party Congress, these fears appeared justified. He proposed to increase natural gas output by nearly half in five years (from 435 billion cubic meters in 1980 to 630–640 billion in 1985), the bulk of the increase to come from West Siberia. Natural gas would provide 75 percent of the net addition to the fuel balance. To reach these targets, the gas industry would spend in the next five years as much capital as it had in the last fifteen years combined, or about 36 billion rubles, more than two-thirds of which would be devoted to building six huge trunk lines containing 20,000 kilometers of 56-inch pipe (a larger diameter than in any other country) between West Siberia and the

[34] Tikhonov's January 1980 report to the USSR Council of Ministers is reprinted in his volume of selected speeches, *Izbrannye rechi i stat'i* (Moscow: Politizdat, 1980), p. 419.

[35] Speech to the October 1980 plenum of the CPSU Central Committee, *Pravda*, 22 Oct. 1980.

[36] The ferrous metallurgy industry, they argued, would require four to seven years of advance preparation, and the machinery sector seven to ten years, before a major gas campaign could be supported effectively. Melent'ev and Makarov, *Energeticheskii kompleks SSSR*, pp. 206–214.

European USSR.[37] One of these lines would continue to Western Europe, supplying up to 40 billion cubic meters of new gas to hard-currency customers.

Brezhnev's strategy was evidently to maintain the share of hydrocarbons in the Soviet energy balance by increasing the proportion of gas while allowing that of oil to drop. The planners' 1985 oil targets show that the rising cost of oil had begun to hit home, because they held back the 1985 oil output target to 630 million tons. At first glance, this seems a modest goal; in fact, it was the level originally set for 1980 at the beginning of the previous plan.[38] This target implied that the share of oil in the Soviet fuel balance would decline from 44 to 39 percent, the gap to be made up with natural gas.[39] Even so, the oil industry would continue to claim the largest share of energy investment: 43 billion rubles, or an increase of 63 percent. As Chapter 4 will argue, however, even such a large increase in investment was not enough to offset rising oil costs, in view of the oil industry's low productivity, and the seemingly modest 1985 output target was in danger from the start.

Coal and nuclear power too were given prominent roles in the official script, but about these there was even more room for doubt. West of the Urals Soviet planners were counting on nuclear power to provide the entire increment to electrical generating capacity in the European USSR. This required bringing about 4.3 gigawatts of new nuclear capacity on line each year, an ambitious pace that, as subsequent events have proved, strained the capacity of engineers and builders to maintain quality and safety.[40] As for coal, the Eleventh Plan provided for a continued transfer of the coal industry east of the Urals to offset the decline of its traditional center in the Donbas. This new strategy rested on the enormous lignite deposits of the Kansk-Achinsk Basin in Krasnoiarsk Province. But to develop the basin's energy and bring its resources to users would require extensive investment in special boilers,

[37] Statements by then Gas Minister V. A. Dinkov, "Gazovaia promyshlennost' na marshe piatiletki," *Ekonomicheskaia gazeta*, no. 2 (1982), p. 2, and "West Siberia's Gas," *Novoe Vremia*, no. 19 (1982), p. 19.

[38] The planned increase in oil investment was announced in *Neftianoe khoziaistvo*, no. 4 (1982), p. 6. Initial targets for the Tenth Plan are taken from the text of the main guidelines, as reprinted in *XXVyi, S"ezd Kommunisticheskoi Partii Sovetskogo Soiuza* (stenograficheskii otchet) (Moscow: Izdatel'stvo politicheskoi literatury, 1976), vol. 2, pp. 226ff.

[39] Melent'ev and Makarov, *Energeticheskii kompleks SSSR*, p. 165.

[40] The nuclear program was heavily criticized in Soviet sources even before the near-meltdown at Chernobyl' in 1986. In the event, the rate of addition of new capacity averaged just under 3 gigawatts per year from 1981 to 1986. *Narodnoe khoziaistvo SSSR za 70 let* (Moscow: Finansy i statistika, 1987), p. 161.

transmission lines, and new technologies for synthetic fuels. Clearly, for both coal and nuclear power the payoff would come slowly.

For the near term, therefore, Brezhnev was counting on gas. To the 1981 Party congress he announced:

> I consider it necessary to single out the rapid development of Siberian gas output as a task of first-rank economic and political importance. The deposits of the West Siberian region are unique. The largest of them—Urengoy—has such gigantic reserves that it can meet for many years both the internal needs of the country and its export needs, including exports to the capitalist countries.[41]

But how carefully had these targets been thought through? During the previous year there had been unusually open controversy, not just over the energy program but over the entire Eleventh Plan. In the sharp disagreements over investment policy energy, as the fastest-growing and hence most disruptive claimant, must have been the most heavily debated of all. And the leaders evidently shrank before the enormous sums their initial energy goals required. When the final version of the plan was unveiled in the fall of 1981, all the preliminary energy output targets announced in the draft version had been cut back—but not gas, whose priority only grew stronger. In November 1981 Brezhnev described the six major Siberian gas pipelines as "without a doubt the central construction projects of the five-year plan." And he added, "They must be finished on time without fail."[42] The shift to gas appears to have been one of the few things that could command a consensus. Yet, as we shall see in Chapters 6 and 7, the suddenness and scale of the gas campaign took the industry by surprise. Instead of one crash campaign in Siberia, there would now be two.

Before assessing the burden of Brezhnev's energy policy, we should pause to reflect on his remarkable behavior. In effect, Brezhnev seized control of energy policy in 1977 and retained the leading role in it until his death. The crash oil and gas campaigns were his. But to judge from their reserved reactions, other major leaders like Kosygin and Baibakov were not convinced that so extreme a response was necessary. Indeed, as the next three chapters will argue, the Brezhnev oil and gas campaigns did a great deal of damage. A plausible case can be made that a slower, more methodical, and more balanced approach—aiming in particular for stabilization of oil output rather than continued expansion—might have produced a healthier situation a decade later.

Why did Brezhnev reject such a course? He was undoubtedly afraid

[41] *Pravda*, 24 Feb. 1981, p. 5.

[42] *Pravda*, 18 Nov. 1981.

of an energy shortage; as we shall see, that danger was real enough. But there may have been other motives as well. In the mid- to late 1970s, as the performance of the economy deteriorated, Brezhnev's policies and authority were under growing attack from several quarters. Though Kosygin's health was failing, he evidently joined Brezhnev's critics, and public polemics broke out between them, suggesting renewed competition within the leadership for the first time in a decade, mainly over the question of who would bear the blame for the administration's failures.[43] Brezhnev responded with new policy initiatives, evidently aimed at reasserting his authority and strengthening his control. The energy campaigns were probably part of this larger strategy. And if the CIA's first report on Soviet oil was indeed a catalyst, that would fit logically within this line of explanation. By 1977 detente was already going sour. The CIA report not only alarmed the leaders; it undoubtedly offended their national pride as well, a most useful emotion for Brezhnev's purposes. These factors help to account for the suddenness and sweep of the Brezhnev energy campaign:[44] the responses were vigorous because the point was precisely to show vigor. Undoubtedly, the same motives are not foreign to Gorbachev, as we shall see.

The Growing Burden of Energy

Behind the oil and coal crises lay a larger problem: a general rise in Soviet energy costs, which began in 1970 and accelerated sharply in the second half of the decade. Energy resources are wasting assets, but the inevitable rear-guard battle against diminishing returns can be fought well or badly. An extractive industry can contain rising costs by increasing its efficiency through innovation, improved management, and vigorous exploration. Soviet energy policy, as we shall see, employed these tactics poorly. As a result, a sector whose technology and operations in 1970 were reasonably well suited to its circumstances had by 1980 fallen into serious trouble. To keep energy output growing, Soviet leaders were obliged to keep increasing the share of energy in total

[43] This theme has been developed by several scholars who have analyzed the late Brezhnev period. See in particular George W. Breslauer, "Reformism, Conservatism, and Leadership Authority at the 26th Party Congress," in Seweryn Bialer and Thane Gustafson, eds., *Russia at the Crossroads: The 26th Congress of the CPSU* (London: George Allen and Unwin, 1982), pp. 71–73.

[44] By the time of Brezhnev's report to the Twenty-sixth Party Congress in 1981, Breslauer writes, "Energy simply dominated the speech, to such an extent that I am tempted to propose that Brezhnev embraced it as the heroic campaign of the decade, by which he would retain the policy initiative and demonstrate his policy effectiveness." Breslauer, "Reformism," p. 73.

industrial investment. This trend was especially striking at the margin: in the second half of the 1970s energy had already absorbed 46 percent of the growth in industrial capital spending. But that was only the start.[45] By the beginning of the 1980s the emergency oil response of 1977 had grown into a massive Siberian energy offensive that threatened to monopolize most of the growth in Soviet industrial investment.

In November 1981 Gosplan chairman N. K. Baibakov announced that energy investment would grow by 44 billion rubles, or 50 percent, between 1981 and 1985. This total, when combined with the record low growth announced for total investment (10.4 percent over five years),[46] implied that energy was to absorb fully two-thirds of all new Soviet investment during the coming five-year plan. The same low-investment diet was not imposed on Soviet industry, which was planned to grow by 23 percent; but even so, the share of energy in the planned increment of industrial investment came to a whopping 85.6 percent![47] One can imagine the long faces in many an industrial ministry in Moscow as the implications of the new energy investment targets for the Eleventh Plan sank home.

Such large increases in investment show that the planners had realized that marginal energy costs were climbing fast, but had they understood just how fast? At first glance, their energy output goals seem realistically modest (table 2.2). The 1985 target for oil was essentially the same as the one that the planners, back in 1976, had hoped to reach in 1980, and the coal target was actually lower. "In recent years," wrote a high Gosplan official, "capital investment in exploration, extraction, and transportation of energy has grown 50 percent faster than energy output itself, and in the oil and gas industries 60 to 100 percent

[45] Energy investment in this example and in table 6.4 is calculated inclusive of transmission, using figures on gas pipeline investment from A. D. Sedykh and B. A. Kuchin, *Upravlenie nauchno-tekhnicheskim progressom v gazovoi promyshlennosti* (Moscow: Nedra, 1983) and on oil pipeline investment from Tretyakova and Heinemeier, "Cost Estimates." Industrial investment is taken from *Narodnoe khoziaistvo SSSR v 1980g*. In absolute terms, energy investment in the first half of the 1970s is taken as 57.8 billion rubles and in the second half as 81.5 billion (both in pre-1982 prices), yielding an increment of 23.7 billion in 1976–1980. The increment in total industrial investment during the same period was 51.1 billion rubles.

[46] Western analysts still do not understand why this extraordinarily low target was chosen or whether it was ever meant seriously. In an earlier speech on the preliminary draft of the five-year plan, in February 1981, Brezhnev had announced an investment growth target of 12 to 15 percent. *Pravda*, 24 Feb. 1981.

[47] Baibakov speech, *Izvestiia*, 18 Nov. 1981. This figure is derived by dividing the announced 44 billion ruble increment for energy by the 23 percent growth in industrial investment, i.e., 51.4 billion rubles.

TABLE 2.2
1985 Energy Production Targets as Set in 1981

	1980 (actual)	*Draft Eleventh Plan*	*Final Eleventh Plan*
Oil (mtnat)	603	620–640	630
Coal (mtnat)	716	770–800	775
Gas (bcm)	435	600–640	630
Electricity (Bkw-hr)	1,294	1,550–1,600	1,555
hydropower (Bkw-hr)	184	230–235	230
nuclear (Bkw-hr)	73	220–225	220

SOURCES: 1980 data: *Narodnoe khoziaistvo SSSR v 1980g.*; Eleventh Plan data: *Izvestiia*, 18 Nov. 1981.

KEY: mtnat = millions of natural tons; bcm = billions of cubic meters; Bkw-hr = billions of kilowatt-hours.

faster."[48] Yet events in the first half of the 1980s, as we shall see, showed that marginal costs were rising even faster than the planners had allowed for.

To appreciate what this implied for the economy as a whole, one must also take into account the capital and manpower requirements of supporting industries and the expenditures associated with consuming energy as well as supplying it. Table 2.3 reproduces the calculations of a Siberian energy expert to give the flavor of some of the numbers circulating in policy circles in Moscow. In 1980, these numbers say, direct investment in energy supply required 22.5–23 billion rubles, but indirect investment for energy consumption added another 50 to 60 percent to basic fuel investment, distributed as shown in the table. Thus energy, which in the narrow sense took up about 50 percent of Soviet industrial investment in 1980[49] and 5.5 percent of the work force,[50] by the broader definition claimed as much as 80 percent of total (not marginal) industrial investment and 13 to 15 percent of total employ-

[48] A. A. Troitskii, "Osnovnye napravleniia razvitiia toplivnoenergeticheskogo balansa elektroenergetiki strany," *Teploenergetika*, no. 5 (1981), pp. 2–4.

[49] This is a larger share than in table 2.1 because the definition of investment used here includes transmission and probably all exploration as well. Total industrial investment in 1980 (pre-1982 prices) was 46.5 billion rubles. *Narodnoe khoziaistvo SSSR v 1980g.*, p. 338.

[50] Work force in 1980 is taken as 112.5 million. *Narodnoe khoziaistvo SSSR v 1980g.*, p. 357.

TABLE 2.3
The Broad Burden of Energy Investment, 1980

	Capital Investment (billions of rubles)	*Manpower (millions of workers)*
Production, transformation, and distribution of energy resources	22.5–23.0	6.0–6.4
fuel supply*	16.0	2.9
centralized heat and electricity supply (Minenergo)†	4.0	NA
power plants and boilers belonging to individual agencies (excluding Minenergo)	2.5–3.0	3.1–3.5
Ancillary branches, supporting operation and growth of fuel-and-power complex	4.0–5.0	5.5–6.5
Investment required for energy consumption	7.0–9.0	3.5–4.1
TOTALS	33.5–37.0	15.0–17.0

SOURCE: Iu. D. Kononov, "Toplivno-energeticheskii kompleks v sisteme narodnokhoziaistvennykh sviazei," *Ekonomika i organizatsiia promyshlennogo proizvodstva*, no. 4 (1983), p. 20. Kononov's analysis is given in fuller form in his chapter in Melent'ev and Makarov, *Energeticheskii kompleks SSSR*, pp. 197–227.

* Includes exploration, extraction, processing, and transmission. This total is considerably larger than the one listed in the official handbook, which without electrical power comes to about 11 billion rubles for 1980.

† Ministry of Power and Electrification.

ment! These numbers simply strain belief. Nevertheless, the Siberian's point must have been clear in Moscow: the load placed on the economy by a further abrupt acceleration of energy investment, amounting to a 50 percent increase over five years, would be backbreaking.

To run ahead of our story a bit, how did investment actually turn out by the end of the five year plan? The leaders abandoned their overall low-investment diet almost immediately. Total investment grew by 17.5 percent during the Eleventh Plan, instead of the 10.4 percent initially envisaged.[51] But industrial investment, which had been slated to grow by 23 percent, was held back to 19.6 percent.[52] In other

[51] This was still low by historical Soviet standards. Investment growth in the Tenth Plan had been 27.5 percent.

[52] *Narodnoe khoziaistvo SSSR v 1985g.*, p. 367.

words, the leaders relaxed their investment constraint primarily in sectors other than industry, particularly in transportation and construction, while tightening it further for industry itself.

Energy investment, on the other hand, conformed to the five-year target fairly closely, growing by only a little less than the 50 percent originally announced for it (table 2.4). In the end, the increase in energy investment between 1981 and 1985 absorbed over a third of total investment growth, though substantially less than originally planned. *But energy absorbed nearly 90 percent of the 44 billion ruble increment allocated to industry, leaving the rest of the industrial sector with*

TABLE 2.4
Growth of Actual Energy Investment, 1976–1985
(in billions of pre-1982 rubles)

	Tenth Plan	*Eleventh Plan*
Oil	26.4	45.2
Coal	9.8	11.6
Gas	10.3	14.5
Electricity	19.4	24.3
Gas pipelines	12.1	22.5
Oil pipelines	3.5	3.0
Exploration*	3.5	4.6
TOTAL	85.0	125.7 (+47.9%)

SOURCES: Gas pipelines: B. L. Krivoshein and P. I. Tugunov, *Magistral'nyi truboprovodnyi transport* (Moscow: Nauka, 1985), p. 10; oil pipelines: guesstimate based on Tretyakova and Heinemeier, "Cost Estimates for the Soviet Oil Industry"; all others: *Narodnoe khoziaistvo SSSR v 1985g.*

NOTE: Pre-1982 prices have been estimated by deflating the Eleventh Plan numbers by the ratios between new prices and old prices used for Tenth Plan numbers in the official handbook, industry by industry.

* Here exploration investment is limited to a rough estimate of the Ministry of Geology's funding from the central budget, as explained in Chapter 3.

essentially stagnant investment budgets. One particularly significant implication, examined in detail in Chapter 7, is that the engineering sector (or machine-building industry, in Soviet vocabulary) was squeezed to pay for the energy campaign, particularly the oil and gas service sector and other industrial support for the oil and gas campaigns.

Within the energy sector, investment in electrical power and oil grew somewhat faster than planned, while investment in coal and gas grew more slowly. Overall, however, divergences from the plan were small. This fact in itself is remarkable, given that an extended succession crisis was taking place at the same time, which produced three new General Secretaries between 1982 and 1985. Although we shall see that priorities did fluctuate somewhat with the changes of leadership, the overall consistency of policy in the first half of the 1980s suggests a broad consensus within the leadership, at least over near-term policy. Yet it is clear in retrospect that the consensus was a thin surface under which pressures were building, pressures that would soon lead to new priorities under Gorbachev.

But the growing investment burden bought much less additional energy than had the previous five-year plan, because of sharply rising unit costs. In the first half of the 1970s a 38 percent increase in investment had yielded a 28 percent increase in energy production; in the first half of the 1980s a 48 percent investment rise produced only 13 percent more energy (table 2.5). In broad terms, then, it took nearly three times

TABLE 2.5
Investment Growth versus Increases in Energy Output

Growth in Energy Output		*Growth in Investment*		*Marginal Ratio P/I*
1975/70	28%	1971–1976	38%	1 to 1.35
1980/75	21	1976–1980	41	1 to 2.00
1985/80	13	1981–1985	48	1 to 3.70

SOURCES: Growth in energy output is calculated from the energy balances given in *Narodnoe khoziaistvo SSSR v 1985g.*, p. 53 (taken as the sum of extraction [*dobycha*], hydropower, and other sources [*prochie postupleniia*]). Growth in investment is taken from table 2.4 above and from *Narodnoe khoziaistvo SSSR v 1980g.*, plus estimates for gas and oil pipeline investment from Sedykh and Kuchin, *Upravlenie nauchno-tekhnicheskim progressom*, and Tretyakova and Heinemeier, "Cost Estimates for the Soviet Oil Industry." This procedure appears to assume that all investments made during a given period produce results by the end of that period, which of course is not the case. Nevertheless, it is a first approximation of the major trends.

as much investment growth to produce and deliver an additional unit of energy in 1981–1985 as it had in 1970–1975.

Despite their more modest objectives, the steepness of this cost trend still took the leaders by surprise. In 1981 they had anticipated a 17 percent rise in energy production; by 1985 they had realized an increase of only 13 percent, distributed as shown in table 2.6. Natural gas accounted for nearly all of the net increase (95 percent), causing a dramatic drop in the share of oil in the Soviet energy balance.[53] The substitution of gas for oil, as we shall see in greater detail in Chapter 7, was the major development of the first half of the 1980s, as it will continue to be for the rest of the century.

The dramatic growth of energy investment, combined with the continuing high-priority flow of resources to the defense industry,[54] sheds new light on the reasons for the disastrous performance of the Soviet economy during the decade 1975–1985. Energy and defense, with a little help from bad weather, dominated Brezhnev's economic policy in the second half of his reign, paralyzing industrial modernization, especially in the civilian machinery sector.

Facing the Dilemmas of Energy Policy, 1982–1988

Even before Brezhnev's death in 1982, the enormity of the investment burden in Siberian oil and gas, combined with the rapidly deteriorating cost trends in energy production, stimulated new efforts to define a more balanced and long-term strategy. The emergency response of 1977 had staved off a downturn in oil output, and the gas campaign launched in 1980 stabilized the share of hydrocarbons in the Soviet energy balance. But the result was a policy still fixated on supply, seemingly oblivious to runaway energy demand, and thus condemned to ever more costly operations in ever more remote wilderness. The leadership had every incentive to start thinking about conservation.

[53] In absolute numbers, natural gas provided 245.7 mtce (millions of tons of coal equivalent) out of a total net increase of 259 in 1981–1985. *Narodnoe khoziaistvo SSSR v. 1985g.*

[54] Robert Campbell has examined the flows of material resources and manpower within the engineering sector during the decade 1975–1985 and has concluded that the nine military-industrial ministries continued to receive a growing share, despite what appears to have been the leaders' belief, from 1981 on, that they were slowing the growth of defense spending. See Robert W. Campbell, "Resource Stringency and the Civilian-Military Resource Allocation," in Timothy J. Colton and Thane Gustafson, eds., *Soviet Soldiers and the State: Civil-Military Relations from Brezhnev to Gorbachev* (forthcoming, 1990).

TABLE 2.6
Energy Output Growth, 1980–1985

	1980 (actual)	*1985 (plan)*	*1985 (actual)*
Oil (mtnat)	603	630	595
Coal (mtnat)	716	775	726
Gas (bcm)	435	630	643
Electricity (Bkw-hr)	1,294	1,555	1,544
hydropower (Bkw-hr)	184	230	215
nuclear (Bkw-hr)	73	220	167

SOURCES: 1980 and 1985 actual data: *Narodnoe khoziaistvo SSSR v 1985g.*; Eleventh Plan data: *Izvestiia*, 18 Nov. 1981.

Brezhnev himself, in the last years of his life, devoted gradually more space in his speeches to energy conservation.[55] In 1979, he commissioned a panel of experts, under the chairmanship of Academy of Sciences president A. P. Aleksandrov, to develop a long-term energy program.[56] Even as the oil and gas campaigns continued to grow, experts began to debate a twenty-year plan to rebalance energy policy toward conservation. But so long as Brezhnev lived, it was the voice of the short term that shaped decisions.

Brezhnev's death opened the way for a host of reform ideas that had been debated for years. But few of them, as Brezhnev's successor, Iurii Andropov, admitted, were ready to implement. The energy program was one of the few exceptions, since by 1982 the Aleksandrov Commission had been at work for several years. Andropov seized upon the draft energy program as one of his first policy initiatives. In his opening speech as General Secretary, in November 1982, he hinted that he planned to put conservation and fuel switching ahead of energy supply. In April 1983 the Politburo approved the draft energy program,[57] and

[55] His speeches to the November 1979 and October 1980 plenums of the Party Central Committee contained strong words in favor of energy conservation (L. I. Brezhnev, *Leninskim kursom* [Moscow: Izdatel'stvo politicheskoi literatury, various years], vol. 8, pp. 200 and 473), and over the same period two major decrees appeared on recovering waste heat and on saving raw materials and energy.

[56] Melent'ev and Makarov, *Energeticheskii kompleks SSSR*, p. 5. During the second half of the 1970s Aleksandrov had chaired a similar commission to study the long-term development of electrical power. I do not know whether the new commission was a continuation or an outgrowth of the previous one, or whether it was entirely new.

[57] "V Politbiuro Tsk KPSS," *Pravda*, 9 Apr. 1983.

in June Andropov unveiled it before the Party Central Committee, describing it as an epoch-making event, a "GOELRO for today's conditions."[58]

As Andropov's health failed rapidly from the summer of 1983 on, official pronouncements from the Politburo continued to stress conservation and fuel switching.[59] A program to displace oil by converting power plants to gas, which had been a dead issue before 1983, came to life under Andropov and continued after 1984, along with other new measures to promote conservation (these are discussed in detail in Chapter 9). Oil investment, which had grown rapidly since 1977, suddenly flattened in 1983 and 1984 (table 2.7). These points suggest that Andropov seriously intended to reorient energy policy; and although no new initiatives were taken under Chernenko, he did not reverse what Andropov had begun.

Events between 1982 and 1984, however, showed how risky and expensive such a course would be. The Soviet nuclear program fell behind schedule and required emergency transfusions of capital.[60] Meanwhile, coal output continued to stagnate while deteriorating in quality.[61] Most serious of all, West Siberian oil output, which had been slowing since 1980, actually began declining in 1983. The reprieve bought by the Brezhnev emergency oil campaign was over.

Politicians and planners, debating the targets of the upcoming Twelfth Plan amid the uncertainties of a succession of successions, now faced in more acute form than ever a dilemma they had hitherto managed to postpone. The hydrocarbon-based policy pursued since the

[58] The expression GOELRO (State Program for the Electrification of Russia) referred to one of the earliest experiments in countrywide planning in the 1920s. See L. A. Melent'ev, *Ocherki istorii otechestvennoi energetiki: razvitie nauchno-tekhnicheskoi mysli* (Moscow: Nauka, 1987), ch. 2. Its use by Andropov was intended not only to invoke hallowed precedents but also to suggest the landmark quality of what Andropov had in mind. In fact, though, GOELRO's real significance was as the forerunner of the five-year plans. Andropov's invocation of GOELRO was an unwitting suggestion that he still thought in terms of large, centrally directed campaigns.

[59] Thus the November 1983 plenum of the Central Committee and a Politburo meeting that preceded it adopted measures to conserve oil products and commented on the rapidly rising cost of oil production. "V Politbiuro TsK KPSS," *Pravda*, 29 Oct. 1983.

[60] For an overview, see Theodore Shabad, "Nuclear Power Developments," *Soviet Geography* 25 (January 1984), pp. 63–64.

[61] For details on trends in coal quality, see Chapter 9. In 1986 *Narodnoe khoziaistvo SSSR* began taking account of the decline in coal quality in reporting coal output. Whereas the 1985 handbook gave 1985 coal output as 487 million tons of standard fuel (mtst, or "coal-equivalent," i.e., 7,000 kilocalories per ton), the 1986 handbook revised the 1985 figure downward to 440 mtst.

TABLE 2.7
Oil Investment, 1976–1985
(excluding transportation; in billions of pre-1982 rubles)

Tenth Plan (1976–1980):	26.4 (+ 65.0%)
Eleventh Plan (1981–1985):	45.2 (+ 71.0%)
1981:	8.1 (+ 19.0%)
1982:	8.7 (+ 7.4%)
1983:	9.1 (+ 4.6%)
1984:	8.9 (– 2.2%)
1985:	10.4 (+ 17.0%)

SOURCE: *Narodnoe khoziaistvo SSSR*, various years.

NOTE: In 1984 *Narodnoe khoziaistvo* began reporting investment data in new prices; I have therefore adjusted them downward by 11 percent to approximate pre-1982 prices. Eleven percent is the difference between Tenth Plan totals as given in pre-1982 prices (in *Narodnoe khoziaistvo SSSR v 1980g.*) and in post-1982 prices (in *Narodnoe khoziaistvo SSSR v 1985g.*). I have used this difference to approximate the pre-1982 price base for oil investment numbers given in new prices (1984 and 1985). This is a rough-and-ready method that gives only general trends and may not agree in detail with other sources. See Chapter 4, note 69.

beginning of the 1960s, oriented almost entirely toward increasing energy supplies instead of limiting demand, promised only a steadily steepening slope of cost and risk. Yet shifting to a policy based on conservation and oil displacement would be no less expensive, at least in the first decade or two, and possibly even riskier, because reducing consumption in industry would require renewing a substantial part of the country's capital stock. Simultaneously, a system that was accustomed to treating energy as a cheap commodity would have to change its habits, attitudes, incentives, and signals—a slow process at best, and at any rate an uncertain one. Political priority and resources would have to be removed from the supply side and transferred to the demand side. This would create a difficult and lengthy adjustment period, during which energy supplies would lag but energy demand would still be high. The only safe way to cross the divide was through a combination of more investment increases, reduced energy exports, and restricted consumption at home—a painfully expensive formula.

Soviet leaders, as aware as anyone of the inertia and rigidity of their own system, understandably thought twice before taking the plunge.

Yet the longer they delayed, the more painful the transition would finally be. The record of the last three General Secretaries is quickly summed up: Brezhnev flinched and played safe; Andropov appeared prepared to venture forward but hardly had time to get started; and Chernenko, like a ghost flitting briefly across the scene, left no trace.

Yet the succession of moribund leaders did not dull debates over policy; it sharpened them. One symptom of the intense energy politics in 1983–1984 was that the Aleksandrov Commission's energy program, announced in June 1983, was not made public until March 1984, one month after Andropov's death.[62] When it finally appeared, the proconservation stance encouraged by Andropov had been watered down.[63] In particular, the published program called for oil and condensate output to keep growing to the year 2000 (some of the Aleksandrov Commission's experts, on the contrary, had stressed oil's high cost and uncertainty, hinting that output should be allowed to peak), and it was vague about the conservation measures to be undertaken in the second half of the 1980s.[64] In short, the program showed several signs of retreat to an energy policy still heavily based on oil, undoubtedly reflecting a combination of weakened leadership at the top and the worrisome events of 1983 and 1984.

Nevertheless, even in this weakened form the program marked an important advance in energy policy. For the first time, it offered a guide for managing the risky transition to a consumption-oriented strategy and brought together the voices of the long term and the short. The essence of the strategy (described at greater length in Chapter 7) was to divide the turn to conservation into two stages, one of preparation (1983–1990) and one of active execution (1990–2000).

The energy program also conveyed the unpleasant news that this combined approach would cost more money, thus increasing the bur-

[62] *Ekonomicheskaia gazeta*, no. 12 (March 1984), centerfold.

[63] This inference is based on a comparison of the published program with the recommendations of the energy experts upon whose work the energy program was based. A summary of the group's data and recommendations was published in book form in 1983. See L. A. Melent'ev and A. A. Makarov, *Energeticheskii kompleks SSSR*, pp. 5–6. For a shorter exposition, see D. B. Vol'fberg and A. A. Makarov, "Ratsional'noe ispol'zovanie i ekonomiia toplivno-energeticheskikh resursov," in D. G. Zhimerin, ed., *Sovremennye problemy energetiki* (Moscow: Energoatomizdat, 1984), pp. 59–83.

[64] The program called only for "creating the preconditions" (*sozdat' predposylki*) by 1990 for a transition to coal and conservation. The Aleksandrov Commission's experts, in contrast, had been quite specific about taking steps immediately to improve measurement, oversight, accountability, and incentives, to retire inefficient equipment, to use waste heat, and to enhance fuel quality, especially that of coal. See Melent'ev and Makarov, *Energeticheskii kompleks SSSR*, pp. 99–100.

den of energy still further in the short term, at precisely the moment when the claims of other sectors were mounting. Indeed, the program projected that for the remainder of the century the energy sector would absorb a much larger share of total investment than ever before (table 2.8).

Initial Choices under Gorbachev, 1985–1988

Even before he became General Secretary, Mikhail Gorbachev appeared eager to restructure industrial policy and to escape the vise of ever-increasing investment in energy supplies. In those two respects, the outlines of his future policy were taking shape as early as April 1983, when he was already a full member of the Politburo and looming as the heir apparent. On the highly visible occasion of Lenin's birthday, Gorbachev, in one of his first major policy speeches, put the machinery sector at the top of his priority list, ahead of energy. In contrast, speaking on the same occasion a year later, Dolgikh, the Central Committee secretary for heavy industry and energy, returned energy to first place and put machinery third after agriculture. Baibakov, announcing the 1985 plan to the Supreme Soviet in November 1984, also put energy ahead of the machinery sector. The difference in priorities could not have been made clearer than when, the following April, Gorbachev rose to deliver his first policy speech as General Secretary. His order of investment priorities, which was to become familiar over the following years, put the machinery sector first, followed by food, consumer goods, and social welfare. Energy supplies he did not mention at all.[65]

Over the following three months Gorbachev presented to his audiences a wish-list of investment policies that clearly rejected the Brezhnevian supply-side approach, although he did not associate it publicly with Brezhnev's name until two years later. Exclaiming over the rising costs of oil, Gorbachev called for a massive reorientation of capital toward conservation—not only of energy but of all natural resources—and toward modernization and reconstruction of existing plant rather than new starts.[66] The machinery sector would become the

[65] "O sozyve ocherednogo XXVII s"ezda KPSS i zadachakh, sviazannykh s ego podgotovkoi i provedeniem" (address to the Central Committee Plenum, 23 April 1985), reprinted in M. S. Gorbachev, *Izbrannye rechi i stat'i* (Moscow: Politizdat, 1987), vol. 2, pp. 7–28.

[66] "Nastoichivo dvigat'sia vpered" (speech to members of the Leningrad Party organization, 17 May 1985), reprinted in Gorbachev, *Izbrannye rechi i stat'i*, vol. 2, p. 75. Gorbachev told his audience that the cost of developing new output capacity had increased by 70 percent in ten years. Ironically, as we shall see in the next chapter, his figure was almost certainly a substantial underestimate, perhaps by a factor of three.

TABLE 2.8
Energy Investment as a Share of Total Soviet Investment (energy program forecast, 1983)

Years	*Percentage*
1960–1980	13–14
1981–1985	18–19
1985–2000	20–22

SOURCES: 1960–1985: Melent'ev and Makarov, *Energeticheskii kompleks SSSR*, p. 158; 1985–2000: energy program, *Ekonomicheskaia Gazeta*, no. 12 (1984).

NOTE: Ancillary investment, especially on the consumption side, is not included.

major new growth point in Soviet investment, while the share of capital spending on extractive industries would be stabilized.[67]

Gorbachev, like Andropov, was facing the dilemmas of Soviet resource policy that Brezhnev had ducked. But how far and how fast would he dare to go? Events challenged him immediately. Late in 1984, despite the frantic efforts of the oil industry, Soviet oil output began to fall, and the decline accelerated in the winter and spring of 1985. Cold weather in the winter of 1985 both impeded oil extraction and added to its consumption, leading to a sharp drop in Soviet oil exports for that year. World oil prices, which had been declining slowly since their peak in 1981, plummeted at the end of 1985. In the same year the dollar began to fall against other major currencies. Overnight the windfall oil-and-dollar profits the Soviets had been enjoying for years were wiped out. Soviet terms of trade in 1986, in terms of crude oil versus West German manufactured equipment, dropped by 60 percent from the level of 1983.[68] As a result, the Soviet leaders faced a familiar conflict

67 "Korennoi vopros ekonomicheskoi politiki Partii" (speech to a meeting at Central Committee headquarters on acceleration of scientific and technological progress, 11 June 1985), reprinted in Gorbachev, *Izbrannye rechi i stat'i*, vol. 2, pp. 116–117.

68 Ed A. Hewett, "Soviet Energy Policy at Mid-Decade," in *PlanEcon Long-Term Energy Outlook* (Washington, D.C.: PlanEcon, Inc., Fall 1986), p. 3.

between near-term and long-term policy, but even more pressingly than eight years before.

These energy troubles coincided with a tough battle over priorities in the next five-year plan. The struggle had evidently begun even before Gorbachev's accession. In 1984 and the first half of 1985 the Politburo rejected draft after draft of the Twelfth Five-Year Plan, as Gosplan and the ministries resisted shifting resources on the scale Gorbachev demanded.[69] The overall result was a political compromise that gave each side what it wanted, mainly by summing everyone's priorities and avoiding hard choices. In particular, the plan called for high growth and improved quality simultaneously. The result was a five-year plan that most Western observers (and most Soviet planners as well) dismissed from the start as unworkable.[70] Planned investment in energy supply continued to bound ahead (as we shall see in more detail below). If Gorbachev's hope had really been to stabilize the share of extractive industry in Soviet investment, he had lost his battle.

How did this happen? It would be a mistake to see the compromise purely as the result of rear-guard resistance by conservatives, although there was plenty of that. Rather, over the course of 1985 the new leadership was forced, step by step, to come to terms with its constrained inheritance. This point can be seen clearly in one of the most important issues at stake in the debates over the Twelfth Plan during the summer and fall of 1985: the new leaders' future policy toward Siberia.

During the 1970s Siberia became the Soviet Union's main source of energy.[71] But the crash growth of the Siberian energy industry unbalanced the economy of the entire region. Most of the 40 percent increase in capital investment planned for Siberian industry in the first half of the 1980s was absorbed by oil and gas in Tiumen' Province. Other branches of industry, even ones that played essential support roles for energy development, either received small increases in investment or faced outright cuts.[72] This bias in favor of extractive industries had long marked Moscow's policy toward Siberia (even though it had been officially deplored by leaders and planners alike), but since the mid-1970s the scale had become positively lopsided.

[69] Ed A. Hewett, "Gorbachev's Economic Strategy: A Preliminary Assessment," *Soviet Economy* 2, no. 1 (March 1986), pp. 285–312.

[70] "Gorbachev's Economic Reform: A *Soviet Economy* Roundtable," *Soviet Economy* 3, no. 1 (1987), pp. 40–53.

[71] For one review in a large literature, see B. P. Orlov and V. N. Kharitonova, "Zapadno-Sibirskii neftegazovyi kompleks v odinnadtsatoi piatiletke," *Ekonomika i organizatsiia promyshlennogo proizvodstva*, no. 6 (1985), pp. 37–51.

[72] A. G. Granberg, "Strukturnye sdvigi i intensifikatsiia promyshlennosti Sibiri," *Ekonomika i organizatsiia promyshlennogo proizvodstva*, no. 6 (1985), p. 11.

The result by the mid-1980s was not only a serious regional problem but a national one as well. Raw energy from Siberia was being shipped thousands of miles to the European USSR, where it was processed and consumed, producing materials and equipment that were then shipped back to Siberia. One of the most important ways to conserve energy, Siberian experts had long argued, was to relocate energy-intensive industries east of the Urals. Indeed, this had been official policy since the early 1970s. But the policy had remained a dead letter, and the imbalance was growing worse.[73]

Never shy in speaking out for the interests of their region, Siberian economists and scientists in the first half of the 1980s began campaigning to change Moscow's policy. Formal submissions to Gosplan and the Politburo were accompanied by a wave of popular books and articles.[74] The Siberian reformers' argument went to the core of the policy dilemma: the share of Siberian investment going to the energy sector must be cut, and the economy of the region must be rebalanced.[75] The share of processing and machinery industries in the Siberian economy must be increased. Infrastructural development, especially roads, housing, and amenities, should get higher priority. All this implied that the rate of growth of Siberian industry, which, though higher than the national average, had been steadily losing its lead, should speed up again, and the overall investment priority of Siberia should be increased.[76] This was essentially the Gorbachev program in Siberian regional dress; and as the Gorbachev leadership took shape and debate over the Twelfth Five-Year Plan intensified, the Siberians were optimistic that their ideas would be adopted in Moscow.[77]

The Siberian reformers' campaign reached its peak in July in a highly

[73] A. G. Granberg, Abel Aganbegian's successor as director of the Institute for the Economics and Organization of Industrial Production in Novosibirsk, summarized the deterioration of the Siberian position in processing industries: "From 1965 to 1982 Siberia's share in the output of mineral fertilizers declined from 5.9 to 2.1 percent, in plastics and synthetic resins—from 16.4 to 10.7 percent, in synthetic fibers—from 17.8 to 11.5 percent, in paper—from 3 to 1.9 percent, in chemistry and petrochemicals—from 13 to 9.2 percent." Granberg, "Strukturnye," p. 13.

[74] Among the popular works, see Aganbegian and Ibragimova, *Sibir' na rubezhe vekov*. The technical works were developed under the aegis of a special multidisciplinary research program headed by Aganbegian. Called "Sibir'," the plan had been adopted in an early version by the Siberian division of the USSR Academy of Sciences in 1980.

[75] See Granberg, "Strukturnye," p. 12.

[76] Ibid., p. 4. According to Granberg, Siberian industry grew 21 percent faster than the national average in 1966–1970, 17 percent faster in 1971–1975, 15 percent faster in 1976–1980, but saw its lead drop further in the first half of the 1980s.

[77] The present author attended a meeting in Novosibirsk in April 1985, at which delegates who had just returned from Gorbachev's first policy meeting (*soveshchanie*) at Central Committee headquarters spoke openly of their optimism.

publicized national conference in Novosibirsk attended by numerous government and Party leaders,[78] but not Gorbachev. The senior figure present, Vitalii Vorotnikov, a member of the Politburo and then prime minister of the Russian Federation, delivered the keynote speech.[79] To the Siberians it must have come as a dash of cold water, for instead of endorsing the pet theses of the Siberians, to which he gave hardly a nod, Vorotnikov dwelt almost exclusively on oil and gas.[80] A few weeks later the Politburo adopted a resolution that acknowledged the Siberians' views but likewise put energy first by allocating a 60 percent increase to West Siberian energy investment.[81]

Gorbachev himself addressed the issue in early September during a three-day tour of the West Siberian gas and oil fields. It was the first visit to the area by a General Secretary since Brezhnev seven years before. Speaking to a nationwide audience from Tiumen', with a gallery of high officials behind him, Gorbachev strongly endorsed the Siberians' views.

To Siberian ears, the General Secretary's words must have sounded far more encouraging than Vorotnikov's. (Indeed, the Russian premier was not present.) But stripped of its embellishments, the General Secretary's real message was essentially the same. Despite his rhetorical support for the Siberian reformers' arguments, Gorbachev was more concerned about the desperate near-term importance of oil. "Tiumen' 's misfortunes give the economy a fever," he said, and he endorsed higher targets for oil output and more investment to match.[82]

To be sure, Gorbachev's words also showed him determined to break with the wasteful, shortsighted, and destructive pattern of the recent campaigns. Henceforth, he said, Tiumen' oil and gas would be devel-

[78] The conference was widely featured in the Soviet press. See, for example, "Sibir': strategiia uskoreniia," *Sovetskaia industriia*, 19 July 1985.

[79] In October 1988 Vorotnikov was transferred from the post of chairman of the RSFSR Council of Ministers to that of chairman of the Presidium of the RSFSR Supreme Soviet.

[80] "Razvitie proizvoditel'nykh sil Sibiri i zadachi uskoreniia nauchno-tekhnicheskogo progressa." The only full text of the speech was published in *Sovetskaia Sibir'*, 20 July 1985, but a slightly abridged version is available in *Izvestiia Sibirskogo Otdeleniia Akademii Nauk SSR*, seriia ekonomiki i prikladnoi sotsiologii, No. 1, vypusk 1 (1986), pp. 10–22.

[81] "V Politbiuro TsK KPSS," *Pravda*, 9 Aug. 1985. This report of the 8 August meeting mentions a 60 percent increase in construction work for the Siberian oil and gas complex. Other than that, no specific numbers were announced. In a speech in Tiumen' in early September, however, Gorbachev confirmed that the Politburo had decided on a substantial hike, from around 50 billion rubles in the Eleventh Five-Year Plan to 82 billion in the Twelfth. "Sibiri—uskorennyi shag," reprinted in Gorbachev, *Izbrannye rechi i stat'i*, vol. 2, pp. 233–254.

[82] Ibid.

oped on a healthier, more rational basis, including better housing and amenities, infrastructure, and industrial support. "We are going to give Tiumen' a second wind," he declared. In short, faced with the opposing claims of the energy sector and the Novosibirsk line, Gorbachev did what he could to blend them, attempting to soften the dilemmas of change by a two-stage approach. In this respect his stance in Tiumen' was no different from the rest of his economic policy; nor was it essentially different from the approach of the Aleksandrov Commission's energy program.

Nevertheless, the fact remains that the man who six months earlier had hinted that he would strive to reduce the burden of energy investment and liberate resources for a vast restructuring of the economy now found himself on the same hook as Brezhnev, and he responded in essentially the same way: investment in Tiumen' oil and gas was to be stepped up again. Throughout the fall the message became still clearer as the press stressed the top priority of Siberian oil and gas and the primacy of the energy sector in Soviet economic policy.[83] Meanwhile the Novosibirsk themes faded away.[84]

The draft five-year plan figures for 1986–1990, released in the fall of 1985, were consistent with these signals. They called for an increase in oil production as well as substantial overall growth in energy supply. The final version of the plan, published in June 1986, picked the middle to high end of the ranges given in the draft (table 2.9).

These targets, even more than their predecessors of five years before, were ominously ambitious. The Twelfth Plan projected an increase of about 16 percent in fuels production—only slightly less than the 17 percent increase that the Eleventh Plan had called for.[85] But to achieve this growth, Prime Minister N. I. Ryzhkov announced in June, the

[83] See the report of a meeting of Party secretaries at Central Committee headquarters in late September, devoted to the capital investment program in Siberia, in *Pravda*, 28 Sept. 1985. See also "Neft' i gaz Sibiri," *Sotsialisticheskaia industriia*, 4 Oct. 1985, and "S pozitsii obshchei zainteresovannosti," *Sotsialisticheskaia industriia*, 5 Nov. 1985.

[84] By November Academician V. A. Koptiug, the head of the Academy's Siberian division, had retreated from his positions of the previous summer. See "Nauka—Sibiri," *Izvestiia*, 20 Nov. 1985. Compared to Koptiug's speech the previous July, the November article was strikingly different. Koptiug made no mention of relocation of energy-intensive industries, his references to Siberian machine building were perfunctory, and he had nothing to say about the development of processing industries. That was not the end of the story, however. As we shall see in Chapter 6, the objective of developing processing industries in West Siberia is being pursued through a network of joint ventures in plastics and petrochemicals.

[85] Matthew J. Sagers, "Oil Production Costs in the USSR," in *PlanEcon Long-Term Energy Outlook* (Washington, D.C.: PlanEcon, Inc., Fall 1987), p. 43.

TABLE 2.9
Five-Year Energy Output Targets, 1985–1990

	1985 (actual)	*1990 (draft)*	*1990 (final)*
Oil (mtnat)	595	630–640	635
Gas (bcm)	643	835–850	850
Coal (mtnat)	726	780–800	795
Electricity (Bkw-hr)	1,544	1,840–1,880	1,860
hydropower (Bkw-hr)	215	NA	245
nuclear (Bkw-hr)	167	390	390

SOURCES: 1985: *Narodnoe khoziaistvo SSSR za 70 let*; 1990 draft: *Pravda*, 9 Nov. 1985; 1990 final: *Pravda*, 19 June 1986.

energy sector would receive a 35 percent increase in investment.[86] This was hardly likely to be enough. Because of the rising marginal cost of new energy over the previous decade, the planned increase in energy output appeared to require at least a 50 percent increase in investment.

There must have been some conflict over this point during the preparation of the five-year plan, because Prime Minister Ryzhkov, at the Twenty-seventh Party Congress three months before, had announced a 47 percent increase for energy production and transportation, a sum more in line with actual cost trends. But this heavy commitment was evidently rejected between March and June 1986.[87] Even so, a 35 percent increase in energy investment, when considered alongside the 23.6 percent increase projected for total investment, meant that the burden of energy investment was still growing, absorbing nearly one-quarter of the planned total increase in investment.[88] Though precise figures are not available for planned industrial investment,[89] the fact

[86] A recent source suggests that the five-year plan provided for a 46 percent increase in gas and oil investment combined, 1990 over 1985. See M. I. Kamenetskii et al., *Ekonomika neftegazovogo stroitel'stva* (Moscow: Nedra, 1988), p. 11.

[87] Ryzhkov's speech to the Twenty-seventh Party Congress appears in *Pravda*, 4 Mar. 1986. It is not certain that the "35 percent" and "47 percent" figures mentioned at various times are based on the same definition of the energy complex, since Soviet statisticians evidently switched definitions sometime in 1986.

[88] According to the final version of the Twelfth Plan, announced in *Pravda* on 19 June 1986, the total increment to capital investment will be 190 billion rubles. The energy sector will increase from 133 billion to 180 billion, or by 47 billion rubles, i.e., about 25 percent of the total.

[89] See Robert E. Leggett, "Soviet Investment Policy: The Key to Gorbachev's Program for Revitalizing the Soviet Economy," in U.S. Congress, Joint Economic Com-

that it typically runs at about one-third of total investment suggested that the energy sector would absorb between two-thirds and three-quarters of the growth there, less than in the Eleventh Plan but still a severe obstacle to Gorbachev's industrial modernization program and to his ambitious goals for the machinery sector. In fact, after the first three years of the Twelfth Plan (1986–1988), energy investment had already grown by 26 percent, well ahead of the planned pace.[90]

Meanwhile, on the demand side, the five-year plan and the accompanying projections to the year 2000 were surprisingly laconic about conservation. On the one hand, the fifteen-year targets were ambitious: national income would double, but energy consumption would grow by only 43 percent. Such savings would require a program of unprecedented vigor, but the plan did not spell out how it would be achieved. The following year Gorbachev presented to the Party's Central Committee a comprehensive package of economic reforms (their major features and implications for energy conservation are discussed in Chapter 9).[91] It is already clear, however, that the reforms, despite their radical intent, represent a compromise package that will be implemented slowly at best. In particular, price increases for energy are only at the discussion stage. A more fundamental problem is that the reforms still fail to choose between high growth and quality of growth. As a result, energy savings are not likely to come quickly; in the meantime, after three years of Gorbachev's acceleration strategy, energy consumption has been growing as fast as ever.[92]

So far, then, while the new Gorbachev leadership has discussed the dilemmas of energy policy more forthrightly than its predecessors, it has hesitated to act. Its first five-year plan retained the previous emphasis on energy supply while failing to allocate enough resources to reach its targets; and as in the previous two five-year plans, it has been obliged to add more resources to the energy sector than originally called for. At

---

mittee, *Gorbachev's Economic Plans* (Washington, D.C.: USGPO, 1987), vol. 1, pp. 244–245.

[90] See Chapter 6 for comparisons with investment in the engineering sector. It could be that the five-year plan provided for a heavy "loading" of energy investment in the first two years of the plan, followed by a fall-off in the last two years. In 1988 energy investment growth slowed to 6.6 percent (*Izvestiia*, 21 Jan. 1989).

[91] The package of decrees adopted in June and July 1987 was published in book form as *O korennoi perestroike upravleniia ekonomikoi: sbornik dokumentov* (Moscow: Politizdat, 1987). A summary presented to the Central Committee in late June appeared in the press as "Osnovnye polozheniia korennoi perestroiki upravleniia ekonomikoi," *Pravda*, 27 June 1987.

[92] See Chapter 7.

the same time, the new leadership has adopted ambitious targets for economic growth that have already caused energy consumption to bound ahead, but it has not yet begun a vigorous, coherent conservation program.

Were these failures due to divisions within the leadership or to opposition from a conservative bureaucracy? The evidence of conflict over the Twelfth Plan was clear enough, as planners and ministry officials throughout 1985 and into 1986 resisted the ambitious targets demanded by the Politburo. But in the end the deeper explanation is that the new leaders themselves were constrained just as Brezhnev was in 1977 and 1980–1981. Alternatives based on coal will not be ready for another decade. Nuclear power continues to experience difficulties, illustrated most dramatically by the tragedy of Chernobyl' but also by the chronic lag of nuclear construction behind plan targets and by rising public opposition to nuclear power. The one saving grace is the all-important gas bridge, but it cannot carry the entire energy economy alone for more than a few years. Therefore, in 1985–1986, as before, the leaders undoubtedly came to the conclusion that they had no choice but to invest whatever it took to maintain oil production. Most probably, this decision was made reluctantly but unanimously.

As the leadership begins wrestling over priorities for the Thirteenth Five-Year Plan (1991–1995), it is clear that Gorbachev intends to keep moving down the path of radical reform, and several signs suggest he will make important changes in energy policy. He has called for a major shift of investment resources toward the food and consumer-goods sectors in the 1990s;[93] and although he has not indicated just how resource cuts would be apportioned between defense and heavy industry, it would be surprising indeed if the energy sector were not a principal target. The surprise personnel changes that Gorbachev sprang on his administration at the end of September 1988 included the retirement of V. I. Dolgikh and relative demotions for V. I. Vorotnikov and N. V. Talyzin (although the latter two remain members of the Politburo, as full and candidate member respectively). Since all three were identified with the conservative priorities set in the Twelfth Plan, the changes underscored Gorbachev's desire for new directions in the next one. Dolgikh's departure may turn out to be especially significant. As Party secretary for heavy industry and energy, Dolgikh was the main executor of Brezhnev's policy; he probably remained an advocate of a supply-oriented approach down to the end, and in his views on conser-

[93] See Gorbachev's speech to the July 1988 plenum of the CPSU Central Committee, "O prakticheskoi rabote po realizatsii reshenii XIX Vesoiuznoi partiinoi konferentsii," *Pravda*, 30 July 1988.

vation he was reluctant to consider price reform,[94] despite a glaring lack of progress in energy efficiency in the first three years of the Twelfth Plan.[95] At this writing (winter 1989) a comprehensive review of Soviet energy policy is under way, which is expected to recommend radical changes in energy investment and consumption, beginning with sharp increases in energy prices.[96] (See the Epilogue for an account of the changes announced as this book was going to press.)

But Gorbachev does not appear to have made up his mind on a more fundamental problem with major implications for energy efficiency, that of choosing between faster growth and more efficient growth. Reform-minded economists now openly criticize the Twelfth Plan's attempt to pursue both objectives at once,[97] but although Gorbachev himself speaks out against "gross growth," he seems reluctant to make an open decision to slow down. Yet this is crucial. So long as the planners continue to push for faster growth, it will be nearly impossible to make gains in energy efficiency or in overall energy consumption.

In the final section of this chapter, we shall draw up a balance sheet of Soviet energy policy over the last fifteen years. But first we turn to one of the most important elements in that policy, the role of foreign trade.

The International Factor in Soviet Energy Policy

Equal to domestic consumption as a force driving Soviet energy policy is foreign trade. Between 1970 and 1988 the volume of net Soviet energy exports increased nearly 270 percent, and now exports account

[94] See V. I. Dolgikh, "Otnoshenie k resursam—vazhneishii kriterii perestroiki v ekonomike," *Pravda*, 11 July 1988. This article is discussed in Chapter 7.

[95] The energy intensity of the Soviet economy continued to rise between 1985 and 1988; see table 7.1. See also N. K. Baibakov (who, despite his retirement from Gosplan, remains a counselor of the Council of Ministers), "Problemy energosberezheniia," *Ekonomicheskaia gazeta*, no. 18 (1988). Similarly, trends in savings of all raw materials, including metals, also lagged behind the five-year plan targets. B. Pavlov, "Rost i struktura ekonomiki," *Ekonomicheskaia gazeta*, no. 14 (1988).

[96] Supporting studies for this review were commissioned in 1986 or 1987, with the aim of producing a new energy program. An overview of these studies was published in *Izvestiia Akademii Nauk SSSP, Seriia Energetika i Transport*, no. 4 (1988). See especially the survey article by A. A. Makarov, "Novyi etap razvitiia energetiki SSSR," pp. 17–27.

[97] For the most colorful statement of the case, see Nikolai Shmelev, "Novye Trevogi," *Novyi Mir*, no. 4 (1988), pp. 161 and 166. Shmelev, however, is far from having Gorbachev's ear, and it is much more significant that Leonid Abalkin, thought to be one of Gorbachev's economic advisers, spoke out on the same theme at the Nineteenth Party Conference (*Pravda*, 30 June 1988). Gorbachev responded critically to Abalkin's speech, however, and one of the reasons may have been Gorbachev's continued ambivalence on this question.

for over 16 percent of total Soviet energy production, including 30 percent of its oil.[98]

This high export share is obviously an important element of the Soviet energy crisis; if the export share had remained, say, at its 1960 level (about 8 percent), then the supply-side pressure on the energy sector would now be much less severe and the transition to a conservation-oriented policy would be less expensive. But the revenues from energy exports play a crucial role in Soviet foreign trade: at the beginning of the 1980s, they accounted for as much as 80 percent of Soviet hard-currency income; and despite the worldwide fall in energy prices in recent years, their share is still about 75 percent.[99]

But is this hard currency bought at too high a price? As we shall see in Chapter 8, this issue has been a controversial one for a long time and for several reasons. But from a strictly economic point of view, there could be little doubt throughout the 1970s that it made sense to increase exports of oil, the marginal cost of which was then far lower than the world price. As late as 1980, when world prices were around $30.00 per barrel, the marginal cost of Soviet oil was about $7.00.[100] It is no wonder that in the 1970s Western economists faulted the Soviets for not exporting more. But after the mid-1980s the situation changed dramatically. By 1986, world prices had dropped to less than half the 1981 levels, but the marginal cost of Soviet oil had nearly doubled. Even if world prices recover somewhat in the early 1990s, Soviet oil exports will soon be fetching less than they cost to produce.

A second issue that has emerged since the beginning of the 1980s is that many Soviets are disappointed with the uses to which the hard currency has been put. In June 1987 Gorbachev, for the first time, used the example of energy to link his criticism of Brezhnev's foreign-trade policy to a sweeping indictment of Brezhnev's overall management of the economy. He accused him of masking the worsening economic situation with massive exports of energy and of wasting the hard-currency proceeds mainly on "current tasks" instead of economic modernization.[101] In short, Brezhnev had squandered his oil income.

[98] PlanEcon, Inc., and *Narodnoe khoziaistvo SSSR za 70 let*, pp. 105 and 641. The reappearance of these numbers in the Soviet statistical annual in 1987 marked the first time the Soviets had published data on oil exports in physical quantities since 1976. For an analysis, see Matthew J. Sagers, "News Notes," *Soviet Geography* 28 (November 1987), pp. 695–701.

[99] A detailed analysis will be found in Jonathan P. Stern, *Soviet Oil and Gas Exports to the West: Commercial Transaction or Security Threat?* (Aldershot: Gower, 1987), pp. 35–38.

[100] Sagers, "Oil Production Costs in the USSR," pp. 43–54.

[101] Speech to the Central Committee of the CPSU, "O zadachakh po korennoi perestroike ekonomikoi," *Pravda*, 26 June 1987.

In fact, Brezhnev used his abundant oil and his windfall energy profits for a number of useful purposes, which could be justified politically if not always economically: to buy grain to feed Soviet cattle, to cushion the impact of the two world oil shocks on his East European clients, and, as Khrushchev had done, to gain fast starts in policy areas of interest to him, such as purchases of foreign plants to make passenger automobiles and synthetic fibers. But although the volume of foreign trade expanded, the system through which it was conducted did not change. As Chapters 6 and 8 will show, decisionmaking in foreign energy trade remained opportunistic, changeable, and inconsistent. In particular, Brezhnev did not use his hard-currency revenues to modernize the oil and gas sectors themselves (apart from a handful of exceptions, chiefly gas transmission). Thus the international aspect of Soviet energy policy provides another illustration of the interaction of system and leadership in the genesis of the energy crisis.

Gorbachev, despite his condemnation of Brezhnev, faces strong pressures to act as Brezhnev did, yet he lacks the same hard-currency bonanza. Western analysts believe that the only way he can finance a rapid modernization of Soviet industry without cutting consumers' standard of living is through massive imports of Western technology financed with foreign bank loans.[102] So far, Gorbachev has followed this advice only in part: he has increased foreign borrowing (net Soviet indebtedness has quadrupled in four years)[103] and cut back grain imports from the West, while keeping oil production and exports at peak levels. As the Thirteenth Five-Year Plan approaches, controversy over these policies is growing. But at this writing, Gorbachev's policy on energy exports still largely resembles Brezhnev's.

The Balance Sheet

What is the record of Soviet energy policy since 1970? First, there is no denying the Soviets' formidable achievements. As they enter the second half of the 1980s they are the world's leading producers of oil and gas, and their position will not be challenged in this century. These resources have been won from arctic tundra and swamp, thousands of miles from the country's major concentrations of population and industry. The Soviets have been equally impressive in transporting oil and gas westward to the European USSR and to the rest of Europe. One

[102] Jan Vanous and Bryan Roberts, "Time to Choose between Tanks and Tractors," *PlanEcon Report* 2, nos. 25–26 (June 1986).

[103] Net bank debt (defined as net debt to the Bank for International Settlements area) grew from $5.3 billion in 1984 to $24 billion in 1988. See "Soviet Economic Performance in 1988," *PlanEcon Report* 5, nos. 6–7 (17 February 1989), p. 5.

should not underestimate the gritty determination and political energy that these successes have required.

But from the perspective of the broader economic health of the country, Soviet energy policy has been a source of disruption. Between 1975 and 1990 the energy sector will have absorbed around two-thirds of all the growth in Soviet industrial investment.[104] Soviet imports, financed by energy exports, enabled Soviet leaders to postpone reforms. In effect, Soviet industrial policy has been energy policy, and that remains just as true for Gorbachev, so far, as for his predecessors.[105]

Was there no alternative? Let us deal first with the supply side. On the broadest strategic level, Soviet policy on energy supplies has not been unsound. As any economist would have recommended, the Soviets have developed the most attractive sources first: from oil they have moved to gas and nuclear power, while preparing (though slowly) new options for coal in the next century. In the oil and gas fields, they have opened up the largest and most accessible deposits first, again the most rational course from the economist's point of view. Especially when compared to the energy policies of most Western governments during the same period, Soviet policy on energy supplies, at least in its broad design, has been reasonably logical and coherent.

But it has had three major weaknesses. The first is the failure to deal with the demand side, to develop a conservation policy. As we shall see in Chapter 7, Soviet energy consumption remains tied to economic growth, and oil consumption, in particular, remains excessively high.

Second, energy decisionmaking has been unbalanced. Hydrocarbons have been excessively favored over coal and nuclear power, Tiumen' Province over the rest of Siberia, development over exploration, field operations over industrial support, short-term output over sound infrastructural development (such as housing and roads), and autarky

[104] This is admittedly a rough estimate, but it is almost certainly on the low side. The increment in annual industrial investment is about 35 billion rubles (from 45 billion in 1975 to about 80 billion in 1990). The increment in annual energy investment is about 22 billion rubles (from 13 billion in 1975 to about 35 in 1990). *Narodnoe khoziaistvo SSSR za 70 let*, pp. 328 and 330. If one allows for the fact that the handbook's definition of energy spending is a narrow one, one arrives at an estimate in the neighborhood of two-thirds.

[105] It is difficult to say whether the share of the energy sector in total Soviet investment is abnormally large compared to other major industrial countries. A glance at investment statistics of selected Western countries suggests that it is not, but establishing a comparable series is beyond this author's competence. (The interested reader might refer to the valuable compendium published by the Organization for Economic Cooperation and Development (OECD), *Industrial Structure Statistics, 1985* [Paris: OECD, 1987].) In any case, what is more significant *politically* is the energy sector's share at the margin, and that is what I have emphasized here.

over interdependence—in short, there has been a chronic favoring of the near term over the long, the safe over the risky, and narrow objectives over broad ones. These biases, in the long run, have worked against the Soviets' own aims and narrowed their options.

Third, policy design is only weakly connected to execution, and as a result Soviet energy policy has been unpredictable in implementation. Over the last fifteen years it has tilted uneasily between plan and improvisation, long-term strategy and near-term expediency, complacency and panic, underresponse and overresponse. Decisionmaking has lurched from the oil campaign in 1977 to the gas campaign in 1980–1981, then to the oil slowdown in 1983, followed by its acceleration again in 1985–1986, while nuclear and coal have been through similar ups and downs.

These constant shifts have aggravated a tendency to pursue short-sighted policies. Bureaucracies engage in a ceaseless scramble to deliver the crash results demanded of them. As we shall see in the next several chapters, efficiency has been sacrificed to speed; fields have been prematurely exhausted; supporting industries have been neglected; and Siberia has been plundered. One is reminded of the hero of Jules Verne's *Around the World in Eighty Days* on his last desperate lap to London, frantically feeding his wooden paddle-steamer to the ship's boiler.

Finally, Soviet energy policy has failed to make efficient or coherent use of the world economy, alternately under- and overexporting fuels, importing either too little equipment or the wrong kinds, and underanticipating and overresponding to external political and economic developments. For the first time in a half-century the world economy is beginning to play a major role again in Russia's internal, civilian affairs. Under Brezhnev foreign issues began to affect domestic decisionmaking, and vice versa, in such key sectors as agriculture, machinery, and, above all, energy. But the pattern of interaction in energy, as we shall see in Chapters 6 and 8, illustrates how little Soviet decisionmaking adapted to the new situation.

The combined result of these features is that energy policy has been in a permanent state of emergency since the mid-1970s. So far, the leaders have shrunk from the dangers and difficulties of trying to curb inefficient and undisciplined energy consumption, and consequently they have been driven toward ever greater investment to develop ever more costly supplies. The vicious circle of imbalances continues to worsen under Gorbachev. The paradox of Soviet energy policy is that it has produced crisis amid plenty, a crisis that is ultimately self-inflicted.

What might a better policy have looked like? It would be bold indeed for a Western observer to take sides on the technical controversies that have swirled around Soviet energy policymakers in recent decades (although in the pages that follow I have found it hard to resist an editorial comment or two). Since this is a book about politics and policymaking, to ask what a better policy might have been is really to ask what the leaders should reasonably have known, indeed, what they *did* know, and what broad course their information should have suggested.

At the beginning of the 1970s two aspects of energy should have been apparent to Soviet leaders and planners. First, the entire center of gravity of Soviet energy supply was already moving eastward across the Urals, while consumption remained concentrated in the west. That meant higher costs in store for every part of the fuel and power industry—higher exploration and development costs in more remote areas, and a much heavier transportation burden from field to furnace. Second, the gains in consumption efficiency that had accrued from the mass conversion from coal to oil over the previous fifteen years (and from a handful of other developments, discussed in Chapter 7) were nearing an end, as they were bound to do.

The first trend spelled higher unit costs on the supply side; the second, diminishing efficiency gains on the demand side. In short, trouble was foreseeable. It is hard to resist the thought that the crisis that followed could have been prevented by a fairly simple combination of stitches in time, requiring neither an all-wise leadership nor a bottomless treasury: an earlier commitment to gas and long-distance gas transmission, a modernization program in the oil and gas service and equipment sector, and a more systematic use of foreign low-technology equipment and, especially, services. As energy costs mounted, even the most elementary conservation and fuel-switching measures could have laid the basis for a demand policy. Energy prices should have been raised more sharply and frequently than they were, and consumers should have been made to feel them directly and tangibly through meaningful incentives and penalties. More oil should have been displaced by other fuels and exported. Consumption should have been metered, using imported meters if Soviet industry could not be coaxed into producing them. Energy conservation should have been included as a criterion in equipment and factory design, with targets and incentives attached. None of these measures required a political millennium; neither do they now. They would have required more energy investment, but not the heavy burden the Soviet leaders carry today.

This is the policy that Soviet experts today say should have been pursued; indeed, it is the policy that most of them advocated from the early 1970s on. Soviet leaders and planners paid lip service to it. But it is not the policy that was carried out. Why?

The first level of explanation is the leadership itself. The coal-and-nuclear policy advocated in 1975 was Kosygin's; the hydrocarbon campaigns of 1977–1982 were very much Brezhnev's own. The turn toward conservation and fuel switching that began in 1983 matched Andropov's thinking, and Gorbachev's ideas (if not his actions so far) point in the same direction. Ever since 1977, when energy became an emergency issue, it has occupied the General Secretary's personal attention. To what extent, then, can the characteristics of Soviet energy policy be ascribed to the leaders themselves?

The second level of explanation is the organizational mechanism through which energy policy is conducted. The mechanism is dominated, like the rest of the Soviet economy, by large, vertically organized state agencies. Though the top leaders may make the major decisions, the preparatory and implementation stages are polycentric. Horizontal integration is poor. The planning system for energy, as in the rest of the economy, is torn between long-range goals and short-term targets. To what extent do these account for the policies pursued?

The third level of explanation is the natural and man-made environment. The Soviets are blessed with phenomenal energy reserves, but that has not always been the prevailing perception; through the 1950s Soviet planners had to invest heavily in energy to offset what then appeared to be an indifferent natural endowment. The present split between Siberian supply and European demand is due, at the origin, not to bad planning but to the speed with which those earlier sources have faded and the newer ones have come to the fore. To what extent have circumstances such as these driven Soviet energy policy?

The challenge of explanation lies not only in distinguishing levels of analysis but also in showing the ways in which they combine. Why, for example, did the Soviet leaders disregard their own experts' warnings of disaster in Siberia in the 1970's? Part of the answer may lie in the legacy of energy scarcity inherited from the 1940s and before, which led a conservative energy establishment to make consistently bearish forecasts about Siberian prospects in the 1960s—a pessimism reinforced by the tendency of Soviet ministries to talk poor and bargain for low targets. Once the wealth of Siberia dawned on leaders and planners, the pessimists were discredited and the optimists were in favor at court. Sober caution could get a hearing only in the long-term plans—until 1977. Thus did past history, natural setting, bureaucratic behavior, and the leaders' perceptions act upon one another, and we shall see many other patterns.

The trouble is that Gorbachev's energy options are growing more constrained than ever. Nuclear power, in particular, has emerged as a serious problem. In the wake of the partial meltdown at Chernobyl' in the spring of 1986, the Soviets have had to modify their graphite-core nuclear power plants to improve their safety, and this has cut electrical output. In 1989, according to Prime Minister Ryzhkov, such losses, added to delays in the nuclear construction program, will cost 30 million tons of coal equivalent, which will have to be made up with oil and gas. This number could increase in the future, because the entire nuclear program has come under increasing public attack, and several projects have been postponed or delayed. If nuclear power is unable to play the role scripted for it in the energy program of 1984, oil and gas production will have increase further to make up for the shortfall.

The issues of leadership and system intertwine at all levels. Nevertheless, in the end, the value of the analysis lies in what it tells us about the prospects for change, and for that we must reach some fundamental judgments. Is the ultimate explanation for the Soviet energy crisis a failure of political will? Is it the tendency of the system to blow apart any long-term strategy the leaders may devise? Or is the problem the speed with which the technological and economic issues evolved, combined with the inertia and dysfunctions of the country's inherited material infrastructure? Is improvement possible, or is the outlook for more of the same? In the following chapters we pursue these questions through the analysis of specific cases, before returning to the major questions of this study in the final chapter.

THREE

ORIGINS OF THE FIRST SOVIET OIL CRISIS, 1970–1982

The Soviet Union is far and away the world's leading oil producer. Its reserves, between 6.5 and 10.5 billion tons (more precise estimates are a closely held Soviet state secret), exceed those of any other country except Saudi Arabia and possibly Kuwait,[1] and many of the country's most promising regions remain to be explored. There is no question that the Soviet Union will remain first in oil output well into the next century.

Yet the Soviet oil industry has been in serious trouble for over a decade. Its afflictions run like a fault line through the landscape of Soviet energy supply, generating periodic tremors that shake careers all over Moscow. Twice in the last decade the leaders have been forced to rush emergency manpower and resources to West Siberia to prevent a sharp decline in oil output, and they may have to do so again in the 1990s. Oil remains the main danger zone in Soviet energy policy and the most demanding claimant on the leaders' capital.

Because of these troubles, Western forecasts have repeatedly claimed that Soviet oil output would soon peak and decline for good. In 1977 the Central Intelligence Agency, in a series of highly controversial reports, predicted a peak in 1980, to be followed by a sharp drop, which would cause the Soviet bloc to become net importers of energy by the middle of the decade.[2] Clearly, the latter did not come to pass, but the first part of the prediction correctly saw trouble: after growing steadily through the 1970s, production stagnated from 1980 to 1983, then fell slightly in 1984 and more sharply in 1985,[3] before recovering in 1986–

[1] Central Intelligence Agency, Directorate of Intelligence, *Handbook of Economic Statistics*, CPAS 88-10001 (Washington, D.C.: USGPO, September 1988), p. 110. See also same, *USSR Energy Atlas*, GI 85-10001 (Washington, D.C.: January 1985). The conversion ratio between barrels and tons is taken as 7.6 barrels per ton.

[2] Central Intelligence Agency, *The International Energy Situation: Outlook to 1985*, ER77-10240 (Washington, D.C.: April 1977), *Prospects for Soviet Oil Production*, ER77-10270 (Washington, D.C.: April 1977), *Prospects for Soviet Oil Production: A Supplemental Analysis* (Washington, D.C.: July 1977).

[3] Strictly speaking, if one excludes natural gas liquids (NGL) from oil proper (Soviet statistics lump them together), the latter actually peaked in 1982. NGL output has grown

1988 (table 3.1). By the risky standards of oil forecasting, the CIA's analysts came close. They spotted the impending Soviet oil crisis ahead of any other foreign observers, although Soviet oil men had been making similar warnings for years.

But the CIA would have come even closer if Soviet leaders had not awakened to the threat when they did. Beginning in late 1977, Brezhnev declared an oil emergency, sharply shifted the oil industry's resources into West Siberia, and then followed up with a flood of additional money and manpower. Soviet investment in oil nearly doubled between 1977 and 1982, Brezhnev's last years (table 3.2). This story reminds us that in the short run oil production and additions to reserves depend mainly on how much money and resources are spent on them.

What was the source of the oil crisis? The purpose of this chapter is to examine the origins of the Soviet oil industry's troubles and the consequences of the first emergency response of 1977–1982, while the next chapter will examine the second oil crisis of 1982–1985 and the aftermath.

First, a brief overview of the geography of Soviet oil is essential. Broadly speaking, the Soviet oil industry has gone through three generations, and may now be on the threshold of a fourth. The first, beginning before the 1917 Revolution, was based on the oil resources of the North Caucasus and Azerbaijan, particularly the oil city of Baku, whose history is closely tied to the origins of the Russian Social Democratic movement and Stalin's early career as a revolutionary. After World War II, the center of the oil industry moved to the Volga Basin and the Ural Mountains. Finally, in the 1960s, the development of the first West Siberian oil fields, based mainly in the province of Tiumen', began the present era in Soviet oil development, which brought the Soviet Union to undisputed first place among the world's oil producers.

Throughout the 1970s the share of West Siberia in Soviet oil output grew dramatically, until by 1980 West Siberia accounted for 52 percent of the national total. By the first half of the 1980s, production from the older Soviet oil regions was fading at a steady 10–12 million tons a year, but this decline was more than offset by annual increases on the order of 20 million tons per year from West Siberia. The share of West

rapidly in recent years, from 9 million tons in 1975 to nearly 31 million in 1987. See Matthew J. Sagers, "Refinery Throughput in the USSR," U.S. Department of Commerce, Bureau of the Census, Center for International Research, CIR Staff Paper no. 2 (Washington, D.C.: May 1984), p. 10, updated in same, "News Notes," *Soviet Geography* 29, no. 4 (April 1988), p. 424.

TABLE 3.1
Soviet Output of Oil and Condensate, 1975–1990

	1975	*1976*	*1977*	*1978*	*1979*	*1980*	*1981*	*1982*	*1983*	*1984*	*1985*	*1986*	*1987*	*1988*	*1990 (plan)*
Total USSR	490.8	519.7	545.8	571.5	585.6	603.2	608.8	612.6	616.3	613	595.3	614.8	624.2	624	635
Tiumen' Province	141.4	175.0	211.1	245.7	274.4	303.8	324.0	342.0	366.2	NA	352.7	376	398	404	425

SOURCES: All Union: *Narodnoe khoziaistvo SSSR*, various years; for 1988: *Pravda*, 22 Jan. 1989. West Siberia: through 1979: *Tekhnicheskii progress v neftianoi promyshlennosti v desiatoi a piatiletke*, p. 90; 1980–1988: *Soviet Geography*, "News Notes," various years.

TABLE 3.2
Soviet Oil Investment, 1971–1985
(billions of pre-1982 rubles)

Ninth Plan		*Tenth Plan*		*Eleventh Plan*	
Year	*Total*	*Year*	*Total*	*Year*	*Total*
1971	2.76	1976	4.12	1981	8.1
1972	3.00	1977	4.45	1982	8.7
1973	3.08	1978	5.27	1983	9.1
1974	3.32	1979	5.86	1984	8.9
1975	3.80	1980	6.80	1985	10.4
TOTAL	16.0		26.4		45.2

SOURCES: *Narodnoe khoziaistvo SSSR*, various years.

NOTES: After 1980 the Central Statistical Administration dropped the second decimal.

From 1984, investment statistics were reported in a new post-1982 price base. These have been converted to the older price base by using a deflator of 11 percent. From 1986, *Narodnoe khoziaistvo* has ceased reporting oil investment separately. I have not attempted to continue the series beyond 1985. See Chapter 4, note 69.

Siberian oil has continued to grow rapidly, reaching nearly two-thirds of total Soviet production in 1986. Thus the overall performance of the Soviet oil industry depends crucially on West Siberia. A fourth generation may be on the way, based on new oil provinces in the northeast Caspian Basin, and possibly offshore sites in the Barents and Kara seas north of the Arctic Circle. But for the balance of this century the role of West Siberia will remain central.

The drama of Soviet oil policy has been the premature weakening of the West Siberian province, and therefore most of the analysis in the next two chapters will focus on the politics of West Siberian oil, especially in the key oblast'[4] of Tiumen'. Beginning in the mid-1970s, the rate of growth of West Siberian output slowed sharply, and from late 1983 to early 1986 output actually declined. From 1986 through 1988 the situation improved markedly, but it is clear that the golden age of West Siberian oil has passed. The most eloquent measure of that is the

[4] The Russian word *oblast'*, for a geographic-administrative unit, is usually translated as "province." To avoid confusion with the technical term "oil province," I have used the Russian word throughout.

depletion rate, the term oil men use to denote the share of new oil output required to offset yearly declines from older fields. By 1985 the depletion rate in West Siberia had risen to 85 percent.[5] Thus in the second half of the 1980s almost all of the anticipated gross increase in West Siberian output has been required simply to stay even, while production from the rest of the country has continued to decline. Nationwide, this means that the Soviet oil industry must bring into production more than 100 million tons of new capacity annually.[6]

The first Soviet oil crisis, beginning in 1977, was above all due to faulty exploration policy, and this chapter will deal primarily with that aspect of the problem. Exploration began to falter more than a decade before the leaders realized they were in trouble, though West Siberian oil experts had started sounding the alarm as early as 1970. But these were years of abundance in the Soviet oil industry; the major West Siberian fields were new and growing fast, and Soviet planners evidently did not take the exploration problem seriously.

In 1976 and 1977 Soviet leaders began to realize that because of accumulated weaknesses in exploration their picture of West Siberian reserves and prospects was highly uncertain. The near-term prospects looked unpromising and largely unproven, and the long-term ones were clouded by controversy among the experts. As G. P. Bogomiakov, first secretary of the Tiumen' Oblast' Party committee (*obkom*), put it the following year, there was an enormous range of opinion among geologists and oil men about the future prospects of Tiumen' Oblast', "from the extreme pessimists to the extreme optimists."[7] Thus Brezhnev's decision in late 1977 to throw the oil industry's resources into West Siberia was, at least as far as anything beyond the near term was concerned, a plunge into the unknown. In the early 1980s a major reappraisal of reserves took place, which led to a downgrading of many previously solid-looking prospects.

To explain how this situation came about, one must account for several apparent contradictions. On the one hand, Moscow was guilty of complacency; but one can also show that there had been steady high-level controversy over exploration policy since at least 1970, that several

[5] S. N. Starovoitov, ed., *Problemy razvitiia Zapadno-Sibirskogo neftegazovogo kompleksa* (Novosibirsk: Nauka, 1983), p. 81.

[6] *Neftianik*, no. 3 (1988), p. 3.

[7] G. P. Bogomiakov, "Novyi etap—novye zadachi i problemy," *Oktiabr'*, no. 4 (1978), p. 187. Somewhat later Siberian economist B. P. Orlov commented, "We are obliged to place large hopes on fields that haven't been discovered yet." Orlov, "Dal'neishee razvitie zapadno-sibirskogo neftegazovogo kompleksa," *Planovoe khoziaistvo*, no. 8 (1980), pp. 15–16.

high-placed leaders were made aware of the problem early, and that spending for oil exploration grew rapidly and steadily. Logistics and technology for exploration were poor, yet during the 1970s Soviet oil geologists had made major strides in improving both. Geologists concentrated most of their effort in older regions, while most of the new reserves came from West Siberia; yet, if West Siberian exploration and development had been sound in the first place, this might have been appropriate policy. The first task of this chapter is to sort out these puzzles.

The second source of the oil crisis was the unbalanced development of the West Siberian oil province, which was then sharply aggravated by the very vigor of the Brezhnevian crash response. Much of the emergency effort was devoted to drilling, indeed mostly for development rather than exploration. The Ministry of the Oil Industry doubled its total drilling nationwide, from under 13 million meters in 1977 to over 23 million in 1982. In Siberia the increase was even more startling, from under 4 million meters in 1977 to nearly 13 million in 1982.[8] At the same time, exploratory drilling in West Siberia expanded hardly at all. This enabled the oil industry to save the annual output plans but prepared further trouble for the future.

This unbalanced approach worsened the fundamental problems that had contributed to the original crisis. The oil industry failed to use the time so dearly bought to lay a sound basis for its future. The result was a second oil crisis, culminating in the sharp downturn of 1985. This time it was Gorbachev who was forced to react with a new round of emergency measures and a further acceleration of spending, which restored output in 1986 to its earlier maximum. But as of mid-1989, the industry's underlying problems remain, and oil output has begun to weaken again, which suggests that a third crisis may not be far off.

This brings us to the double dilemma of Soviet oil policy over the last decade. On the one hand, it is clear that Soviet leaders, for all practical purposes, can maintain oil output at current levels or higher as long as they choose to pay the rapidly mounting price. So far they have resolutely done just that. But their very determination has produced a chronic campaign atmosphere that has made costs rise even faster than they would under a more systematic, long-term policy. Simultaneously, the oil campaign absorbs resources that could have been used elsewhere in the energy sector or in the economy as a whole. With each passing

[8] For 1977: J. Richard Lee and James R. Lecky, "Soviet Oil Developments," in U.S. Congress, Joint Economic Committee, *Soviet Economy in a Time of Change* (Washington, D.C.: USGPO, 1979), vol. 1, pp. 581–585; for 1982: *Neftianoe khoziaistvo*, no. 3 (1983), p. 4. See the Appendix on drilling statistics at the end of this book.

five-year plan, the horns of the dilemma grow sharper as costs continue to rise.

The first oil crisis of 1977–1978 is the key to understanding the situation the Soviets are facing today, and the industry's prospects depend on how successful it has been in alleviating those earlier problems. Has exploration in Siberia now pulled out of its long stagnation? Is there better agreement and less uncertainty today about West Siberian prospects? Our search for answers begins with a review of the major issues in the exploration controversy as they developed to 1977. We then turn to the Soviet responses to the oil crisis up to 1982.

Our second task is to draw out the broader lessons of the oil crisis for our understanding of Soviet decisionmaking. Who or what was to blame? Could the leaders have acted to resolve the conflicting information they were getting? What combination of rationality and miscalculation can explain why the world's largest oil producer has been thrown into turmoil twice in one decade, and may be again?

At the Core of the First Oil Crisis: Exploration

The connections between reserves, exploration, and production in the petroleum industry are complex. On the whole, since more spending buys more exploration, reserves grow with investment. But a decade may elapse between discovery and production, and many a prospect fails to materialize. Once the major finds in a new province have been made, marginal returns fall off quickly and risks rise. Thus exploration belongs to a class of policy problems in which decisionmakers are buying expensive but uncertain information about a stream of future returns. A policymaker under pressure to boost near-term output will be tempted to favor development and skimp on exploration, and with a little wishful thinking he may convince himself that reserves are more certain than they really are.

Within the exploration process itself there are further tough choices. An "upstream-oriented" exploration program—one that stresses broad geophysical surveys but neglects proving up known prospects and preparing them for development—produces near-term uncertainty and hampers production; but a program with the opposite bias will soon run out of long-term prospects and thus fails to prepare for the future. The choice of time horizons, geographic regions, and technology not only produces knowledge about the stream; in a sense it shapes the stream itself. Designing an exploration program is a balancing act, and an expensive one—in the Soviet case it involves about one-third of all the capital going into oil and gas.

Who Does What and Where? And Who Pays?

To follow what happens in exploration policy, one must keep clearly in mind the different agencies involved, the kind of exploration they do, and how they are funded. Soviet oil and gas exploration is divided among three main agencies: the Ministries of the Gas Industry (MGP), of the Oil Industry (MNP), and of Geology (Mingeo).[9] Mingeo's share of all exploratory drilling for gas and oil has been growing steadily since the beginning of the 1970s, from about 40 percent to 61 percent in 1987,[10] with the oil industry picking up most of the rest. This reflects the fact that, broadly speaking, MNP and MGP explore the older provinces and Mingeo the newer ones.[11] One important implication for what follows is that the MNP has taken little responsibility for oil exploration in West Siberia. Geophysical work for oil exploration is subordinated jointly to the Ministries of Oil and Geology, while the Gas Ministry has had its own geophysical service since 1971.[12]

Also important for tracking policy are choices between the "upstream" and "downstream" phases of exploration. Soviet geologists distinguish among three stages. (1) The first stage in the investigation of a promising new region is large-scale surveying through geophysical investigation and corehole drilling. This stage extends from the identification of promising new geological formations to the mapping of new structures. (2) Promising structures are then explored further by drill-

[9] Until September 1987 the Ministry of Geology was a Union-Republic ministry and thus had republic-level counterparts (e.g., the RSFSR Ministry of Geology) as well as a Union-level headquarters (the USSR Ministry of Geology) that sets overall policy. In the fall of 1987, as part of a wave of similar changes, the republic-level units were eliminated and the ministry became a single all-Union body. References in this chapter to the Ministry of Geology designate the entire Union-Republic organization unless otherwise specified.

[10] *Narodnoe khoziaistvo SSSR v 1987 godu* (Moscow: Finansy i statistika, 1988), p. 563. It has been reported that MNP has committed itself to increasing its exploratory drilling effort in West Siberia in the Twelfth Plan. Iu. Perepletkin, "Surgut: pervye rezul'taty," *Izvestiia*, 4 Sept. 1986.

[11] M. M. Brenner, *Ekonomika geologorazvedochnykh rabot na neft' i gaz v SSSR* (Moscow, Nedra, 1979), p. 76. In the second half of the 1970s Mingeo did about one-third of all its oil drilling in West Siberia, while MNP performed only about one-thirtieth of its drilling there; the difference is probably even more lopsided today. A. A. Trofimuk, "Neft' i gaz Sibiri," *Sotsialisticheskaia industriia*, 1 July 1980.

[12] Offshore development, as we shall see in Chapter 5, belonged to the Gas Ministry as well between 1978 and 1987 but at the beginning of 1988 was transferred back to the Oil Ministry. V. A. Dinkov, "Uskoriat' tempy perestroiki," *Neftianoe khoziaistvo*, no. 4 (1988), p. 4.

ing prospecting wells (*poiskovoe burenie*). Reserves identified at this stage become part of what Soviet geologists call "prospective reserves" (*perspektivnye zapasy*), commonly designated as C_2 (corresponding roughly to the categories of "possible" or "inferred" reserves in Western practice). (3) Prospects are then "proved up" to demonstrate the actual presence of commercially exploitable quantities of oil through drilling of outlining wells (*razvedochnoe burenie*). Reserves confirmed at this stage are classified as "industrial reserves" (*promyshlennye zapasy*), designated as C_1 (corresponding to the categories of "probable" or "calculated" reserves in Western practice). As a new field is prepared for production and reserves are confirmed with actual development wells, they enter the categories of A and B reserves (a somewhat looser category than the Western "demonstrated" or "measured").[13] As one moves downstream, prospects become more certain and reserves more precise. But simultaneously there is a high attrition rate as many prospects, on closer examination, turn up dry or unprofitable. This has been a large and growing source of uncertainty in West Siberia, where from the 1960s to the early 1980s the share of C_2 reserves that make it to higher categories has dropped from 7.6 percent to somewhere around 1.5 percent.[14] Needless to say, the quality standards applied to each class of reserves, and the resulting degree of uncertainty attached to each, are crucial policy issues.

Funding for exploration comes from two sources. Geophysical surveying and mapping (including corehole drilling), which are conducted mostly by Mingeo, are funded directly from the state budget.[15] This category accounts for 20–30 percent of total spending on gas and oil

[13] For discussions in Soviet literature of the various categories of reserves and stages of exploration, see the following sampling: I. P. Lavrushko and T. N. Smolenchuk, "Kharakteristika neekspluatiruemykh promyshlennykh i perspektivnykh zapasov nefti SSSR" *Geologiia nefti i gaza*, no. 3 (1983), pp. 7–11; V. I. Korchagin, V. V. Pechnikov, and V. Ia. Shirokov, "Osnovnye tendentsii razvitiia regional'nykh geologo-geofizicheskikh rabot na neft' i gaz v SSSR," *Geologiia nefti i gaza*, no. 6 (1983), pp. 24–28; and N. I. Buialov and V. I. Korchagin, "Etapy provedeniia geologorazvedochnykh rabot na neft' i gaz i sootnoshenie zatrat po vidam rabot na primere Zapadnoi Sibiri," *Ekonomika neftianoi promyshlennosti*, no. 7 (1982), pp. 22–24. For Western discussions, see Robert W. Campbell, *The Economics of Soviet Oil and Gas* (Baltimore: Johns Hopkins University Press, 1968); and same, *Trends in the Soviet Oil and Gas Industry* (Baltimore: Johns Hopkins University Press, 1976); CIA, *USSR Energy Atlas*, p. 13; and Arthur A. Meyerhoff, "Soviet Petroleum: History, Technology, Geology, Reserves, Potential, and Policy," in Robert G. Jensen, Theodore Shabad, and Arthur W. Wright, eds., *Soviet Natural Resources in the World Economy* (Chicago: University of Chicago Press, 1983), pp. 327–330. I have also drawn from Leslie Dienes, "The Soviet Oil Industry in the 12th Five-Year Plan," *Soviet Geography* 28, no. 9 (November 1987), pp. 617–655.

[14] Dienes, "Soviet Oil Industry," p. 629.

[15] *Ekonomika neftianoi promyshlennosti*, no. 8 (1982), pp. 12–15. The state collects a

exploration.[16] Subsequent exploratory stages (so-called deep drilling), in contrast, are considered capital investment by the Ministries of Gas and Oil; and when the actual work is performed by the Ministry of Geology, it is under contract to the other two ministries. We should observe that in Western practice much of the latter category would be handled by production departments and not considered "exploration" at all; yet it makes up close to 40 percent of Mingeo's drilling.[17]

These divisions of task and turf have policy consequences that played a role in the oil crisis of the 1970s and continue to do so today. Since West Siberian exploration is primarily the responsibility of Mingeo, most Soviet commentators agree that blame for the reserves crisis of 1976–1977 falls in the first instance on the geologists.[18] But MNP's organizations in West Siberia were also to blame: having no stake in exploration, they competed with the geologists for manpower and resources to support development, thus weakening still further the exploration effort. Geologists, since they are rewarded for fulfilling the annual "additions to reserves" targets in each category, tend to overstate reserves; oil men, who are responsible for producing reserves, have an opposite incentive to understate them in order to obtain more manageable production targets. As a result, there is chronic conflict between Mingeo and MNP over reserves, and the official figures are bargained compromises.[19] The Oil and Gas Ministry leaders, since they must fund exploratory drilling from their capital budgets, face difficult choices between long-term and short-term goals, which they tend to resolve in favor of the latter, that is, in favor of production and the most down-

"geological exploration fee" from the Oil and Gas Ministries, which partly covers the budget portion of the Ministry of Geology's funding. This fee currently provides about 2 billion rubles per year. See Albina Tretyakova and Meredith Heinemeier, "Cost Estimates for the Soviet Oil Industry: 1970 to 1990," U.S. Bureau of the Census, Center for International Research, CIR Staff Paper no. 20 (Washington, D.C.: June 1986).

[16] The relative shares of upstream and downstream phases of exploration vary sharply from region to region and over time, and therefore so do the proportions of "budget-funded" versus "contract-funded" exploration. Thus, in West Siberia the share of budget-financed exploration (i.e., upstream exploration) has fallen steadily from the 1948–1965 period, when it averaged 48.8 percent of total spending, to just under 19 percent during the decade of the 1970s. Starovoitov, ed., *Problemy*, p. 60.

[17] Dienes, "Soviet Oil Industry," p. 628.

[18] Gorbachev himself, when he visited Tiumen' in September 1985, appeared to hesitate on this point. In his speech on nationwide television he criticized the geologists sharply for their complacency (*shapkozakidatel'stvo*), but the *Pravda* version of his speech the next day removed almost all criticism of the geologists. *Pravda*, 6 Sept. 1985.

[19] Alexei Makhmoudov, *The Soviet Oil and Gas Industries (Problems of Reserve Estimation)* (Falls Church, Va.: Delphic Associates, Inc., 1986), pp. 68–71.

stream sort of exploration. And while the bias toward development is partially offset by having much of the early exploration effort financed directly from the state budget to Mingeo, the latter must fight its own battles with the central planners, since surveying and mapping do not show the near-term payoffs that planners look for when they hand out resources.

Background to the Crisis

The Soviet oil crisis of the late 1970s, though it took its most important and controversial form in West Siberia, was born out of larger problems with oil exploration nationwide dating back to the late 1960s. First, total exploratory drilling slumped for oil and gas in 1968 and after, and did not return to 1967 levels until 1980 (table 3.3). Other key indicators showed outright declines: exploratory wells completed, new oil structures discovered, and new deposits identified as commercially exploitable all dropped between the mid-1960s and the mid-1970s (table 3.4). From the beginning of the 1970s, the Ministries of Oil and Geology began reporting nearly every year that they had not met the goal for gross additions to industrial reserves.[20]

The immediate cause of these declines was that exploration teams were obliged to drill deeper, travel to more remote places, and work in more complex formations. Drilling costs rose correspondingly: between 1966 and 1977 the cost of a meter of exploratory hole rose 230 percent.[21]

These trends reflected the natural aging of the Soviet oil industry, particularly in the older European and Central Asian zones (table 3.5). The newer oil provinces of West Siberia were less affected by increasing depths, but even there the cost per meter of exploratory drilling nearly doubled over roughly the same period.[22]

In response to the aging of the industry, Soviet geologists (except in West Siberia, as we shall see) were moving upstream in search of more productive areas, giving more stress to earlier stages of exploration (surveying, mapping, and prospecting) and less to the later stages

[20] In addition, Robert Campbell observed in the mid-1970s that industrial reserves ($A + B + C_1$) appeared to have been growing less rapidly than output since 1965, and within that category the share of $A + B$ was dropping relative to C_1. Campbell, *Trends*, pp. 12–13.

[21] Brenner, *Ekonomika geologorazvedochnykh*, p. 159.

[22] Average cost per exploratory meter in West Siberia more than doubled between the Eighth and the Tenth Five-Year Plans, while average well depth increased only 24 percent during the same period. However, the average of the Tenth Plan includes the three frantic years 1978–1980, during which cost per meter rose sharply. Starovoitov, ed., *Problemy*, p. 59. These figures include oil only, all performers.

TABLE 3.3
Exploratory Drilling for Oil and Gas, 1961–1987
(all performers; millions of meters)

Year	*Total*	*Oil*	*Gas*	*Year*	*Total*	*Oil*	*Gas*
Seventh Plan				Tenth Plan			
1961–1965	*24.7*	*16.5*	*8.1*	1976–1980	*26.7*		
				1976	5.2	3.6	1.6
Eighth Plan				1977	5.2	3.6	1.6
1966–1970	*26.2*	*16.2*	*10.0*	1978	5.2	3.6	1.6
1967	5.8			1979	NA		
1968	5.1			1980	5.9		
1969	4.9						
1970	5.1	3.3	1.9	Eleventh Plan			
				1981–1985	*32.2**		
Ninth Plan				1981	6.2		
1971–1975	*26.1*	*17.8*	*8.3*	1982	6.2		
1971	5.3			1983	6.5		
1972	5.1			1984	6.5		
1973	5.2			1985	6.8		
1974	NA						
1975	5.4	3.8	1.6	Twelfth Plan			
				1986–1990			
				1986	7.2		
				1987	7.8		

SOURCES: For total drilling before 1974: Campbell, *Trends*; for 1975: Hewett, *Energy Economics*; for 1976–1978: average from Brenner, *Ekonomika geologorazvedochnykh*, p. 88; for 1970 and 1980–1986: *Narodnoe khoziaistvo SSSR*, various years. For the breakdown between oil and gas, Brenner, pp. 87, 89, and 93. Seventh, Eighth, and Ninth Plans: Brenner, pp. 86–88; Tenth Plan: *Ekonomicheskaia gazeta*, no. 5 (1983), p. 1; Eleventh Plan: *Narodnoe khoziaistvo SSSR*, various years.

* Dinkov, *Neft' SSSR*, p. 148, reports a 1981–1985 total of 29.2 million, which may refer to oil only, leaving 3 million meters for gas.

(proving up and predevelopment). The share of drilling in the latter category (*razvedochnoe burenie*) dropped steadily, from 49 percent in the Seventh Plan (1961–1965) to 36 percent in the Ninth Plan (1971–1975).[23] At the upstream end of the spectrum, stratigraphic and parametric drilling (*oporno-parametricheskoe burenie*) rose more than eightfold, from 0.24 million meters in 1961–1965 to a peak of 2.07 million meters in 1971–1975, or from less than 1 percent of overall exploratory drilling to about 8 percent.[24]

[23] Buialov and Korchagin, "Etapy provedeniia geologorazvedochnykh," pp. 22–24.

[24] Korchagin et al., "Osnovnye tendentsii razvitiia regional'nykh geologo-geofizicheskikh," pp. 26–27. Unfortunately, I have no information concerning total

TABLE 3.4
Gas and Oil Structures Discovered and Drilled,
New Fields Identified, 1961–1975
(countrywide; all performers)

Period	*Structures Discovered*	*Prepared for Drilling*	*Drilled*	*New Fields Identified*	*Exploratory Oil Wells Completed*
1961–1965	2,316	1,672	1,585	NA	7,117
1966–1970	2,035	1,971	1,721	453	6,074
1971–1975	2,047	1,861	1,778	388	5,973

SOURCE: Brenner, *Ekonomika geologorazvedochnykh*, pp. 82, 92.

Such upstream exploration is expensive and has more demanding requirements for equipment and know-how, and the geologists worked hard to adopt new tools and techniques. Use of the turbodrill, increasingly unwieldy and inefficient at greater depths, fell from nearly two-thirds of oil exploration meterage to less than one-half between 1970 and 1980, while rotary drilling increased correspondingly.[25] Geophysical methods began to displace corehole drilling; advanced seismic-reflection techniques, especially the common-depth-point process, started to appear;[26] and Soviet geologists turned to field computers for seismic data processing (at the beginning of the 1980s, about two-thirds of those computers were still imported).[27] Though Soviet exploration technology still lagged badly behind Western standards, geologists and planners must have hoped that the productivity decline could be stabilized or even reversed. Indeed, the geologists were not entirely unsuccessful: commercial drilling speed (meters per drilling rig per month), after declining sharply between 1967 and 1972, resumed a slow increase through 1977, although this was at least partly an artifact of the greater share of West Siberian drilling, with its initially easier conditions (table 3.6).

investment shares in various stages of geological work. If anything, relying on drilling shares as a surrogate measure understates the trend toward earlier stages of exploration.

[25] *Ekonomika neftianoi promyshlennosti*, no. 9 (1982), p. 10.

[26] *Geologiia nefti i gaza*, no. 1 (1982), p. 21, reports that in 1975 50 percent of all Soviet seismic work used the common-depth-point method (CDP), while *Ekonomika neftianoi promyshlennosti*, no. 1 (1982), pp. 9–12, reports that during the Tenth Plan (1976–1980) 90 percent of all seismic work used CDP. For Western commentary on Soviet capabilities in this field, see, for the 1970s, Meyerhoff, "Soviet Petroleum," pp. 316–317, and, for the 1980s, Dienes, "Soviet Oil Industry," pp. 634–635.

[27] *Geologiia nefti i gaza*, no. 11 (1982), p. 8.

TABLE 3.5
Average Depths of
Completed Exploratory Wells
(oil and gas; all performers; in meters)

	1960	*1970*	*1977*
Countrywide	1,845	2,560	2,827
Azerbaijan	2,668	4,074	4,307
Ukraine	2,618	4,313	4,660
Kazakhstan	NA	2,913	3,348
Tuzkmenistan	2,358	3,414	3,724

SOURCE: Brenner, *Ekonomika geologorazvedochnykh*, p. 90.

Yet, despite these efforts at adaptation, Soviet exploration teams were not finding enough oil. Top leaders were well aware of the mounting problems even in the early 1970s. In 1971, outlining the targets of the Ninth Five-Year Plan before a gathering of the Supreme Soviet, Prime Minister Kosygin announced that exploration would be strengthened, and the language of the plan itself concurred.[28] Investment in oil and gas exploration jumped sharply. Indeed, spending for exploration grew rapidly throughout the period 1961–1975. But what is equally significant is that exploration's share of total gas and oil investment declined steadily (table 3.7). In other words, Soviet leaders had begun to show awareness of the problem in the first half of the 1970s, but their response was weak.

The Neglect of Siberia

The main part of this puzzle is still missing. The single most important reason the performance of Soviet oil exploration declined in the mid-1970s was that Mingeo in Moscow systematically gave most of its attention to the older oil-producing regions rather than to West Siberia, where every new well yielded far more oil. The contrast between West Siberia and an older region such as the North Caucasus tells a striking story (table 3.8). By the mid-1970s West Siberia was providing more than two-thirds of gross additions to $A + B + C_1$ reserves with only about 15 percent of the total investment in drilling effort (table 3.9). On the face of it, sound policy would seem to have called for

[28] *Gosudarstvennyi piatiletnii plan razvitiia narodnogo khoziaistva SSSR na 1971–75 gody* (Moscow: Politizdat, 1972), p. 105.

TABLE 3.6
Commercial Drilling Speed, Oil and Gas Exploration, 1967–1987 (meters per rig per month; all performers)

1967	380	1980	403*
1970	342	1985	444*
1972	329	1986	476
1975	363	1987	518
1977	370		

SOURCES: For 1967, 1972: Campbell, *Trends*, pp. 16–17; for 1970, 1975, 1977: Brenner, *Ekonomika geologorazvedochnykh*, p. 168; for 1980 and 1985–1987, *Narodnoe khoziaistvo SSSR*, various years.

* Dinkov, *Neft' SSSR*, p. 150, gives 462 and 487, respectively, suggesting less improvement in 1980–1985.

shifting more of the exploratory effort to West Siberia as early as 1970. This failed to happen for several reasons.

First, top leaders, beginning with Kosygin, had become alarmed because the older oil fields of the European USSR had begun to decline much faster than anticipated. (From 1971 to 1975, oil output outside Siberia dropped by 261 million tons/year, instead of the planned 150 million tons.)[29] As early as 1971, while presenting the main lines of the Ninth Five-Year Plan to the Supreme Soviet, Kosygin had stressed the importance of exploration in the European part of the USSR.[30] In this he echoed the views of many geologists and oil men, including a rising oil executive from the Ural oil region around Perm', N. A. Mal'tsev, who would become oil minister just in time to preside over both oil crises.[31] The older regions still produced the bulk of Soviet oil; valuable

29 Summary figures on gross and net additions to capacity, and resulting depletion rates, can be found in Ed A. Hewett, *Energy, Economics and Foreign Policy in the Soviet Union* (Washington, D.C.: Brookings Institution, 1984), ch. 2.

30 *Gosudarstvennyi piatiletnii*, p. 105.

31 The views of advocates of more exploration in the European USSR are discussed in Han-ku Chung, *Interest Representation in Soviet Policy-Making: A Case Study of a West Siberian Energy Coalition* (Boulder: Westview Press, 1987), pp. 65–66. Mal'tsev was minister of the oil industry from April 1977 to February 1985.

TABLE 3.7

Investment in Gas and Oil Exploration, 1966–1985

	Billions of Rubles	*Share of Total Oil and Gas Investment*
1966–1970	7.7	45
1971–1975	10.5	36
1976–1980	14.1	25
1981–1985	18.6	21

SOURCES: 1961–1978: Brenner, *Ekonomika geologorazvedochnykh*, pp. 151–152; 1979: A. A. Trofimuk, "Pervye rezul'taty primeneniia priamykh metodov poiska i razvedki neftianykh i gazovykh mestorozhdenii v Sibiri," *Vestnik Akademii Nauk SSSR*, no. 11 (1981), p. 11; 1980–1985: *Narodnoe khoziaistvo SSSR*, relevant years.

NOTE: I am assuming as a rough approximation that the figure used for "capital investment in exploration" in *Narodnoe khoziaistvo SSSR* represents in each case about 75 percent of total spending on gas and oil exploration (for the reasons explained in the text), so I have added one-third to the *Narodnoe khoziaistvo* figure to produce the rough comprehensive total used in the table. Total oil and gas investment is defined inclusive of transmission (as in table 2.4), with a correction added for the inferred oil and gas budget of Mingeo. All figures are in pre-1982 prices.

TABLE 3.8

Ratio of Shares of New Reserves to Exploratory Oil Drilling in West Siberia and North Caucasus, 1961–1980

	Seventh Plan 1961–1965	*Eighth Plan 1966–1970*	*Ninth Plan 1971–1975*	*Tenth Plan 1976–1980*
North Caucasus	0.25	0.30	0.10	0.11
West Siberia	6.00	4.70	4.60	3.40

SOURCE: N. I. Buialov and V. I. Korchagin, "Otnositel'naia effektivnost' geologorazvedochnykh rabot na neft' i gaz i ee znachenie dlia planirovaniia," *Ekonomika neftianoi promyshlennosti*, no. 11 (1982), pp. 14-15.

NOTE: A ratio of 1 would represent a perfect balance of effort and discoveries; less than 1 suggests more exploration than warranted by discoveries; greater than 1 suggests not enough.

TABLE 3.9
Shares of West Siberia in Oil Exploration Inputs
Compared to Its Contribution to Reserves
(percentages)

Shares of West Siberia in:	*Seventh Plan 1961–1965*	*Eighth Plan 1966–1970*	*Ninth Plan 1971–1975*
Total exploratory investment (oil and gas)	9.7	12.0	14.2
Drilling meterage (oil only)	6.5	12.9	14.9
Wells completed (oil only)	7.6	14.9	16.5
Gross additions of industrial oil reserves ($A+B+C_1$)	30.7	61.0	69.7

SOURCE: Brenner, *Ekonomika geologorazvedochnykh,* pp. 153, 92, 88.

production infrastructure and manpower was in place there; and the oil produced was located closer to points of use than Siberian oil was. Consequently, there were compelling reasons for trying to discover more reserves in the older oil provinces.

Second, so many prospective reserves had been discovered in West Siberia in the previous decade that it was hard to imagine that the region's prospects were threatened. Indeed, planners undoubtedly considered the reserves-to-production ratio in West Siberia to be so high that accelerating exploration there would be a waste of resources. In addition to these sound reasons there were some unsound ones. Most of the equipment and manpower of Mingeo was still located in the older regions, and simple bureaucratic inertia slowed the transfer of resources west of the Urals. Above all, the rationale of the exploration policy hinged on the assumption that the reserves situation in West Siberia was basically accurate and sound. But from 1970 on, that point was increasingly in dispute.

Controversy in West Siberia, 1970–1977

As the performance of the older oil regions deteriorated, Tiumen' oil men and geologists faced mounting pressure from the authorities in Moscow to increase output. Targets rose unremittingly, faster than the West Siberians thought wise, faster than new reserves were being discovered, and far faster than the rate at which planners were willing to increase supporting investment. In both 1970 and 1975 the planners set aside the cautious preliminary five-year targets recommended by local oil men and substituted sharply higher ones. As table 3.10 shows,

TABLE 3.10
Five-Year Oil Targets for Tiumen', 1975 and 1980
(millions of tons)

	1975 *(set in 1970–1971)*	*1980* *(set in 1975–1976)*
Tiumen' oil men's recommendations	70–75	250–260*
Five-year plan	120–125	300–310
Final output	141.4	303.8

SOURCES: This table is a composite of information contained in *Ekonomika i organizatsiia promyshlennogo proizvodstva* (*EKO*), no. 3 (1979), p. 15, no. 6 (1977), pp. 35–36; Gurari, "Neft' i gaz Zapadnoi Sibiri"; Bogomiakov, "Novyi etap," p. 188; Starovoitov, ed., *Problemy*; F. Salmanov, "Opiraias' na prognozy"; V. Lisin, "Proschety v raschetakh," *Pravda*, 3 Apr. 1984; Aganbegian and Ibragimova, *Sibir' na rubezhe vekov*.

* This figure was itself the result of earlier pressure from above. As early as 1970 a Central Committee/Council of Ministers "Directives" decree had called for a 1980 output target for West Siberia of 230–260 million tons.

the planners got away with it in the Ninth Plan (1971–1975), which encouraged them to do the same again in the Tenth (1976–1980), when they were not so lucky. The higher the targets climbed, the greater the disparity grew between ends and means.

From about 1970, Siberian geologists began warning that the higher targets could not be met unless exploration were sharply stepped up and new reserves added. F. G. Gurari, then deputy director of West Siberia's leading geological institute, observed that few of the fields discovered so far had been proved up. He cautioned, "Forecast reserves are not confirmed reserves. They must be verified by exploratory deep drilling."[32] The chief of Tiumen' 's geological service, Iu. G. Erv'e, calculated at the same time that to meet the planners' 1980 target would require a doubling of "industrial" reserves (that is, the "proven and probable" category, $A + B + C_1$) between 1971 and 1975. But in the previous three years, he pointed out, the rate of discovery of new fields had dropped sharply, as had their average size.[33]

Planners did not totally ignore these warnings. Capital investment in West Siberian oil and gas exploration tripled between 1965 and

[32] F. G. Gurari, "Neft' i gaz Zapadnoi Sibiri: perspektivy, problemy," *Priroda*, no. 1 (1971), pp. 16–23.

[33] Iu. G. Erv'e, interview in "Tiumenskie razgovory," *Neftianik*, no. 1 (1971), pp. 2–7.

1975.[34] But the tripling of funds did not buy a corresponding increase in performance: exploratory oil drilling meterage increased barely more than 25 percent between the Eighth and Ninth Plans (from 2.09 million meters to 2.65 million; see table 3.11), while the number of exploratory oil wells completed grew even more slowly, by about 6.5 percent.[35]

Furthermore, each new well and each new field added fewer new reserves, especially industrial reserves in the proven and probable category. The average field discovered in Tiumen' between 1971 and 1975 held 40 percent as much prospective reserves (that is, $A + B + C_1 + C_2$) as the average Tiumen' field discovered before 1966 but only 27 percent as much industrial reserves (i.e., $A + B + C_1$).[36] An inventory conducted in 1980 showed that fields discovered in 1971–1975 represented only 20 percent of total industrial reserves in West Siberia, while fields discovered before 1966 still held over 58 percent.[37]

In 1975 the situation was not yet perceived as desperate because West Siberian reserves were still growing; prospective reserves ($A + B + C_1 + C_2$), in particular, grew by nearly 40 percent between the Eighth and Ninth Plans.[38] But industrial reserves were not keeping pace, and both categories of additions to reserves were far outstripped by the growth of West Siberian production, which nearly quintupled between 1970 and 1975.[39] Moreover, Siberian oil men were already beginning to argue that the geologists' reserves were inflated in every category, a claim we shall explore in the next chapter.[40]

Some Western observers have interpreted these debates as evidence of an interregional struggle for priority, pitting officials in West Siberia against their counterparts in the European USSR.[41] It is true that many West Siberians were strong boosters of accelerated oil and gas explora-

[34] F. Salmanov, "Chtoby plast ne skudel," *Pravda*, 17 Dec. 1982. Salmanov's figures are corroborated by the data already cited from Brenner, *Ekonomika geologorazvedochnykh*, p. 153, which show that over roughly the same period West Siberia's share of exploratory investment grew by 50 percent even as the national total was doubling, thus yielding roughly a tripling. Further rough corroboration comes from Starovoitov, ed., *Problemy*, pp. 59 and 60.

[35] Brenner, *Ekonomika geologorazvedochnykh*, p. 92. But Starovoitov, ed., *Problemy*, p. 59, says about 16 percent. Though the Starovoitov figure is more recent, Brenner's data are more detailed and thorough, so I am accepting them as more likely to be correct.

[36] Starovoitov, ed., *Problemy*, p. 61.

[37] Ibid., pp. 61 and 62.

[38] Ibid., p. 59.

[39] Ibid., p. 63.

[40] Chung, *Interest Representation*, pp. 69–70.

[41] See in particular ibid.

TABLE 3.11
Oil Exploration in West Siberia, 1961–1975
(primarily by Glavtiumengeologiia)

Years	*Exploration Wells Completed*	*Exploratory Drilling (thous. meters)*
1961–1965	541	1,074
1966–1970	932	2,087
1971–1975	983	2,654

SOURCE: Brenner, *Ekonomika geologorazvedochnykh*, pp. 88–92.

tion and development in their region. But this episode also shows that the West Siberians did not form a single group and frequently held opposing views (as we shall see again in later chapters). An explanation based on regional interest groups does not capture the complexity of the motives involved.

Elsewhere in the country the primary cause of declining productivity in exploration was the rapid increase in average well depths. That was not the main problem in West Siberia, where the average well was shallow to begin with and was not getting much deeper (only 13 percent between the Eighth and Ninth Plans). Yet over the same period the cost of one meter of exploratory hole increased by more than half.[42] The explanation could only be that working conditions for the geologists were getting tougher: more remote areas (though still primarily in central Tiumen'), more difficult geological formations, and smaller fields. From the early 1970s, West Siberian geologists were meeting their targets for additions to industrial reserves ($A + B + C_1$) by smaller and smaller margins.[43]

In sum, by the mid-1970s many West Siberians perceived an impending crisis, and authorities and experts were divided over how to react. There were two possible courses.

SEARCH FOR NEW OIL PROVINCES?

Siberia had had a history of lucky strikes, and the most tempting choice was to redouble the search for new provinces to the north and east, in the hope that they would contain new giants. Calls to that effect began

[42] Starovoitov, ed., *Problemy*, p. 59.
[43] S. Vtorushin and A. Murzin, "Iskat' novye klady," *Pravda*, 10 Aug. 1977.

coming from the oil industry early in the 1970s. An economist in the Oil Ministry wrote in 1973:

> In the decade of the 1980s the oil resources of the Middle Ob' will be insufficient for further expansion of oil output. Development of the oil resources of the northern region of West Siberia is being moved to the forefront. . . . In this vast territory . . . we must create a giant new base for oil production, which in its volume of output will be no smaller than that of the Middle Ob' region. In the decade 1981–1990 a new oil region must be created in East Siberia.[44]

The following year the oil minister himself, Valentin Shashin, added his voice:

> We face as never before the issue of the need to discover enormous new oil provinces equal to the Urals-Volga and West Siberia. East Siberia, the Caspian Depression, and the shelves of seas and oceans, which have enormous potential for the growth of reserves, may be such regions. But at present we are alarmed by the fact that the USSR Ministry of Geology is not drilling enough exploratory wells in new prospective provinces.[45]

It is significant, in the light of the events of 1977–1978, that top decisionmakers were witnesses to the growing alarm of the oil industry as early as 1973. Attending a meeting on oil and gas exploration in November 1973, top officials and specialists in the industry, as well as Party Secretary V. I. Dolgikh and Gosplan Deputy Chairman A. M. Lalaiants—both responsible at top levels for energy policy then as now—heard the first secretary of the Tiumen' province organization, B. Ie. Shcherbina, criticize the geologists for their "slow pace of work in the new and highly promising regions in the northern part of Tiumen' Province."[46]

But little changed. Almost no diversion of effort took place to unex-

[44] *Ekonomika neftianoi promyshlennosti*, no. 6 (1973), p. 9.

[45] *Neftianoe khoziaistvo*, no. 3 (1974), p. 4. See also an article by Shashin in *Sotsialisticheskaia industriia*, 6 June 1974, in which he develops substantially the same point.

[46] *Pravda*, 23 Nov. 1973. Less than a month later Shcherbina was promoted to Moscow to head the Ministry for Construction of Oil and Gas Enterprises (MNGS). Shcherbina's spectacular career since the late 1960s has been based entirely on the Siberian oil and gas industries. In 1983, largely in reward for his key role in overseeing organizing the gas pipeline campaign in the early 1980s, Shcherbina was promoted to deputy chairman of the USSR Council of Ministers, where he is responsible for energy affairs.

plored areas in the north of Tiumen' Province[47] let alone to those of East Siberia.[48] As the then head of Gosplan's Oil and Gas Department, Iu. V. Filanovskii, put it a few years later, the West Siberian geologists had "holed themselves up in their base settlements and delayed for five to seven years the move to new areas."[49]

The local geologists complained that they were short of resources because Mingeo was discriminating against West Siberia in favor of the older oil-producing regions. The available figures bear them out. Until 1966 funding for such upstream operations as mapping and geophysical exploration in West Siberia had been roughly equal to capital investment for downstream exploratory drilling; from 1966 to 1975 the latter spurted ahead while the former declined (even in absolute terms), so that during the 1970s mapping and geological exploration accounted for less than one-fifth of all spending for oil exploration.[50] Thus the trend in West Siberia contrasted sharply with the growing emphasis on upstream exploration that was simultaneously taking place in the rest of the country. The immediate consequence was that the West Siberians failed to share even in the limited technological improvements that were aiding geophysical exploration elsewhere. The West Siberians complained, for example, that while modern seismic equipment was reaching teams in other parts of the country, their repeated requests to the USSR Ministry of Geology went unheeded.[51]

Why was there not more real support for upstream exploration in Siberia? One reason is that geologists throughout the country were at odds over West Siberia's prospects. From the late 1960s, the Soviet

[47] One way of showing this is to look at trends in base-point and parametric drilling (*oporno-parametricheskoe burenie*), which accompanies the upstream stages of exploration and should therefore tend to be concentrated in new regions. The share of such drilling, though it increased slightly in the first half of the 1970s, remained well under 1 percent of total exploratory drilling in West Siberia (Korchagin et al., "Osnovnye tendentsii," p. 27), though, as we saw earlier, it was rising rapidly elsewhere in the country at that same moment.

[48] Figures given in Brenner, *Ekonomika geologorazvedochnykh*, p. 88, show that exploratory drilling in East Siberia during the Ninth Plan fell to less than half the level of ten years before.

[49] Iu. V. Filanovskii, "Zapadno-Sibirskii neftegazovyi kompleks: rezul'taty i perspektivy," *Planovoe khoziaistvo*, no. 3 (1980), p. 21.

[50] Starovoitov, ed., *Problemy*, p. 60. The claim that budgetary allocations to Glavtiumengeologiia declined in absolute terms from 1968 to 1977 is made in Vtorushin and Murzin, "Iskat' novye klady." The reader will recall that upstream operations are funded out of budgetary allocations to the Ministry of Geology from the state budget, while downstream operations are regarded as capital investment, funded through the Ministries of Oil and Gas.

[51] Vtorushin and Murzin, "Iskat' novye klady."

geological establishment taught that north of the 64th parallel in Tiumen' Province one would find gas and gas condensate in plenty, but little oil.[52] Many West Siberian geologists insisted that this was wrong and that oil would be found under the gas. As the 1970s went on, the West Siberians added other promising locations to support their claim that most of the region's oil potential was still unmapped.[53] Local Party authorities joined the technical dispute on the side of their scientists. Thus V. N. Tiurin, then first secretary of Yamal-Nenets Autonomous Okrug (the administrative entity that contains most of the Middle Ob' Basin), criticized the

> more than a few open and hidden opponents who think that the Tiumen' geologists have discovered everything that can be discovered, and who advise that one should not, as they put it, yield to illusions, and in essence do everything to curtail the exploration of new deposits. Such judgments disorient geologists.[54]

The then second secretary of the Tiumen' Party obkom, at about the same time, sounded a similar note:

> Even today voices still resound, asserting that commercial-grade deposits of oil cannot be found. These assertions are made despite scientific prognosis: they do not take into consideration world practice and the discovery by our geologists, for example, of the Russkaia, Gubkin, and Urengoy deposits.[55]

Nevertheless, official priority in oil exploration, especially in geophysical mapping and other upstream operations, continued to favor the older oil-producing regions. This bias did not actually produce any major increase in exploratory oil drilling in the European part of the country on the part of either the Ministry of Geology or the Ministry of Oil. But the Europe-first policy probably did retard the shift of exploratory effort to West Siberia.

The West Siberians persisted in their efforts to reverse this policy,

[52] References to this position occur in Gurari, "Neft' i gaz Zapadnoi Sibiri," and Filanovskii, "Zapadno-Sibirskii neftegazovyi kompleks."

[53] A. A. Trofimuk and I. I. Nesterov, "Prirodnye uglevodorody Sibiri: prognoz i osvoenie," *Vestnik Akademii Nauk SSSR*, no. 9 (1979), pp. 78–83.

[54] V. N. Tiurin, *Oktiabr'*, no. 4 (1976), p. 138.

[55] Gennadii Shmal', *Sovetskaia Rossiia*, 22 Dec. 1976. Shmal' followed his patron Shcherbina to the Ministry for Construction of Oil and Gas Enterprises (MNGS) in the early 1980s. By 1984 he appeared as deputy minister (*Stroitel'stvo truboprovodov*, no. 3 [1984], p. 6), and by 1985 he had become first deputy minister (*Sotsialisticheskaia industriia*, 1 Sept. 1985). As of spring 1989, that is still his position; see his by-line in *Stroitel'stvo truboprovodov*,, no. 2 (1989).

and by 1975 they succeeded in making some headway. The directives for the Tenth Five-Year Plan (1976–1980) called for an increase in oil exploration and specified that it should be focused "above all in the Middle Ob' Basin and in the north of Tiumen' Province."[56] By this time, however, oil men were beginning to suspect that no new giants would be discovered soon, and they began to advocate falling back toward the only alternative available: to develop the multitude of smaller fields—many of them still uncertain prospects—lying beyond the known giants of the Middle Ob' Basin. This approach came to be known as the "second-stage" strategy.

PROVE UP THE SMALLER SIBERIAN FIELDS?

In the early 1970s the West Siberian oil industry rested on a dangerously narrow base. Out of some seventy-five prospective fields discovered by 1970,[57] only eleven had been developed for production, and proving up the latter had absorbed much of the exploration effort up to that time.[58] Fully 72 percent of the exploratory drilling in West Siberia during the Eighth Plan (1966–1970) had been *razvedochnoe*, that is, of the downstream variety that supports development.[59] This was a rational strategy as far as it went, based on the sensible proposition that the richest fields should be developed first. But the result by the early 1970s was that the burden of meeting the soaring output targets imposed on the Tiumen' oil industry would be borne by a handful of fields, above all, the supergiant Samotlor.

Samotlor is one of the wonders of the oil world and has been the mainstay of the Soviet oil industry for the last decade and a half. It began producing in 1969 and soon outstripped all forecasts. By 1975 it had reached 87 million tons a year[60] and was still growing fast. Its crucial role can be judged by the fact that the Nizhnevartovsk Oil Association, within which Samotlor is located, supplied 89.6 million tons of the total 116.6 million tons of the net increase in West Siberian output during 1971–1975, or 77 percent.[61]

It would have been sound policy to attempt to lessen this imbalance in the early 1970s by shifting exploration policy toward fields outside the Middle Ob' Basin, to prepare the way for new production in the second half of the 1970s. Indeed, this became official policy. The share

[56] Vtorushin and Murzin, "Iskat' novye klady."

[57] Gurari, "Neft' i gaz Zapadnoi Sibiri," p. 16.

[58] Starovoitov, ed., *Problemy*, p. 64.

[59] Korchagin et al., "Osnovnye tendentsii," p. 27.

[60] Starovoitov, ed., *Problemy*, p. 69.

[61] Ibid., p. 69.

of outlining (*razvedochnoe*) drilling was held back and that of prospecting drilling (*poiskovoe*) grew to 42 percent or, in absolute numbers, from 0.59 million meters to 1.1 million.[62] Eight new small fields were brought into production by 1975. But the redeployment of effort proved to be limited: three-quarters of the region's exploratory deep drilling for oil remained confined to the Middle Ob' region. By 1975 the Tiumen' oil industry remained dependent on the largest two or three fields, and especially Samotlor.

The chief issue at this time was how far Samotlor could be pushed. Gosplan, reluctant to accelerate oil spending in West Siberia any further, preferred to believe that output from Samotlor could keep growing for several more years. The deputy chief of Gosplan's Oil and Gas Department was quoted in *Pravda* as exclaiming: "The Siberians—they're terrific! Some other oil regions have let us down, but the plan will still be met. Tiumen' will cover."[63] But Tiumen' oil men thought that Samotlor would peak in 1977 at 100 million tons a year. Under pressure from Moscow, they reluctantly increased their 1980 estimate to 120 million tons. Gosplan was still not satisfied. As a *Pravda* correspondent reported:

> Gosplan for the time being is putting all its hopes on regions that have already been developed, particularly Samotlor, and they keep inquiring, "Since it turned out to be capable of yielding 120 million tons a year instead of 100, then why can't we extract 150 from it?" "Impossible," answer the people in Tiumen', "unless you want a sharp decline in a few years. . . ." Then criticism of a different sort starts to circulate, aimed at the geologists, "Why can't you discover just one more Samotlor?"[64]

The oil men were accused of trying to set comfortable targets for themselves; Viktor Muravlenko (then head of the Tiumen' oil industry) and others who tried to restrain Gosplan's enthusiasm, earned the nickname "upper-bounders" (*predel'shchiki*).[65] Their efforts were unavailing. In the second half of 1975 the planners overrode the objectors and sharply increased the 1980 targets for both Samotlor and for Tiumen' as a whole.[66]

This caused a flood of warnings from Tiumen' authorities, who

[62] Derived from a combination of Korchagin et al., "Osnovnye tendentsii," p. 27, and Brenner, *Ekonomika geologorazvedochnykh*, p. 88.

[63] A. Murzin, "Vsled za Samotlorom," *Pravda*, 11 June 1975.

[64] Ibid.

[65] L. Levitskii, R. Lynev, Iu. Perepletkin, "Trudnye milliony," *Izvestiia*, 27 May 1985.

[66] Farman Salmanov, "Opiraias' na prognozy," *Pravda*, 19 Feb. 1976.

brought the issue back to exploration and the development of the small outlying fields. On this point at least, all the West Siberians appeared united. The province's first Party secretary, G. P. Bogomiakov, warned midway in 1975: "Tiumen' is capable of increasing its output, in a stable and planned fashion, to even 200, 250, or 300 million tons of oil. But only under one condition: we must get ready right now, immediately, to go forth to new fields."[67] Viktor Muravlenko warned that if the Central Committee's targets were to be met, it would be necessary to bring into production sixty-two new fields in the Tenth Five-Year Plan.[68] The head of the Tiumen' geological service, Farman Salmanov, drew the implication: to turn prospects into reality would require bringing annual exploratory meterage in West Siberia up to 2 million meters year, a fourfold increase.[69]

After much argument the West Siberians ended up with half a loaf, or rather a promise of one. The planners' high 1980 output target stayed the same, but priority and support for West Siberian exploration were officially raised.[70] Some effects of the shift began to be noticed in Tiumen' at the beginning of 1977, as more equipment started to arrive for West Siberian exploration.[71] But on the whole, subsequent Soviet criticism suggests that the shift was more in words than in substance, and no great infusion of capital followed.[72] Total exploratory meterage in West Siberia, which had been 500,000 meters in 1976[73] (about the same as the annual average of the previous five-year plan), probably did not increase much in 1977. In 1976, 1977, and perhaps 1978, for the first time, West Siberian geologists failed to meet the annual plan target for gross additions to industrial reserves.[74] Then even the planners had to acknowledge they had a problem.

[67] Cited in Murzin, "Vsled za Samotlorom."

[68] V. Muravlenko, "Dal'she, za Samotlor," *Sotsialisticheskaia industriia*, 1 Jan. 1976.

[69] Salmanov, "Opiraias' na prognozy."

[70] The new policy was implemented in a CPSU Central Committee/USSR Council of Ministers decree at the end of 1976. "O merakh po dal'neishei podgotovke razvedannykh zapasov nefti, gazokondensata i prirodnogo gaza v Zapadnoi Sibiri," *Izvestiia*, 12 Dec. 1976. Whether coincidence or not, in 1976 the former chief of the Gosplan Oil and Gas Department was replaced by a career oil manager, V. I. Filanovskii, formerly chief of the capital construction department of the Ministry of Oil. Filanovskii has since returned to the Oil Ministry, where he is now first deputy minister, but throughout the period of the first oil crisis he was in charge of oil and gas policy at Gosplan.

[71] Vtorushin and Murzin, "Iskat' novye klady."

[72] This is an inference from Brenner, *Ekonomika geologorazvedochnykh*, p. 153, who writes, "From 1976 to 1978 the role of West Siberia in gross additions to oil reserves remained completely the same, under relatively small capital investments."

[73] *Pravda*, 14 Dec. 1980.

[74] A. A. Geniush, deputy director of the Tiumen' geological service for economic

Thus the oil crisis of 1977–1978 had been brewing since the beginning of the 1970s. It combined several ingredients. The West Siberian oil industry rested on too narrow a base. No new giants had been discovered (and indeed, none has been discovered in Siberia since 1974). Known prospects, consisting mostly of smaller fields outside the settled zone, were not proved up, so that by the mid-1970s the oil industry lacked a reserve of new fields fully outlined and ready for development. Meanwhile, the planners, scrambling to cover shortfalls elsewhere in the country, pushed Samotlor and the handful of other West Siberian fields too hard. By 1975–1976 the protests of local oil men and geologists had begun to bring a response from Moscow in the form of increased investment and logistical support for exploration, but it was too little and too late to avert trouble.

Who was to blame? In the first instance the geologists, since they were responsible for exploration. They were divided among themselves, and they provided the leaders with conflicting information. The oil industry deserves its share of the blame, too, since it was the source of funding for much of the geologists' downstream drilling. And although oil men grumbled about the unreliablility of the geologists' reserve estimates, they do not appear to have confronted the geologists head-on; instead, they negotiated compromise estimates with them.

A distant foreign observer, and a layman at that, should resist the temptation to pass judgment on highly complex technical issues. Nevertheless, the broad outlines of the problem seem clear enough in retrospect: by the mid-1970s Soviet exploration was failing to give Soviet leaders and planners the information needed for sound decisions. One cannot resist the thought that the leaders might have been more curious about a debate that was frequently conducted within their presence. Instead, they clung too long to the hope that exploration in the European USSR would pay off; then they preferred the easy solution of overproducing the handful of Siberian giants in the increasingly vain hope that more giants would soon be on the way. The system generated uncertain information and conflicting incentives, but in the end failure was due to the leaders' passivity and wishful thinking. It may be true, as the economist tells us, that the ant and the grasshopper differ only in their social rate of time preference, but there is still such a thing as simple improvidence.

---

affairs, speaking at a meeting in Tiumen' in mid-1978, suggested that the geologists, after missing the target in 1976 and 1977, might fall short in 1978 as well. "Tiumen': kompleks i ego grani," *Ekonomika i organizatsiia promyshlennogo proizvodstva*, no. 3 (1979), pp. 3–15.

The Brezhnev Emergency Response, 1977–1982

The geologists' failure to meet their reserves targets was not the only bad news from the Siberian oil fields in 1976 and 1977. The industry also reported sharp declines in the flow rates of new wells, especially in the crucial Nizhnevartovsk region within which Samotlor was located, abrupt increases in the West Siberian depletion ratio (that is, the percentage of new output required to compensate for declines in older fields), and, above all, sometime in 1977 the beginning of a decline in the growth rate of West Siberian output.[75] If one adds to that the simultaneous collapse of the coal industry—the centerpiece of the energy policy adopted in 1975—and the disappointing growth of nuclear power, one can readily imagine that Soviet leaders required little help from Western analysts to realize that their energy policy was in serious trouble. What is striking is not only that Brezhnev was so slow to react but that the other leaders were slower still.

Development, 1977–1980

The Soviet oil industry's success in stabilizing oil output after 1977 was due overwhelmingly to two factors. The first was a massive increase in development drilling. The second, and even more important, was a drastic shift of effort toward West Siberia. Whereas in 1977 less than 25 percent of the oil industry's drilling effort had gone into West Siberia, by 1982 West Siberia's share was well over half.

This shift to West Siberia was crucial because every new well in West Siberia still yielded more oil than the older fields of the Volga and the North Caucasus (see table 3.12). Moreover, most of the West Siberian oil fields then under development lay at shallow depths, and the rock was fairly easy to drill. As a result, a drilling brigade could drill nearly three times more hole in a year in West Siberia than the national average.[76]

The easier conditions in West Siberia also enabled the Soviets to skirt some of the chronic problems of their drilling technology, especially the defects of the turbodrill, which becomes less and less desirable to use at increasing depths. And since the historic advantage of the turbodrill for

[75] Data on new-well flow rates, depletion ratios, output per meter of development drilling (broken down according to the various producing regions of Tiumen'), and a graph of overall output trends in West Siberia will be found in Starovoitov, ed., *Problemy*, pp. 64, 81, and 82.

[76] In 1981, for example, the West Siberian figure was 45,000 meters per brigade versus 16,000 meters in the rest of the country. The West Siberian figure comes from *Ekonomicheskaia gazeta*, no. 5 (1982), p. 2; the all-Union figure is derived from *Neftianoe khoziaistvo*, no. 12 (1982), p. 66.

TABLE 3.12
New Well Flow Rates
(tons/day)

	1975	*1978*	*1980 (forecast in 1979)*	*1980 (actual)*	*1985 (actual)*
USSR	58.5	48.4	45.0	38.0	26
West Siberia	148.7	90.6	71.1	66.2	39

SOURCES: For 1978 and 1980 (forecast): Filanovskii, "Zapadno-Sibirskii neftegazovyi kompleks," p. 23; for 1975 and 1980: Starovoitov, ed., *Problemy*, p. 67; for 1985: Dinkov, *Neft' SSSR*, p. 148.

NOTE: For 1975, Filanovskii gives 162.0 tons/day, but this appears to be a mistake. Starovoitov's numbers are confirmed in Dinkov, p. 102.

the Soviet oil industry has been that it has less exacting requirements for high-quality pipe and drill bits, the massive move to West Siberia postponed those problems as well. During the decade from 1970 to 1980, the share of the turbodrill in total development drilling actually rose from 81.8 percent to 87.1 percent (table 3.13).

Such a remarkable increase in development drilling, together with so radical a shift in priorities to West Siberia, would have been difficult to forecast in 1977, the year before the stepped-up oil campaign began. How was it achieved? From 1978 through 1981, the drilling increases were obtained in classic "extensive" manner, that is, through massive additions and transfers of manpower, resources, and funding.

TABLE 3.13
Use of Different Drill Types in the Soviet Oil Industry, 1970–1980
(percentages)

	Development		*Exploratory*		*Total*	
	1970	*1980*	*1970*	*1980*	*1970*	*1980*
Turbodrill	81.8	87.1	63.8	48.1	76.4	82.1
Rotary	14.8	11.1	34.5	51.5	20.8	16.3
Electric	3.4	1.8	1.7	0.4	2.8	1.6

SOURCE: *Ekonomika neftianoi promyshlennosti*, no. 9 (1982), p. 10. I am unable to reconcile these data with those given in Dinkov, *Neft' SSSR*, p. 149. These suggest, however, that the dominance of the turbodrill increased still further from 1980 to 1985.

Two new practices brought hundreds of thousands of additional workers to Tiumen' and Tomsk provinces from older oil regions.[77] First, new workers were added to the permanent drilling teams of the Tiumen' oil industry. While nationwide the number of oil-drilling brigades attached to the Ministry of the Oil Industry grew by only 23.2 percent from 1976 to 1982,[78] the number of brigades attached to MNP's agency for Tiumen' (Glavtiumenneftegaz) in Tiumen' nearly doubled during roughly the same period (table 3.14). Since MNP did little exploration in Siberia, almost all of these new workers were used to boost development drilling.

In addition to these increases in the permanent complement of the Tiumen' industry, temporary teams were flown in from older areas. Since 1977, when the system began, the contribution of such outside forces has been crucial: flown-in teams from Tatariia, for example, drilled 1.3 million meters during the Tenth Plan,[79] and contingents from Bashkiriia contributed even more.[80] All told, drilling teams on loan from outside West Siberia contributed 10 million meters of hole (mainly development) by the end of 1981, roughly one-fourth of the total in West Siberia.[81]

For Western observers this resort to flown-in manpower was the greatest single surprise of the Brezhnev emergency oil policy. At first the role of the flown-in teams was difficult to spot because they remained subordinated to their home organizations and because their work in Siberia was credited toward target fulfillment back home—an apparent political sweetener to give the older regions an incentive to help out in Siberia. But once Soviet sources began publishing figures on the subject, it became clear that the fly-in method has been—and is increasingly—one of the essential elements of the oil industry's performance since 1977.

The Brezhnev emergency response rescued the 1980 output plan. Thanks to the tripling of development drilling that took place in West Siberia between 1975 and 1980, the West Siberian industry produced 313.6 million tons of oil in 1980, a little above the low end of the five-

[77] A. Aganbegian, "Toplivo Sibiri," *Pravda*, 1 Aug. 1983.

[78] *Oil and Gas Journal*, 27 June 1982, p. 27, from Soviet sources.

[79] *Neftianoe khoziaistvo*, no. 12 (1982), p. 12.

[80] Ibid., no. 2 (1983), p. 7. According to Ie. V. Stoliarov, director of the Bashkir oil industry, Bashkir drilling brigades drilled 3 million meters from 1977 to 1982.

[81] R. T. Bulgakov (former director of Glavtiumenneftegaz), "Zapadnaia Sibir'—osnovnaia neftegazodobyvaiushchaia baza strany," *Neftianoe khoziaistvo*, no. 12 (1982), pp. 13–15.

TABLE 3.14
Oil-Drilling Brigades Attached to Glavtiumenneftegaz, 1976–1981

End 1976	70
End 1979	106
End 1980	119
End 1981	138

SOURCE: *Ekonomika neftianoi promyshlennosti*, no. 4 (1982), pp. 17–18.

NOTE: The only absolute number this article actually gives is the figure for 1981. It also gives the number of brigades added during 1977–1979, 1980, 1981, and planned for the Eleventh Plan. The absolute numbers given in the chart are derived from these, but should probably be taken as approximate only.

year target set in 1976. There is little doubt that if the leaders had not responded as they did in 1977–1978, Soviet oil output would have peaked around 1980.

But the gains wrung between 1978 and 1981 were costly. As inexperienced and inadequately trained drillers were thrown into the ranks, productivity declined. The flown-in drilling teams, though manned by experienced workers, were hampered by fatigue and disorientation from poorly organized air transportation and inadequate housing.[82] Both the local teams and the fly-ins were increasingly deployed to remote locations, which caused further logistical snarls and increased nonproductive time. In Nizhnevartovsk, the most important of the Tiumen' oil associations, commercial drilling speed (meters per rig per month) dropped by 37 percent, mostly because nonproductive time rose from 25 to 50 percent of the drillers' time budget. But even mechanical speed (meters drilled per hour during productive time) declined by 9 percent.[83] Overall, because of the declining productivity,

[82] A. Laletin, "Samoletom na rabotu i obratno," *Trud*, 8 June 1982.
[83] *Ekonomika neftianoi promyshlennosti*, no. 4 (1982), p. 6.

the average cost of a production well in West Siberia doubled from 1975 to 1980.[84]

More significant for the long-term future of West Siberian oil was the indirect impact of the Brezhnev campaign on all other West Siberian oil operations. Investment in the Tiumen' oil industry was sharply rechanneled toward drilling and away from ancillary and infrastructural tasks, such as well completion and maintenance, installation of lifting equipment, housing and amenities, and construction of roads. Thus, while total productive investment in oil development and production in West Siberia increased 2.8 times between 1975 and 1980 and drilling investment increased 3.4 times, ancillary construction and road construction grew only half as fast. The share of housing construction in West Siberian oil investment, never large to begin with, declined from 9.1 percent in the Ninth Plan to 6.6 percent in the Tenth.[85]

The impact of these lopsided priorities could be observed almost immediately. Capital tied up in uncompleted projects soared from 558 million rubles in 1975 to 1,302 million by 1980.[86] Uncompleted wells doubled from 350 to over 700, and many of those officially listed as completed were poorly built, requiring repair and insulation before they could be put into operation.[87] The relative lack of attention given to installation of pumps and gaslift equipment delayed the process of mechanizing production, so that by 1980, 80 percent of West Siberian wells were still free-flowing (though with the aid of pumped-in water, a technique known as waterflooding).[88] Housing space available to oil workers by 1980 was only one-third of the national average, and for workers from ancillary ministries (particularly geologists) it was worse.[89] The one bright spot in infrastructural development was the growth of railroad capacity, which went from 3 percent of the oil industry's supply needs to 33 percent in five years, thus relieving the overburdened river-transport system.[90] The West Siberian oil industry, in short, was solving its immediate problem—that of producing the massive increase in drilling required by Moscow—but storing up further trouble for the future through unbalanced development.

Another portent of future trouble was that the West Siberian industry continued to rest on a small base, despite efforts to broaden it. The

[84] V. A. Dinkov, *Neft' SSSR, 1917–1987* (Moscow: Nedra, 1987), p. 102.

[85] Starovoitov, ed., *Problemy*, pp. 67, 73, 83.

[86] Ibid., p. 45.

[87] Derived from *Ekonomika neftianoi promyshlennosti*, no. 3 (1982), p. 22.

[88] Starovoitov, ed., *Problemy*, p. 66.

[89] Ibid., p. 76.

[90] Ibid., p. 70.

number of producing fields did grow from nineteen in 1975 to forty-six in 1980,[91] but by 1980 nearly half the output of Tiumen' Province still came from Samotlor, whose output was pushed from 87 million tons in 1975 to 154.6 million in 1980, far beyond the limits that Siberian oil men had been advocating only a few years before.[92] Yet the industry had little choice: however quickly the flow rates of new wells in the established Siberian fields declined, those of newly developed fields proved lower still (table 3.15).

In holiday speeches oil industry spokesmen were fond of claiming that they had made major gains in efficiency nationwide while meeting the emergency, but one must beware: for the years 1978–1980 these apparent gains were artifacts of the move to West Siberia. The continued growth of oil output between 1977 and 1980 nationwide was achieved with only about a 10 percent increase in manpower over the course of the Tenth Plan, but it should be clear that this result was due mainly to the one-time gains produced by the geographic shift and not to fundamental improvements in the oil industry.[93] Within West Siberia itself, efficiency dropped.

Exploration, 1977–1980

In just four years (1977–1980) the Ministry of the Oil Industry more than tripled its drilling in West Siberia, but its involvement in Siberian exploration hardly grew at all.[94] Instead, the burden fell almost entirely on the Ministry of Geology, which managed to boost exploratory drilling for oil in West Siberia from about 0.4 million meters in 1976 to about 0.9 million in 1980. (These numbers are inferred from the data presented in table 3.16.) Of the total volume of West Siberian exploratory drilling for oil in 1976–1980, which grew some 30 percent from 2.65 million meters in the first half of the 1970s to about 3.5 million meters in the second half,[95] only about 0.5 million was the work of MNP.[96]

[91] Ibid., p. 64.

[92] Derived from ibid., pp. 64 and 65.

[93] The estimate of 10 percent is derived from the information that oil output per worker grew 19.3 percent during the Tenth Plan. *Ekonomika neftianoi promyshlennosti*, no. 12 (1981), p. 4. Since total oil output increased by 31 percent over the same period, one can then calculate a figure for the increase in the labor force.

[94] In 1977 MNP drilled 3.8 million meters in West Siberia; in 1980, 12.9 million. In contrast, the scattered data for MNP exploration suggest that its contribution in West Siberia remained less than 100,000 meters per year.

[95] The first figure comes from Brenner, *Ekonomika geologorazvedochnykh*, p. 88. The second is a guesstimate based on "K Tiumenskomu millionu," *Pravda*, 14 Dec. 1980.

[96] This is another guesstimate. Trofimuk, "Neft' i gaz Sibiri," writes that in the late

TABLE 3.15
New Well Flow Rates in Tiumen' Fields (tons/day)

Date of Field Development	*New Well Flow Rate*	
	1975	*1980*
Prior to 1971	177	75.6
1971–1975	121	72.3
1976–1980	—	54.7

SOURCE: Starovoitov, ed., *Problemy*, p. 67.

The geologists could have sent more teams to West Siberia than they did. (Mingeo moved only about 10 percent of its drilling capacity east of the Urals during this period, much less than MNP.) But as they began moving from the center of the Middle Ob' Basin to smaller and more remote fields, they quickly ran into tougher conditions, which limited the rate at which the effort could be expanded. As a result, the efficiency of West Siberian exploration declined even more drastically than that of development (table 3.17). The geologists had been undersupplied and underequipped for years; they could not respond as quickly as MNP's development teams to a sudden influx of resources.

Just as development dominated exploration overall, so within exploration most of the increased effort was directed toward downstream operations—to provide information to support the rapid increase of development drilling. Thus the share of *razvedochnoe* drilling, which had declined to 57 percent of West Siberian exploratory drilling (oil and gas combined) in the Ninth Plan (1971–1975), rose sharply to 66 percent in the Tenth (1976–1980), most of that increase presumably coming in the last three years of the plan.[97] Even within exploration, in other words, the bias was toward near-term results.

1970s MNP was putting only about one-thirtieth of its exploratory effort into West Siberia. Roughly the same range of meterage can be inferred from a description of exploration by Glavtiumenneftegaz in *Geologiia nefti i gaza*, no. 11 (1982). The article states that Glavtiumenneftegaz completed 183 exploratory wells in Tiumen' in the Tenth Plan period. If one assumes an average depth of 2,700 meters (a representative depth, as reported in *Tekhnicheskii progress v neftianoi promyshlennosti v desiatoi piatiletke* [Moscow: Nedra, 1981]), then one arrives at a total of just under 0.5 million meters for the second half of the 1970s.

[97] Korchagin et al., "Osnovnye tendentsii," p. 27.

TABLE 3.16
Trends in Exploratory Oil Drilling in West Siberia, 1976–1980
(thousands of meters)

	Mingeo	*MNP*	*Total*
1976			500
1977	600		
1978			
1979	763		800
1980			1,000
1976–1980		$\leq$500	

SOURCES: For Mingeo: Filanovskii, "Zapadno-Sibirskii neftegazovyi kompleks," and Iudin, *Sotsialisticheskaia industriia*, 3 Mar. 1978; for MNP: *Geologiia nefti i gaza*, no. 11 (1982); for the total: "K Tiumenskomu," defined as "oil exploration."

Meanwhile, the debates over West Siberian reserves raged on. In 1979 an influential Tiumen' geologist exclaimed:

> The more insistently the question is raised about exploration of oil in the Siberian tundra, the more skeptics appear in the way of the geologists. . . . Never once have the forecasts of the Tiumen' scientists been refuted in practice. On the contrary, more than once reality has exceeded the most daring of them. . . . Life shows that the Tiumen' geologists have earned the right to special trust.[98]

Behind the plea for "special trust," however, lay a reluctant concession that the Tiumen' geologists had not yet succeeded in justifying their predictions, and in particular their claim that more oil bonanzas would be found as teams moved north. At about the same time, Glavtiumengeologiia's chief economist stated that half of the region's planned output for 1985 would have to come from fields that had not yet been discovered.[99] In 1980, as five-year targets once again came up for debate, the unnamed skeptics had still not come around. Farman Salmanov, chief of Glavtiumengeologiia, acknowledged that, if anything, the controversy was growing: "In the second stage of development of West Siberia there are no fewer disputes than before. . . . I cannot agree with those who try to show that we have reached a peak in

[98] I. Nesterov, "Pravo na doverie," *Pravda*, 22 July 1979.
[99] A. A. Geniush in "Tiumen': Kompleks i ego grani," p. 15.

TABLE 3.17
Deterioration of Performance Indicators in Glavtiumengeologiia, 1975–1978

	Commercial Speed (meters/rig-mo.)	*Completion Time (days/well)*	*Meterage per Rig (meters/yr.)*	*Labor Productivity (meters/man)*
1975	1,230	155.8	3,755	44.5
1978	1,005	216.5	3,306	37.3

SOURCE: Filanovskii, "Zapadno-Sibirskii neftegazovyi kompleks," p. 21.

Tiumen'. "[100] Salmanov went on to hint that the skeptics were located high in Moscow's planning and policymaking circles.[101]

The worrisome reserves trend in West Siberia failed to improve. Although gross additions to prospective reserves ($A + B + C_1 + C_2$) increased slightly from the Ninth to the Tenth Plan, the more immediately important category of industrial reserves ($A + B + C_1$), which had been one of the chief concerns of 1976 and 1977, continued to lag.[102] No new giant fields were discovered; instead, additions to reserves came either from further exploration of established fields or from increasingly unattractive new locations. The latter showed a revealing discrepancy between potential and proven reserves: the average new field discovered during 1976–1980 was reported to contain only 39 percent as much prospective reserves ($A + B + C_1 + C_2$) as the average field discovered before 1966 and only 12.3 percent as much industrial reserves ($A + B + C_1$).[103] Such a gap between confirmed and unconfirmed reserves could only stimulate further skepticism and controversy about the region's prospects. Meanwhile, even such unconfirmed addi-

[100] Farman Salmanov, "V sporakh rozhdaetsia . . . neft'," *Sotsialisticheskaia industriia*, 12 July 1980.

[101] Ibid. We have seen that many of the most important players (Baibakov, Mal'tsev, Dolgikh) had spoken or written in favor of further effort in the European USSR and that the USSR Ministry of Geology appeared to share their preference. But this attitude was probably shifting at the time. Thus, in an article published in 1980, the new chief of Gosplan's Oil and Gas Department, V. I. Filanovskii, appeared to endorse the Tiumen' position when he wrote that exploration conducted during the Tenth Plan had refuted the theory that there was no oil to be found north of the 64th parallel. Filanovskii, "Zapadno-Sibirskii neftegazovyi kompleks," p. 19.

[102] Starovoitov, ed., *Problemy*, pp. 59 and 61. In 1980 Academician A. A. Trofimuk, one of the leading authorities on Siberian oil and gas, wrote that the "ratio of output to additions to reserves is worse than in the other regions." Trofimuk, "Neft' i gaz Sibiri."

[103] Starovoitov, ed., *Problemy*, p. 62.

tions were growing much more expensive to discover: during the Tenth Plan one ton of gross additions to prospective reserves ($A + B + C_1 + C_2$) cost 3.3 times what it had ten years before.[104] Reluctant planners began to realize that to dispel the uncertainty surrounding West Siberia's oil future in the 1980s would require a further substantial increase in exploration expenditure, particularly for upstream operations.

From One Crisis to the Next

In 1980–1981, as the leaders and planners reviewed the results of the three-year crash effort and debated their strategy for the Eleventh Five-Year Plan (1981–1985), three facts must have been evident to them. First, the shift to West Siberia had enabled the industry to skim dramatic one-time gains from the region's shallower wells, higher new well flow rates, simpler geological formations, and greater concentration of production in a few large fields. These advantages, though fading steadily, still remained great. Sound strategy, therefore, called for continuing the transfer of the industry's resources to Siberia while limiting the decline of the older regions.

Second, the impact of the previous three years on the efficiency of the oil industry in West Siberia had been disastrous. Unless the rocketing costs could be slowed, even doubling oil investment in the region in the first half of the 1980s would not be enough to enable West Siberian output to offset declines elsewhere.

Third, the previous three years had confirmed the weakness of exploration crews in Tiumen' and had failed to dispel uncertainty over West Siberian prospects. (On the contrary, there began an intensified debate that soon led to a radical downward revision of reserves estimates.) Moreover, the immediate need for downstream exploration to support development of new fields was preventing the geologists from stepping up the search for new prospects. It was far from clear whether the region's claimed potential would ever be confirmed, but the only way to find out was to invest still more.

Was Brezhnev right to react as he did? By the classic Soviet test, he was: he met the plan. But in responding with an all-out campaign, he delayed a more methodical attack on the root causes of the oil problem. The consequences were soon to be felt.

104 Ibid., p. 59.

FOUR

THE SECOND OIL CRISIS, 1982–1988

By the time Brezhnev died in 1982, the Soviet oil industry appeared to have contained the threat of a decline in oil output. Production still rose steadily, if far more slowly than in the late 1970s. But the appearance of stabilization was deceptive. The oil industry owed its growth mainly to the continuing transfer of development drilling capacity to West Siberia. The planners and ministers had failed to use the resulting respite to raise the oil industry's efficiency, to reinforce its industrial base, to increase exploration and accelerate the development of new Siberian fields, or to improve infrastructure in and around the oil fields, such as housing, roads, and powerlines. At the same time, the Siberian strategy drained resources away from the older oil provinces elsewhere in the country, thus slowing the introduction of new recovery techniques. The main result of five years of Brezhnev's crash oil program, in short, was to aggravate the previous imbalance of the oil industry and thus to prepare further trouble.

The sharp decline in oil output that began in late 1984, followed by an unexpectedly strong recovery from early 1986 to the present, raises all over again the question of the role of leadership and its effect on performance. What caused the second oil crisis? What made it pass? Will there be a third one?

In 1980–1981, as they debated the shape of the next five-year plan, leaders and planners were caught between the economy's unquenched demand for oil and oil's fast-rising cost. To keep the share of oil in the energy balance at its 1980 level would have required a 1985 target of 717 million tons and more than a tripling of oil investment. The planners decided instead on a more modest goal of 630 million tons, which was, in fact, the level originally set for 1980 at the beginning of the previous plan. But the extra capital allocated to reach it (about 17 billion rubles, or an increase of 63 percent over the previous five-year plan) was inadequate from the start. In subsequent postmortems, the planners were accused of having ignored information on the rapidly rising costs of exploration and development submitted to them by the oil industry and to have based their plans on the much lower cost figures of earlier years.[1] But the leaders cannot escape ultimate blame. The seeming modesty of the five-year oil target concealed what later turned out to be a good deal of wishful thinking. The decisions made then suggest that leaders and planners had barely begun to focus on the cost problem and had not developed any real strategy for dealing with its causes.

Instead, they evidently continued to count heavily on the existing Tiumen' oil fields. The same jousting between planners and local oil men that had characterized the debate over oil targets five years before was repeated. The oil men's initial offer of 340 million tons for Tiumen' was rejected by Moscow because it would have meant not only falling far short of the national target but also accepting the possibility of an outright decline.[2] As in the previous two five-year plans, the planners responded by raising sharply the oil industry's initial proposed target for Tiumen', this time by about 35 to 40 million tons (table 4.1). Subsequently, as the older oil regions fell behind the planned pace, the Tiumen' target was raised even higher, to nearly 390 million tons.[3]

Information available to the planners must have told them how difficult such growth would be. The reports of local oil specialists showed that by 1985 West Siberia would reach a depletion ratio of more than 85 percent (that is, more than 85 percent of the gross increase in West Siberian output would have to offset declines elsewhere in the region),

[1] I. Gostev, "Oilfield Reliability," *Sovetskaia Rossiia*, 11 Jan. 1986 (trans. in Foreign Broadcast Information Service, *Soviet Union Daily Report*, Supplement 010, 15 Jan. 1986, p. S1). One would give a great deal to know more about the cost estimates the planners actually used. Retrospective estimates by Western analysts suggest that from 1970 to 1980 the average production cost of a ton of oil had increased from 7.9 rubles per ton to 12.5, or about 58 percent. But the marginal cost had skyrocketed, from around 14 rubles per ton to 53, and was continuing to rise steeply. See Matthew J. Sagers, "Oil Production Costs in the USSR," in *PlanEcon Long-Term Energy Outlook* (Washington, D.C.: PlanEcon, Inc., Fall 1987), pp. 50–51. A Soviet estimate, based on the development costs for one ton/year of new production capacity, shows a more moderate rate of cost growth, reflecting the low depletion rates and the greater share of high-yielding young oil fields in the Soviet cost structure of the early 1970s. V. I. Dolgikh, "Otnoshenie k resursam—vazhneishii kriterii perestroiki v ekonomike," *Pravda*, 11 July 1988.

[2] The oil men's recommendation of 340 million tons for Tiumen' would have meant about 350 million tons for West Siberia as a whole. V. Lisin, "Proschety v raschetakh," *Pravda*, 3 Apr. 1984. Adding the 240–245 million ton target ultimately set for the rest of the country would have yielded a total 1985 target of 590–595 million tons. In fact, actual output in 1985 was 365.8 million tons for West Siberia but only 229.5 million for the rest of the country. *Soviet Geography* 30, no. 4 (April 1989), p. 308.

[3] A. G. Aganbegian, *Zapadnaia Sibir' na rubezhe vekov* (Sverdlovsk: Sredne-Ural'skoe knizhnoe izdatel'stvo, 1984), p. 25, gives the 1985 West Siberian target as 400 million tons. *Soviet Geography* 26, no. 4 (April 1985), p. 300, cites 390 million tons for Tiumen' and 402 for West Siberia.

TABLE 4.1
Five-Year Oil Targets for Tiumen', 1985 and 1990
(millions of tons)

	1985 (set in 1980–1981)	*1990 (set in 1985–1986)*
Tiumen' oil men's recommendations	340	
Five-year plan	375–380	410–425*
Final output	352.7	

SOURCES: 1985 targets: Lisin, "Proschety v raschetakh"; 1990 target: Chirskov in *Stroitel'stvo truboprovodov*, no. 2 (1986), p. 4.

* Tiumen' obkom First Secretary Bogomiakov, in the television version of Gorbachev's appearance in Tiumen', 6 September 1985, gave 410–420.

the new well flow rate would drop to little over 40 percent of its 1980 level, and the marginal capital cost of each ton of gross addition to capacity would rise to 2.3 times the 1980 level (table 4.2).

But, given the targets assigned to it, the oil industry had no alternative to the West Siberian campaign strategy. The Oil Ministry planned to triple its drilling in West Siberia by 1985, leaving little increase for the rest of the country.[4] Total oil investment was similarly biased toward West Siberia: out of the total increase of nearly 17 billion rubles scheduled for the oil industry in the Eleventh Plan, West Siberia was slated to receive about two-thirds.[5]

[4] Total drilling by MNP in West Siberia, which had exceeded 27 million meters in 1976–1980 (S. N. Starovoitov, ed., *Problemy razvitiia Zapadno-Sibirskogo neftegazovogo kompleksa* [Novosibirsk: Nauka, 1983], p. 64), was slated to increase to 75–77 million meters in 1981–1985 (*Ekonomika neftianoi promyshlennosti*, no. 3 [1982], p. 4; *Neftianoe khoziaistvo*, no. 4 [1982], p. 3). As it turned out, MNP drilling in West Siberia fell considerably short of planned tripling. Annual drilling rates only doubled between 1980 and 1985, from 8.4 million meters to a little over 17 million. Still, this represented about 80 percent of the total increase in MNP drilling countrywide. For 1980, see *Neftianoe khoziaistvo*, no. 3 (1983), p. 4. For 1985, V. A. Dinkov says that oil drilling in West Siberia grew 2.2 times, but it is unclear whether he includes only MNP drilling; see Dinkov, *Neft' SSSR, 1917–1987* (Moscow: Nedra, 1987).

[5] The nationwide increase is derived from *Neftianoe khoziaistvo*, no. 4 (1982), p. 6; the West Siberian share is derived from the information that the region's oil investment was scheduled to double during the Eleventh Plan (S. D. Ageeva and B. P. Orlov, "Nekotorye cherty investitsionnogo protsessa v zapadno-sibirskom neftegazovom komplekse," *Izvestiia Sibirskogo Otdeleniia Akademii Nauk SSSR* [seriia obshchestvennykh nauk], no. 11 [1982], pp. 85–89), together with the statement that West Siberia was to receive half of the total oil investment during the same period (*Neftianoe khoziaistvo*, no. 3 [1982], p. 4). Investment trends tend to reflect drilling trends, since drilling currently accounts for over 40 percent of MNP's total investment.

TABLE 4.2
Decline of Major West Siberian Oil Indicators, 1970–1985

Year	*Depletion Ratio (%)*	*New Well Flow Rate (tons/day)*	*Capital Costs Per Ton/Yr of Gross Addition to Capacity (1970 = 100)*
1970	26.9	111.8	100.0
1975	34.7	148.7	NA
1980	49.0	66.2	150.0
1985*	85.7	39	345.0

SOURCE: Starovoitov, ed., *Problemy*, pp. 64, 67, 68, 81; for 1985: Dinkov, *Neft' SSSR*, p. 148.
* Forecast in early 1980s.

Underlying this approach was the hope that the "Siberian fix" would work again, without endangering output in the older oil regions. The industry claimed that even as the shift to West Siberia was going on, it could also improve its productivity—an unlikely prospect so long as it was forced to devote all its attention to meeting production plans. In retrospect, then, the 1981–1985 oil plan was based in no small part on wishful thinking and political pressure, and it was in serious danger from the start.

The Crisis of 1982–1986

Fresh Trouble in West Siberia

New troubles were not long in appearing. In 1982, for the first time in its history, the Tiumen' oil industry failed to meet its yearly output plan. The ministry hastily "corrected" the target downward, and the matter was not made public.[6] But in each of the following three years the shortfall worsened, and by the end of the Eleventh Plan Tiumen' had fallen about 30 million tons short of the 390 million ton target set five years before.[7] Indeed, Tiumen' oil output, after reaching 1 million

[6] V. Lisin, "Proschety v raschetakh."

[7] In 1983 Tiumen' came up 3 million tons short of the annual plan (*Sotsialisticheskaia industriia*, 24 Feb. 1984); in 1984, about 5 million (*Izvestiia*, 7 Dec. 1984); and in 1985, over 20 million (*Sotsialisticheskaia industriia*, 7 Aug. 1985). These specific numbers have little meaning as such, however, since the annual plans for Tiumen' are frequently revised, sometimes several times in one year. What matters is that they show that the planners and reality were drawing farther and farther apart. (Actual Tiumen' output in 1985 is reported as 352.7 million tons in *Soviet Geography* 29, no. 4 [April 1988], p. 425.)

tons per day in 1984, was unable to hold at that level; by the end of the year it had already begun to decline. This meant that overall Soviet oil output was bound to fall: unless Siberia produced regular increments of at least 12–14 million tons every year, declines in the older oil regions of the country could not be offset. That is exactly what happened in late 1984 and in 1985.

The most eye-catching symptom of trouble in Tiumen' was an epidemic of idle wells. By the end of 1985, one out of six of Tiumen' 's nearly 30,000 wells was not producing.[8] By accepted industry practice, 2,000 idle wells would have been considered normal; but by January 1986 there were about 5,000,[9] accounting for a shortfall of between 10 and 15 million tons of output a year. Many of these wells had been drilled in the hectic years after 1977, and the quality of the work had been poor; the bill was now coming due, especially at Samotlor, where 1,000 of the idle wells were located. Samotlor finally peaked in 1980 at 155 million tons a year; and despite the local oil men's frantic efforts to keep it from slipping, it accounted for most of Tiumen' 's shortfall over the next five years.[10]

The other major symptom of new trouble in West Siberia was the industry's failure to develop new fields fast enough to support production goals. The "second-stage strategy," in other words, was not working; as a result, the older fields were being severely overproduced.[11] The initial five-year target for 1981–1985 had called for eighty new fields, but this was quickly revised down to thirty[12] and then to twenty-six.[13] By 1985 only twenty-four new fields had been brought on line,[14]

[8] Soviet accounts differ widely on the specific numbers, although they agree on the overall picture. Iu. Belanov and V. Kremer, "Trudnaia neft'," *Sotsialisticheskaia industriia*, 7 Aug. 1985; Iu. Perepletkin, "Pogoda na zavtra," *Izvestiia*, 11 Feb. 1986; unattributed news item in *Pravda*, 12 Feb. 1986; "Vse skvazhiny—v stroi!" *Sotsialisticheskaia industriia*, 15 July 1986; V. Kozlov, "Neft' Zapadnoi Sibiri," *Planovoe khoziaistvo*, no. 8 (1986), p. 43; G. Bazhutin, V. Zhiliakov, and V. Kremer, "Preodolenie," *Sotsialisticheskaia industriia*, 7 Sept. 1986.

[9] Perepletkin, "Pogoda na zavtra."

[10] L. Levitskii et al., "Razryv," *Izvestiia*, 28 May 1985.

[11] Gostev, "Oilfield Reliability."

[12] The initial target appeared in *Sotsialisticheskaia industriia*, 21 May 1980, and the revised one in same, 5 Sept. 1982, both as cited in *Soviet Geography* 26, no. 4 (April 1985), p. 300.

[13] L. Levitskii et al., "Trudnye milliony," *Izvestiia*, 27 May 1985.

[14] Ia. Ali-Zade et al., "S chego nachinaetsia promysel," *Sotsialisticheskaia industriia*, 1 Feb. 1986; see also *Izvestiia*, same date. Unfortunately, Soviet estimates vary widely. Thus Starovoitov, ed., *Problemy*, p. 64, lists a total of 46 fields in operation as of 1980; Leslie Dienes, "The Soviet Oil Industry in the 12th Five-Year Plan," *Soviet Geography* 28, no. 9 (November 1987), cites a source by V. I. Graifer giving 77 fields in production in 1985. The implied increase of 31 fields for 1981–1985 is, of course, at variance with the numbers given by Ali-Zade.

and they contributed much less than anticipated. All told, the shortfall from this cause alone was 10 to 15 million tons a year.[15]

These two symptoms—the epidemic of idle wells and the failure to develop output from new fields—accounted for most of the gap between actual production and the five-year goal.

Panic and Purge in Tiumen'

As the situation worsened in Siberia, Moscow reacted in panic. A familiar search for scapegoats began, confined at first to Nizhnevartovsk (the most serious trouble spot) but soon widening to the rest of Tiumen'.[16] In 1982 and 1983 all but one or two of the twenty administrative heads in Nizhnevartovsk were fired.[17] In February 1985 the minister of oil himself, N. A. Mal'tsev, was replaced by the former minister of gas, V. A. Dinkov, and a new wave of purges hit West Siberia, beginning with the head of the Tiumen' oil industry. This time, instead of promoting a field man (as had always been the case in the past), the new minister sent in a planner/economist, V. I. Graifer, from Moscow.[18] Over the next year most of the top command of the Tiumen' industry, and several hundred of the next level of managers, were fired.[19] The average tenure of a chief engineer in a production division dropped to just over one year.[20]

By the end of 1985 local oil men were becoming understandably gun-shy, and the industry reported problems in getting good people to

[15] Iu. Perepletkin, "Rezervy neftianogo plasta," *Izvestiia*, 7 Dec. 1984.

[16] As many a bureaucrat will testify, it pays to be reassigned before the roof falls in. Rishad Bulgakov, who as head of the Tiumen' oil industry (Glavtiumenneftegaz) since 1977 had presided over the Brezhnev campaign, was transferred to Moscow in the spring of 1981. His successor, R. I. Kuzovatkin, was a Tiumen' veteran who had previously served in Nizhnevartovsk (*Pravda* 11 June 1975) and headed Iugansk (*Izvestiia* 11 Feb. 1986). Bulgakov resurfaced in late 1985 as deputy chief of Gosplan's Oil and Gas Department (*Sotsialisticheskaia industriia*, 29 Dec. 1985), where at this writing he is working still.

[17] Perepletkin, "Rezervy neftianogo plasta."

[18] Graifer was head of the Oil Ministry's Administration of Economic Planning from 1976 to 1985. Central Intelligence Agency, Directorate of Intelligence, *Directory of Soviet Officials: National Organizations*, various years.

[19] *Pravda*, 24 Dec. 1985. There were few identifiable promotions or survivals. One noteworthy exception was the head of the successful Iugansk oil association, Iu. N. Vershinin, who rose to become chief engineer of Glavtiumenneftegaz. *Ekonomicheskaia gazeta*, no. 40 (1983), p. 8; *Sotsialisticheskaia industriia*, 20 May 1984; and *Izvestiia*, 27 May 1985. Another survivor was V. Bogdanov, head of Surgutneftegaz. *Sotsialisticheskaia industriia*, 7 Aug. 1985. As of spring 1986, the general directors of five of the six main Tiumen' oil associations were L. Filimonov (Nizhnevartovsk), V. Bogdanov (Surgut), N. Zakharchenko (Var'egan), V. Gorodilov (Noiabr'sk), and V. M. Nikolaev (Iugansk). I have no information for Krasnoleninsk.

[20] Levitskii et al., "Razryv."

fill the leading positions in Tiumen'. In fact, it was difficult to tell how much of the turnover in the top ranks was the result of firings or of resignations ahead of the axe. The press wrote hopefully that the merry-go-round had halted,[21] but in early 1986 managers were still changing with "kaleidoscopic speed" at Samotlor,[22] and the top thirty positions at Var'egan also changed hands.[23]

The Tiumen' Party obkom was also hard hit, a result both of the oil crisis and the wider "cleansing" (*ochishchenie*) simultaneously going on in Party organizations around the country during Gorbachev's first year.[24] Miraculously, the first secretary, Gennadii Bogomiakov, kept his job, most likely as a result of protection from Deputy Prime Minister Boris Shcherbina, Bogomiakov's predecessor in Tiumen' and apparent patron.

The tide of replacements was but one symptom of mounting pressure from ministry headquarters. Waves of commissions descended on Nizhnevartovsk from MNP headquarters in Tiumen' and Moscow, as many as ten at a time and nearly three hundred in 1985 alone.[25] They extracted promises from the local managers to pump harder, then flew off again. The ministry made constant nervous changes in targets. But the one thing that did not change was the pressure to produce. It was

[21] Ibid.

[22] V. Kuz'mishchev et al., "Trevogi i nadezhdy Samotlora," *Pravda*, 28 Jan. 1986.

[23] Bazhutin et al., "Preodolenie." Var'egan was a troubled corner of Nizhnevartovsk that had been established as an independent association only the previous year.

[24] In particular, the secretary for oil and gas, E. G. Altunin, was replaced in the spring of 1985 by V. V. Kitaev (*Sovetskaia Rossiia*, 20 Apr. 1985), and the secretary for cadres, V. I. Erofeev, by Iu. Klat. In addition, several gorkom first secretaries appear to have been replaced, notably at Noiabr'sk (where the current first secretary, V. Shestakov, is first mentioned in *Sotsialisticheskaia industriia*, 1 Feb. 1986), Nizhnevartovsk (S. I. Denisov; first mention, *Pravda*, 5 Sept. 1985), Tiumen' City (V. G. Kholiavko; first mention, *Izvestiia*, 28 Feb. 1985), and Nefteiugansk (M. Metakov; first mention, *Pravda*, 17 Sept. 1986). The second secretary of the Tiumen' obkom, G. M. Goloshchapov, is first mentioned in *Izvestiia*, 28 Feb. 1985, and the first secretary of the Khanty-Mansiisk okruzhkom, V. A. Churilov, is first mentioned in *Pravda*, 5 Sept. 1985. Finally, the chairman of the Tiumen' oblispolkom, V. V. Nikitin, was replaced some time in 1985 by N. I. Chernukhin (Nikitin is last mentioned in this position in *Pravda*, 17 Feb. 1985, while Chernukhin appears in the list of delegates to the Twenty-seventh Party Congress in February 1986). Not all of the incumbents were necessarily demoted; Nikitin, for example, was promoted to Moscow as the first deputy chairman of the RSFSR State Agro-Industrial Committee (Twenty-seventh Party Congress delegate list), which suggests that the oblispolkom chairman's responsibilities in Tiumen' may be agricultural instead of industrial.

[25] Ia. Ali-Zade et al., "Ostrye ugli Samotlora," *Sotsialisticheskaia industriia*, 28 Jan. 1986; also Ia. Ali-Zade et al., "Komandirovka kuratora," *Sotsialisticheskaia industriia*, 11 Apr. 1986.

felt to such a point, indeed, that in some new fields desperate managers were producing oil from exploratory wells.

Local officials reacted by systematically misreporting outputs, and phony data flowed up the ranks in response to the threats flowing down. As the central press poured on criticism of the disarray in the oil fields, the local Party apparatus in Nizhnevartovsk (the site of the worst trouble) attempted to squelch it, an early case of local resistance to *glasnost'*.[26] When Gorbachev visited Tiumen in the fall of 1985, he accused local officials of lying, and he wagged his finger at them, exclaiming, "That won't do, comrades!" (*Tak nel'zia, tovarishchi!*).[27]

But the year 1985 also witnessed the beginning of a long-term review of oil policy and an attempt to change course. In the following sections we shall examine more closely the causes of the second oil crisis and then turn to the Gorbachev leadership's response and its results.

Causes of the Second Oil Crisis

In its immediate causes, the second oil crisis was substantially different from the first one. Above all, the events of 1977 had been tied to problems in exploration policy. Moscow's soaring expectations had been rudely jolted. No new giants had been discovered, existing prospects had not been proved up, and proven reserves had been exaggerated. The panic one senses in Soviet sources of the time was due to sudden and acute uncertainty.

In contrast, the second crisis was one of development and production, caused by the oil industry's longstanding failure to improve productivity and aggravated by accumulated gaps and imbalances in Siberian oil development, particularly the lopsided stress on development drilling of the previous five years. These causes had been long in the making. Ironically, their effects may have been aggravated by Andropov's attempt to hold back oil investment in 1983–1984: since about three-quarters of all oil investment goes into development drilling and field preparation, any sudden slowdown in funding, in the absence of other offsetting measures, was bound to be felt quickly.

As we review the list of the oil industry's problems, the interesting question is how the same list must have looked to the new Soviet leadership taking shape in 1983–1985. In particular, how much of the industry's disarray was directly traceable to the political laxness of Brezhnev's last years? What role must the new leaders have seen for

[26] This charge was made by the Party second secretary, Egor' Ligachev, at the Twenty-seventh Party Congress. See *XXVIIyi. s"ezd Kommunisticheskoi Partii Sovetskogo Soiuza, stenograficheskii otchet* (Moscow: Politizdat, 1986), vol. 1, p. 236.

[27] Tiumen' speech, *Pravda*, 7 Sept. 1985.

short-term measures, the "human factor" policies that Gorbachev touted in his first two years as General Secretary?

DRILLING

Expansion of development drilling remained the core of the oil industry's strategy in the first half of the 1980s, as the industry continued the drive to transfer its drilling teams and resources to West Siberia. The Oil Ministry's five-year plan called for a near doubling of its total drilling in 1981–1985, mostly concentrated on development,[28] but a tripling in West Siberia, almost exclusively for development.[29]

But the ministry fell short of its drilling targets. In Tiumen' drilling only doubled instead of tripling as planned;[30] as a result, the number of new wells there fell short also, by nearly 1,500. Most of the shortfall was presumably in the newer oil fields, as the industry concentrated its resources on the previously developed areas.[31]

Even so, this was a remarkable performance. Countrywide, the number of new operating oil wells commissioned grew by 80 percent over the previous five-year period (table 4.3), while in West Siberia the growth rate was 250 percent. At the same time, the drillers' productivity, though recovered somewhat from the decline of 1977–1980, did not return to the levels of 1975.[32] Consequently, the only way the industry could increase its drilling volume was to bring in more personnel and rigs; and it was forced to do so in far larger numbers than it had originally planned, relying mainly on the same two mechanisms described in the previous chapter: adding to the permanent complement of the West Siberian oil industry and flying in massive numbers of temporary workers from other oil regions. From 1980 to 1985 the number of drilling brigades attached to Glavtiumenneftegaz grew from

[28] Oil industry total drilling was 71 million meters in 1976–1980. The five-year plan called for an increase to 130 million in 1981–1985. *Sotsialisticheskaia industriia*, 5 Sept. 1982.

[29] Oil Ministry drilling in West Siberia, almost entirely for development, was a little over 27 million meters in 1976–1980 (26.8 for development and about 0.5 million for exploration). The five-year plan target for 1981–1985 in West Siberia was 75–77 million meters. See *Ekonomika neftianoi promyshlennosti*, no. 3 (1982), p. 4, and *Neftianoe khoziaistvo*, no. 4 (1982), p. 3.

[30] Kozlov, "Neft' Zapadnoi Sibiri," p. 32. What Kozlov actually says is that the 1985 drilling level was double that of 1980.

[31] Ibid., p. 33.

[32] Dinkov, *Neft' SSSR, 1917–1987*, ch. 6, shows the improvement from 1980 to 1985. But see V. Kniazev, "Na ostrie dolota," *Pravda*, 27 Sept. 1986, for a statement that for the period 1975–1985 as a whole monthly meterage per brigade, commercial and mechanical speed, meterage per bit, and time budgets all showed net declines.

TABLE 4.3
New Production Oil Wells Commissioned, 1971–1987 (thousands)

1971–1975	20.8
1976–1980	29.8
1981–1985	53.6
1986 } 1987 }	14.3

SOURCE: *Narodnoe khoziaistvo SSSR v 1987g.*, p. 285.

119 to 282, compared to the 219 originally planned.[33] As for flown-in oil workers on temporary duty, by 1985 their numbers had swelled to between 40,000 and 50,000, and they accounted for close to 40 percent of all drilling in Tiumen' (up from about one-quarter in the previous five-year plan), as well as 25 percent of well repair work.[34] This influx of workers swamped the industry's already meager program for housing and services, causing morale to drop and labor turnover to increase and hampering efforts to improve productivity.

Moreover, apart from the problems of labor and housing, low productivity in drilling was caused by poor material supply, infrastructure, and management. Pipe, bits, and muds were of poor quality; rigs were open to the cold; road-builders failed to prepare the way; line crews lagged in laying powerlines; drillers sat waiting for key parts to arrive—these stories are familiar from similar complaints throughout the economy. Soviet oil men had found ways of adapting in the past. The classic case was the Soviet use of the turbodrill, which does not require the same high standard of quality in bits and pipe as the Western rotary drill.[35] Another successful adaptation through ingenuity was the grow-

[33] The original five-year plan target is given in *Ekonomika neftianoi promyshlennosti*, no. 4 (1982), pp. 17–18. The actual 1985 figure comes from Kniazev, "Na ostrie dolota." He says that the number of brigades had grown "by" 282 since 1975, which would put the total well over 310. I believe that may be a mistake and have used the lower number.

[34] V. I. Graifer, quoted in B. Sidorenko, "Problemy Tiumenskoi nefti," *Ekonomicheskaia gazeta*, no. 9 (1986); L. Levitskii et al., "Chelovek na severe," *Izvestiia*, 16 Sept. 1985; and Belanov and Kremer, "Trudnaia neft'."

[35] Robert W. Campbell, *The Economics of Soviet Oil and Gas* (Baltimore: Johns Hopkins University Press, 1968), pp. 94–95 and 106–120.

ing use of cluster wells, a technique in which several wells are drilled from a single location. But with drilling scheduled to double again in the second half of the 1980s, Soviet drillers seemed to have run out of short cuts. The only systematic way to attack the problem of falling productivity in drilling was to improve the volume and quality of equipment. We analyze what happened in Chapter 6.

WELL OPERATION AND MAINTENANCE

As any oil field ages, the underground pressure drops and the flow rate declines. When that happens, oil must be helped to the surface either by raising the underground pressure artificially or by installing pumps, a process Soviet oil men refer to as "mechanization." In West Siberia flow rates were initially so high that no mechanization was needed (other than pumping water into the fields, a technique known as "waterflooding," which the Soviets traditionally employ from the very beginning of development). By the late 1970s, however, new well flow rates had declined dramatically (table 3.12). Yet the oil industry put so much stress on drilling that it neglected the mechanization program.

The Soviet oil industry has long relied on the traditional sucker-rod pump, which is considered inadequate to cope efficiently with the large volumes of oil mixed with water that result from the Soviets' use of waterflooding. In 1980 over 61 percent of all Soviet wells were equipped with such pumps, which also required 83 percent of all repairs.[36] But at the beginning of the 1980s the oil industry adopted an ambitious program of well mechanization based on more modern equipment, notably gaslift and electric submersible pumps. Similar programs had been adopted in earlier five-year plans, but Soviet industry had proved unable to support them.[37]

Gaslift. Gaslift involves recycling associated gas back into the well to make the oil-water mixture more buoyant so that it rises to the surface faster. Soviet experiments with imported gaslift equipment began in 1972 in West Siberia, and the technique was adopted as a major program in the Eleventh Five-Year Plan.[38] Forty-five hundred gaslift units were to have been installed between 1981 and 1985, at a cost of over 1

[36] V. I. Luzin, *Ekonomicheskaia effektivnost' povysheniia kachestva i nadezhnosti neftepromyslovogo oborudovaniia* (Moscow: Nedra, 1984), p. 42. Dinkov, *Neft' SSSR, 1917–1987*, ch. 6, gives 63.5 percent.

[37] Soviet difficulties with electric submersibles are described in Robert W. Campbell, *Soviet Energy Technologies: Planning, Policy, Research and Development* (Bloomington: Indiana University Press, 1980), pp. 221–225.

[38] *Neftianoe khoziaistvo*, no. 3 (1982), pp. 53–55.

billion rubles,[39] and more than one-third of the new units were to have been located at Samotlor.[40] Subsequently, the goals of the program may have been raised higher still as it became apparent that Samotlor was in serious trouble.[41]

The initial Soviet strategy was to get off to a fast start by relying on Western suppliers for the lift units,[42] while the gas feeder lines and most of the ancillary compressor stations, which pump the associated gas to the wells, would be provided by the Soviets themselves. But the strategy misfired. The designated domestic subcontractor did not produce the compressor stations, and the crews that were to install the gas feeder lines were drawn off to work on the big Siberian gas trunk lines (a side effect, incidentally, of the American embargo of 1981–1982). Some Western compressor stations must have been used instead. By the end of 1985, nearly 1,400 gaslift units were reported in operation at Samotlor, about one-third of the final target. The outcome was somewhat more successful at Surgut, accounting for much of the superior performance of that region.[43] Countrywide, the share of Soviet oil wells equipped with gaslift increased from 2.8 percent to 4.4 percent between 1981 and 1985.[44]

Electric Submersibles. The other key part of the mechanization program was to install more modern and reliable electric submersible pumps. The attraction of electric submersibles is their high capacity,

[39] *Ekonomika neftianoi promyshlennosti*, no. 3 (1982), p. 6.

[40] *Ekonomicheskaia gazeta*, no. 8 (1981), p. 7. On the basis of local interviews, an American correspondent reported in 1981 that 1,400 of Samotlor's 3,000 wells and another 600 at Fedorov would be equipped with gaslift. Robert Gillette, "Russia Expected to Mount Major Drive to Avert Decline in Oil Output," *Los Angeles Times*, 6 Jan. 1981, p. 1.

[41] Later sources mention 3,000 or even as many as 4,000 units scheduled for Samotlor in the Eleventh Plan. *Sotsialisticheskaia industriia*, 2 Mar. 1985, and *Izvestiia* 28 May 1985.

[42] The lift units at Samotlor are French equipment supplied by Technip. A contract with Technip was signed in October 1978 for 850 million francs. Gillette, "Russia Expected to Mount Major Drive."

[43] This account is pieced together from V. Borodin, "Rezervy neftianogo plasta," *Sotsialisticheskaia industriia*, 2 Mar. 1985; Ia. Ali-Zade et al., "Ostrye ugli Samotlora"; V. Kuz'mishchev et al., "Kliuchi ot nefti," *Pravda*, 24 Jan. 1986; A. Zhdanov, "Displei na promysle," *Pravda*, 22 Mar. 1986. By the end of 1985, 14 compressor stations were reported operating, but only one of them was Soviet. The subcontractor in question is the Dzerzhinskii plant in Azerbaijan, which belongs to the Ministry of Chemical and Petroleum Machine-building (for a discussion of the role of the Azerbaijan plants in industrial support for the oil industry, see Chapter 6).

[44] Dinkov, *Neft' SSSR, 1917–1987*, p. 153.

which makes them ideal for the large volumes of oil and water coming from Soviet wells.[45] But until the end of the 1970s Soviet electric submersibles had been very unreliable and required frequent repairs (table 4.4).[46] In 1981–1985 the electric submersible program showed considerable improvement, as the share of wells in Tiumen' equipped with electric centrifuge pumps increased from 18 percent in 1980 to 45 percent.[47]

Well Maintenance and Repair. In the Soviet oil industry (in contrast to Western practice) drillers have traditionally enjoyed the most prestige, while well repair and maintenance crews have had the least.[48] As veteran Soviet oil men like to say, "Where you find oil is at the end of a drillbit," or, "If you have wells, you'll have oil."[49] That viewpoint played a part in the oil industry's stress on drilling after the emergency of 1977, which nearly doubled the stock of oil wells countrywide by 1985.[50] But this fast growth, together with the poor quality of much of the well-finishing work, suddenly turned well maintenance into an urgent problem for which local oil bosses, and the well maintenance crews themselves, were unprepared.

Long neglected by the industry, repair crews in the early 1980s complained that they received lower pay and fewer perquisites than drillers or operators, that they were allocated less equipment support,[51] and that they could not keep up with their fast-growing workload. This was a problem throughout the country,[52] but it was especially severe in

[45] Soviet models can extract 250–500 cubic meters a day (and the better models as much as 700), compared to 30–40 cubic meters for the traditional sucker-rod pump. See A. Gumeniuk (general director of the Komi Oil Association, Komineft'), "Zaiavka neftianogo promysla," *Sotsialisticheskaia industriia*, 7 Aug. 1982.

[46] Campbell, *Soviet Energy Technologies*.

[47] Dinkov, *Neft' SSSR, 1917–1987*, p. 159.

[48] M. Zaripov and A. Podol'skii, "Trudnyi gorizont," *Sovetskaia Rossiia*, 7 and 8 Dec. 1982.

[49] Interview with B. S. Sagingaliev, director of the Emba Oil Association (Embaneft'), "Potentsial Emby," *Kazakhstanskaia pravda*, 4 Sept. 1983. Muravlenko was head of Glavtiumenneftegaz from 1965 until his death in 1977.

[50] The total well stock grew from about 65,000 to about 125,000 during the same period (exploratory and development combined). I have not actually seen a complete set of numbers on the total well stock; these estimates are drawn from occasional references in *Neftianoe khoziaistvo*.

[51] Perepletkin, "Rezervy neftianogo plasta."

[52] As the Eleventh Plan progressed, the older regions found that the rate of repairs was running at only half the planned level. For observations about Tatariia, for example, see R. T. Bulgakov and A. K. Mukhametzianov (respectively, past and current head of the Tatar Oil Association, Tatneft'), "Neftegazodobyviaushchii raion posle ego zenita," *Ekonomika i organizatsiia promyshlennogo proizvodstva* (*EKO*), no. 1 (1981), pp. 110–148.

TABLE 4.4

Average Number of Days between Repairs, 1976–1985
(MNP; countrywide)

Type of Extraction	*1976*	*1979*	*1980*	*1981*	*1982*	*1983*	*1984*	*1985*
Electric centrifuge	230	240	246	260	284	311	334	335
Sucker rod	91	98	110	115	128	140	148	156
Gaslift	516	472	511	560	585	713	757	573
Free flow	773	1,014	1,083	1,253	1,261	1,264	1,276	971

SOURCES: for 1976 and 1979: Mingareev et al., *Tekhnicheskii progress*, p. 106; for 1981–1985: Dinkov, *Neft' SSSR*, p. 158.

West Siberia, where the bias toward drilling was far stronger. As one maintenance chief in Surgut observed, "Headquarters in both Surgut and Tiumen' look through their fingers at our problems."[53] MNP headquarters in Moscow shared the general prejudice; indeed, at the height of the second crisis the ministry actually ordered Tiumen' to shut down its capital-repair units to allocate more manpower to well operation.[54]

Progress in well maintenance and repair depended on other ministries as well, but the low priority attached to it by the oil industry meant that MNP put little pressure on supporting ministries to do their part. A good example is corrosion control. Because of the Soviets' extensive use of waterflooding, their wells produce vast quantities of water laden with salts and other substances that create plugs, deposits, and corrosion. This problem was growing fast, but only about 5 percent of the well stock got anticorrosion treatment[55] because the chemical industry did not produce enough of the necessary chemicals.[56]

Waterflooding. Soviet oil men rely heavily on a production technique known as waterflooding, which involves injecting water into a field to push oil toward the wells and up to the surface. It requires an elaborate network of pumps, pipes, and, frequently, water treatment equipment, as well as (in special situations) boilers for heating water or generating steam. Since the injected water soon breaks through to the oil wells, what comes up to the surface is a viscous mixture of oil, water, and gas that must be separated by additional equipment. As the field ages, the proportion of water in the mixture (the "water cut") increases. In many older Soviet fields the water cut has reached 85 to 90 percent, so that pumped wells in late stages of development are working largely to raise water.

Waterflooding is a well-known technique in other countries, but it is usually reserved for later stages in an oil field's life-cycle. In Soviet practice, however, waterflooding is used from the very beginning of development, and between 85 and 90 percent of all Soviet oil is produced by waterflooding.[57] Soviet oil men claim that it enables the industry to produce 250 million tons more each year than the existing

53 *Sotsialisticheskaia industriia*, 20 Aug. 1983.

54 Levitskii et al., "Razryv"; and V. Kuz'mishchev et al., "Osoboe mnenie Iugantsev," *Pravda*, 14 Feb. 1986.

55 *Neftianoe khoziaistvo*, no. 6 (1982), p. 8.

56 *Sovetskaia Rossiia*, 8 Dec. 1982.

57 R. Sh. Mingareev, G. E. Grigorashchenko, A. P. Smirnov et al., *Tekhnicheskii progress v neftianoi promyshlennosti v desiatoi piatiletke* (Moscow: Nedra, 1981).

development infrastructure (wells, pumps, and so on) could yield otherwise, at a saving of some 25 billion rubles over the last generation.[58] What is beyond dispute is that a new field can be brought up to maximum output faster with waterflooding than without; thus Samotlor reached its peak in ten years. But Soviet oil men claim further that waterflooding also produces higher total recovery than other countries obtain: 43 percent for the Soviet Union versus 33.3 percent for the United States.[59] Thus they classify waterflooding not simply as a means of accelerating output or achieving lower cost (which it does by extending the free-flow period of a well) but as a true means of enhancing recovery.

Western oil men have long been dubious about this last claim. They believe that waterflooding shortens the life of a field, actually reduces total recovery, and sharply raises production costs. The Soviets systematically overproduce their fields to get quick returns, these experts say, and waterflooding is a large part of the problem.

Waterflooding figured prominently in the logic of the CIA's pessimistic 1977 reports on Soviet oil. In particular, the CIA's analysts predicted that unwise waterflooding practices would cause a premature and sharp decline of production at Samotlor. Output at Samotlor did indeed decline after 1980, although it is not clear that waterflooding was directly responsible. More obvious are the indirect effects: waterflooding adds enormously to Soviet requirements for pumps and pipe, thus adding to the already considerable logistical burden. Each year the Soviet oil industry pumps into its oil fields the equivalent of a small river (2.2 billion cubic meters in 1985),[60] consuming about 1 percent of all Soviet electricity for this one purpose alone.[61] Since 1977, the volume of water pumped has doubled, and the water cut has risen from half to over two-thirds.[62] Waterflooding has been used in West Siberia from the start, and the water cut there, while still lower than the national average, has risen quickly.

The Soviets' reliance on waterflooding probably had two conse-

[58] V. M. Iudin (deputy minister of oil in charge of enhanced-recovery programs) and M. L. Surguchev, "Polnoe ispol'zovanie resursov nedr," *Neftianoe khoziaistvo*, no. 12 (1983), p. 54.

[59] "Vozmozhnosti neftianogo plasta," *Ekonomicheskaia gazeta*, no. 8 (1982), p. 2.

[60] *Narodnoe khoziaistvo SSSR v 1985g*, p. 80.

[61] *Neftianoe khoziaistvo*, no. 1 (1983), p. 53. Pumping water in the early 1980s required 13 billion kilowatt-hours per year.

[62] The water cut, reported at 50.8 percent in 1977 (Wilson, *Soviet Oil and Gas*) had risen to 62.2 percent by 1982, the most recent figure I have found. *Neftianoe khoziaistvo*, no. 8 (1983), p. 28.

quences for them in 1982–1985. First, it increased their vulnerability to poor equipment supply and maintenance, particularly because of corrosion. Second, the Soviet oil men's attachment to a technique they know well appears to have helped delay experimentation with newer methods of advanced enhanced recovery. Only the first factor played a major role in 1982–1985, but the second will become increasingly important in the future, and we return to it at the end of this chapter.

HOUSING AND SERVICES

Soviet reviews of the second oil crisis attach great importance to labor problems. The oil industry's policy, like that of most Soviet ministries when opening up new areas, has typically been to concentrate on production facilities and to neglect housing and amenities. As a result, most oil workers, whether temporary or permanent, are lodged in makeshift housing and enjoy few of the most elementary services. Turnover is extremely high, and thus inexperience compounds the problems of equipment and supply, lowering productivity even further.

Yet it is important to observe that the oil industry would not need nearly so much manpower if it used what it has more efficiently, particularly through more and better equipment and infrastructural support. Indeed, if local operations were more efficient, the Soviets might be able to follow North American practice and keep permanent settlements small. Instead, they have engaged themselves, largely involuntarily, in the unique experiment of trying to build large permanent cities at far higher latitudes than any to be found in equivalent areas of North America.[63] Because of the oil industry's poor productivity, these settlements have grown far faster than planned, as new workers are brought in to compensate for shortfalls in other inputs.[64] Much of the housing problem, therefore, is a symptom rather than a cause. These issues are discussed at greater length in the next chapter.

OVERVIEW

Low productivity in drilling, neglected well repair and maintenance, lagging well mechanization, shortsighted production practices, excessive reliance on a handful of older fields—these were the principal

[63] Leslie Dienes, "Employment Structure, Settlement Policy, and the Development of the North Tiumen' Oil and Gas Region," *Soviet Geography* 26, no. 10 (October 1985), pp. 609–622.

[64] In the first half of the 1980s the population of Tiumen' Province grew twice as fast as had been projected. The net increase was nearly 750,000 people, instead of the 370,000 originally planned. G. P. Bogomiakov in V. Kuz'mishchev et al., "Nadezhen li tyl?" *Pravda*, 10 Dec. 1986.

elements in the second oil crisis. They were not new causes; the policies behind them had been characteristic of the industry since the beginning. But to what extent could they be offset through quick measures from a new, more energetic leadership?

In the midst of the debacle of 1984–1985, some oil regions in Tiumen' did better than others. Two oil associations in Tiumen', Iugansk and Surgut, managed to turn in good performances in 1982–1985, in contrast to the collapse of Nizhnevartovsk (table 4.5). According to admiring Soviet press stories, Iugansk did well because it resisted Moscow's demands for unrealistic increases in output. Beginning in the late 1970s, Iugansk oil men adopted, over ministry opposition, a long-term development plan that favored total return over near-term output. Realizing that well operation was going to be the crucial problem ahead, they built up well-repair facilities of their own and stocked them with second-hand equipment bought with their own resources. They rewarded their maintenance crews not for the number of repairs (as was the rule elsewhere in the industry) but for trouble-free wells. They also started a major program to mechanize their wells, so that by 1985 most of Iugansk was equipped with down-hole pumps and the number of idle wells in Iugansk remained small. Somehow they managed these achievements without neglecting development drilling; alone of all the West Siberian oil associations, Iugansk actually increased its drilling productivity. As a consequence of all this, Iugansk came in well ahead of its five-year output target in 1981–1985.[65]

In fact, Iugansk may have owed much of its good fortune to being small enough to escape the pressure imposed on Samotlor. For some unknown reason, it also received better equipment than the rest of the Tiumen' oil industry, notably electric centrifuge pumps that by 1985 produced more than half of Iugansk's oil.[66] But one simple fact shows the limits of the "Iugansk model": in 1981 the chief of Iugansk, R. I. Kuzovatkin, who was credited with having originated much of the Iugansk strategy,[67] was named head of the entire Tiumen' oil industry;

[65] Needless to say, this success story has been generously covered by the Soviet press. See in particular Kuz'mishchev et al., "Osoboe mnenie Iugantsev"; Perepletkin, "Pogoda na zavtra"; Iu. Belanov, "Svoi pocherk," *Sotsialisticheskaia industriia*, 3 Nov. 1985; Iu. Belanov and V. Liakutkin, "A opyt riadom," *Sotsialisticheskaia industriia*, 19 Sept. 1985; Levitskii et al., "Trudnye milliony"; I. Nikolaev, "Sverkh zadaniia piatiletki," *Ekonomicheskaia gazeta*, no. 46 (1985); and M. Makhlin, "Na novom etape osvoeniia prirodnykh bogatstv," *Ekonomicheskaia gazeta*, no. 38 (1985), p. 7. Through the end of 1988, Iugansk has continued to be a leader; see *Soviet Geography* 30, no. 4 (April 1989), p. 311.

[66] Nikolaev, "Sverkh zadaniia piatiletki."

[67] Perepletkin, "Pogoda na zavtra."

TABLE 4.5
West Siberian Oil Output Shares and Yield per Meter Drilled, 1970–1985

	1970		*1975*		*1980*		*1985*	
	O	*Y*	*O*	*Y*	*O*	*Y*	*O*	*Y*
Nizhnevartovsk	8.2	42.3	97.8	32.7	202.5	12.9	160	3.5
Var'egan							15	
Surgut	3.5	8.4	13.2	12.3	48.6	5.5	60	3.6
Iugansk	11.7	12.1	24.8	5.0	45.5	4.5	68	3.3
Krasnoleninsk	4.6	6.1	5.6	14.0	6.2	5.0	6	NA
Noiabr'sk	—	—	—	—	—	—	15	NA
Tomsk	3.4	15.4	6.6	8.6	9.8	4.8	12	2.9
West Siberia overall	31.4	14.0	148.0	20.9	312.6*	8.2	372*	3.5

SOURCES: Starovoitov, ed., *Problemy*, for data through 1980 and the planned yield through 1985. Output data for 1985 from *Soviet Geography* 27, no. 4 (April 1986).

KEY: "O" stands for output in millions of tons per year; "Y" stands for yield in tons per meter of hole drilled. Yield figures for 1985 are plan; all others are actual.

NOTES: The Noiabr'sk and Krasnoleninsk districts were established in 1981 and 1983, respectively; Var'egan was carved out of Nizhnevartovsk in 1985.

* Subsequent reports for 1980 production in West Siberia show 313.6 instead of 312.6 million tons and, for 1985, 366 million tons instead of 372. See *Soviet Geography* 30, no. 4 (April 1989), p. 308.

but he proved unable to transfer his success, or even much of his approach, to the parent organization and in 1985 became himself the chief victim of the second crisis.[68] Nevertheless, the relative success of Iugansk must have suggested that a quick fix could work once more. By the end of 1985, a fairly straightforward combination of measures seemed likely to stem the decline: repair the idle wells, boost the mechanization program, accelerate the development of smaller fields, while simultaneously laying the basis for a longer-term improvement of supply. But at what cost?

The Recovery of 1986–1988

By the end of 1985 most Western analysts would have forecast that Soviet oil output would keep heading downhill. But surprisingly, in 1986 and 1987 the decline was sharply reversed, and production kept growing until mid-1988. This remarkable recovery raised a host of questions. How was it achieved? Could it last?

[68] The same story is being re-enacted in the current five-year plan: Iu. Vershinin, Kuzovatkin's successor at Iugansk and another highly praised manager, was promoted to chief engineer of the Tiumen' oil industry in 1985. So far, he has proved luckier; as of early 1989, he was still on the job (*Sotsialisticheskaia industriia*, 22 Feb. 1989).

The answer to the first question was partly familiar, partly unexpected. The familiar part was a second emergency response in the form of massive new injections of capital and manpower, a striking affirmation of the new leadership's commitment to oil. Oil investment rose by 45 percent during Gorbachev's first four years.[69]

Much of the emergency response has been aimed, as before, at increasing development drilling. Senior Politburo members traveled to oil regions around the country in 1985 and 1986, distributing blame and exhortation, all stressing the vital importance of oil.[70] Thus a large part of the leaders' response was in the most traditional, short-horizon campaign style, and at the end of 1986 the Party first secretary for Tiumen', G. P. Bogomiakov, acknowledged as much. The recovery of 1986, he said, was a classic example of the much-denounced policy of "The plan at any price!" "Extensive methods of development," he added, "remain the order of the day."[71]

Yet alongside the familiar campaign response were faint elements of a new approach. First, the industry evidently attempted to take some of the burden off West Siberia. While the bulk of the 1986–1987 recovery came from there, a little help arrived from the older regions, particularly the Volga-Urals province and Azerbaijan, which stemmed a decade-long decline. The older regions, which had lost 11 million tons a year in the first half of the 1980s, cut their decline to 8 million tons a year in 1986–1988.[72]

Second, leaders began an effort to correct longstanding imbalances in West Siberia. Touring Tiumen' in September 1985, Gorbachev harshly

[69] Unfortunately, Soviet statistical manuals since 1985 have stopped listing oil investment separately from overall energy investment. Oil investment had previously risen by 16 percent in 1985 (*Narodnoe khoziaistvo SSSR v 1985g.*, p. 368). *Kapital'noe stroitel'stvo SSSR* (Moscow: Finansy i statistika, 1988), p. 53, gives oil and gas investment together in 1987 as 19.75 billion rubles, up 20.5 percent from 1985. In 1988, total energy sector investment grew 7 percent over 1987 (*Izvestiia*, 21 Jan. 1989). These numbers together give only a rough impression, but they suggest an increase in oil investment of at least 40 percent under Gorbachev. A press bulletin released by Goskomstat in 1989 confirms this: it gives oil investment in 1989 as 14.46 billion rubles, an increase of 45 percent since 1984.

[70] Thus Party Second Secretary Ligachev in Tatariia: "One cannot overstate the importance of oil to the state." "Utverzhdaia novye podkhody k delu," *Pravda*, 22 May 1986. Gorbachev went to Tiumen' in September 1985, where he observed that shortfalls at Tiumen' "give a fever to the economy"; Ryzhkov traveled to the Tengiz oil field in Kazakhstan in December 1986 (*Pravda*, 10 Dec. 1986); Vorotnikov went to Novosibirsk in July 1985 with a speech stressing oil; not to mention several appearances by candidate Politburo member V. I. Dolgikh, who remained the Central Committee secretary responsible for heavy industry and energy until his retirement on 30 September 1988.

[71] Interview with G. P. Bogomiakov in Kuz'mishchev et al., "Nadezhen li tyl?"

[72] While Siberian output increased by 53.2 million tons/year from 1985 to 1988,

criticized the Tiumen' authorities' neglect of housing and amenities, the ancillary ministries' inattention to infrastructural support, and the shortcomings of suppliers of equipment and oil services. "It is embarrassing," he said in a nationwide television address, "when a drilling foreman addresses us and says that the greatest incentive in Nizhnevartovsk is to be given a ticket to see a movie."[73]

If the words were blunter than in earlier years, the sentiments were familiar, and Gorbachev's audience must have wondered whether anything would really change. But it soon began to appear that something was indeed afoot: Gosplan was ordered to reallocate 500 million rubles of MNGS's Twelfth Plan construction budget to housing, schools, and other "social" facilities countrywide, while the Ministry of Power similarly increased its allocation for housing for its workers in Tiumen' by 50 percent.[74] By the end of 1986, despite determined rear-guard efforts by all the major agencies to hold back housing targets (and some of the usual connivance from Gosplan), pressure from the leadership had forced up the pace of housing construction dramatically.[75] The supply of oil field equipment had also shown small signs of improvement: gaslift equipment and electric submersible pumps began to arrive in larger numbers. The supply of electricity improved when the gas-fired Surgut-2 power plant began operation. In addition, there was a major effort to bring idle wells back into production by flying well-repair and drilling crews to West Siberia.[76]

But righting long-accumulated imbalances will take years, as will improving efficiency in the fields. Therefore the recovery of 1986–1987 was mainly due to what Gorbachev would call "human factor" measures. Of the West Siberian gains in 1986, more than half came from either conventional or one-time expedients (infill drilling—that is, additional drilling of developed fields—and well repair), and less than half from new fields and well mechanization. Despite harbingers of change, the West Siberian emergency response of 1986 was not much

production in the Volga and Urals provinces declined from 143 million tons to 120 million; Azerbaijan increased slightly from 13 million tons/year to 13.6; and Kazakhstan grew from 22.8 to 25.5 million. *Soviet Geography* 30, no. 4 (April 1989), p. 308.

[73] Television version of Gorbachev's speech, 6 September 1985. This sentence was not reprinted in the version published in *Pravda* the next morning.

[74] Iu. Perepletkin, "Surgut: pervye rezul'taty," *Izvestiia*, 4 Sept. 1986.

[75] Kuz'mishchev et al., "Nadezhen li tyl?"

[76] At the beginning of 1985, 100 additional well-repair brigades were sent to Samotlor; their initial impact was slight, however, since many of them arrived without proper equipment and adequate provision for them at the work site. See Levitskii et al., "Chelovek na severe."

different from its predecessor of 1978–1980. The same appears to be true of the older oil provinces, although the reasons for their improved performance are not yet fully understood. As will be clear from a later section, one can discount the role of tertiary oil recovery, which is still at an early stage of development in Soviet oil practice and did not yield more than 5 million tons in 1985. Much of the delayed decline of the Bashkir Oil Association, for example, was due to additional drilling, and the same may turn out to be true of the Volga-Urals region. Some increases came from Azerbaijan and Kazakhstan, which have begun to bring a new generation of fields into production (table 4.6).

What is the outlook for the early 1990s? In Siberia, the gains from repairing idle wells will vanish over the next few years and those from infill drilling will continue to decline. Consequently, the near-term future of the oil industry depends on a familiar equation: Will spending continue to rise? Will the traditional approach prevail? Will output targets be ratcheted higher and higher? Will the pressure to meet them nullify efforts to rebalance the oil industry and make it more efficient?

The information available so far suggests a familiar contest between good intentions and target pressure. The oil industry must expand its total drilling to 200 million meters in 1986–1990, an increase of some 73 million meters (or about 74 percent) over the previous five-year plan, its fastest growth to date.[77] What makes this a race with the devil, of course, is the necessity to keep output growing in the face of high depletion rates. But what if the Gorbachev leadership finally decided to let output fall? It is clear that this is a controversial issue in Moscow. In the first half of 1986 the Soviet press carried statements to the effect that oil output would be stabilized.[78] The oil output target for 1987, announced in the fall of 1986, called for 617 million tons, virtually no increase over 1986.[79] Western observers speculated that the Soviet leaders had decided to abandon their 1990 goal of 635 million tons, which would indeed have meant the end of an era. But oil output bounded well ahead of the plan target in 1987. In 1988, output weakened in the third quarter, and oil output ended the year at the same level as 1987. But this was evidently not yet a change in official policy: in

[77] *Ekonomicheskaia gazeta*, no. 7 (1986), p. 14. MNP's total drilling in 1981–1985, derived from annual reports, was about 127 million meters, versus the 130 called for in the five-year plan.

[78] Thus *Izvestiia*'s economic columnist wrote that "we have reached the point where oil output will not grow any more." *Izvestiia*, 26 Apr. 1986. Similar accounts appeared in *Moscow News*.

[79] Speech by Gosplan Chairman N. V. Talyzin to the Supreme Soviet, announcing the 1987 annual plan. *Pravda*, 18 Nov. 1986.

TABLE 4.6

Soviet Oil and Condensate Production by Region, 1975–1990
(millions of tons per year)

	1975	*1980*	*1983*	*1985*	*1986*	*1987*	*1988*	*1990 (plan)*
USSR	490.8	603.2	616.3	595.3	614.8	624.2	624.3	635
RSFSR	411	547	564	542	561	569	569	565
European Russia	182	149	114	100	98	91	88	72
Komi ASSR	11	19	19	19	19	20	21	17
North Caucasus	24	19	14	11	9	7	6	5
Volga	147	111	81	75	70	64	61	50
Urals*	79	81	69	68	66	62	59	50
Siberia	150.5	317	381	369	397	416	422	443
West Siberia	148.0	313.6	377.8	365.8	394	413	419	440
Tiumen'**	141.4	303.8	366.2	352.7	376	398	404	425
Tomsk	6.6	9.8	11.6	13.1	13.7	15	15	15
Sakhalin	2.5	3	3	3	3	3	3	2.7
Non-RSFSR	80	56	52	53	54	55	55.3	70
Ukraine	12.8	8	7	6	5.6	5.6	5.4	6
Belorussia	8	3	3	3	2	2	1.9	2
Georgia	0.3	3.2	3	2	2	2	0.2	2
Kazakhstan	23.9	18.7	19.5	22.8	23.7	24.5	25.5	39.1
Turkmenia	15.6	8	6	6	5.9	5.8	5.7	5
Other Central Asian	2.1	1.5	1	1	1	2	3.0	1
Azerbaijan	17.2	14	12	13	13	13	13.6	14.5

SOURCE: *Soviet Geography.*

* Bashkir ASSR is included in the Urals.

** Tiumen' output in 1988 includes about 10 million tons of gas condensate produced by MGP.

October 1988 Gosplan chairman Iu. D. Masliukov ratcheted the 1989 target to 631.6 million tons, well above the pace called for in the five-year plan.[80] He invoked problems in foreign trade and nuclear power, which suggests that as late as the fall of 1988 the leadership, was still determined to keep oil output growing. Meanwhile, more and more leading figures in the energy establishment called for allowing oil output to fall.[81]

But even stabilizing oil output will not necessarily mean that Soviet leaders can stop increasing oil investment or slacken their efforts to reform the oil industry: if they make that mistake, they will soon be in trouble again. The future of the industry depends on better technology, exploration, and equipment, which in turn will require capital and continued high political priority. In the next section we examine two of the most important issues for the future, exploration and enhanced oil recovery. Chapter 6 examines a third issue, the quality of equipment support for oil and gas.

Toward a Third Oil Crisis?

Exploration in the 1980s

Reserves were not an immediate issue in the second oil crisis; but the chronic weaknesses of Soviet exploration policy have not been remedied, and both near-term prospects and long-term reserves have grown more uncertain. The problem for decisionmakers is a classic one: How much should one wager in a game against nature? The difference this time is that nature now appears to promise much less than it did in the mid-1970s.

Production continued to dominate exploration in the first half of the 1980s. Though capital spending on exploration for oil and gas increased substantially,[82] its share of total oil and gas investment decreased yearly, continuing the trend of the previous two decades (see table 3.7). The decline may have been arrested in 1986 and 1987, but it is still too early to tell whether this reflects a lasting change in priorities.[83]

[80] Iu. D. Masliukov, "O gosudarstvennom plane ekonomicheskogo i sotsial'nogo razvitiia SSSR na 1989 god," *Pravda*, 28 Oct. 1988.

[81] See for example A. Ie. Sheindlin, *Izvestiia*, 16 Jan. 1989.

[82] Total "capital investment" for geological exploration—the bulk of which is devoted to drilling for oil and gas—grew by 27 percent from 1980 to 1985. *Narodnoe khoziaistvo SSSR v 1987 g.*, p. 563.

[83] In 1986–1987, "capital investment" for geological exploration grew by 20 percent

TABLE 4.7
Exploratory Drilling
for Oil and Gas, 1976–1987
(millions of meters)

	Plan	*Actual*
Tenth Plan		
1976–1980	*28.0*	*26.7*
1980		5.89
Eleventh Plan		
1981–1985	*34.4*	*32.1*
1981		6.17
1982		6.17
1983		6.48
1984		6.46
1985		6.77
Twelfth Plan		
1986–1990	*44.9*	
1986		7.19
1987		7.81

SOURCES: *Narodnoe khoziaistvo SSSR*, various years. The five-year target for 1986–1990 is given in *Ekonomicheskaia gazeta*, no. 21 (1985), p. 6.

Exploratory drilling fell short of the Eleventh Plan target (a 20 percent increase instead of the 29 percent initially called for),[84] although growth was sizable in absolute terms (table 4.7). The bias in favor of the older regions is gradually being overcome. Over half the total increase in 1981–1985 went to West Siberia, where drilling for oil and gas exploration nearly doubled, exceeding 7 million meters.[85] Thus the share of West Siberia in total exploration has climbed steadily over the last ten years, although it is striking that even now over 70 percent of all exploratory drilling still takes place in the older oil regions (table 4.8).

The Ministry of Geology has continued to bear most of the burden of

(*Narodnoe khoziaistvo SSSR v 1987 g.*, p. 563), about the same as total oil and gas investment (*Kapital'noe stroitel'stvo SSSR*, p. 53).

[84] *Ekonomicheskaia gazeta*, no. 5 (1983), p. 1.

[85] Farman Salmanov, "Rezervy geologov Tiumeni," *Sotsialisticheskaia industriia*, 4 Sept. 1985. Both Mingeo and MNP were to double their exploratory drilling in West Siberia by 1985. Mingeo's targets were reported in *Sovetskaia geologiia*, no. 3 (1982), p. 4, while those of MNP can be found in *Geologiia nefti i gaza*, no. 11 (1982), p. 12.

TABLE 4.8
Share of West Siberia in Total Exploratory Drilling for Oil and Gas
(millions of meters)

	Total	*West Siberia*	
1971–1975	26.1	3.1	(11.9%)
1976–1980	26.7	≈4	(≈15)
1981–1985	32.1	≈7	(≈22)
1986	7.2	≈2	(≈30)

SOURCES: Until a volume with reliable series, such as Brenner, *Ekonomika geologorazvedochnykh*, appears, one is forced to rely on fragmentary and inconsistent numbers from journals and newspapers. Total: for 1971–1975, Brenner, p. 86; 1976–1980, inference from *Narodnoe khoziaistvo* (1984), p. 397; 1981–1985, *Narodnoe khoziaistvo SSSR v 1985.* West Siberia: 1971–1975, Brenner, p. 88; 1976–1980, guesstimate from partial figures given in *Pravda* 14 Dec. 1980, *Sotsialisticheskaia industriia*, 3 Mar. 1978, and *Planovoe khoziaistvo*, no. 3 (1980), p. 21; 1981-1985, inference from Salmanov, "Rezervy geologov Tiumeni" (presumably Glavtiumengeologiia only).

exploration, especially in West Siberia, where Mingeo still performs some 90 percent of the exploratory oil drilling.[86] To meet its West Siberian targets, Mingeo continued to transfer its operations east of the Urals, where it now performs nearly 50 percent of its drilling.[87] In contrast, the Ministry of the Oil Industry still directs most of its exploration efforts elsewhere.[88] In short, the traditional allocation of duties among ministries (described in the last chapter), together with its policy consequences, continues to the present.

The main reason that reserves did not figure in the second oil crisis is that the geologists resorted to a quick fix of their own. In the first half of

[86] Kozlov, "Neft' Zapadnoi Sibiri," p. 31.

[87] This estimate is derived from information that Mingeo will increase its drilling in West Siberia by 90 percent in 1986–1990, compared to 40 percent growth for the rest of the country. *Ekonomicheskaia gazeta*, no. 21 (1985), p. 6.

[88] Mingeo accounted for 87 percent of the net increase in oil and gas drilling nationwide between 1980 and 1987. *Narodnoe khoziaistvo SSSR v 1987 godu*, p. 563. Since most of that net increase is presumably concentrated in West Siberia, these figures confirm that the division of roles between Mingeo and MNP in West Siberia has not changed.

the 1980s they gave most of their attention to downstream operations, outlining known prospects and preparing them for production. In this strategy they were successful: they met their assigned five-year target for additions to so-called industrial reserves (that is, $A + B + C_1$),[89] but, as we shall see presently, this achievement came at the cost of further imbalance in the exploration program. Thus the oil industry's continued focus on near-term results in 1981–1985 was matched by the geologists.

The geologists' apparent success did not still quarrels over the region's prospects, not least among the geologists themselves. An effort in 1981 to arrive at a consensus among geologists in various research institutes produced only the careful conclusion that West Siberian reserves of oil, gas, and condensate were "sufficient."[90] As of 1982, according to another source, the forecasts of Siberian oil prospects by various agencies differed from one another by "50 percent and more."[91] But during this period an important decision was made to tighten the official definitions of reserves. New regulations, issued in 1983, made it more difficult for reserves to reach the A and B categories (thus requiring much additional exploratory drilling of industrial reserves in the C_1 class) and created a new C_3 category into which the less reliable portion of C_2 reserves was transferred.[92] The effect of the new rules was to cut down official reserves in all categories, an indirect admission that previous estimates had been inflated.

Despite these changes, oil men remained highly skeptical of the geologists' findings. The disagreements broke into the open in early 1984 at a meeting in Tiumen' of the country's top planners and energy officials. The estimates presented by Farman Salmanov, head of the Tiumen' geological service (Glavtiumengeologiia), were bullish as always, while those presented by the head of Tiumen's oil industry were far more pessimistic. The two officials were instructed to produce a common estimate,[93] but this did not end the disagreements.[94] Now, however, politicians seem more inclined to believe the oil men than

[89] Farman Salmanov made this claim in early 1986 in an undelivered "supplementary" speech appended to the report of the Twenty-seventh Party Congress, *XXVII. s"ezd KPSS, stenograficheskii otchet* (Moscow: Politizdat, 1986), vol. 3, p. 35.

[90] *Sovetskaia geologiia*, no. 3 (1982), p. 4.

[91] Starovoitov, ed., *Problemy*, p. 14.

[92] The 1983 regulations are discussed in Leslie Dienes, "Soviet Oil Industry," pp. 625–627.

[93] Iu. Perepletkin, "Energeticheskii potentsial Sibiri," *Izvestiia*, 24 Mar. 1984. The head of the Tiumen' oil industry, R. I. Kuzovatkin, was replaced in the spring of 1985, but Salmanov has stayed on.

[94] Kozlov, "Neft' Zapadnoi Sibiri," p. 32. This article reports that, whereas the oil men accuse the geologists of inflating reserves to make themselves look good, the geologists

formerly. When he visited Tiumen' in 1985, Gorbachev stated that the ratio of explored reserves to production in West Siberia was no better than in the rest of the country.[95]

Uncertainties over West Siberian reserves, in turn, contribute to uncertainties over the development of new fields. One of the most striking features of recent years is the juggling of targets for new fields, which is being repeated in the Twelfth Five-Year Plan. Thus the oil minister in 1986 called for seventy-seven new fields to be opened up in West Siberia in 1986–1990, but other sources mention between sixty-six and ninety-four. But the development of new West Siberian fields appears to be going faster now than in the first half of the 1980s. Soviet sources reported twenty-one new fields in production in 1986, twenty in 1987,[96] and about eighteen in 1988. But new fields do not automatically mean new oil. New fields, in addition to being increasingly difficult to reach and develop, are typically brought into production before outlining is complete and reserves are confirmed. The result is frequent disappointments, and the contribution of new fields to West Siberian output has been consistently short of expectations.

Finally, disagreements persist over the long-term future of West Siberian oil. On the one hand, many Soviet geologists continue to believe that West Siberia still contains a great deal of undiscovered oil, and Western experts largely agree. The geology—a combination of excellent reservoir rocks and sealed traps—is highly favorable.[97] The region has been explored only about a tenth as much as older oil regions such as Azerbaijan.[98] Even if no new giants are discovered, Tiumen' alone holds many hundreds of fields that would be considered sizable by any but earlier Siberian standards, not to mention more distant prospects in East Siberia or offshore in the Barents and Kara seas. Moreover, many geologists have not given up on the idea that new giants will be discovered below the gas fields of north Tiumen' or in unconventional structures throughout the region.

The trouble is, these expectations are not being confirmed with actual

---

return the charge, blaming the oil men for lowering the reserve estimates in order to excuse their own malperformance.

95 *Pravda*, 7 Sept. 1985, p. 1. It is nevertheless remarkable that while the heads of the local oil industry come and go, the chief of the Tiumen' geologists, Farman Salmanov, survives through thick and thin.

96 *Soviet Geography* 30, no. 4 (April 1989), p. 312.

97 See in particular the work of James W. Clarke of the U.S. Geological Survey. I am indebted to Dr. Clarke for his kind advice and criticism.

98 Geologists have drilled about 16 meters of exploratory hole per square kilometer in West Siberia versus about 140 in Azerbaijan. Sidorenko, "Problemy Tiumenskoi nefti," p. 60.

findings. So far, the record of discoveries in north Tiumen' and in the Barents Sea has been disappointing, yielding gas instead of oil. Complex structures, after raising hopes, have produced some frustrating defeats, notably at Salym and Sutormin (although reserves from such formations account for a large share of the additions to prospective reserves in West Siberia). Neither do more distant prospects, such as East Siberia or the zone around the Caspian Sea, offer any clear alternatives. The old controversies continue to boil, and at the moment the pessimists seem to have the stronger case.[99]

In recent years, geologists have been focusing their attention on the eastern shore of the Caspian Sea. The star of the area is Tengiz, which may hold as much as 2.5 billion tons, making it one of the largest oil fields in the world and nearly equal to Samotlor itself.[100] Tengiz will be a difficult field to develop, however, as will the other eastern Caspian fields, and after initial delays in producing the appropriate equipment itself, the Soviet oil industry has formed several joint ventures with Western companies. (See Chapter 6.)

To dispel these uncertainties, the geologists must increase both the volume and the effectiveness of their upstream effort, and here they are hampered as much as ever by the priorities imposed on them and by their own weaknesses. In the first half of the 1980s downstream exploratory drilling, consisting of outlining work to support production needs, grew 60 percent faster than geophysical work, and the number of new prospects remained static.[101] The geologists' allocation of effort has not changed,[102] largely because the Oil Ministry still balks at doing its own outlining work, despite steady criticism.[103]

[99] The case for the pessimists is summarized in Dienes, "Soviet Oil Industry." For a review of East Siberian oil prospects, see B. V. Robinson, "Economic-Geographic Assessment of Oil Resources in East Siberia and the Yakut ASSR," *Soviet Geography* 26, no. 2 (February 1985), pp. 91–97.

[100] In March 1988 Oil Minister Dinkov made an unusual public announcement of the reserves estimate for Tengiz. It is not known, however, whether it refers to total or recoverable reserves. *Financial Times*, 16 Mar. 1988.

[101] Kozlov, "Neft' Zapadnoi Sibiri," p. 32.

[102] Ibid., p. 31. Critics recommend that the share of prospecting (*poiskovoe*) exploration should be at least 30 percent of total effort in the Twelfth Plan and move toward 50–60 percent thereafter.

[103] In mid-1983 Academician Abel Aganbegian, now one of the leading economic advisers in Moscow but then still director of an economic institute in Novosibirsk, called upon MNP to help out: "The Ministry of the Oil Industry should help the [geologists] by increasing its outlining [*razvedochnoe*] drilling near the developed fields of the Middle Ob' region, so that the geological organizations can move out more quickly to the poorly explored northern regions and increase their volume of prospecting [*poiskovoe*] drilling." Abel Aganbegian, "Toplivo Sibiri," *Pravda*, 1 Aug. 1983.

Soviet critics say the share of exploration in total West Siberian drilling should be closer to 25 percent (it is now about 10 percent), and within the exploration effort geophysical investigation (chiefly by seismic methods) should be half or more of the total investment (it is far short of a third today). But to follow these recommendations would mean sharply improving productivity while simultaneously expanding operations, a difficult trick.

The sources of the geologists' weaknesses are much the same as ten years ago, but their needs have grown. To reach more remote locations and explore more complex formations, they require better transportation and equipment, more manpower, and better incentives. But their greatest need is for modern data-processing equipment. In the mid-1980s Siberian geologists had only enough computer power to process about 10 percent of the raw information coming from their seismic crews,[104] and, lacking adequate technology for geophysical work, they still depended too much on drilling.[105] Since the drillers are themselves underequipped and inefficient, any increase in West Siberian exploration is bound to be expensive in money and manpower. The chief Tiumen' geologist, Farman Salmanov, even as he called for a doubling of exploratory drilling in the second half of the 1980s, conceded in advance that such a policy would require doubling manpower as well.[106]

Although it is impossible for a layman and an outsider to judge the rights and wrongs of technical arguments that have been going on for more than two decades now, certain basic points are clear enough from the Soviet commentary: the reserves picture in Siberia is highly unsatisfactory; Soviet geologists are ill-equipped to provide policymakers with the information they need; and current exploration policy is dangerously lopsided in the direction of current production needs.

The Soviet oil industry offers a classic example of decisionmaking under uncertainty. The leaders must decide how much to invest in a peculiar sort of lottery, in which the main problem is uncertain information about the lottery itself. Should they undertake radical measures to modernize the exploration process, knowing that even if the modernization succeeds the lottery might still be a losing one in the end? Or should they limit their investment, even though there might be a winning ticket in the ground? So far, they have not really done either, and as a result they are paying a great deal for inadequate information.

[104] Kozlov, "Neft' Zapadnoi Sibiri," p. 32.
[105] Ibid. See also Dienes, "Soviet Oil Industry," p. 634.
[106] Salmanov, "Rezervy geologov Tiumeni."

Enhanced Oil Recovery

Soviet planners and politicians frequently speak of enhanced oil recovery as the magic solution of the future. All over the world oil companies are forced to leave unrecovered 40 to 80 percent of the oil known to be present in a field; and in every country oil men are searching actively to increase total recovery. So-called tertiary methods of enhanced recovery involve treating oil-bearing rock with heat, gases, or chemicals, sometimes in conjunction with waterflooding. In the lower forty-eight United States, between a quarter and a half of all remaining recoverable oil will require some combination of these methods.[107] In short, enhanced recovery has become a major part of Western oil practice.

Enhanced recovery in the USSR, in contrast, has had an uneven history, the product of initially overenthusiastic acceptance of foreign experience and incautious use of foreign imports, on the one hand, and inadequate support from supplier ministries and resistance among oil men in the field, on the other. As a result, enhanced recovery went through a premature boom in the mid- and late 1970s, followed by an abrupt bust from which it is only now reviving.

Tertiary recovery suddenly became fashionable in Moscow in the mid-1970s. Enthusiasm for enhanced recovery was especially high among technologists at MNP headquarters, at the State Committee for Science and Technology (whose responsibility includes publicizing successful Western innovations), and above all in Gosplan, where it was seen as a way to take advantage of the established infrastructure in the older oil regions, thus saving on energy investment while slowing the decline of those regions, which had been unexpectedly severe in the first half of the 1970s. The chairman of Gosplan, N. K. Baibakov, appeared especially enthusiastic.[108]

The Soviet partisans of enhanced recovery appear not to have noticed at first that the initial wave of enthusiasm in the United States had been followed by sober second thoughts; by the early 1980s still only a minor fraction of U.S. output came from the new methods.[109] In 1976,

[107] See, for example, the estimates in Exxon's "background series," *Improved Oil Recovery* (New York: Exxon Corporation, Public Affairs Department, 1982). Of the 50–105 billion barrels of recoverable reserves estimated at that time to remain in the United States, 30–75 billion could be produced by primary and secondary methods, while 20–30 billion require tertiary methods (p. 8).

[108] N. K. Baibakov, "Zadacha narodnokhoziaistvennoi vazhnosti," *Ekonomicheskaia gazeta*, no. 11 (1974), pp. 7–8. As Han-ku Chung observes, Baibakov had been interested in enhanced recovery in the early 1960s, when he still headed the oil industry. Chung, *Interest Representation in Soviet Policy-Making: A Case Study of a West Siberian Energy Coalition* (Boulder, Colo.: Westview Press, 1987), p. 57.

[109] Of the 19 million tons produced by the U.S. oil industry in 1982, 14.4 million

with little concrete knowledge, experience, or advance preparation, the Ministry of the Oil Industry launched an ambitious program, conducted by a specially created enhanced-recovery department under a deputy minister, E. Khalimov. The results proved disastrous. Khalimov plunged into purchasing foreign equipment and chemicals, most of which piled up on roadsides or were dumped into spent wells. He then tried to cover up the debacle with faked figures and excuses, but by the end of the Tenth Plan it was clear he had achieved nothing. In 1981, shortly after the Central Committee's Party Control Commission conducted a devastating postmortem, Khalimov was fired.[110]

For the next five years enhanced recovery kept a lower profile. In official ministry prose it was mentioned in respectful tones as the most promising avenue for the future, but the industry clearly was not counting on it for the near term and had no plans for a major contribution from the West. Gosplan chairman Baibakov, unrepentant, acknowledged opposition to tertiary recovery among "some" specialists, who considered it too expensive and not effective, although he himself had not lost faith.[111]

Nevertheless, enhanced recovery was supported through a special fund amounting to about 1 percent the total oil industry fixed-capital investment.[112] All told, spending for enhanced recovery totaled 500 million rubles in the first half of the 1980s.[113] Three specialized institutes were established to promote enhanced recovery, and about 20,000 people were actively engaged in research in the area.[114]

Yet controversy continued to smolder over the proper place of tertiary recovery. The Soviet perception of the Western advances grew more sober as industry experts realized that the enthusiasm of American oil men had also cooled.[115] Planners and technocrats in Moscow remained

---

were recovered through the use of steam. (Chung, *Interest Representation*, citing *Oil and Gas Journal*, 5 Apr. 1982.) By 1986, output attributed to enhanced oil recovery had grown to 27–28 million tons a year, but energy experts saw little prospects for increase unless oil prices recovered substantially. R. Mike Ray et al., "Potential Crude Oil Production from Enhanced Oil Recovery" (unpublished briefing paper, U.S. Department of Energy, Bartlesville Project Office, 16 Sept. 1986).

110 V. Sevast'ianov, "Izderzhki popustitel'stva," *Sotsialisticheskaia industriia*, 4 Oct. 1981.

111 N. K. Baibakov, "Gody bol'shikh svershenii," *Neftianoe khoziaistvo*, no. 12 (1983), p. 5.

112 *Ekonomicheskaia gazeta*, no. 2 (1983), p. 8, and no. 15 (1983), p. 7.

113 Speech by Prime Minister Ryzhkov to the Supreme Soviet, introducing the final targets of the Twelfth Five-Year Plan. *Pravda*, 19 June 1986.

114 Ibid.

115 M. B. Nazaretov, "Opytno-promyshlennye ispytaniia metodov uvelicheniia nefteotdachi v SShA," *Neftianoe khoziaistvo*, no. 2 (1985), pp. 61–63.

committed to tertiary methods because they felt that waterflooding was no longer adequate. But local oil men hung back.[116]

Most of the effort, appropriately enough, was aimed at the older oil fields, particularly in Kazakhstan, Komi, Tatariia, and Baskhiriia.[117] The largest project was in Mangyshlak, where hot water and steam stimulation were used to reduce the viscosity of heavy oils.[118] Next in size was a program in Tatariia, using sulphuric acid. All told, by 1983 some 130 projects were underway at more than a hundred locations in over fifty different fields in all parts of the country.[119]

But the program produced only modest results. By 1985 the enhanced-recovery program, even by the official tally, had fallen short of the five-year target, yielding perhaps 5 million tons in 1985 as opposed to the targeted 8 million (table 4.9). And it is likely that even these results are inflated, because the definition of additional output attributable to such methods is somewhat arbitrary and therefore open to fudging by local officials. It follows, incidentally, that enhanced recovery was not a major factor in the improved performance of the oil industry in 1986–1987.[120]

The suspicion that enhanced recovery has yet to show major results in the Soviet Union is strengthened by the heavy criticism it received in the press. Reporters spoke of homemade methods and slapdash improvisation. Their worst censure was reserved for the program's lead research institute, TatNIINeftemash, which they say faked its results, recalling the unfortunate Khalimov.[121] The chief of oil development for Bashkiriia commented that most of the projects involving detergents and other chemical methods of advanced recovery had not proved cost-effective but hinted that he was under considerable pressure from the ministry to use them.[122]

[116] The following exchange gives the flavor: "The potential of waterflooding as a means of further increasing total productivity is already exhausted," states an article by the Oil and Gas Department of the State Committee on Science and Technology in 1983. *Ekonomicheskaia gazeta*, no. 8 (1983), p. 2. "Far from exhausted," retorted a conference of local oil men at about the same time. "Problemy sovershenstvovaniia razrabotki mestorozhdeniia," *Neftianoe khoziaistvo*, no. 8 (1983), p. 29.

[117] *Ekonomicheskaia gazeta*, no. 8 (1983), p. 2.

[118] *Neftianoe khoziaistvo*, no. 12 (1982), p. 58. Hot-water injection has lost popularity in the United States in favor of steam because the latter carries much more heat.

[119] *Ekonomika neftianoi promyshlennosti*, no. 11 (1982), pp. 8–10.

[120] There have been recent claims that enhanced-recovery methods now contribute up to 30 million tons/year. But, given the checkered history of the program and the difficulty of determining precisely how much of a well's output is due to tertiary recovery, one should beware of inflated claims.

[121] Zaripov and Podol'skii, "Trudnyi gorizont," *Sovetskaia Rossiia*, December 7, 1982.

[122] "Novinka novinke rozn'," *Pravda*, 15 Aug. 1983.

TABLE 4.9
Incremental Production Attributable to Enhanced-Recovery Methods, 1975–1985 (millions of tons/year)

1975	1.5
1980	2.7
1981	2.6
1982	3.0-3.4
1983	4.0
1984	NA
1985 (plan)	8.0

SOURCES: *Ekonomicheskaia gazeta*, no. 2 (1983), p. 8; no. 8 (1983), p. 2; *Neftianoe khoziaistvo*, no. 12 (1982), p. 58; *Oil and Gas Journal*, 16 Apr. 1984.

These assessments reflect a tug-of-war between the planners and technocrats in Moscow and the oil men in the field. The latter favor waterflooding and resent the pressure from above to adopt new methods before they are proven. The Oil Ministry itself, perhaps caught in the middle, has merged the two programs under a single deputy minister, V. Iudin, who speaks of the benefits of using both together.[123]

One is hard put to decide which classic theme of Soviet bureaucratic behavior this episode illustrates best: technological overambitiousness above, resistance to innovation below, overly enthusiastic acceptance of foreign examples and incautious use of foreign imports, or inadequate support from supplier ministries. At all events, it is clear that advanced recovery techniques are still too experimental and too expensive to provide the magic solution that Soviet planners hoped for in the late 1970s. Waterflooding, then, remains the method of choice for enhanced recovery in the Soviet oil industry in the 1980s. Nevertheless, there are signs that the new leadership has renewed hopes for enhanced recovery. The 1990 target for additional production from all such methods has been set at 15 million tons. But in view of the program's rocky history, one can only be skeptical.

[123] As of 1989, Iudin was still on the job. CIA, Directorate of Intelligence, *Directory of Soviet Officials: National Organizations*, LDA 89-10149 (Washington, D.C.: USGPO, February 1989), p. 87.

Conclusion

Since the late 1970s the Soviet oil industry has staved off a decline in oil output by exploiting one-time gains available from shifting the industry's development resources to West Siberia. That trump card having been played twice, Soviet leaders now face essentially the same core problem they did in 1977: the cost of oil has continued to rise rapidly; no new oil giants have been discovered (with the problematic exception of Tengiz); the oil industry's technology is primitive and its industrial base weak; and output remains uncertain unless the leaders are willing to continue pouring ever more capital and manpower into oil.

The essential cause of the problem is also the same as before: the bulk of the Soviet effort since 1977 has gone into a crash increase in development drilling, to the neglect of the industry's other operations. To be sure, there have been some improvements. The base of West Siberian oil production has been broadened compared to seven years ago, as exploration teams have moved out from the established fields of the Middle Ob' Basin to the outlying areas of Tiumen' Province. But the newer fields are smaller and more difficult to explore and develop, and so production there has been lagging behind the plan. The tasks of well mechanization, maintenance, and repair are being addressed more seriously than in the past. A campaign to improve housing, equipment, and infrastructure has begun, but it has not had time to produce results; moreover, its success depends on unceasing top-priority attention and pressure from Moscow.

Who is to blame? Are the culprits also the same as in the 1970s? In that earlier crisis there were no heroes. Siberian exploration teams failed to venture outside the familiar and comfortable Middle Ob' Basin. The Ministry of Geology in Moscow was skeptical that north Tiumen' would yield oil and did not support exploration there. The Ministry of the Oil Industry took little responsibility for Siberian exploration and for that matter was also skeptical about Siberian reserves. Gosplan reinforced MNP's bias toward development by driving Siberian output targets higher and higher. The top leaders themselves, fearing a collapse of oil output, kept the pressure on the oil industry while failing to take steps to make the industry more modern and more efficient. Even the Siberian oil experts and geologists, who deserve credit for having spotted the problem early, should probably share in the blame for the very extravagance of their claims that vast new oil reserves lay just around the corner.

In the mid-1980s, with some differences in detail, the actors and their roles sound much the same. If one were forced to pick a chief villain, one would have to name Gosplan and the top leaders themselves, whose insistence on keeping oil output growing at all costs created the continuous campaign atmosphere that has driven the oil industry for the last twenty years. But to make such an accusation would be to miss the real meaning of the affair. No single group is guilty; the truth is more subtle and more interesting.

Two standards of rationality contend in the Soviet decisionmaking system. The first is the voice of long-term wisdom. It has been saying for fifteen years that Soviet policy should move toward coal, nuclear power, and energy conservation. The other voice is that of short-term caution, which says that oil output cannot be allowed to drop until it can drop safely, lest oil shortages cause energy bottlenecks that would slow down the whole economy.

The voice of the long term is well represented in Soviet institutions, and it rings especially loud in the press. The USSR Academy of Sciences, the State Committee on Science and Technology, the major energy ministries, and Gosplan all have offices and research institutes specializing in long-term energy policy. This is the voice one hears in the official energy program adopted in 1984 and in the revision of it that is under way now. And it has not been without effect: the long-term strategy of Soviet energy policy, as it has evolved since 1980 or so, looks beyond the era of hydrocarbons to a future of coal, nuclear generation, and conservation, and in that respect is soundly conceived.

The trouble comes in the implementation. As one moves from five-year plans to annual ones, the voice of near-term caution grows louder, until its impact on targets and funding priorities is overwhelming. Nowhere has this been more true than in oil. Every year since the beginning of the 1970s the planners have acted as though driven by the fear of imminent disaster in their oil supplies, setting ever higher West Siberian output targets in the five-year plans and then ratcheting them higher still in the annual ones. In the first half of the 1970s it was the unexpected decline of oil output in the older regions that caused them to force the pace in Siberia. In the second half of the decade the fear of a shortfall in Siberia itself drove the campaign into still higher gear, while in the 1980s the fear that alternatives would not be available in time has driven the planners even more urgently. Only at the end of the 1980s, at long last, does it appear that the leadership is ready to let up—yet even now the signals are ambiguous.

One is tempted to side with the reasonable voice of the long term, but the near-term voice has a compelling case too. In the 1970s any Soviet planner who knew his business would have been wary of the scientists' glib talk of the coal-and-nuclear future and skeptical of the oil industry's constant efforts to chisel their targets downward. What he could not dismiss, in contrast, was the certainty of brown-outs and black-outs, hard-currency shortages, and other unpleasantness if oil should run short. In any one year the case was strong for higher oil targets.

But fifteen years of such year-by-year risk avoidance have produced a result that all Soviet decisionmakers would agree is the wrong one: a prematurely aged oil industry with uncertain prospects and inadequate technology; costs out of control owing to years of unbalanced effort and short horizons; a production crisis in West Siberia that requires constant firefighting; and solutions and alternatives still not ready, especially on the consumption side, where Soviet energy efficiency is still the lowest of any industrial nation.

What prospect is there that, at least where oil is concerned, the two voices of the Soviet planning system will agree on the same course? Thanks to the expanded gas program launched in 1981, natural gas is beginning to displace oil and will provide a twenty-year bridge to enable Soviet planners to begin restructuring their energy economy. To take full advantage of this new respite, the Soviet leaders must not lull themselves to sleep again. They must rebalance and modernize the oil industry, accelerate exploration, improve industrial support, and enhance living conditions. If they are deceived by the recent oil recovery, they run the risk of a third oil crisis in the early 1990s.

FIVE

THE SOVIET GAS CAMPAIGN, 1970–1988

Soviet gas policy has been one of the few real success stories of the Soviet economy in the last decade, but it has been a big one. In 1984 the USSR surpassed the United States as the world's largest natural gas producer, and it will keep its lead well into the next century, thanks to explored reserves amounting to as much as 40 percent of the world total. Within the Soviet fuel balance, natural gas has overtaken oil as the USSR's main energy source, and by 1990 it will supply more than 40 percent of all fossil fuel production (table 5.1). Soviet geologists, gas men, and pipeline builders have worked long and hard under some of the world's harshest conditions. Thanks to their efforts, natural gas is playing a crucial role as a "bridging fuel," carrying the Soviet economy from the era of oil toward the coal-and-nuclear future of the next century. If it were not for natural gas, the Soviet economy would now be in serious trouble indeed.

But if the Soviet planners had launched their gas policy sooner, at the beginning of the 1970s, their energy problems would not be so pressing today. Specifically, if the gas bridge had been begun then, the oil industry would not have had to resort to the crash gas campaign it began in 1981. As it is, Soviet energy experts now worry that many of the same mistakes committed in the oil fields are now being repeated for gas. No gas crisis looms for the 1990s; Soviet reserves are much too large for that. But the gas bridge has been made needlessly costly, and it will be become costlier still over the next decade as a result of policies pursued today.

This chapter has two aims. The first is to analyze the policies that have enabled the gas industry to play its present role and to examine the

This chapter is an elaboration and update of an earlier work by this author on the origins and initial results of the gas campaign of 1980–1981. See *The Soviet Gas Campaign: Politics and Policy in Soviet Decision-Making*, R-3036-AF (Santa Monica, Calif.: Rand Corporation, June 1983). The discussion of capital investment has been revised, and a number of earlier errors have been corrected. The earlier detailed review of infrastructural imbalances has been omitted, except for the issues of manpower and settlement policy.

TABLE 5.1
Soviet Gas Output, 1970–1988

	Bcm	*Percentage of Soviet Primary Fuel Output**
1970	197.9	19.1
1975	289.3	21.8
1980	435.2	27.1
1981	465.3	28.4
1982	500.7	29.7
1983	535.7	31.1
1984	587.4	33.3
1985	643.0	35.8
1986	686.0	36.6
1987	727.0	37.7
1988	770.0	NA

SOURCES: *Narodnoe khoziaistvo SSSR*, various years; for 1988: *Pravda*, 22 Jan. 1989.

* Defined as fossil fuel but not primary electricity.

major decisionmaking issues that arose along the way. The second is to look toward the future and to attempt to anticipate how the same policies, if pursued over the next decade, may affect the reliability and cost of gas supplies. One of the most important questions to examine is whether gas is a relatively cheap fuel (as its abundance might suggest) or an expensive one. If the former, then the leaders' growing reliance on gas is sound; if the latter, then their gas-oriented policy will amount to a continuation of the Brezhnev approach.

Strategy and Decisionmaking in the Evolution of Soviet Gas Policy

In the early 1970s few observers would have predicted that within a decade natural gas would play so crucial a role for the Soviets. Long the humble stepchild of the oil industry, the Ministry of the Gas Industry (MGP) since the mid-1960s had had a history of uncertain growth and unmet targets.[1] But in the second half of the 1970s, with the development of the first West Siberian gas fields and the construction of large-diameter transcontinental pipelines, gas became a star performer. In contrast to the worrisome slowdown of oil growth and the collapse of coal, gas boomed ahead and was the only energy source to meet the five-year targets set for it in 1976.

Even so, when Soviet leaders in 1980–1981 announced plans to increase the output of natural gas by nearly 50 percent in five years, most Western observers reacted skeptically. Not only would the massive increment of new gas have to come from the arctic wastes of West Siberia, but delivering it to the European USSR and Western Europe would require six giant pipelines spanning 20,000 kilometers (12,500 miles) with 1,420-millimeter (56-inch) steel pipe, powered by over 10 gigawatts of compressor capacity, the equivalent of ten good-sized electric power plants. To achieve this on such short notice seemed beyond the existing capacities of Soviet industry. As discussed in Chapter 1, Western observers were not the only skeptics; we now know that the sudden step-up in gas targets in 1980–1981 was questioned by Soviet energy experts as well, largely on the same grounds.

Nevertheless, the Gas Ministry and its principal construction agency, the Ministry for Construction of Oil and Gas Enterprises (MNGS), met the challenge. They reached their five-year output target handily and built all six pipelines ahead of schedule; in fact, by the end of the Eleventh Plan in 1985 they were well along on a seventh. As we shall see, they achieved these goals by taking short cuts that are now causing them trouble. Nevertheless, the second half of the 1980s has witnessed equally rapid growth. Gas production is planned to increase from 643 billion cubic meters (bcm) in 1985 to 850 in 1990. So far, gas production has been rising about 7 percent a year, although 1989 has brought early signs of a slowdown.

Yet all is not well in the gas industry. To keep growing at its present pace it must cross the Arctic Circle to new giants at Yamburg and the Yamal Peninsula (see map 2). But Yamburg is behind schedule; instead of supplying the bulk of new Soviet gas in the second half of the 1980s, it will not do so until the beginning of the 1990s. The current growth in gas output still comes mainly from Urengoy, the star of the last five-year plan and the largest gas field in the world; but Urengoy is being

[1] See Jonathan P. Stern, *Soviet Natural Gas Development to 1990* (Lexington, Mass.: D. C. Heath/Lexington Books, 1980), and Robert W. Campbell, *Trends in the Soviet Oil and Gas Industry* (Baltimore: Johns Hopkins University Press, 1976).

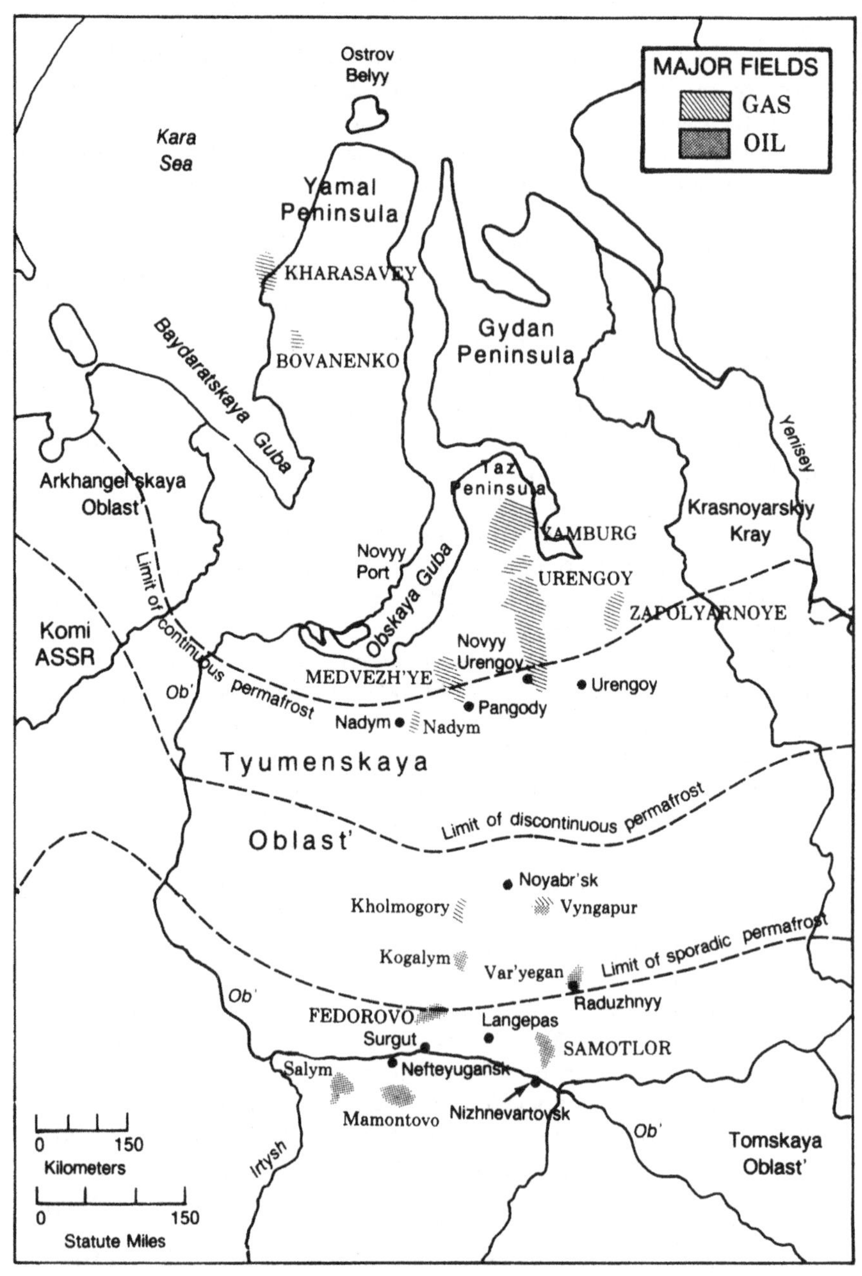

MAP 2. West Siberian Oil and Gas Region. Source: CIA, *USSR Energy Atlas*, January 1985.

pushed far above its planned maximum. Meanwhile, to process and transport the new gas requires as many new pipelines and as much new gas-treatment equipment in the second half of the 1980s as in the first half, and these are more expensive because the conditions are far tougher. In addition, the industry now faces growing costs just to maintain and repair the existing transmission network. Finally, the economy is having increasing difficulty absorbing increments of 40–50 bcm of gas each year.

At bottom, the strategy used by the gas industry has been as unbalanced as that of the oil industry farther south. Housing, roads, and powerlines have been neglected along with infrastructure of all sorts. To observers writing in the Soviet press, the most striking feature of the gas campaign to date is its close resemblance to the earlier history of Soviet oil. In short, the Soviet gas campaign is another case of "extensive" response to crisis and mirrors in its essential features the rest of Soviet energy policy.

What is different this time is that the memory of the oil crisis is present in everyone's mind. *Pravda*'s correspondent in Tiumen', V. Lisin, wrote in 1985 that continued unbalanced development would lead to the same "unpleasant fate" experienced by the oil industry.[2] More recently two economists from the gas industry raised a storm of debate over gas production goals for the year 2000 by warning that the present policy of pushing gas output to the maximum is exhausting the major fields prematurely.[3] The critics acknowledge that the two cases are not exactly the same: the country's huge gas reserves are real, while yesterday's expected oil riches have turned out (so far) to be more modest. The issue is not whether the gas is there but how much it will cost to develop and deliver it. *Pravda*'s editors, commenting on the debate, asked, "Will the generation of the year 2000 be able to afford a trillion cubic meters a year? To maintain the trillion level will require truly gigantic capital investment, which, economists warn us, will grow in almost geometric progression."[4] In effect, the argument is over what economists call the "social rate of time preference": the benefits of forced production today, the critics charge, are overweighted against production lost tomorrow, which will require additional investment to make up later. The "patriots" of the gas industry retort, "There is no

[2] V. Lisin, "Gazovyi potentsial," *Pravda*, 21 Jan. 1985.

[3] I. Tyshliar and V. Gasparian, "Ne nado verit' v mif o 'deshevom gaze,' " *Pravda*, 30 Sept. 1987; same, "Otrasl' na 'forsazhe,' " *Pravda*, 17 Nov. 1987; and same, "Berech' gaz: k voprosu o deshevoi energii," *Pravda*, 1 Feb. 1988.

[4] Tyshliar and Gasparian, "Berech' gaz."

alternative."[5] To which the critics rejoin, "The alternative is conservation, beginning with higher gas prices to the consumer."

An important feature of learning is the choice of symbolic precedents and the language of discourse. For the gas patriots of the 1970s the relevant precedent is the West Siberian epic of the oil industry; for their critics in the 1980s it is the oil epic's dismal sequel. But even more significant is that the critics' arguments are framed in economic terms, while their opponents speak in physical terms of reserves and shortages. Thirty years ago Soviet economists made their timid reappearance in a policy world dominated by technologists;[6] now, under Gorbachev, the economists speak with authority, while the technologists sound old-fashioned and defensive. Economics has become the accepted official language of Soviet policy discourse, and it is the language the current leaders themselves routinely use. As the debate over gas policy heats up at the end of the 1980s, the issues of cost, not geology or technology, will dominate.

Background to the Big Gas Policy

One of the most intriguing questions about the gas bridge policy of 1980–1981 is: Why was it not begun earlier? Did Soviet leaders miss an important opportunity five or ten years before, for which they are paying a high price today? Until the beginning of the 1970s the growth of the Soviet gas industry had been based almost entirely on fields in the European USSR and in Central Asia. Soviet planners and gas men evidently expected this pattern to continue, but from about 1966 on the older fields proved unable to support further growth. Anticipated new reserves failed to materialize, while existing fields began to decline earlier than expected.[7] The growth rate of gas output dropped sharply,[8]

[5] A group of men long associated with the big gas policy appeared with a rebuttal in *Pravda* (1 Feb. 1988), under the revealing title "Samaia dinamichnaia."

[6] One illustration of the return of economists to policy debate in the 1950s, the case of the battle against hydropower under Khrushchev, will be found in the present author's *Reform in Soviet Politics: Lessons of Recent Policies on Land and Water* (New York: Cambridge University Press, 1981), chs. 4, 6, and 7. As Gregory Grossman observed, economic issues had never disappeared from Soviet policymaking (nor could they—after all, scarcity never disappears); but in the absence of economists they were debated by engineers in a peculiar, sub rosa language. See Grossman, "Capital Intensity: A Problem in Soviet Planning" (Ph.D. diss., Harvard University, 1952).

[7] V. I. Botvinnikov, *Problemy razvitiia gazovoi promyshlennosti Sibiri* (Novosibirsk: Nauka, 1983), pp. 23–25.

[8] Annual increments to output had reached 19 billion cubic meters (bcm) a year by 1965 but sank back to 9 bcm by 1972. See A. D. Sedykh and B. A. Kuchin, *Upravlenie nauchno-tekhnicheskim progressom v gazovoi promyshlennosti* (Moscow: Nedra, 1983), p. 5.

and by 1975 the industry fell far short of the five-year target set in 1970.[9]

Meanwhile, starting in the second half of the 1960s, geologists were uncovering fabulous new gas reserves in West Siberia, which in less than five years transformed the map of Soviet gas resources. By 1970 reserves in Tiumen' Province already accounted for more than half of the nationwide total; thereafter West Siberian reserves bounded ahead, while in the rest of the country new discoveries barely kept pace with production (table 5.2). Yet, as we saw in Chapter 1, the leaders of the gas industry were reluctant to take the plunge into West Siberia. It took the first oil crisis to overcome their resistance.

The main reason for such reluctance, according to Soviet critics today, is that the leadership of the gas industry considered Siberian gas too expensive to develop and to ship. In the early 1970s, when the impending rise in the cost of oil was not yet foreseen, the high cost of gas loomed all the larger—so much so that the leaders of the gas industry themselves urged that natural gas be phased out as a boiler fuel and reserved for premium uses.[10]

The costliness of Siberian gas is not hard to explain. Even today most of the northern half of Tiumen' Province is virgin territory, and conditions there make the Siberian gas campaign as tough as anything the Soviets have undertaken in peacetime. But the main bottleneck to expansion and the greatest source of expense has been transmission capacity. Soviet planners and gas men had lagged in moving up to larger pipe and more powerful compressors,[11] and to compound the problem the gas transmission network was inefficiently run.[12] Any large-scale move into West Siberia would require a massive investment in 1,420-millimeter pipe and compressor stations capable of transmitting gas at 75 atmospheres or higher. But Soviet industry could not yet supply

[9] The original five-year target for 1975, based on the assumption that fields in the North Caucasus and the Ukraine would continue to grow, was 320 bcm; but actual output that year was 289.3, and the cumulative shortfall for the entire decade 1965–1975 was over 100 bcm. Sedykh and Kuchin, *Upravlenie nauchno-tekhnicheskim progressom*, p. 7. For Western sources on this period, see Campbell, *Trends*; Leslie Dienes and Theodore Shabad, *The Soviet Energy System: Resource Use and Policies* (New York: Wiley and Sons, 1979); and Stern, *Soviet Natural Gas Development*.

[10] This viewpoint outraged Siberian gas patriots, who criticized MGP leaders for it by name. See, for example, an interview with the first secretary of the Tiumen' obkom, G. P. Bogomiakov, "Tiumenskii kompleks i ego budushchee," *Ekonomika i organizatsiia promyshlennogo proizvodstva*, no. 5 (1976), p. 9.

[11] Sedykh and Kuchin, *Upravlenie nauchno-tekhnicheskim progressom*, pp. 7–12.

[12] Robert W. Campbell, *Soviet Energy Technologies: Planning, Policy, Research and Development* (Bloomington: Indiana University Press, 1980), pp. 204–209.

TABLE 5.2
Growth of Soviet Explored Gas Reserves, 1965–1980
(trillions of cubic meters)

	Tiumen' Province	*USSR Countrywide*	*Siberian Share (%)*
1965	0.3	3.2	9.4
1970	6.9	12.1	57.0
1971	9.3	15.8	59.0
1972	10.6	17.7	59.9
1973	12.2	19.9	61.3
1974	13.9	22.5	61.8
1975	15.2	23.7	64.1
1980	24.9	34.3	72.6

SOURCES: 1965–1975: Botvinnikov, *Problemy*, p. 42; 1980: I. P. Zhabrev, ed., *Gazovye i gazokondensatsionnye mestorozhdeniia. Spravochnik*, 2d ed. (Moscow: Nedra, 1983), cited in *Soviet Geography* 24 (1983), pp. 703–707. These are what the Soviets call "industrial reserves," ($A + B + C_1$), i.e., corresponding roughly to the American concept of "proven and probable."

NOTE: I have not found a more recent official statement on Soviet gas reserves, although they have increased substantially since the 1980 estimate. The *Financial Times International Gas Report*, 5 Aug. 1988, p. 10, quoted a figure of 41.7 trillion cubic meters, but on 10 June 1988 the same source gives 46–50 trillion cubic meters (p. 4).

either in the necessary quantity or quality, so to the list of deterrents to a "big gas" policy was added the unpleasant prospect of massive imports of equipment. The first 1,420-millimeter pipe—imported—did not appear until 1972, and average installed compressor capacity did not pass 4 megawatts until 1975,[13] when the Soviets began importing compressors to equip pipelines from Orenburg and Urengoy.

The gas industry's hesitation to move energetically into West Siberia showed other revealing symptoms. Well into the second half of the 1970s the Gas Ministry continued to invest more resources in the older gas regions than in West Siberia, apparently with the planners' blessing.[14] Gas engineers and planners toyed with various technological fixes

[13] Sedykh and Kuchin, *Upravlenie nauchno-tekhnicheskim progressom*, pp. 121 and 123.

[14] "Ekonomicheskaia effektivnost' kapital'nykh vlozhenii v gazovoi promyshlennosti za 1971–79gg.," in All-Union Scientific Research Institute for the Economics of the Gas Industry (VNIIEgazprom), *Ekonomika gazovoi promyshlennosti*, seriia ekonomika, organizatsiia i upravlenie v gazovoi promyshlennosti (obzornaia informatsiia), no. 10

to lick the transmission problem, such as superlarge pipe, lighter-than-air dirigibles, and even schemes to transport condensates or gas hydrates, which form a sort of snow, packed into capsules. These ideas evidently found enough support in the leadership of Gosplan and MNGS (Nikolai Baibakov, in particular, took some interest, and even Prime Minister Kosygin paid a visit to a pilot plant where the capsule technology was under development) that special research teams and institutes were organized around them, and planning for them was going strong as late as 1976.[15] For a time, the industry—presumably with some encouragement from the top leadership—considered developing the northernmost Yamal fields first for export to the West in the form of liquid natural gas (LNG).[16]

Despite the industry's reluctance, in the end there was no arguing with the growing dominance of West Siberian reserves. Ever since the mid-1960s local Tiumen' authorities had been beating the drum for faster development of Siberian gas, and an important turning point finally came in 1973, when the man who had long been the most enthusiastic Siberian gas booster of all, Tiumen' Obkom First Secretary Boris Shcherbina (who has since risen still higher, to deputy chairman of the USSR Council of Ministers and head of the Council of Ministers' Energy Bureau), was placed in charge of the newly created Ministry for the Construction of Oil and Gas Enterprises, the principal mission of which was precisely to accelerate Siberian gas and oil development.[17]

(1980). In 1975 an editorial in Gosplan's monthly journal emphasized development of gas resources in Central Asia and Kazakhstan, which were "located in more favorable climatic conditions than the north of Tiumen' and can be developed more quickly." "Uskorenno razvivat' toplivno-energeticheskuiu bazu strany," *Planovoe khoziaistvo*, no. 2 (1975), p. 5.

[15] For descriptions of these ideas and a review of the official moves made at the time, see the report by the then deputy director of Gosplan's Project Review Committee (*ekspertnaia komissiia*), veteran gas man Iulii I. Bokserman, "Transport budushchego," *Oktiabr'*, no. 6 (1976), pp. 155–166; and same, "Nevidimye magistrali," *Znamia*, no. 11 (1975), pp. 116–138. Proposals to transport condensate instead of gas can be found in M. A. Styrikovich et al., "Ob optimal'nykh napravleniiakh razrabotki gazokondensatnykh mestorozhdenii Tiumenskoi oblasti," *Vestnik Akademii Nauk SSSR*, no. 7 (1974), pp. 54–57.

[16] There is some confirmation of this in Bokserman, "Nevidimye magistrali," p. 128. He refers to plans to build a port on the Yamal Peninsula to transport gas by LNG tankers to other locations in the Soviet Union. As late as 1978 the Gas Ministry in Moscow was "recommending" to the Tiumen' gas men that they proceed directly to Kharasavei, on the northwestern coast of the Yamal Peninsula, in the first half of the 1980s, with the goal of producing 35 bcm/year from that field by 1985. Ye. G. Altunin, "Strategiiu vybrat' segodnia," *Ekonomika i organizatsiia promyshlennogo proizvodstva*, no. 2 (1979), p. 18.

[17] Esfir Raykher, "Decision-Making in the Soviet Gas Industry" (Falls Church, Va.: Delphic Associates, 1988).

In the first half of the 1970s, despite the gas industry's modest investment in the area, West Siberia contributed 29 percent of the net increase in Soviet gas production, up from 14 percent during the previous five years. This contribution turned the previously unreliable gas industry into a steady performer: MGP has not missed a single annual output target since 1973. But the real turning point came in the second half of the 1970s. Reassured that they could rely on Siberian gas and alarmed by the unexpected lag in oil output and the collapse of coal production, Soviet leaders invested heavily in Tiumen' gas development and pipeline construction (we shall examine the data on investment in the next section). Between 1975 and 1980, natural gas increased its share in the Soviet fuels balance from 21.8 to 27.1 percent,[18] with Siberia providing 92 percent of the growth.[19]

The stage was now set for the big gas campaign of the 1980s. But the industry's reluctance to move into Siberia in the first half of the 1970s had several lasting effects. It meant a shorter period of preparation before the 1980–1981 campaign began. When the big push came, the machine-building industry was not ready with the necessary compressors, pipe, and other equipment; consequently, the gas industry was obliged to rely largely on imported equipment, at least for transmission. New technologies that might have cut transmission costs were rejected in the interest of speed. One may question, of course, whether the agencies involved would have made good use of the extra five years if they had had them; but the industry's poor preparation contributed to the imbalance of the gas campaign in the first half of the 1980s, forcing a lopsided emphasis on pipeline construction at the expense of sound infrastructure for development.

Investment Data

The most important single measure of the real priority of any program is the amount of money actually spent on it; and in the Soviet case one must look beyond money to the material resources and manpower actually allocated. Ambitious five-year investment plans, announced with fanfare at Party congresses, often shrivel up when the time comes to translate them into annual budgets and competing ministries begin to push and shove in the corridors of Gosplan and the Party Central Committee. Since the mid-1970s, as declining growth rates have cut the expansion of new budget resources, high-level political battles over spending have become especially fierce. During Gorbachev's first year

[18] *Narodnoe khoziaistvo SSSR v 1984g.*, p. 166. This figure omits primary electricity production.

[19] Botvinnikov, *Problemy*, p. 23.

the war of the numbers became plain for all to see, as the Politburo rejected a half-dozen drafts of the Twelfth Five-Year Plan.[20] But this was a departure from the norm: in traditional Soviet practice the more controversial or unsettled numbers are, the fewer of them appear in print.

The gas campaign is a case in point. Soviet authorities, to this author's knowledge, never announced a clear investment target for the gas campaign of 1981–1985, and so far the same has been true for the Twelfth Plan under Gorbachev. We have five-year investment targets for the energy sector as a whole,[21] and one-year targets for oil, coal, and electrical power for 1986,[22] but the leaders' gas investment priorities for the period 1986–1990 remained a mystery.

The reasons for controversy may well be different in 1985–1986 from what they were five years before. In 1980–1981 the leaders' plans for the gas campaign called for investment to increase sharply, as a share both of total energy and of total industrial investment. But the cost estimates for meeting the assigned output targets, as we shall see, were highly uncertain. Therefore controversy reflected uncertainty as well as competition. In 1985–1986 the uncertainty may have been less, but the competition was greater.

Two main questions will concern us in this section. First, in view of the resources actually allocated to gas, has the leaders' real commitment matched their rhetoric? And second, have those resources been sufficient to support reasonably balanced development of the industry? In short, has gas investment policy been rational?

GAS INVESTMENT TO 1980

The record of gas investment to 1980 is now reasonably well documented.[23] From 1966 to 1980 gas investment grew rapidly, from 4.05

[20] Ed A. Hewett, "Gorbachev's Economic Strategy: A Preliminary Assessment," *Soviet Economy* 2, no. 1 (March 1986).

[21] N. I. Ryzhkov, "O gosudarstvennom plane ekonomicheskogo i sotsial'nogo razvitiia SSSR na 1986–1990 gody," *Pravda*, 19 June 1986.

[22] V. V. Dementsev, "O gosudarstvennom biudzhete SSSR na 1986g. i ob ispolneniii gosudarstvennogo biudzheta SSSR na 1984g.," *Ekonomicheskaia gazeta*, no. 48 (1985), centerfold.

[23] A brief note on gas investment numbers: Even when published statistics are available, it is difficult to derive a single, "best" series. Different Soviet authors include or exclude pipeline investment, exploratory and development drilling not actually performed by MGP crews, construction done by contractors from other ministries, decentralized capital investment, and so-called nonproductive expenditures. Some use current prices, others constant prices tied to various base years. Since this section is concerned mainly with comparing the various statements of gas industry leaders, I have decided to rely on

billion rubles in the Eighth Plan to 19.3 billion in the Tenth (table 5.3). Investment in transmission grew even faster, from 2.6 billion rubles to 12 billion during the same period.

CONFLICTING PROJECTIONS FOR GAS INVESTMENT, 1981–1985

At the beginning of the Eleventh Plan two indirect statements by gas industry leaders tell us what they thought (or hoped) they were going to get. At the 1981 Party Congress in February, the veteran gas minister S. A. Orudzhev stated that the gas industry would spend as much in the coming five-year plan as it had in the last three plan periods combined, which added up to around 33.5 billion rubles. Orudzhev died two months later and was succeeded by the more junior of his two first deputies, V. A. Dinkov. In August, Dinkov used a different formula: gas investment in the Eleventh Plan would double that of the Tenth, implying about 38.5 billion rubles.[24] It is not clear why the two men used different figures. Was Dinkov lobbying for—or had he been promised—more funds than Orudzhev a few months before? If so, was it because he had redone his sums and realized he needed more money to meet his assigned targets? Or was he using a different definition of investment? That is unknown.

By working backward from what we know of Soviet estimates of pipeline costs at the time, we can arrive at five-year investment forecasts for 1981–1985 in the same range as those implied by Dinkov. A frequently cited Soviet rule of thumb was that the six 1420-millimeter pipelines scheduled for the Eleventh Plan would cost roughly 1 billion rubles per 1,000 kilometers.[25] With a five-year target of 21,000 kilome-

MGP numbers and conventions. MGP statistics are given in current prices and exclude a portion of exploratory and development drilling but include pipeline investment. The series published in the annual handbook of the Central Statistical Administration, *Narodnoe khoziaistvo SSSR*, is given in constant prices and includes all gas-related drilling but excludes investment in pipeline construction. I have found invaluable the work of Albina Tretyakova and Meredith Heinemeier, in "Cost Estimates for the Soviet Gas Industry, 1970 to 1990," U.S. Bureau of the Census, Center for International Research, CIR Staff Paper no. 19 (Washington, D.C.: June 1986).

[24] For the first estimate, see Orudzhev's speech at the Twenty-sixth Party Congress, reported in *Pravda*, 2 Mar. 1981. Dinkov's formula comes from Dinkov, "Zveno energeticheskoi programmy," *Sovetskaia Rossiia*, 1 Aug. 1981.

[25] See, for example, Boris Shcherbina, "Glavnye magistrali toplivnoi energetiki," *Stroitel'stvo truboprovodov*, no. 12 (1982), p. 6. The lowest figure I have seen was from *Pravda* correspondents V. Lisin and V. Parfenov, "Energiia tiumenskogo severa," *Pravda*, 2 May 1982, who used a range from 2.5 to 3.0 billion rubles per line. A second estimate, from early 1981, came from the then deputy director (now director) of the Institute for

ters of 56-inch pipeline, then, the gas industry faced transmission investment of about 21 billion rubles, plus a certain additional amount for lesser pipelines, say, 6 billion rubles (which assumes that the lesser pipelines would cost about as much per kilometer as the average for the previous five-year plan), for a total of 27 billion. If one further assumes that transmission was expected to account for 70 percent of total gas investment (as Gas Minister Dinkov stated on several occasions),[26] the projected total investment for the gas industry in 1981–1985 would be 38 to 39 billion rubles.

Some authoritative sources mentioned even higher figures, particularly for pipeline investment, which suggested that cost estimates for the gas campaign remained unsettled well into the first half of the 1980s. The chairman of the USSR Bank for Construction, for example, stated in 1982 that for the six main lines from Urengoy the planners had allocated a total of 31 billion rubles,[27] or 1.5 billion rubles per 1,000 kilometers, 50 percent more than the estimates cited earlier. Similarly, *Pravda* once gave the cost of the Urengoy-Uzhgorod export line as 7.6 billion rubles, or about 1.7 billion rubles per 1,000 kilometers.[28] Evidently some people in Moscow thought the gas campaign could cost as much as 50 billion rubles.[29] But such estimates were probably on the pessimistic side. By extrapolating from known cost

---

the Organization and Economics of Industrial Production of the Siberian division of the USSR Academy of Sciences, who projected 3–4 billion rubles per line. A. Granberg, "Narodnokhoziaistvennaia effektivnost' uskorennogo razvitiia proizvoditel'nykh sil Sibiri," *Planovoe khoziaistvo*, no. 5 (1981), p. 76. A somewhat higher figure came from A. Lalaiants, deputy chairman of Gosplan for energy affairs ("Bazovyi kompleks," *Pravda*, 30 Dec. 1981), who put the cost at 3–5 billion rubles "and more." All these figures agreed roughly with Shcherbina's rule of thumb, if one allows for the fact that the six pipelines have lengths ranging from 2,500 to 4,500 km.

[26] V. A. Dinkov, "Gazovaia promyshlennost' na marshe piatiletki," *Ekonomicheskaia gazeta*, no. 2 (1982), p. 2; and same, "Neotlozhnye zadachi otrasli," *Gazovaia promyshlennost'*, no. 1 (1982), p. 19. A statement by TASS uses the figure two-thirds instead of 70 percent. Foreign Broadcast Information Service, *Soviet Union Daily Report*, 13 Jan. 1982. This represented an increase over the last two five-year plans, when transmission costs represented 60.6 percent of total gas investment (1971–1975) and 62.6 percent (1976–1980). Sedykh and Kuchin, *Upravlenie nauchno-tekhnicheskim progressom*, p. 8.

[27] M. S. Zotov, "Vazhnye zadachi finansirovaniia i kreditovaniia kapital'nogo stroitel'stva," *Finansy SSSR*, no. 4 (1982), p. 4.

[28] "Urengoy-Uzhgorod: pervaia tysiacha kilometrov," *Pravda*, 4 Oct. 1982.

[29] Indeed, the CIA's own estimates, based on statements from Moscow, were on the high side of this range, at 49 billion rubles. See Robert Leggett, "Soviet Investment Policy in the 11th Five-Year Plan," in U.S. Congress, Joint Economic Committee, *Soviet Economy in the 1980s: Problems and Prospects*, (Washington, D.C.: USGPO, December 1982), vol. 1, p. 137.

TABLE 5.3

Capital Investment in the Gas Industry, 1966–1980
(MGP definition, millions of current rubles)

	Exploratory Drilling	*Production*	*Transmission*	*Gas Treatment*	*Underground Storage*	*Other*	*Total*
Eighth Plan 1966–1970	63.3	1,019.1	2,597.2	59.4	44.6	266.3	4,049.9
Ninth Plan 1971–1975	280.8	2,745.2	6,169.0	459.6	91.5	433.6	10,179.7
Tenth Plan 1976–1980	684.0	4,535.5	12,065.7	654.7	277.7	1,056.9	19,274.5

SOURCE: Sedykh and Kuchin, *Upravlenie nauchno-tekhnicheskim progressom*, p. 8.

NOTE: These figures appear to cover "productive" investment only and exclude "unproductive" investment charged to the gas industry, such as housing and services. Various sources mention figures of about 21 billion rubles for productive and unproductive together in 1976–1980, but I have found no comprehensive series as detailed as this one.

trends in the gas industry, the American analyst A. Tretyakova produced a forecast in roughly the same range as Dinkov.[30]

Incidentally, these figures included only *direct* investment in the gas campaign, that is, capital expenditures actually charged to MGP and MNGS. A full reckoning would have included indirect items, such as capital investment in electrical power (the Power Ministry was supposed to invest 3 billion rubles in the West Siberian oil and gas complex during the Eleventh Plan),[31] roads, and dock facilities. Consequently, the full gas investment bill was far higher than the sums we are trying to reconstruct here, which are those of MGP alone.

ACTUAL INVESTMENT, 1981–1985

In the end, how much did the Gas Ministry actually get from 1981 to 1985? Unfortunately, MGP has not yet published a full series. However, one can reconstruct what that series would look like by starting from the numbers published in the standard statistical handbook and applying the appropriate corrections. This procedure suggests that the industry invested about 34.5 billion rubles (in pre-1982 prices), of which pipelines accounted for 22.5 billion.[32] In short, the gas industry may have received somewhat more than Orudzhev said he thought he

[30] See Tretyakova and Heinemeier, "Cost Estimates," p. 5. Tretyakova's total forecast was actually 41 billion rubles, but one must subtract 2–3 billion in non-MGP drilling to reproduce a MGP-type number.

[31] V. Lisin, "Sbivshis' s shaga," *Pravda*, 21 Jan. 1983.; also V. P. Kuramin, "V goru semero vezut," *Sotsialisticheskaia industriia*, 28 Oct. 1982.

[32] I have used pre-1982 prices throughout, because the point of the exercise is to compare actual investment with the 1981 forecasts. Differences between the *Narodnoe khoziaistvo* numbers for the Tenth Plan in pre-1982 prices (as published in the 1980 edition) and in post-1982 prices (as published in the 1985 edition), suggest that one should apply a deflator of about 10 percent to reproduce Eleventh Plan gas investment numbers in pre-1982 prices. Taking the reported Eleventh Plan total of 15.9 billion rubles from *Narodnoe khoziaistvo v 1985 g.*, then, and applying a 10 percent deflator, one arrives at an Eleventh Plan total (in pre-1982 prices) of 14.5 billion rubles. Since MGP numbers do not include drilling performed by other organizations, I subtracted a guesstimate of 2.5 billion rubles to yield a total for gas extraction of 12 billion. Next, a Soviet source gives 22.5 billion invested in pipelines (B. L. Krivoshein and P. I. Tugunov, *Magistral'nyi truboprovodnyi transport* [Moscow: Nauka, 1985], p. 10), which appears to be in pre-1982 rubles. Adding this to the adjusted development figure above yields an "MGP-style" total of 34.5 billion.

An even cruder procedure, for what it may be worth, produces results in the same range. Using the fragmentary MGP numbers reported in Gustafson, *Soviet Gas Campaign* (table 4 and the accompanying note), yields three points on a curve. Since then, the gas industry has published one more number: MGP's investment target for 1985 was 10.7 billion rubles (*Gazovaia promyshlennost'*, no. 3 [1985], p. 4), presumably in post-1982 prices. After applying a rough 10 percent deflator to convert to pre-1982 prices, one obtains another point on the curve. The result for 1981–1985 adds up to about 35 billion rubles.

was going to get (33.5 billion) but considerably less than what Dinkov, possibly on the basis of sounder second thoughts about the costs of the impending campaign, claimed he needed (38.5 billion).

One can interpret these results in two ways, one "political" and the other "technical." The political approach is to view any differences between stated intentions and final results as evidence of shifting priorities at the top. By that standard, if we recall (from Chapter 1) that the entire energy sector ended up in 1985 about as planned, the gas industry's priority may have slipped a bit as time went by, while that of electrical power and oil may have gained.

That conclusion would be surprising, because the central event of the early 1980s was the American embargo of 1981–1983, which caused the political priority of the gas pipeline program to increase dramatically. Why, then, would the priority of the gas industry have slipped? On the contrary, all the circumstantial evidence suggests that it grew. The Soviet explanation is that dramatic improvements in the efficiency of pipeline construction made it possible to meet the plan targets at modest cost; but, as we shall see, that claim should be viewed skeptically. The more likely explanation is that bottlenecks in domestic compressor production (discussed in Chapter 6) prevented the pipeline builders from installing as much capacity as the plan had originally called for. In short, the gas industry may have been unable to spend all the capital that had been allocated to it. Two additional constraints in the field may have further prevented the gas industry from using its capital: a lag in gas drilling and a general shortfall in building infrastructure in the gas fields.

This reminds us of an important point to bear in mind when we try to scrutinize investment numbers for possible policy meanings. Investment outcomes depend not simply on shifts in political priority at the top but also on the various constraints encountered along the way, particularly a ministry's capacity to absorb the capital allocated to it.[33]

[33] One indirect measure of absorptive capacity is the capital tied up in uncompleted projects. In the gas industry this quantity more than tripled between 1971 and 1979, passing from about 1 billion rubles to about 3.6 billion, of which slightly more than half was pipelines. "Ekonomicheskaia effektivnost'," p. 10. More recent, separate figures for the gas industry are not yet available, but those published for the gas and oil industries combined show that capital tied up in incomplete projects (many of which are under contract to MNGS) continued to climb steadily in absolute terms throughout the first half of the 1980s (from 8 billion rubles in 1980 to 11 billion in 1985) but declined as a share of total investment (from 82 percent of annual investment in 1980 to 71 percent in 1985). *Narodnoe khoziaistvo v 1985g.*, p. 371. For 1986, *Narodnoe khoziaistvo* did not give numbers in rubles but showed that incomplete construction had climbed once again to 74

GAS INVESTMENT IN THE SECOND HALF OF THE 1980s

What resources is the gas industry receiving to meet its targets in the second half of the 1980s? The Twelfth Plan (1986–1990) began as the previous one had, without any firm announcement of investment targets for gas. There are some signs that the planners wanted to slow the growth of gas investment. The gas industry was slated for a small percentage increase in 1986.[34] Another sign of an intended slowdown in gas investment compared to oil was that MNGS's plan for contract work in West Siberia was scheduled to grow twice as fast for oil as for gas from 1986 to 1990.[35] Yet seven major new trunk lines were planned for 1986–1990,[36] and gas output was scheduled to rise from 643 bcm in 1985 to 850 bcm in 1990. At this writing (spring 1989), the gas industry and its builders have been moving along well ahead of schedule: gas output grew by nearly 20 percent in 1986–1988 and at the present pace could hit 865 bcm by 1990. Thirty-four thousand kilometers of gas pipelines were added to the country's network in 1986–1988, well ahead of the rate of the last five-year plan.[37] But all this costs money. Since MGP is doing more and more of its work in

---

percent of total investment. *Narodnoe khoziaistvo SSSR za 70 let*, p. 332. In 1987 it remained at 73 percent (Goskomstat SSSR, *Kapital'noe stroitel'stvo SSSR* [Moscow, 1988], p. 69).

34 Planned investment for 1986 was 11.3 billion rubles (*Gazovaia promyshlennost'*, no. 12 [1985], p. 4), compared to a plan target of 10.7 billion for 1985 (*Gazovaia promyshlennost'*, no. 3 [1985], p. 4). *Narodnoe khoziaistvo SSSR* has unfortunately ceased reporting energy investment by sector. Beginning in 1986, it began reporting only a single aggregated number for the entire "energy complex," the definition of which has evidently also changed.

35 Investment in construction and assembly work (SMR) by MNGS in West Siberia was scheduled to grow from 15.2 billion in the Eleventh Plan to 23.9 in the Twelfth, or 60 percent, but the oil portion of that budget was planned to grow from 4.2 to 8.0 billion, or 90 percent. If one assumes that all of the remainder is allocated to gas work, then the gas portion was planned to grow from 11.0 billion in the Eleventh Plan to 15.9 billion in the Twelfth, or 45 percent. V. G. Chirskov, "Kursom intensifikatsii," *Stroitel'stvo truboprovodov*, no. 2 (1986), p. 4. This shift in part reflected a planned downgrading in the relative priority of pipeline construction, compared with the last five-year plan. According to the same source, the share of "above-ground" construction was to rise from 51 percent in 1985 to 65 percent in 1990.

36 The minister of MNGS said six (*Stroitel'stvo truboprovodov*, no. 2 [1986], p. 4), but he may have been counting the first Yamburg pipeline, begun in 1985, as part of the last five-year plan.

37 Data for 1986 come from *Narodnoe khoziaistvo SSSR za 70 let*, pp. 163 and 353, and for 1987 and 1988 from year-end reports in *Pravda*, 24 Jan. 1988 and 22 Jan. 1989. The target for 1986–1990 is 50,000 km, according to MNGS Minister V. S. Chernomyrdin, speaking at the World Gas Conference in Washington, D.C., June 1988.

permafrost zones, each new field and each new pipeline is bound to be more costly than the last.[38] Thus, to keep up with fast-rising marginal costs, gas investment must be growing at least as fast as that of the energy sector as a whole, but at this point further information is not available.

Official discretion on gas investment may be the result of new restrictions on the release of economic information adopted under Andropov, or it may indicate that the issue of investment remains as controversial and unsettled today as it was five and ten years ago. It is not yet possible to tell which. Therefore, in order to see the real direction of gas policy and evaluate its prospects, one must look deeper, at the level of implementation and the actual allocation of material resources and manpower.

Policy Issues and Potential Bottlenecks

Because it was launched so suddenly and with so little preparation, the gas campaign has suffered from many of the same symptoms of imbalance we observed in the case of oil. Several of these have been described in my earlier work on gas policy and will not be repeated here. This section will look at two further policy issues: gas transmission and the development of the Yamal Peninsula. Our aim is to establish the reasons for the imbalance and to evaluate its likely effects on gas costs and reliability in the near future.

Pipelines

Pipelines and transmission have been the headline stories of Soviet gas policy for the last fifteen years. Until the mid-1970s inadequate transmission capacity had been the chief constraint on the growth of the gas industry, and the cost of pipeline development had been the principal deterrent to the large-scale exploitation of West Siberian fields. By 1980 the situation had improved, but mainly because of imported pipe and equipment. Thus the spectacular expansion of the pipeline network

[38] Thus capital costs for transmission have almost doubled in the last decade, from 66 rubles per 1,000 cubic meters of transmission capacity in 1971–1975 to 121.3 rubles in 1981–1985. Krivoshein and Tugunov, *Magistral'nyi truboprovodnyi transport*, p. 10. This reflects the increasing distances over which gas is piped. Costs per unit of throughput (cubic meters × kilometers), in contrast, have steadily declined as a result of larger pipe diameters and more powerful compressors. In the Twelfth Plan, however, average distances will continue to increase, thus requiring more capital investment per unit of volume shipped.

[39] In early 1989 Goskomstat issued a press bulletin giving MGP investment in 1988 as 10.52 billion rubles. For the reasons given in note 23, it is not possible to evaluate this number without knowing what it includes.

announced for the first half of the 1980s struck most observers, including Soviet ones, as overambitious, especially the 1,420-millimeter large-diameter trunk lines scheduled to bring Siberian gas to the European USSR.

Not surprisingly, pipeline construction targets remained unstable in the first two years of the 1981–1985 campaign. Overall, the trend was toward lower numbers, as planners grappled with the realities of implementation. An initial goal of 50,000 kilometers of new trunk line, published in March 1981,[40] was cut to 38,000 by November;[41] and the targets for new 1,420-millimeter pipe dropped from 26,000 kilometers to the low 20s.[42] The initial plan to build seven major 1,420-millimeter lines from Urengoy was reduced to six.

Some of the instability was apparently due to differences between Siberian gas boosters and the pipeline builders (now led by the former first secretary of the Tiumen' Obkom, Boris Shcherbina), on the one hand, and the more conservative leadership of the Ministry of the Gas Industry, which was holding out for lower gas targets.[43] The Soviet agencies were also divided between two competing compressor technologies (this issue is discussed in Chapter 6) and over the routing of

[40] "Razvitie gazovoi promyshlennosti: obzor," *Ekonomicheskaia gazeta*, no. 13 (1981), p. 2.

[41] By the beginning of September 1981, *Pravda* began to use the figure 40,000 (6 Sept. 1981), and in October the new lower figure was confirmed in *Ekonomicheskaia gazeta* ("Razvitie truboprovodnogo transporta," no. 43 [October 1981], pp. 1–2).

[42] The initial figure of 26,000 km appeared in S. A. Orudzhev, "Zadachi rabotnikov gazovoi promyshlennosti na 1980 god," *Gazovaia promyshlennost'*, no. 2 (1980). It was cited also in an address by Iurii Baranovskii (until 1988 head of the Soviet gas export trading organization, Soiuzgazeksport), "Development of the Gas Industry of the Soviet Union and Possibilities of Increase in Exports of Natural Gas to Western Europe," paper delivered at the European Gas Conference, Oslo, Norway, 25 May 1981. The later figures can be found in "Razvitie truboprovodnogo transporta," *Ekonomicheskaia gazeta*, no. 43 (October 1981).

[43] Thus Gas Minister Dinkov, in August 1981, used the figure 19,000 km for the six major pipelines from Siberia. Dinkov, "Zveno energeticheskoi programmy." But as late as the winter of 1982 the MNGS house journal kept quoting the earlier, higher numbers. A. K. Dertsakian, "Tsentral'nye stroiki piatiletki," *Stroitel'stvo truboprovodov*, no. 2 (1982). Somewhat later Shcherbina boasted that the Soviet Union would not only complete the six pipelines called for in the plan by 1985 but would even build a seventh for good measure—thus also harking back to the original draft targets. *Financial Times*, 8 Sept. 1982, quoting a TASS release. Shcherbina then repeated the boast ("Glavnye magistrali toplivnoi energetiki," p. 7), and it was echoed by *Pravda*'s Tiumen' correspondent, V. Lisin ("Sever, kotoryi sogrevaet," *Pravda*, 25 Oct. 1982), and in another TASS release on 4 November 1982 (Foreign Broadcast Information Service, *Soviet Union Daily Report*, 5 Nov. 1982). MGP itself may have been internally divided on this question. At a fairly late date S. Kashirov, a deputy minister of gas with responsibility for pipelines, still used the higher figures for new trunk lines, thus echoing MNGS positions. "Chetkii ritm," *Sotsialisticheskaia industriia*, 27 Dec. 1981.

the new lines. For some years MGP officials had been split between a northern route and a southern one, each "represented" by a different design institute with competing northern and southern jurisdictions. According to a former Soviet gas economist, Gas Minister Orudzhev favored the northern route because it would be cheaper to build and to operate; his then first deputy, V. Dinkov, advocated the southern on the grounds that it would be more accessible for construction crews and supplies.[44] Eventually, the first of the six major trunk lines followed the northern route; but after Dinkov became minister, the remainder followed the southern.

What was not in question was the top priority of the core of the gas pipeline program, despite Brezhnev's death and the subsequent parade of three successors in less than three years. One of the main reasons, without a doubt, was the challenge of the American compressor embargo of 1981–1983. For three years gas pipelines held the front page of every Soviet newspaper, and the Kremlin's indignation over Washington's attempted leverage probably did more to resolve interagency disputes and overcome obstacles than any Soviet energy czar could have done. By the end of 1985 MNGS had met its most important targets: the total gas transmission network grew by 38,600 kilometers;[45] and on the all-important 1,420-millimeter trunk lines, MNGS laid over 20,000 kilometers of pipe, weighing 15 million tons, with a transmission capacity of 200 billion cubic meters a year.[46] Thus over the last decade the length of 1,420-millimeter large-diameter gas pipeline in service in the Soviet network has grown strikingly (table 5.4).

But although MNGS achieved miracles in laying pipe, it was less successful with the compressor stations. It took only six months on the average to lay 100 kilometers of pipe, but it took seventeen to twenty months to complete a compressor station. Thus by late 1985 the compressor stations for the Urengoy-Uzhgorod export line were still not finished, even though pipe laying had been completed two years before,[47] and it was clear that the compressor stations for the later lines of the 1981–1985 plan would not be completed until well into the second half of the 1980s. If one accepts the ministry's official claims, by the end of the five-year plan in 1985 MNGS had installed about 86 percent of

[44] Raykher, "Decision-Making."

[45] B. L. Krivoshein, "Truboprovodnyi transport v stranakh mira," in Vsesoiuznyi institut nauchnoi i tekhnicheskoi informatsii, *Itogi nauki i tekhniki: seriia Truboprovodnyi transport* (Moscow: 1986), vol. 11, p. 5. I am grateful to Robert Campbell for bringing this source to my attention.

[46] Interview with Deputy Minister of MNGS G. Sudobin, "Vperedi—Yamburg," *Sotsialisticheskaia industriia*, 19 May 1985.

[47] "Kontrasty trassy," *Sotsialisticheskaia industriia*, 20 Aug. 1985.

TABLE 5.4
Large-Diameter Pipe in the Soviet Gas Network, 1972–1985 (1420 mm)

	Length (kilometers)	*Percentage of Total Trunk Line Length*
1972	NA	1.2
1975	3,630	3.7
1976	4,320	4.2
1977	NA	5.9
1981	15,990	11.8
1982	20,650	14.3
1983	26,370	17.0
1984	31,170	18.9
1985	35,330	20.2

SOURCES: Krivoshein, "Truboprovodnyi transport"; Campbell, *Soviet Energy Technologies*; and Sedykh and Kuchin, *Upravlenie nauchno-tekhnicheskim progressom*, p. 21.

the new compressor capacity originally assigned to it in 1981. Whereas the five-year plan targets in 1981 called for 25,000 megawatts of new compressor capacity, the final figure came closer to 21,500 (table 5.5).[48] But most of the shortfall was concentrated in the six 1,420-millimeter large-diameter trunk lines, for which compressor capacity was originally planned at about 18,000 megawatts[49] but probably ended up at less than 15,000.[50]

To make up the deficit, MNGS was obliged to resort to some shortcuts. One of these brought major savings: MNGS built most of the

[48] The five-year plan figure appears in "Razvitie truboprovodnogo transporta," *Ekonomicheskaia gazeta*, no. 43 (October 1981). The actual figure for 1981–1985 is derived from information in Krivoshein, "Truboprovodnyi transport v stranakh mira," p. 9, that total installed capacity increased by 2.2 times in 1981–1985. Since total installed capacity in 1980 is reported by Sedykh and Kuchin, *Upravlenie nauchno-tekhnicheskim progressom*, p. 10, to be 18,000 megawatts, the 1985 capacity is 39,600. (A small portion of the shortfall may be due to retirement of older compressor capacity.)

[49] The only plan figure I have found for the six Siberian trunk lines is "more than 20,000 megawatts" (*Krasnaia zvezda*, 16 Feb. 1982), but that number appears to assume seven lines instead of six. In that case 18,000 appears closer.

[50] The final installed capacity is given in Sudobin, "Vperedi—Yamburg," although I am skeptical that the MNGS numbers reflect compressor capacity actually available at the end of 1985.

TABLE 5.5
Expansion of Compressor Capacity for the Gas Pipeline Network, 1970–1985 (megawatts)

	Total Capacity	*Capacity per 100 km*
1970	3,400	5.2
1975	8,230	8.3
1980	18,000	12.7
1985	39,600	21.5

SOURCES: Sedykh and Kuchin, *Upravlenie nauchno-tekhnicheskim progressom*, p. 10; Krivoshein, "Truboprovodnyi transport," p. 9. For 1980, Krivoshein and Tugunov, *Magistral'nyi truboprovodnyi transport*, p. 16, give an estimate of 12.9.

Siberian portion of all six trunk lines along a single corridor, thus making maximum use of scarce manpower and infrastructure and allowing the operators to pool compressor capacity.[51] Other shortcuts were more costly. Concentrating its resources on the large-diameter trunk lines, MNGS pulled resources away from other major programs, such as the pipe laying for gaslift systems in the oil fields, piping for gas-gathering networks at Urengoy, spur lines to bring gas to power plants to displace fuel oil, and gas treatment plants to purify the raw gas before shipment.

The most important compromise was to distribute available compressor capacity evenly throughout the trunk-line system and thus to begin operation without the usual spare capacity. MNGS also spaced its stations farther apart than the customary 100 kilometers. Through such measures it was able to bring each new line up to capacity within a year after pipe laying was completed.

But the gas industry has had to pay a price, as we shall see, in diminished reliability and efficiency. Soviet gas pipelines have long suffered from low efficiency and reliability. In the late 1970s Robert

[51] B. Trofimov, an official of the Tiumen' obkom, claims this idea originated with the Tiumen' Party authorities. Trofimov, "Formirovanie tiumenskogo neftegazovogo kompleksa," *Planovoe khoziaistvo*, no. 9 (1981), pp. 84–88. A. N. Kolotilin mentions the same initiative, but not the role of the Party. Kolotilin, "Zapadnaia Sibir': gazovye magistrali piatiletki," *Gazovaia promyshlennost'*, no. 11 (1981).

Campbell diagnosed the network's problems as due to a combination of breaks and leaks in the line pipe, fouling with condensate and water, inefficient and unreliable compressors, and inadequate storage at the delivery end of the line. (This last item is discussed in Chapter 7).[52]

The available evidence suggests that, if anything, the problems have worsened over the last decade. First, Soviet sources report that in the mid-1980s the 1,420-millimeter trunk lines experienced about twenty-eight stoppages per year, each one averaging over one hundred hours.[53] How much gas production is lost depends on what reserve compressor capacity is available and how many parallel trunk lines run alongside the nonworking one. According to Soviet calculations, if one assumes for each compressor station four working compressors and two in reserve, then the overall loss of gas output from stoppages should be no more than 2 to 2.5 percent of total deliveries. But if each compressor station has four working compressors and only one in reserve, then the shortfall rises to more than 8 percent. This is likely to have been the case recently, in view of the industry's lag in installing compressors on the main trunk lines.

Second, it appears plausible that the trunk lines are fouled, because the rate of installation of gas treatment plants at Urengoy, which strip the raw gas of water and gas liquids before it leaves the field, also lagged behind the plan. Each of the fourteen plants working there by 1985 was one or two years late in coming on line; therefore a certain portion of the output from Urengoy, the largest Soviet field, has probably been shipped raw. By the beginning of the current five-year plan (1986–1990), Urengoy was producing around 300 bcm per year, but gas treatment capacity was unlikely to have been more than about 220–240 bcm, so the untreated portion shipped through the lines was on the order of 60–80 bcm a year and probably growing.[54]

[52] Campbell, *Soviet Energy Technologies*, pp. 204–209.

[53] Krivoshein and Tugunov, *Magistral'nyi truboprovodnyi transport*, p. 227. This figure is derived from the information that the frequency of outages "at the present time" is 8×10^{-4}/km-yr. Since the total length of 1,420-mm gas pipeline reached 35,300 km in 1985, the total number of stoppages was therefore about 28.

[54] The estimate of 14 treatment plants may be generous. The Soviet press reported that an eleventh plant began operation in the fall of 1985. *Izvestiia*, 22 Oct. 1985. Soviet reporters spoke of a "chronic lag" in this department (*Pravda*, 21 Jan. 1985), and there were no further reports of new plants until the summer of 1986, when a local gas official spoke of a "fifteenth" plant under construction at Urengoy. M. Umanskii, "Direktor ne terpel fanfar," *Sotsialisticheskaia industriia*, 29 Aug. 1986.

The average capacity of gas treatment plants at Urengoy was given in 1983 as 14 bcm per unit. V. Filatov and R. Saifulin, "Yamburg—brat Urengoia," *Ekonomicheskaia gazeta*, no. 46 (1983), p. 9. Assuming at a rough guess that units 10 through 14 averaged 20 bcm/year, total gas treatment capacity at Urengoy may have been 220 bcm/year.

Reliability problems in transmission add to the cost of natural gas. Soviet calculations suggest that short-term interruptions in gas supply cost as much as 6,000 rubles per 1,000 cubic meters in lost production in the heavy and electrical machine-building sectors, and between 1,000 and 3,000 rubles in other major branches of heavy industry. At those rates, even the 2 percent shortfalls mentioned earlier would inflict billions of rubles of losses on gas consumers. This problem could grow far worse if recent Soviet reports of problems with compressors (discussed in Chapter 6) presage further declines in reliability in the years ahead.[55]

Thus, in the end, the skeptics of 1980–1981 were both right and wrong. Like those who predicted a peak in oil output for 1980, they underestimated the capacity of the Soviet system to mobilize its forces and throw them into the breach. But just as in the Siberian oil fields, the price of near-term success was long-term imbalance. The gas industry must now spend money to offset the side effects of the campaign, principally in its transmission network. But in addition, the earlier imbalance forces the campaign itself to continue, as the industry moves north into the Yamal Peninsula.

Decisionmaking over Yamburg and the Yamal Peninsula

The future of the Soviet gas industry in the 1990s and beyond lies in the far north of Tiumen' Province, beyond the Arctic Circle, at Yamburg and the other giants of the Yamal Peninsula. Though not so large as Urengoy, these are formidable fields by any other standard. The most recent published Soviet estimates, from 1980 (see table 5.6), are certain to have grown, as more reserves have been discovered.

The important point about these new fields is that as one travels the 530 kilometers north from Urengoy to Yamburg one crosses an invisible climatic and geological divide. Occasional patches of permafrost to the south become an unbroken expanse to the north; gravel and stone for roads become scarce; and the ice-free season for river shipping shrinks to two months or less. South of the line, 2–10 percent of all working days are lost because of weather conditions (work officially stops, under Soviet rules, when the temperature drops to −40° and the wind speed rises to 15 meters per second); north of the line, lost workdays become far more frequent under continuous gales and mercury readings as low as −60°.[56] As a Tiumen Party official once re-

[55] Krivoshein and Tugunov, *Magistral'nyi truboprovodnyi transport*, p. 232.

[56] A. V. Epishev, "The Impact of Geographical Conditions and the Need for Environmental Protection in the Development of the Natural Gas Industry in the Northern USSR," *Izvestiia AN SSSR* (seriia geograficheskaia), no. 4 (1979), pp. 52–63; translated in *Soviet Geography* 22, no. 2 (February 1981), pp. 67–80.

TABLE 5.6
Proven and Probable Reserves ($A + B + C_1$) of the Major Siberian Gas Fields, 1980 (trillions of cubic meters)

Urengoy	7.8
Yamburg	4.1
Zapoliarnoe	2.6
Bovanenko	2.2
Kharasavei	0.8

SOURCE: Zhabrev, ed., *Gazovye.*

marked, Urengoy is "little flowers" by comparison with Yamburg, and the Yamal fields to the northwest are even worse.[57]

This divide has important consequences for decisionmaking. It implies that the gas industry must make major technological and logistical adjustments, not simply to be efficient but to make any headway at all. Innovations that have been marooned for years in the bureaucracy now become urgent imperatives: pipelines must be cooled and buildings must be raised off the permafrost so as not to melt the frozen soil beneath; equipment must be adapted to the cold; large buildings must be shipped in prefabricated modules. Yet the story of development at Yamburg so far is a familiar tale: the adaptations are not ready, work has lagged behind schedule, and bureaucratic pressure for fast results is mounting. It is most unlikely that these problems will actually constrict the growth of gas production. The gas industry and its supporting ministries will conquer Yamburg and the Yamal Peninsula as they did Urengoy. But if they do so through essentially the same brute-force approach, the new Siberian gas will be far more costly than the old.

The lag at Yamburg originated in bureaucratic battles that began in the 1970s and continued into the early 1980s. At issue was the proper sequence of development in north Tiumen'. Should the Gas Ministry concentrate on Urengoy or press on right away to the more northerly fields, Yamburg and Kharasavei? The initial sequence of gas development envisioned by ministry planners in the late 1970s called for more or less simultaneous development of Urengoy and the more northerly fields of the Yamal Peninsula, beginning with Yamburg. (This proposal may have been a last leftover of earlier hopes that Western capital could

[57] "Urengoi—eto eshche tsvetochki." Altunin, "Strategiiu vybrat' segodnia."

be enlisted in Siberia to develop LNG facilities served by the more northerly fields.[58]) In early negotiations with the West Europeans in 1980 over a new East-West pipeline, it was initially understood that the gas would be drawn from Yamburg, and the project was commonly referred to in the Western press as the "Yamal" pipeline.[59] In the fall of 1980, Soviet press articles spoke of reaching an output level of 100 bcm a year from Yamburg by 1985.[60]

But during 1980 Yamburg faded from the front page while development targets for Urengoy grew steadily. In February 1981, when Brezhnev unveiled his gas program, he mentioned only Urengoy; and in August 1981 MGP announced officially that Yamburg would take second place to Urengoy.[61] The final version of the Eleventh Plan, adopted in November 1981, called for all six of the trunk lines scheduled for construction to originate from Urengoy, including the export line to Western Europe. Yamburg was zeroed out of the annual plans of both MGP and MNGS for 1981, and the Ministry of Transportation Construction (Mintransstroi), though it had been instructed to begin building docking facilities to serve the field, failed to get started.[62] For the moment, Yamburg was going nowhere.

Several factors appear to explain the postponement. Siberian gas boosters, and especially the Tiumen' Party obkom under Shcherbina and Bogomiakov, had long argued for a southern strategy based on Urengoy, aimed primarily at domestic markets. The argument that Yamburg gas had priority because it was reserved for export, they dismissed with a snort. ("What?" exclaimed the Tiumen' Party secretary responsible for gas, "Does it have a different smell?"[63]) Their most forceful argument was that, because of the exceptionally difficult conditions in the north, gas from Yamburg and Yamal would cost a fortune.[64] Economic studies conveying the same message were circulating at least as early as 1979,[65] and they were evidently used to good effect

[58] Initial Soviet interest in an American proposal to ship West Siberian gas to the United States is described in Chapter 8.

[59] Strictly speaking, Yamburg is located on the Taz Peninsula, on the east bank of the Ob' estuary, while the Yamal Peninsula lies on the west bank. But in a looser sense the entire region can be referred to by the name of Yamal, since it lies in the administrative entity known as the Yamalo-Nenetskii okrug.

[60] "Gazovyi kompleks," *Sotsialisticheskaia industriia*, 19 Sept. 1980.

[61] Dinkov, "Zveno energeticheskoi programmy."

[62] V. Lisin, "Gaz Sibiri," *Pravda*, 15 June 1981.

[63] Altunin, "Strategiiu vybrat' segodnia," pp. 17–18.

[64] According to Altunin, "Strategiiu vybrat' segodnia," every increment of new capacity of 35 bcm/year from north Yamal would cost 1.5 billion rubles more than the equivalent volume taken from Urengoy.

[65] Epishev, "Impact of Geographical Conditions."

by a contingent of "south-firsters" inside MGP, which evidently included then First Deputy Minister Dinkov.[66] When Dinkov succeeded Gas Minister Orudzhev in early 1981, he brought with him a new generation committed to big gas.

But the really decisive factor was probably the Kremlin's decision to launch the gas campaign. Suddenly the Gas Ministry, which had been arguing for a more leisurely pace, was told to increase annual gas output by 200 bcm in five years. Only one field could do the job: Urengoy.

Development of Urengoy had been approved only four years before, in early 1977, and commercial production had begun in the spring of 1978.[67] Initial growth plans were almost leisurely. In May 1980 *Pravda* reported that Urengoy would "eventually" reach a peak output rate of 180 bcm a year.[68] But the official targets soon began to mushroom, recalling the escalation of output goals at Samotlor in the 1970s. By September 1980 the "eventual" target had reached 200–250 bcm,[69] and over the winter the eventual target became "the 1985 target" and continued escalating, from 250 bcm by March 1981[70] to 270 by April 1981.[71] By October 1981 one could find unofficial statements that implied a 1985 target of as much as 275 bcm.[72]

Local gas men were not quite so bullish on Urengoy, again recalling the reluctance of oil men at Samotlor to be stampeded by the push for higher targets. The head of gas development operations at Urengoy, I. S. Nikonenko, estimated in May 1981 that Urengoy would reach 250 bcm only by 1990; and he did not predict annual increments greater than 25 bcm,[73] whereas only two months before *Ekonomicheskaia gazeta* had published targets that implied growth from Urengoy of 40 bcm a year.[74]

But all agreed that Urengoy could not continue to play the same role in the second half of the 1980s and beyond; therefore the postpone-

[66] Dinkov, "Gazovaia promyshlennost' na marshe piatiletki," hints as much.

[67] L. Kostylev and V. Noskov, "Pis'ma iz Urengoia," *Sotsialisticheskaia industriia*, 22 and 23 Jan. 1980.

[68] Lisin and Parfenov, "Energiia tiumenskogo severa."

[69] "Gazovyi kompleks," *Sotsialisticheskaia industriia*, 19 Sept. 1980.

[70] B. P. Orlov, "Razvitie ekonomiki Sibiri na otdel'nykh etapakh sotsialisticheskogo stroitel'stva," *Izvestiia sibirskogo otdeleniia AN SSSR* (seriia obshchestvennykh nauk), no. 11 (1982), pp. 61–70.

[71] This was the figure used by Baranovskii, "Development of the Gas Industry," who in all such figures was echoing Orudzhev, "Zadachi rabotnikov gazovoi promyshlennosti."

[72] Lisin, "Gaz Sibiri."

[73] A. Gramolin, "Chas Urengoia," *Komsomol'skaia Pravda*, 7 and 9 May 1981. For a profile of Nikonenko, see V. Lisin, "Zhemchuzhina tundry," *Pravda*, 6 June 1982.

[74] "Razvitie gazovoi promyshlennosti," *Ekonomicheskaia gazeta*, no. 13 (March 1981), p. 2.

ment of Yamburg could only be brief. Within a year the debate over timing, priorities, and strategy began anew. Cautiously criticizing the Tiumen' obkom's earlier opposition to moving to the northern fields, a *Sovetskaia Rossiia* correspondent in early 1982 lined up a string of testimonials from local gas experts, emphasizing the dangers of ***not*** making the move. He concluded, "If we're going to crack the Yamburg nut, we have to at least put it into our mouths."[75]

At this point, in 1982, there was clearly a wide gap between official plans and reality. The Gas Ministry's five-year plans still called for commercial output to begin at Yamburg by 1984 and to reach a level of 36 bcm by 1986.[76] MNGS still intended to build one and perhaps two 56-inch lines from Yamburg southward during the Eleventh Plan, to connect with the network leading out of Urengoy.[77] But gas men and pipeline builders were reluctant to get started because they were already finding it difficult to meet their current targets at Urengoy. Although 3.5 billion rubles had reportedly been provided for Yamburg in the Eleventh Plan, Gosplan showed no great sense of urgency either.[78] And without pressure from Gosplan, all the participating agencies had an open invitation to delay.

Finally, in the winter of 1982 MGP took the plunge, sending a team overland to Yamburg to establish the first base camp and begin digging an access canal to it from the future dock site on the Ob' estuary, four kilometers away.[79] But MGP was alone. Mintransstroi, having failed to begin building docks in 1981, delayed again in 1982, despite public exhortation from Gas Minister Dinkov.[80] Transportation construction crews argued that local river fleet officials had refused to approve the designs for the docks.[81] This was a crucial source of delay, since the most ready access to the site would be by water. During the first year, 1982, only 20,000 tons of supplies were unloaded, using makeshift facilities.[82]

[75] I. Ognev, "The Road to Yamburg," *Sovietskaia Rossiia*, 13 Mar. 1982; translated in *Current Digest of the Soviet Press* 39, no. 9 (1982). Under Brezhnev, we should remember, it was highly unusual for a local correspondent to criticize a Party official directly, and Ognev does not. He refers to Tiumen' Energy Secretary Altunin only indirectly as the man who four years earlier had been director of the Gas Ministry's agency in Tiumen' (Tiumengazprom).

[76] Ognev, "Road to Yamburg."

[77] Dertsakian, "Tsentral'nye stroiki piatiletki."

[78] Ognev, "Road to Yamburg."

[79] A chronology of the first three years appears in *Ekonomika i organizatsiia promyshlennogo proizvodstva* (*EKO*), no. 4 (1985), pp. 48–49. For a detailed description, see L. Levitskii et al., "Mladshii brat Urengoia," *Izvestiia*, 31 May 1985.

[80] Dinkov, "Gazovaia promyshlennost' na marshe piatiletki," p. 3.

[81] Ognev, "Road to Yamburg."

[82] *Pravda* editorial, 6 June 1985.

Access via road and rail was likewise held up. A project for a 183-kilometer road from Medvezh'e was paralyzed by disputes until 1984 or 1985, partly because of struggles for precedence between the Nadym and Urengoy gas organizations (the former having jurisdiction over Medvezh'e): both claimed the honor of being the main support point for Yamburg. Nadym had been the initial choice, but the issue was finally decided in favor of Urengoy. Only then did construction begin.[83]

A similar battle took place over a proposed 530-kilometer railroad line from Novyi Urengoy to Yamburg. For three years Gosplan's transportation department, which had consistently opposed further railroad building in north Tiumen', held out against the new line, while Gosplan's Tiumen' office argued for it, until finally the project was approved by higher authority in late 1983.[84] Construction of the new line began in 1984 but moved more slowly than previous lines had, because of the exceptionally difficult terrain and climate.[85] As a result of these delays, the supply strategy for Yamburg was thrown off. Until the road and railroad were completed sometime in 1987, the river port in the Ob' estuary was the sole major delivery point, whereas under the original plan it was supposed to handle only about half of the supply traffic.[86]

Meanwhile, delays continued to plague the river port. Of the 2 million tons of supplies planned for 1983, only about 50,000 were threaded through the docks, then still at an early stage of construction.[87] In 1984 there was only slight improvement: the plan still called

[83] The initial designation of Nadym was reported in V. Strizhev, "Shkola khoziaistvovaniia," *Izvestiia*, 15 Feb. 1982, the switch to Urengoy in Levitskii, "Mladshii brat Urengoia." Disputes over the proposed road from Nadym to Yamburg are described in Filatov and Saifulin, "Yamburg—brat Urengoia"; the construction of the new road from Urengoy was reported in *Ekonomicheskaia gazeta*, no. 41 (1985).

[84] Iu. I. Topchev, "Intensifikatsiia v soiuze s ekologiei," *Ekonomika i organizatsiia promyshlennogo proizvodstva* (*EKO*), no. 4 (1985), p. 41. Four years earlier, the same official had reported that the Urengoy-Yamburg line was dead. "Problemy gazovogo kompleksa," *Ekonomicheskaia gazeta*, no. 24 (1981). As late as the spring of 1983 the head of the Urengoy gas organization, I. S. Nikonenko, told reporters that there would be no rail line to Yamburg. *Ekonomika i organizatsiia promyshlennogo proizvodstva* (*EKO*), no. 5 (1983), p. 55. Although Gosplan headquarters in Moscow opposed the railroad, Gosplan's territorial office in Tiumen' (whose history is related in Chapter 9) lobbied in favor of it. Filatov and Saifulin, "Yamburg—brat Urengoia."

[85] *Pravda*, 1 June 1985, reported that 5 kilometers and one bridge had been completed. An interview with the minister of transportation construction in the fall of 1985 made no claims of progress. *Ekonomicheskaia gazeta*, no. 41 (1985), p. 10.

[86] Filatov and Saifulin, "Yamburg—brat Urengoia." Supplying Yamburg by helicopter is said to be exceptionally difficult because of bad weather. As of early 1986, there was no airport for fixed-wing craft, although there was a plan to develop one. *Sotsialisticheskaia industriia*, 7 Jan. 1986.

[87] The 2 million ton estimate comes from an interview with the chief engineer at the

for 2 million tons, but only 250,000 could be unloaded.[88] In the summer of 1984 the USSR Council of Ministers, alarmed by the slow progress, stepped in with a decree declaring Yamburg the Gas Ministry's top priority for the Twelfth Five-Year Plan and prescribing a series of special measures to improve supply for the site.[89] Immediately after the 1984 decree MGP and MNGS began to give more priority to Yamburg, beginning with the creation of special agencies.[90]

At this point, the beginning of commercial development had slipped to 1986,[91] but there were still further delays in store. By the beginning of 1985 only "a few tens of millions of rubles" had actually been invested in Urengoy, out of the roughly one billion required to launch commercial production[92] and out of the total of four billion planned for Yamburg to 1990.[93] The rest of the year brought little improvement. The first drilling brigade, which had arrived in 1983, took ten weeks (three times longer than planned) to drill the first hole. By the end of 1985 it had managed only twelve wells, and drilling was proceeding at about one-tenth the planned rate, even with the help of a second brigade, which finally arrived in the summer.[94]

When General Secretary Gorbachev toured the Siberian oil and gas fields in September 1985, he had especially harsh words for the agencies in charge of construction at Yamburg:

> Every time new tasks arise in the development of the oil and gas complex, we are forced to take emergency, firefighting measures and to allocate a lot of extra money. And now it's happening again: when we need large prefab units to develop the gas industry beyond the Arctic Circle on an accelerated basis, MNGS turns out once again to be unprepared.[95]

What Gorbachev was referring to was the single largest headache facing

---

Yamburg site, G. A. Shemraev, "Ia znaiu—gorod budet," *Ekonomika i organizatsiia promyshlennogo proizvodstva* (*EKO*), no. 2 (1984), p. 149.

[88] Filatov and Saifulin, "Yamburg—brat Urengoia."

[89] *Izvestiia*, 23 Aug. 1984.

[90] In September 1984 MGP created Yamburggazdobycha to handle gas development and production. Its counterpart construction contractor, Glavyamburgneftegazstroi, subordinated to MNGS, was established in November 1984. Topchev, "Intensifikatsiia v soiuze s ekologiei," pp. 42–43.

[91] V. A. Dinkov, "Effektivnost' ispol'zovaniia gaza," *Ekonomicheskaia gazeta*, no. 12 (1984), p. 2.

[92] Lisin, "Gazovyi potentsial."

[93] Shemraev, "Ia znaiu—gorod budet," p. 151.

[94] Iu. Belanov and V. Zhiliakov, "Truden put' k zapoliarnomu gazu," *Sotsialisticheskaia industriia*, 7 Jan. 1986.

[95] *Pravda*, 7 Sept. 1985.

builders at Yamburg: how to deliver and assemble the seven immense gas treatment units planned for the field. Conventional Soviet construction techniques were out of the question; the only possible course was to ship prefabricated modules. Each gas treatment plant at Yamburg is designed with an annual capacity of 28 bcm (versus 7 bcm at Medvezh'e and 14 at Urengoy),[96] and consists of twenty-three modular pieces, each weighing between 150 and 300 tons. These had to be floated on pontoons down the Ob' River from a staging site near Tiumen' City[97] to the docks serving Yamburg, then mounted on air cushions and towed twenty-eight kilometers to the field.[98]

The initial plan was to have the first two plants assembled and running by the end of 1985, but the final decision in favor of the prefab approach was not made until the beginning of 1983,[99] and two years later the first prefab pieces were still being assembled and shipped from staging points in southern Tiumen'. The pontoons were in short supply, and not all the modules could be sent off before ice closed the river in the fall of 1985.[100] The ones that arrived had to be dragged across the ice to the site because the air cushions still existed only on paper.[101] The first plant was completed in the summer of 1986, the second one in 1987,[102] and a third began processing gas in early 1988.[103]

The gas treatment plants were not the only problem demanding new approaches; the harsh conditions of Yamburg required adaptations at every turn. Cement froze in the mixers and had to be shot through with steam as it turned. Pipelines required 300 tons of reinforced concrete "pins" every 100 kilometers to keep the pipe sections from swimming on the permafrost. Wells had to be sunk in clusters. Much more automation was required throughout the site.[104] Some of these innovations required imported equipment. For example, it was essential to refrig-

[96] Filatov and Saifulin, "Yamburg—brat Urengoia."

[97] Iu. Siniakov, "Yamburg—nachalo novoi gazovoi magistrali," *Sovetskaia Latviia*, 25 Jan. 1985. Seventy to 80 percent of the assembly work was done at this site. *Gazovaia promyshlennost'*, no. 4 (1985), p. 5.

[98] V. Kotov, "Na Yamburge rabochaia pogoda," *Pravda*, 19 Jan. 1986.

[99] *Ekonomika i organizatsiia promyshlennogo proizvodstva* (*EKO*), no. 11 (1983), p. 64.

[100] Interview with Iu. Topchev, "Ispytyvaet Zapoliar'e," *Sotsialisticheskaia industriia*, 10 Sept. 1985.

[101] Topchev, "Intensifikatsiia v soiuze s ekologiei," p. 38.

[102] G. Bazhutin, "Pochemu zastrial karavan," *Sotsialisticheskaia industriia*, 16 July 1986.

[103] "Gazovyi 'konveier,' " *Pravda*, 30 Jan. 1988. By mid-1989 a fourth plant had begun operation and a fifth and sixth were under construction.

[104] For details, see B. D. Batozskii and N. G. Portianko, "Yamburg—zapoliarnyi region gazovoi promyshlennosti," *Gazovaia promyshlennost'*, no. 6 (1985), pp. 5–7.

erate the gas in the pipelines, to prevent the permafrost from melting under the heat of the compressed gas. In the northern part of Urengoy, where such cooling was also required, the Soviets bought equipment from a French firm, Sofregaz.[105] Officials at Yamburg had expressed the "hope" that a Soviet model would be used at Yamburg;[106] but Soviet efforts had been spotty in the past, and French equipment was used at Yamburg as well.

As a result of the cumulative disputes and delays at Yamburg, the start of commercial output was pushed back from 1984 to 1987 (although a symbolic amount began flowing in 1986). Once output began, it also grew more slowly than industry planners had anticipated. Whereas Urengoy took seven years to reach its planned peak (that is, 1978–1985), Yamburg was supposed to achieve the same stage in only four.[107] But by early 1985 local officials were beginning to speak again of seven or even eight years. During his trip to Siberia in the fall of 1985, Gorbachev still forecast that Yamburg would supply all of the increase in Soviet gas output in the second half of the 1980s,[108] implying an output level of about 200 bcm a year by 1990, and at this writing that is still the official goal.[109] But by the spring of 1986 newspaper accounts retreated to formulas like "practically all"[110] or "most" of the increment.[111] In 1987 Yamburg produced 28 bcm, suggesting that it is unlikely to reach more than 150 bcm a year by 1990. The governing constraint is probably not pipeline capacity, since the current five-year plan calls for six large-diameter trunk lines from Yamburg by 1990, and there is no reason to doubt MNGS's ability to build them (although compressor capacity is another matter). Rather, as we have seen, the main problem is site development, especially the installation of gas-processing capacity. Still, Yamburg is now beginning to play its assigned role of supplying the main increment to Soviet gas production, but about three years behind schedule.

In the meantime, the gas industry had to find output increases of 40–50 bcm a year from some other source. That meant forcing output at Urengoy. Instead of a peak output of 250–270 bcm, as originally anticipated, Urengoy has already been pushed beyond 325 bcm and

[105] A. Kuvshinnikov, "Kholodil'nik dlia vechnoi merzloty," *Izvestiia*, 13 May 1986.

[106] Shemraev, "Ia znaiu—gorod budet," p. 153.

[107] Siniakov, "Yamburg—nachalo novoi gazovoi magistrali."

[108] Gorbachev, speech in Tiumen', *Pravda*, 7 Sept. 1985.

[109] V. S. Chernomyrdin, minister of MNGS, speaking at the World Gas Conference, Washington, D.C., June 1988.

[110] Belanov and Zhiliakov, "Truden put' k zapoliarnomu gazu."

[111] Iu. Perepletkin, "Pogoda na zavtra," *Izvestiia*, 11 Feb. 1986.

may be forced higher still.[112] What would be the consequences of pushing Urengoy to as much as 400 bcm a year or more? The Soviet press has occasionally speculated that the results might be similar to those at the supergiant oil field Samotlor, which was damaged by the excessive demands placed on it. Indeed, the history of dire predictions goes back to 1982, when *Pravda* first began denouncing the practice of forcing production at Urengoy.[113] Sound strategy would call for the developers to sink wells along the entire width of the field; but because well drilling has been lagging, they have been working a corridor only 8 to 12 kilometers wide, tapping the richest part of the field. Coming back later to work the neglected "shoulders" will be difficult and inefficient. Observers warned that the combination of forcing the output of existing wells and restricting development to the richest middle corridor would exhaust Urengoy prematurely.

Western gas experts, however, point out that gas fields, as a general rule, are less delicate than oil fields and are not as easily damaged by overly rapid production. There is no particular technical reason why the field's shoulders cannot be developed later; the principal consequence of above-plan production is simply that Urengoy's reserves will be used up earlier. If that is correct, then the gas industry's present approach, however unintended at the outset, may not in fact be irrational. Soviet critics apparently disagree, insisting that accelerated production at Urengoy will cut total recovery.[114]

What worries the planners more about Urengoy is whether the gas industry can muster enough drilling brigades to maintain the pace required there. Development drilling has been a bottleneck at Urengoy from the beginning, partly because the productivity of Siberian drilling brigades in the gas industry is much lower than that of brigades in the oil industry.[115] Commercial speeds have stagnated since the early 1980s, so increases in development meterage can be achieved only by sending in more drillers. This should not be a fundamental problem, since gas drilling in Tiumen' still accounts for only about one-fifth of the industry total.[116] But the gas industry may hesitate to transfer drillers to Siberia because they may be bid away by the oil industry,

[112] In 1988 Urengoy produced 325 bcm. *Soviet Geography* 30, no. 4 (April 1989), p. 317.

[113] V. Lisin and V. Parfenov, "Zhemchuzhina tundry," *Pravda*, 6 June 1982.

[114] Tyshliar and Gasparian, "Ne nado verit' v mif o 'deshevom gaze'."

[115] For details, see Gustafson, *Soviet Gas Campaign*.

[116] Gas drilling statistics, unfortunately, are not easy to pin down. In 1985 MGP drilling (exploratory and development combined) was about 2.3 million meters. (According to *Gazovaia promyshlennost'*, no. 3 [1985], p. 4, the 1985 plan target was 2.5 million.

whose drilling volume in Siberia is over thirty times that of the gas industry, mostly concentrated in more southerly and better settled areas.

What do these problems add up to? It is unlikely that the gas industry will experience fundamental problems at Urengoy or elsewhere for another decade because the fields involved are so large. The real message of the delays at Yamburg applies to the mid-1990s, and it can be summed up as follows. The gas fields beyond the Arctic Circle represent an enormous leap in difficulty, to which the gas industry must respond soon with improved technology and management.[117] After Yamburg, the going will get even tougher. For example, Bovanenko, the next field in line after Yamburg,[118] floods regularly to a depth of 1.5 to 2 meters. For lack of suitable gravel and rock for roads and drilling islands, developers must bring in 50 million cubic meters of foundation from 400 kilometers away or develop a synthetic mesh to do the job instead. Compressor stations should be located four times farther apart than they are now, which will call for correspondingly higher transmission pressures. Permanent settlements for workers will be out of the question; all labor will have to be flown in and out. Right now MGP is far from being able to meet these challenges. Yamburg is a warning that has not yet been heeded.

The basic reason is familiar. The pressure for immediate growth has forced the gas industry to concentrate on near-term targets and to push more distant ones into the background. The postponement of Yamburg in 1980–1981 and the slowness of its revival in 1982–1984 may have been worsened by the political turmoil of three successions in the Kremlin, plus two at the top of MGP and one in MNGS.[119] The abundance of Soviet gas resources is so great that gas men can recoup

---

Assuming a fulfillment rate of 93 percent—roughly the record of the previous two years—gives a result of 2.3 million.) For 1985 the actual gas drilling record in Tiumen' (Glavtiumengazprom only) was 0.493 million meters. *Gazovaia promyshlennost'*, no. 2 (1986), p. 6.

[117] See P. Borodavkin, "Trudnyi gaz Iamala," *Izvestiia*, 4 May 1986. According to Prime Minister N. I. Ryzhkov, speaking in Tiumen' in May 1988, the plans adopted in 1986 for new engineering approaches and technology for the Yamal offensive were in disarray by 1988. Ryzhkov, "Razvitiiu Zapadnoi Sibiri—sozidatel'naia energiiu perestroiki," *Pravda*, 15 May 1988.

[118] Bovanenko is expected to begin commercial production in 1991. Interview with Gas Minister V. S. Chernomyrdin, *Gazovaia promyshlennost'*, no. 4 (1988), pp. 2–4.

[119] The late S. A. Orudzhev was replaced by V. I. Dinkov in 1981; then in 1985 Dinkov became minister of oil and was succeeded by V. S. Chernomyrdin, who had been chief of gas operations in Tiumen'. At MNGS, B. Ye. Shcherbina became deputy prime minister in January 1984 and was followed by his former first deputy, V. G. Chirskov.

their mistakes by forcing production at existing fields. But the implication is that costs will rise rapidly once they finally tackle the more northerly sites, and rising costs put the logic of the cheap gas bridge in question.

It is easy to criticize the gas industry and its political bosses for "irrational" shortsightedness in squeezing Urengoy and putting off development of the Yamal Peninsula. But such a policy could be considered quite rational from two points of view. First, it could simply represent a "social time preference" that esteems present benefits and applies a high discount rate to future ones. Second, the policymakers may simply reason that they need a big bridge fast, to give themselves a quick start in displacing oil. Either choice is defensible. But the main question is whether the respite was used well. This chapter and the next two argue that it was not.

The Issue of Manpower

The Soviet planning system is traditionally described by Western observers as "taut." It is especially so in the oil and gas industries, as the planners push the ministries toward inexorably higher output targets, first in the five-year plans and then in the annual ones. The result is a characteristic style of development, particularly in virgin areas: workers sleep in temporary quarters, bump along over temporary roads, and live by the light of temporary generators. The conditions described in Soviet accounts of the north Tiumen' gas fields strike the Western reader as barely controlled chaos—and most workers make their stay as temporary as they can.

These problems have generated constant controversy among the players, pitting local interests in north Tiumen' (including the local Party apparatus) against those of ministry headquarters and central planners in Moscow, and the oil and gas industries against one another. What is special about the north Tiumen' campaigns is both the scale of the effort and the difficulty of the region. To reach the remote, uninhabited wilderness of north Tiumen', supplies must be threaded through narrow lifelines that are open only part of the year; and elementary infrastructure must be built in a region that until recently had none. Yet these are not sophisticated technological problems; the real issues are priorities and management.

In this section we consider as an example the most pressing and controversial of these problems: manpower.[120] Manpower is in short

[120] This section extends the discussion of other sources of imbalance in Gustafson, *Soviet Gas Campaign*.

supply throughout the Soviet Union, although, as all Soviet sources freely admit, that is because it is inefficiently employed and distributed.[121] The gas and oil industries are prime examples: since their technological levels are low, they overuse labor, most of which is still concentrated in the regions where the two industries first grew up. As the center of oil and gas production has shifted to Siberia, the ministries involved have had difficulty getting workers to follow. Local authorities in the older areas (including local oil and gas officials themselves) resist the removal of key units and fight against the downgrading of their areas, forcing the oil and gas ministries to resort to extraordinary and controversial measures. Conflict over manpower policy and the related issues of housing and amenities have produced some of the loudest polemics of the politics of Siberian oil and gas, both in Moscow and in Tiumen'.[122]

HOW MANY WORKERS?

First, how many people are engaged in the Tiumen' gas industry, compared to the oil industry farther south? At the beginning of 1987 the Yamal-Nenetsk Autonomous Region (*okrug*) listed an urban population of 330,000, some 245,000 more than seven years before and 60,000 more than the previous year.[123] If one assumes that virtually the entire increase was caused by the gas campaign, then the total working population associated with Siberian gas can be taken at roughly 260,000. Of that number, only about one-third work directly for MGP. The rest are geologists (Mingeo), construction workers (MNGS), and employees of the other thirty-odd ministries active in the gas campaign.[124] In contrast, the number of workers associated with the Tiu-

[121] For valuable background on Soviet manpower policy, see Peter Hauslohner, "Managing the Soviet Labor Market: Politics and Policymaking under Brezhnev" (Ph.D. diss., University of Michigan, 1984).

[122] Soviet economists and demographers have written several valuable studies. One of the best is A. D. Khaitun, *Ekspeditsionno-vakhtovoe stroitel'stvo v Zapadnoi Sibiri* (Leningrad: Stroiizdat, 1982). For an excellent analysis by a Western scholar, see Leslie Dienes, "Employment Structure, Settlement Policy, and the Development of the North Tiumen' Oil and Gas Region," *Soviet Geography* 26, no. 10 (October 1985).

[123] *Narodnoe khoziaistvo SSSR, 1922–1982*, p. 17, and *Narodnoe khoziaistvo SSSR za 70 let*, p. 391.

[124] In 1982 there were some 60,000 geologists working in West Siberia ("Zapadnaia Sibir': nadolgo li khvatit resursov?" *Sotsialisticheskaia industriia*, 16 Apr. 1982) and 25,000 employees in the electrical power sector in Tiumen' Province (Lisin, "Sbivshis' s shaga"). At the beginning of 1986 MNGS listed 200,000 employees throughout the West Siberian oil and gas complex. V. G. Chirskov, "Kursom intensifikatsii," *Stroitel'stvo truboprovodov*, no. 2 (1986), p. 2.

men' oil industry (both directly and indirectly) is about three times as large.[125]

Workers come to north Tiumen', initially attracted by higher wages, but most of them do not stay more than a year or two. As a general rule, the farther north one goes, the more transient the labor force. For the two principal oil and gas regions of Tiumen' Province (the Khanty-Mansiisk and Yamal-Nenetsk *okrugi*), turnover in recent years has averaged about one-third,[126] but in the newer gas regions there are reports of 50 percent annual turnover and higher.[127] The problem is especially severe for construction crews, in which annual turnover in the early 1980s was close to 100 percent.[128] As a result, though the oil and gas regions of Siberia have averaged a net growth of about 40,000 people a year since the mid-1960s, the actual gross migration (that is, total in and out) each year is more likely 240,000,[129] and the difference is growing. Since the cost of training, moving, and housing one worker is reported to average 25,000 rubles,[130] one can well imagine why the authorities are concerned.

THE HOUSING PROBLEM

The main reason for high turnover is bad living conditions owing to a consistent neglect of housing and communal services. From 1976 to 1985 these two categories accounted for less than one-tenth of total oil- and gas-related investment in Tiumen' Province, about 5 billion out of 50 billion rubles.[131] At the beginning of the 1980s, average housing space per capita in the oil and gas regions was 6 square meters, two-

[125] In the early 1980s there were reported to be about four times as many employees of MNP as of MGP in West Siberia. A. Anan'ev and A. Silin, "Obespechenie predpriiatii i stroek Zapadno-Sibirskogo neftegazovogo kompleksa rabochei siloi," *Planovoe khoziaistvo*, no. 1 (1984), p. 95. My estimate assumes that there are proportionately fewer construction workers supporting MNP, principally because as a relatively "mature" extractive industry MNP requires less construction. Thus in the Eleventh Plan about 70 percent of MNGS construction work in West Siberia was devoted to the gas industry and only 30 percent to the oil industry. Chirskov, "Kursom intensifikatsii."

[126] Dienes, "Employment Structure," p. 611.

[127] In 1985 *Izvestiia* reported that two-thirds of the workers who come to the northern part of West Siberia (essentially the gas region) stay barely more than one year. *Izvestiia*, 16 Sept. 1985.

[128] Khaitun, *Ekspeditsionno-vakhtovoe stroitel'stvo v Zapadnoi Sibiri*, p. 11.

[129] Dienes, "Employment Structure," p. 611.

[130] *Izvestiia*, 16 Sept. 1985. This figure is frequently cited in the Soviet press, although I do not know its origin or the basis on which it was calculated.

[131] Dienes, "Employment Structure," p. 617.

thirds of the legal minimum.[132] There may have been some improvement in the first half of the 1980s for Tiumen' Province as a whole. According to Gorbachev's own reckoning, 8.6 million square meters were built in 1981–1985, representing a gross addition of about 3.5 square meters per capita in five years. Yet everyone from Gorbachev on down continues to speak of the housing shortage as the area's most serious problem. The apparent discrepancy between perception and reported achievement is probably due to the fact that a good deal of the space officially listed as housing is actually occupied by administrative offices.[133]

The gas industry, because it is located farther north, has more trouble with building contractors than does the oil industry farther south. MGP workers in Novyi Urengoy, the base city for the Urengoy gas field, were supposed to receive over 1 million square meters of new housing during 1981–1985[134] but ended up far short. In recent years housing construction for the gas industry has been growing faster than for the oil industry, but at present rates it will take several more years to catch up.

POLICY ISSUES INVOLVED IN HOUSING AND MANPOWER

To deal with the problem of manpower, the oil and gas ministries and the associated construction ministry have used two expedients: either housing workers in permanent base areas within the region and sending them on temporary duty to outposts in the field (the so-called *vakhtovyi metod*) or flying in workers on a two-week rotation from regions outside Siberia (the *ekspeditsionnyi metod*). The latter method is especially widespread in the oil industry; by 1985, as we saw in Chapter 4, flown-in crews accounted for 40 percent of all drilling and 25 percent of well repairs and maintenance in Tiumen'—altogether more than 50,000 workers.[135] MNGS has made extensive use of both systems for pipeline construction.[136] By the end of 1983 about 200,000 workers in Tiumen' were employed under one or the other system.[137] This has been

[132] Ibid.

[133] L. I. Gubina, "Obespechennost' zhil'em naseleniia Tiumenskoi oblasti i problema zakrepleniia kadrov," in S. N. Starovoitov, ed., *Problemy razvitiia Zapadno-Sibirskogo neftegazovogo kompleksa* (Novosibirsk: Nauka, 1983), p. 219.

[134] Ye. Altunin, *Gazovaia promyshlennost'*, no. 12 (1982), p. 27.

[135] Iu. Belanov and V. Kremer, "Trudnaia neft'," *Sotsialisticheskaia industriia*, 7 Aug. 1985. For a summary review of the impact on drilling performance from 1977 to 1987, see R. G. Shevaldin, "Zapadnaia Sibir': itogi vakhtovo-ekspeditsionnogo metoda za 10 let," *Neftianoe khoziaistvo*, no. 1 (1988) 3–5.

[136] Khaitun, *Ekspeditsionno-vakhtovoe stroitel'stvo v Zapadnoi Sibiri*, p. 22.

[137] Anan'ev and Silin, "Obespechenie predpriiatii."

the crucial margin of difference in preventing manpower shortages from becoming a bottleneck in both the oil and gas campaigns, and it will remain so for the indefinite future.

The fly-in system has proven especially controversial. It arose more or less by improvisation in the mid-1970s because initial plans had overestimated the ease of attracting manpower to the region.[138] The fly-in system spread fast during the first oil crisis. In 1977 MNP began assigning to associations in areas with declining production a quota of work to be fulfilled in Siberia. At first this practice concerned drilling teams primarily, but the method soon spread to other specialties as well.[139]

Why is the oil industry relying more on fly-ins while the gas industry is trying to build permanent settlements? On the face of it, one would have expected the opposite, because the more developed infrastructure of the southern Tiumen' area should be better suited to supporting a permanent population than the northern region, and labor turnover has been more severe in the gas than in the oil region. One reason may be that the two ministries have had different histories. In the previous generation of oil fields, in the Ural and Volga regions, MNP built large permanent settlements, but with the usual lag, so that by the time the housing was completed the fields were already declining. Although the housing is now full, many of the occupants are unemployed; indeed, they are among those who are being flown on temporary duty to Siberia today. As one Soviet article asks, "Must we repeat this experience in West Siberia?" Another reason is that the oil industry's great period of Siberian growth is behind it. Its future, unlike that of the gas industry, seems to promise a multitude of small fields and few giants. For the oil industry, therefore, the fly-in method has an obvious appeal.[140]

Among local Siberian authorities, however, the fly-in system has become increasingly unpopular, even for manning pipelines.[141] They complain that the fly-in system brings them the wrong kinds of workers, with the wrong attitudes. Local gas men line up with the local Party authorities against ministry headquarters and planners in Moscow in advocating a policy of stabilizing the work force in more permanent

[138] Khaitun, *Ekspeditsionno-vakhtovoe stroitel'stvo v Zapadnoi Sibiri*, pp. 9 and 19.

[139] Iu. K. Bot, "Osobennosti razvitiia tiumenskogo neftagazovogo kompleka i formirovaniia ego trudovykh resursov," in Starovoitov, ed., *Problemy*, pp. 208–209.

[140] Ibid., pp. 202–204.

[141] The large pipeline corridors leading out of Urengoy, consisting of as many as six parallel lines running along a common corridor, require compressor station crews and maintenance units that may number 500 people and more per station. Altunin, "Strategiiu vybrat' segodnia," p. 14.

settlements. The first Party secretary of the Yamal-Nenetsk district (in which the north Tiumen' gas fields are located) expressed a typical local attitude:

> Human values cannot always be translated into the language of economic categories. The experts reckoned that the "expedition" method for oil exploration would pay for itself within three or four years. But such gains here and now may end up costing us large losses in the future. The temporary worker often has a mentality that is alien to society [*neset chuzhduiu obshchestvu psikhologiiu*], a consumer-minded approach to the job, and a plundering attitude toward nature. A person like that has no reason to take good care of expensive equipment. In short, many temporary workers tend to work for themselves and give little in return.[142]

The fly-in system, moreover, is hard on the workers and bad for efficiency. Two *Pravda* correspondents, observing that oil workers were flown in from as far away as Moldavia and the Crimea, wrote that their productivity was lower than that of the locally based teams, because of fatigue and jet lag, lack of acclimatization to the area, and so on,[143] and that this led to problems of morale. Temporary teams flown in to oil fields typically work fifteen days on and fifteen days off; construction crews in both industries (particularly pipeline construction) work twenty days on and ten days off. Soviet experience has been that skilled workers and brigade leaders cannot keep up that kind of pace—a serious problem, since these are the categories of workers and specialists that are apparently the most difficult to draw to Siberia in the first place.

Meanwhile, the two industries face another problem: despite the high turnover in the region, many families do end up settling in north Tiumen', creating unintended communities of permanent residents in places the authorities had initially planned only as outposts. Thus a decade ago the giant gas field Medvezh'e was to be supported from the base town of Nadym, using a settlement at nearby Pangody as an outpost. Workers who attempted to settle their wives and children at Pangody found them forcibly returned to Nadym by the authorities. But eventually the pressure to settle was too strong, and Pangody

[142] K. Mironov, "U istokov gazovykh rek," *Pravda*, 17 Apr. 1981.

[143] Lisin and Parfenov, "Energiia tiumenskogo severa." For a vivid description of the reasons oil workers reach Siberia in less than top physical shape, see A. Laletin, "Samoletom na rabotu i obratno," *Pravda*, 8 June 1982. The *Trud* correspondent traveled with oil workers from Bashkiriia to Tiumen' and shared with them the sleepless nights, the long waits for delayed planes and buses, and the lack of accommodations along the way.

in 1985 had a permanent, if uncomfortable, population of 15,000 people.[144]

In planning the development of Urengoy the gas men similarly lagged in providing for the development of Novyi Urengoy, the major base for the field. The first brick apartment buildings started going up only in 1980, built with bricks brought from the European USSR that reportedly cost one ruble apiece. Until then, those who were lucky lived in rough-hewn wooden houses; the rest slept in bunk houses at their work places. In the field, MGP and MNGS used mobile dormitories—small wagons on wheels that did not keep out the cold.[145] The population mushroomed quickly. From 1,000 in 1976 it jumped to 79,000 by the end of 1986 and is still growing fast.[146] There are no parallel examples elsewhere in the world of such large permanent cities at such northerly latitudes.[147]

Now the same issue confronts the planners once more at Yamburg. Local officials have been arguing for a permanent settlement there,[148] on the model of earlier fields; and there exists a "general plan" for Yamburg that projects a settled population of 25,000.[149] Party authorities at Novyi Urengoy are urging that the Yamburg settlement there be given official status as a city.[150] But official policy is still fluid. Meanwhile, the history of Pangody and Novyi Urengoy is being reenacted: at this writing there are already several thousand people at Yamburg, but housing and amenities are getting the lowest priority.

Faced with the drawbacks of the fly-in policy and of "wildcat" towns emerging spontaneously in high-cost locations, the government has attempted to find a solution somewhere in between. Since 1981 the official aim has been to reduce the volume of long-distance fly-ins and to emphasize instead "outpost settlements" (*vakhtovye poselki*) located close to work sites, from which workers would be rotated periodically to "base cities" (*bazovye goroda*) no more than 150–200 kilometers away, where their families would live.[151] In May 1982 new regulations

[144] Levitskii et al., "Mladshii brat Urengoia."

[145] Accounts of these conditions are legion in the Soviet press. Almost any of the sources cited above contains examples.

[146] The 1976 figure comes from Kostylev and Noskov, "Pis'ma iz Urengoia," the 1986 one from *Narodnoe khoziaistvo SSSR za 70 let*, p. 398.

[147] As Leslie Dienes observes, Novyi Urengoy is located in a region climatically analogous to Canada's Great Bear Lake but is much more marshy and unpleasant. Dienes, "Employment Structure," p. 618.

[148] Shemraev, "Ia znaiu—gorod budet," p. 153.

[149] Levitskii et al., "Mladshii brat Urengoia."

[150] Ibid.

[151] "Vakhta na severe," *Pravda*, 14 Nov. 1981, p. 1.

were published to spell out the guarantees and benefits to which the *vakhtoviki* were entitled. The regulations were revealing: their authors felt obliged to specify, for example, that workers at outposts must receive three hot meals a day and that women with children under the age of eight could not be assigned to outpost duty "without their consent."[152]

In effect, this policy aims to replace the long commute with a short one, thus building up a permanent workforce in the area, but not at remote, high-cost locations. So far, however, this policy has not worked noticeably better than the others. The root problem is the unwillingness of the planners and ministries to allocate resources to housing and amenities. The local Party officials, while concerned about the welfare of their areas, lack the power to reallocate resources. Moreover, since they are ultimately judged on the performance of the local industries, they ultimately share the latter's obsession with output. As a result, housing and amenities fall between the cracks.

Since 1985, however, the General Secretary himself has entered the picture. When Gorbachev visited Tiumen' Province in the fall of that year, he strongly endorsed the goal of slowing turnover by building more housing and improving local living conditions. The ultimate goal of state policy, he declared, should be to transform Siberia into "a pleasant place to live." After sharply criticizing the oil industry for failing to attend to the welfare of oil workers in Siberia, Gorbachev warned the gas industry against repeating the same mistakes.

Curiously, Gorbachev's most interesting remarks, though shown on nationwide television, did not appear in the *Pravda* version of his speech.[153] Thus on television Gorbachev described the ministries as the chief culprits, but he pinned a large share of the blame on the local Party authorities as well, especially the Tiumen' obkom. He urged the Party authorities "not to give in to any economic planners if they forget" about the priority of providing "normal living conditions" for the workers; and he warned that unless Siberian oil and gas construction projects also provided for people's comfort, "the consequences and the damage are unavoidable. We shall have production facilities, capacities, and jobs standing idle, producing nothing. Why then are we building these enterprises?"

So Gorbachev's commitment to a new policy seemed firm, yet it

[152] "Vakhtovyi metod organizatsii rabot," *Ekonomicheskaia gazeta*, no. 21 (1982), p. 16.

[153] This was a noticeable feature of the handling of Gorbachev's public addresses in his first two years, suggesting shaky staff organization at first and possibly also an uncertain consensus in the Politburo.

remains puzzling why his remarks were so heavily edited in the press. In particular, Gorbachev's televized speech detailed a whole series of targets for the coming five-year plan, including an increase of close to 50 percent in housing construction for Tiumen' Province.[154] But these goals were omitted in the press as well.

Despite Gorbachev's intervention the running debates over manpower and housing in Tiumen' are bound to continue, because the tensions are built in to the situation itself. For the foreseeable future more manpower will be needed than can be properly accommodated or induced to move permanently. Consequently, there is no quick alternative to temporary crews. But there are deeper reasons for favoring temporary rotations over permanent settlement. The oil and gas campaigns are an immense, one-time investment in a region that has only one major resource: hydrocarbons. When the gas and oil are gone, the region may not return to arctic oblivion, but the planners are clearly worried about those potential ghost towns of the future that today's pioneers, at a cost of tens of billions, are now building. This is not a new theme in Soviet discussions, but it flares up each time a new field is opened. Behind this is the old (and still controversial) question of how to deal with Siberia: to settle and develop it permanently or to grab its resources and run.

What are the consequences for the gas industry? Manpower problems, especially in MNGS, are an important cause of the shortcomings routinely reported at Urengoy: a "chronic lag" in development drilling, two or three years' worth of unfinished construction projects, plan fulfillment rates for construction on the order of 22 percent, and the like.[155] Yet it appears that the impact on gas output is minor, except perhaps that a certain amount of unprocessed gas is shipped raw through the pipelines. The gas wealth of the north Tiumen' fields is so great that, so far, they forgive the most serious mistakes, even more than the oil fields to the south.

Conclusions

In several respects the recent history of the Soviet gas industry resembles that of oil a decade before. The development of Siberian resources in both industries began only after much initial reluctance, skepticism, technical debate, and bureaucratic foot-dragging. Then Siberian oil and

[154] According to Gorbachev, the 8.6 million square meters of housing space built in 1981–1985 would be increased to 14.6 million in 1986–1990. Television version of Gorbachev's Tiumen' speech, 6 Sept. 1985.

[155] V. Lisin, "Gazovyi potentsial."

gas operations both grew at a feverish pace, under constant pressure from planners in Moscow who ratcheted output targets higher and higher, far outpacing the local specialists' own recommendations. Exploration and the advance preparation of new fields began to be neglected in favor of development, especially by the oil and gas ministries themselves. Infrastructure, housing, and amenities received consistently low priority. Technological levels, low to begin with, improved little, and industrial support for both industries (as the next chapter will show) remained poor. Finally, both industries were slow to confront new challenges when these required new skills and new approaches. The result in both cases has been needlessly high costs.

The two industries' experience is similar in one more respect: developing Siberian fields required dealing with some of the toughest natural conditions in the world. Yet, because the two industries had found some of the world's largest fields, they were rewarded more magnificently than anyone could have imagined. In short, the experience of Siberian oil and gas shows why the campaign approach is a constant temptation in Soviet decisionmaking: the initial conditions appeared to require it; the initial successes seemed to justify it; and the unique wealth of Tiumen' Province long concealed its costs.

But the similarities end there, at least for now. Known Soviet gas reserves in Tiumen' are so much larger than known oil reserves that the gas industry is unlikely to pay the same price for its mistakes that the oil men farther south did. Both industries may continue to use the campaign approach; but whereas the predictable consequence on the oil side will be exorbitant cost and recurrent crisis, only the former fate awaits the gas industry in this century, unless Moscow unwisely slows down investment in gas and pipelines.

One reason a crash approach has been necessary in the gas industry is that bureaucratic friction and nearsighted planning delayed the move to Siberia in the early 1970s and then the advance across the Arctic Circle in the first half of the 1980s. The first of these delays was especially costly; if the big gas policy of 1980–1981 had begun five or ten years earlier, much of the damaging pressure on the Siberian oil industry could have been avoided. All the participants share in the blame, except the geologists who uncovered the fabulous North Tiumen' gas reserves and the local officials (especially those of the Tiumen' Party obkom) who urged their rapid development. The gas industry lacked resolve; the planners and scientists lacked vision; the leaders lacked foresight. But in the end, responsibility falls on the leaders: just as they should have reacted to the impending oil problem as early as 1973, so should they have begun massive gas development before 1976. They had the information; they could weigh the dangers; they had access to foreign equipment—and yet they dallied.

The gas campaign also illustrates the gap between the Soviet decisionmaking system's capacity to learn and its ability to act on its learning. By 1980–1981 it was clear to all how heavy a price the oil industry was paying for its unbalanced approach to Siberian development. Yet the gas industry then repeated much the same pattern, first at Urengoy, and now at Yamburg. The reasons in both cases are much the same: the pressure for fast gains in output and the failure to provide for balanced and consistent industrial and technological support. Thus learning proceeded, but adaptation failed to follow.

By the late 1990s the marginal costs of delivered natural gas could well approach those of oil today—that is, they may well exceed average world prices.[156] The Soviet gas bridge will become very expensive as the economy moves toward the next century. In gas as in oil, therefore, the country's energy future depends on improved industrial support and conservation. These are our next topics.

[156] Marginal cost estimates for Soviet gas are tricky because they fluctuate. Matthew Sagers estimates that the marginal production cost of Soviet gas at the well head in 1986 was around 10 rubles per ton of oil equivalent, or roughly $1.30 per barrel. But transmission costs bring this figure up dramatically at the point of delivery: pipelines, as we have seen, account for 70 percent of gas investment and consume about 10 percent of gas output.

Prime Minister N. I. Ryzhkov, speaking in Tiumen' in May 1988, stated that production costs for West Siberian oil and gas were 50 percent higher than for the rest of the country. This is surely a mistake, in view of the higher productivity of work crews in the region. But Ryzhkov's statement may reflect the very large burden of energy transmission. See Ryzhkov, "Razvitiiu Zapadnoi Sibiri."

SIX

INDUSTRIAL SUPPORT FOR THE OIL AND GAS CAMPAIGNS: THE INTERACTION OF DOMESTIC POLICY AND IMPORT STRATEGY

One of the most important reasons for the Soviet energy crisis has been deficient industrial support. Most of the equipment used by the Soviet oil and gas industries is obsolete in design and fabrication; deliveries are unreliable; and one-third to one-half of what arrives in the field is defective. These three problems together—obsolete technology, uncertain supply, and low quality—explain much of the low productivity of the oil and gas industries and the attendant consequences: excess manpower, unbalanced effort, and high costs.

Business as usual, the reader may say, and a classic illustration of the command system at its most mischievous. But as this chapter will show, bad industrial support for the oil and gas industries was made worse by specific policies and priorities of the Brezhnev administration, in particular a systematic neglect of the relevant machinery ministries and an inconsistent policy on imports for the oil and gas industries.

Therefore, on the face of it, even limited reform should lead to improvement. From the moment Gorbachev came to power in 1985, the new leadership put top priority on reforming and modernizing the machinery sector. The five-year plan for 1986–1990 provided for an immense increase in investment in the eight civilian machinery ministries,[1] and these ministries were among the first to switch to the new economic mechanism adopted in the summer of 1987. Industrial support for the oil and gas sectors is an important part of this program: when Gorbachev visited Tiumen' in the fall of 1985, he put special emphasis on the problems of equipment and supply.

But it will take time before the effects of the machinery program are felt. Meanwhile, the effort creates a powerful new claimant for invest-

[1] In 1987 and 1988 a series of decrees reduced the number of civilian machinery ministries from 11 to 8.

ment resources. Moreover, it is unclear how much of the new machinery investment will go for energy-related equipment. The machinery program favors eye-catching high technologies, not the more modest ones needed by the oil and gas industries. Finally, the combination of massive increases in investment with radical changes in the economic system is proving disruptive; indeed, the whole machinery program is off to a poor start.[2] For these reasons the quality of industrial support may well deteriorate further.

But why was industrial support for the oil and gas sectors allowed to become such a bottleneck in the first place? Why was the crash oil and gas program not accompanied by a crash program in the corresponding branches of machinery? Failing that, why did the Soviet leaders not turn systematically to imports to help remedy the problem? This chapter will show that while Soviet policymakers under Brezhnev did not sit idly by, their responses were improvised and contradictory. Their behavior illustrates the characteristic inability of the Brezhnev leadership to develop a coherent strategy for a sector in which domestic and foreign suppliers are combined.

Dimensions of Trouble in Industrial Support

Changing Requirements for Industrial Support

Three big changes have driven the oil and gas industries' equipment requirements in the last ten years: first, their expanded scale of operations; second, the increasingly remote and harsh locations in which they work; and third, the greater depths, smaller size, and more complex geology of new fields. Consequently, the oil and gas industries have needed both better equipment and much more of it, as the following list shows.

Gas Industry

1. Arctic welding techniques, pipe layers, excavators, insulated and corrosion-proof pipe
2. Gas-turbine drives and compressors, refrigeration and gas-processing plants
3. Wide-bore wells.

[2] Andrew J. Matosich and Bonnie K. Matosich, "Machine Building: *Perestroyka*'s Sputtering Engine," *Soviet Economy* 4, no. 2 (April-June 1988), pp. 144–176.

Oil Industry

1. Field equipment for seismic exploration, offshore equipment, technology for enhanced oil recovery. Equipment for high-pressure and high-sulfur environments.
2. New rigs for cluster drilling, better drill bits and muds, better-quality drill pipe, downhole pumps and gaslift equipment. Improved logging equipment. Control systems.
3. Expanded secondary refinery capacity: hydrocracking, catalytic cracking. Chemicals for corrosion control and enhanced oil recovery; drilling muds.

Few of the items on this list call for high technology. Offshore development, enhanced oil recovery, and seismic exploration do require large jumps in the technological levels of industrial support. But mostly the oil and gas industries need traditional equipment with improved designs, better alloys, and more modern manufacturing methods that are well within the capabilities of the best Soviet industries. The problem, as we shall see, is that the oil and gas service industries are among the weakest parts of the civilian Soviet machinery sector. Faced with simultaneous requirements for increased reliability, innovation, and quantity, they have mainly delivered quantity. The statistical handbooks hint at this when they show that the gross value of output of equipment for oil-field development, oil and gas exploration, and oil and gas refining has increased sharply since the mid-1970s, while the number of prototypes of new equipment and the percentage of new machinery in total output have stagnated (table 6.1).

Reviewing specific types of equipment, we find essentially the same picture. The one relatively bright spot is drilling, which has been the Oil Ministry's top priority since the beginning of the oil campaign in late 1977. In West Siberia cluster drilling, in which numerous slanting wells are drilled from a single site and a single rig, has spread rapidly. New rigs for cluster drilling get good grades from the field,[3] and this is one reason the oil industry has been able to keep drilling meterage growing rapidly, even though the total number of rigs produced annually has not increased much in ten years.[4]

[3] G. S. Popov (deputy minister of the petroleum industry), "Ravnenie na liderov," *Sotsialisticheskaia industriia*, 4 Sept. 1983. Their producer, the Uralmash association in Sverdlovsk, has been widely praised. Uralmash is one of the largest conglomerates in the country and is the place where the present prime minister, Nikolai Ryzhkov, made his early career. The Uralmash model in question is the BU-3000-EUK. A. Aganbegian, "Toplivo Sibiri," *Pravda*, 1 Aug. 1983; *Oil and Gas Journal*, 27 June 1983; Iu. N. Vershinin, "Impul's vstrechnogo plana," *Ekonomicheskaia gazeta*, no. 40 (1983), p. 8.

[4] Soviet output of drilling rigs for development and exploration rose from 480 in 1970 to 570 in 1985, before dropping back to 546 in 1986 and 553 in 1987. *Narodnoe*

But in other respects industrial support for drilling leaves much to be desired. Conventional Soviet rigs are criticized by the users as heavy, inefficient, and unreliable, falling far short of world standards.[5] Many models developed in the 1950s are still in production.[6] A perennial source of dissatisfaction among drillers is the poor quality of drill pipe and casing pipe. Scattered figures suggest that about 10 percent of the delivered pipe is defective.[7] Drill bits are likewise reported to have quality problems, and special-purpose bits (for example, for low-speed turbodrills) have been slow to reach the fields.

Industrial support appears still less satisfactory as one looks beyond drilling to other development operations. Poor well finishing and mechanization, which were among the most important reasons for the bad performance of the West Siberian oil fields in the first half of the 1980s, are blamed on delays in equipment supply that can run as much as a decade behind plan targets.[8] Production of downhole pumps, in particular, has stagnated (especially when compared with the tremendous increase in the number of wells),[9] and even the highest-priority programs (such as the electric submersibles described in Chapter 3)

---

khoziaistvo SSSR v 1987 godu (Moscow: Finansy i Statistika, 1988), p. 133. Even the vaunted Uralmash BU-3000-EUK is available only in small numbers, but some Western observers believe that the oil industry has had some success in lengthening the average service life of its rigs.

[5] The head of West Siberian geological exploration, Farman Salmanov, criticizes Soviet rigs (including those made by Uralmash) as being 70 percent heavier than foreign models. As a result, they can be moved only when the ground is frozen, and thus they are frequently idle. *Pravda*, 14 Jan. 1986. An article on the parent ministry in charge of rig production, Mintiazhmash, charges that none of the ministry's rigs matches world standards. M. Berger et al., "Prospekt Kalinina, 19: Pis'ma iz ministerstva. 3: Tekhnika," *Izvestiia*, 18 Dec. 1986. For complaints that recent models are actually less reliable than older ones, see M. Makhlin, "Na novom etape osvoeniia prirodnykh bogatstv," *Ekonomicheskaia gazeta*, no. 38 (1985), p. 7. In addition to Uralmash, the other main Soviet producer of drilling rigs is the Volgograd Drilling Technology Plant (VZBT). M. Nikolaev, "Burovye zhdut sovremennuiu tekhniku," *Ekonomicheskaia gazeta*, no. 7 (1986), p. 14.

[6] Nikolaev, "Burovye zhdut sovremennuiu tekhniku."

[7] More recently Gorbachev used the same figure in criticizing the high defect rate of a major supplier in Azerbaijan, although other suppliers, such as the Severskii Pipe Plant in Sverdlovsk Province, he described as doing better. Gorbachev speech in Tol'iatti, 8 April 1986, in M. S. Gorbachev, *Izbrannye rechi i stat'i* (Moscow: Politizdat, 1987), vol. 3, p. 340. Yet in mid-1986 the collegium of the Ministry of the Oil Industry continued to complain about the low quality of drill pipe and casing pipe. *Sotsialisticheskaia industriia*, 11 June 1986.

[8] This was notoriously the case at Samotlor. L. Levitskii et al., "Razryv," *Izvestiia*, 28 May 1985.

[9] In 1970, Soviet production of downhole pumps was 77,000 units; in 1980, 91,600; and in 1986, 92,100. *Narodnoe khoziaistvo SSSR v 1987 godu*, p. 132.

TABLE 6.1

Some Gross Value Indicators of Industrial Response to Increased Requirements in the Oil and Gas Industries, 1970–1987

	Gross Output of Equipment for Oil Development and Oil and Gas Exploratory Drilling (1970=100)	*Gross Output of Equipment for Oil and Gas Refining (1970=100)*	*Oil-Field Equipment (millions of rubles)*	*Number of Prototypes of New Equipment**	*New Machinery Models (as a percentage of total output)†*
1970	100	100	92	64	6.6
1975	160	146	123	47	NA
1980	230	202	201	53	5.0
1985	317	267	229	56	4.9
1986	340	286	248	42	4.7
1987	352	296	241	39	NA

SOURCE: *Narodnoe khoziaistvo SSSR*, various years.

* This figure refers to "energeticheskoe oborudovanie," which presumably includes the entire fuels and energy sector.

† This category refers to the Ministry of Chemical and Petroleum Machine-building as a whole.

have shown little response, despite a decade of urgent pleas from oil men.[10] The picture is broadly the same for gaslift equipment (also discussed in Chapter 3).[11] Overall, between one-third and one-half of all equipment for well finishing and operation is rated as defective on arrival.

To defend themselves against their suppliers, the oil and gas ministries have assembled a small army of repairmen, working in factory-sized shops, to put newly arrived equipment in working condition before it is used in the field. By 1986 the Tiumen' oil industry alone had 8,000 people serving this function, and their numbers were growing rapidly.[12] But this stopgap measure has hardly made up for the manufacturers' refusal to provide postdelivery service or an adequate supply of spare parts.[13]

As one moves down the oil industry's priority list to programs that the oil and gas ministries themselves have treated as secondary, industrial support virtually disappears. The worst shortfalls have been in well

[10] One of the principal producers of electric submersibles is the Borets factory in Moscow. This once-famous enterprise had declined badly by the early 1980s. But a new director in 1984 and an ambitious retooling program may have brought some improvement after 1986. See D. Murzin, "Otkrovenno i konstruktivno," *Sotsialisticheskaia industriia*, 20 Mar. 1986; Iu. Medvedev, "Borets delaet vybor," *Pravda*, 18 Oct. 1986; and V. Kapel'kin, "S kogo i kak prosit'," *Sotsialisticheskaia industriia*, 12 June 1986. Yet, as of the first half of 1986, oil men remained critical of Soviet-made electric submersibles: most were poor in quality, and the best ones were available only in small numbers. See V. Kuz'mishchev et al., "Partnery," *Pravda*, 9 Feb. 1986; and an interview with the chief engineer of the Bashkir Oil Association, A. Syrtlanov, "Iskat' obshchuiu vygodu," *Sotsialisticheskaia industriia*, 24 May 1986. For background on the history of Soviet troubles with electric submersibles, see Robert W. Campbell, *Soviet Energy Technologies: Planning, Policy, Research and Development* (Bloomington: Indiana University Press, 1980).

[11] A frank and detailed analysis appears in V. Borodin, "Rezervy neftianogo plasta," *Sotsialisticheskaia industriia*, 2 Mar. 1985. See also "Adresovano neftianikam," *Pravda*, 12 Sept. 1981; and "Vtoroe dykhanie neftianogo plasta," *Izvestiia*, 23 Oct. 1983. According to Borodin, as of the end of 1984 compressors for the Samotlor gaslift program were all imported. The domestic plant that was supposed to produce them had managed to ship only three "experimental" units by late 1983. In 1986 the Ministry of Chemical and Petroleum Machine-building sent its flagship plant, the Frunze NPO in Sumy, into the fray (Kapel'kin, "S kogo i kak prosit'"). But as of the beginning of 1989 the first unit from Sumy was not yet operational (*Soviet Geography* 30, no. 4 [April 1989], p. 311).

[12] D. Melikov, "Spros strogii, spravedlivyi," *Sotsialisticheskaia industriia*, 22 Feb. 1986. The consequences for performance are dramatic: the average electric submersible pump in Soviet oil fields requires repair every hundred days or so (*Tekhnicheskii progress v neftianoi promyshlennosti v desiatoi piatiletke* [Moscow, Nedra, 1981], p. 106); but if the pumps are put in proper condition by the oil industry beforehand (as at Iugansk in West Siberia), the time between repairs nearly quadruples (*Ekonomicheskaia gazeta*, no. 40 [1983], p. 8).

[13] Nikolaev, "Burovye zhdut sovremennuiu tekhniku."

maintenance and repair, which, as we have seen, has been the oil industry's lowest-priority program. For this type of equipment the defect rates approach 50 percent.[14] The result has been a vicious circle of low priority and low performance. Thus, when the oil industry finally started a crash program of well repair in 1986, it was held up by a lack of supporting equipment.[15]

Corrosion control, to mention another example, is a special problem in the Soviet oil industry because of the wide use of waterflooding as a development technique.[16] Corrosion prevention is supposed to be a billion-ruble-a-year program, but in reality it falls far short of that level.[17] The Ministry of the Petrochemical Industry, whose job it is to produce corrosion inhibitors, struck corrosion prevention from its programs for the Eleventh Five-Year Plan (1981–1985), and both Gosplan and the State Committee for Science and Technology went along with the decision.[18] The Ministry of Ferrous Metallurgy likewise resists requests to produce corrosion-resistant pipe for the high-sulfur oils and gases of the Caspian Basin and Kazakhstan.[19] The Oil Ministry has been obliged to do what it can on its own, with some success in the older oil-producing regions, such as Tatariia and Bashkiriia.

A final example is special arctic equipment. As the oil and gas industries move north and east, the climate grows worse, and local workers need equipment specially designed or adapted to arctic conditions. Officially, at least, there is a category of output labeled "KhL" (for the Russian word *kholod*, cold), intended for operation at 40 degrees below zero and under. But in practice most northern operations use conventional equipment,[20] and Siberian oil and gas men expect little help from outside. As the head of Tiumen' gas development put it: "For construc-

[14] Iu. Belanov et al., "Tekhnika dlia neftianikov," *Sotsialisticheskaia industriia*, 7 July 1984.

[15] Interview with First Deputy Oil Minister V. Iu. Filanovskii-Zenkov, in *Sotsialisticheskaia industriia*, 24 Mar. 1986.

[16] Pipes used in waterflooding systems at Samotlor, for example, are said to last only a year, whereas with proper protective coatings they would last ten times longer. See I. A. Ognev, "Kakie mashiny nuzhny promyslu," *Sotsialisticheskaia industriia*, 26 June 1984. A more detailed treatment will be found in B. S. Lobanov et al., "Osnovnye napravleniia bor'by s korroziei neftepromyslovogo oborudovaniia," *Neftianoe khoziaistvo*, no. 2 (1985), pp. 6–9.

[17] M. Zaripov and A. Podol'skii, "Trudnyi gorizont," *Sovetskaia Rossiia*, 7 and 8 Dec. 1982.

[18] Ognev, "Kakie mashiny nuzhny promyslu."

[19] T. Mukhamed-Rakhimov, "Put' k kaspiiskoi nefti," *Izvestiia*, 7 Sept. 1983; also A. Galin, "Dragotsennoe kol'tso Prikaspiia," *Pravda*, 22 Dec. 1983.

[20] A. B. Sukhovskii et al., "Tekhnika dlia Sibiri i severa," *Ekonomika i organizatsiia promyshlennogo proizvodstva* (*EKO*), no. 3 (1984), pp. 81–91.

tion we'll take anything, even if not specially made for arctic conditions—we've almost forgotten about that kind."[21]

In sum, the pattern of shortages and low quality that plagues Soviet oil and gas men is not random but mirrors the priorities of the oil and gas industries themselves: development gets preference over exploration, drilling over well finishing and mechanization, and well sites over "peripherals" such as power supply and roads. Equipment required for immediate production is in better supply than that needed for maintenance, prevention, or longer-term support. Near-term expediency predominates over longer-term efficiency.[22] We shall see in the next section how some of these priorities are transmitted to suppliers.

Why has industrial support been so remarkably poor? The first part of the answer is that behind the poor supply is a domestic machinery sector in crisis.

Portrait of a Sector in Crisis

Prior to the 1917 revolution the Russian oil industry, concentrated around Baku in Azerbaijan, relied entirely on imported equipment. The Soviet oil service sector originated in the 1920s and 1930s and, after marking time during World War II, grew rapidly in the 1950s and 1960s.[23] But whereas the center of the postwar oil industry moved to the Volga Basin and then to West Siberia, the oil service sector remained in the birthplace of the industry. Today, 70 percent of Soviet equipment for producing oil and gas still comes from Azerbaijan, principally from the city of Baku.[24] A secondary cluster of plants is located in the Volga-Kama Basin, the site of the oil industry's second generation. Very little of the oil and gas industries' support comes from West Siberia.

Most equipment for the oil and gas industries, particularly that intended for well operation, is manufactured by the Ministry of Chemical and Petroleum Machine-building (Minkhimmash). Drilling rigs are the responsibility of the Ministry of Heavy and Transport Machine-building (Mintiazhmash),[25] while most domestic pipe comes from the

[21] Ivan Spiridonovich Nikonenko, director of Tiumengazdobycha, quoted in "Tsena golubogo zolota," *Ekonomika i organizatsiia promyshlennogo proizvodstva* (*EKO*), no. 5 (1983), p. 56.

[22] A noteworthy exception is gas transmission, which is treated later in this chapter.

[23] N. P. Umanchuk, "VNIIneftemashu—40 let," *Khimicheskoe i neftianoe mashinostroenie*, no. 8 (1987), p. 4.

[24] "Neftianikam—dobrotnoe oborudovanie," *Sotsialisticheskaia industriia*, 9 Feb. 1986.

[25] In July 1987 Mintiazhmash was merged with the Ministry of Power Machinery (Minenergomash). However, during the period covered by this study the two ministries were separate entities; I therefore use the former names.

Ministry of Ferrous Metallurgy (Minchermet).[26] But these names of large conglomerates tell us little, apart from the fact that responsibility for oil and gas service belongs to parent ministries with many other competing missions. For a more precise picture of the industry's problems, it will help to focus briefly on the most important cluster of actual producers, Minkhimmash's industrial association for petroleum machine building, called Glavneftemash.

Glavneftemash produces as much as two-thirds of the oil-field equipment used in the Soviet Union. Its fifteen enterprises, clustered in and around Baku, employ over 20,000 workers.[27] In the twelve years or so since the beginning of the Brezhnev oil program it has tripled its output, which makes it the fastest-growing division of Minkhimmash. But its growth has been based almost entirely on existing capacity; there has been little investment in new plant or modernization of old. When the Soviet press began paying special attention to Glavneftemash in 1986 (after Gorbachev's strong criticism of industrial suppliers in Tiumen' the previous fall), it painted a sorry picture of inefficiency and disarray: Glavneftemash's plants were primitive and dirty, its machinery out of date, its operations poorly mechanized, and its research and development facilities, such as they were, taken over for current production. Glavneftemash was working at 99 percent capacity, but its output was antiquated and substandard.[28]

[26] A fourth important supplier, much less frequently mentioned, is the Ministry of Defense Industry (Minoboronprom).

[27] F. K. Salmanov, "Optimizm i optimizatsiia," in *Tiumenskii meridian* (Moscow: Politizdat, 1983), p. 85. I have identified ten of the fifteen: Zavod im. Leitenanta Shmidta, Zavod im. Dzerzhinskogo, Bakinskii rabochii, Kishlinskii Mashinostroitel'nyi Zavod, Zavod Neftepromyslovogo Mashinostroeniia im. Montina, Azerbaidzhanskii Truboprokatnyi Zavod im. Lenina, Zavod im. Kirova, Ishimbaiskii Zavod, Mashinostroitel'nyi Zavod im. Kasimova, Bakinskii Mashinostroitel'nyi Zavod im. Sardarova.

Minkhimmash operates more than a dozen other enterprises that provide industrial support to the oil and gas industries. I have located ten: NPO Volgogradneftemash (whose major unit, the Petrov plant, is located in Baku), the Barnaul Plant for Geological and Exploration Equipment, the Kuibyshev Association for Drilling Machinery, the Saratov Plant for Petroleum Machinery, the Petroleum Machinery Plant in Izhevsk, the Al'metevsk Electric Submersible Plant, the Borets Plant in Moscow, the Turbobur Plant in Perm' Oblast', the Krasnyi Molot Plant in Groznyi, and the Salavatneftemash Association in Bashkiriia. In addition, the ministry's two flagship associations, the Kriogenmash NPO in Moscow Province and the Frunze NPO in Sumy (Ukraine), though not primarily dedicated to the oil and gas industries, produce important items for them, such as gas-turbine drives for gas pipeline compressors.

[28] See in particular Melikov, "Spros strogii, spravedlivyi"; for a slightly earlier picture, see Belanov et al., "Tekhnika dlia neftianikov." According to Belanov, at least half the machine tools in Glavneftemash consisted of worn-out general-purpose cutting tools.

With the beginning of the Twelfth Five-Year Plan's high-priority program of machinery investment in 1986, pressure mounted on Minkhimmash to bring Glavneftemash up to standard. The minister declared that henceforth the oil and gas sector would be his agency's top priority.[29] There followed a familiar flurry of bureaucratic activity: half the association's plant directors were fired;[30] a blizzard of investigative commissions descended on Glavneftemash and other suppliers; speeches by high officials resounded at Party Central Committee headquarters in Moscow;[31] and the Party city committee (*gorkom*) in Baku, prodded by criticism from Moscow,[32] responded in time-honored fashion by launching a "quality program" for Glavneftemash, monitoring its progress with yet more meetings.[33] The Oil Ministry, as the principal customer, sent Siberian emissaries to Baku in 1986 to establish a quality-control office, which displaced Glavneftemash's own inspectors and began rejecting defective equipment as it came off the assembly line.[34] (This behavior contrasts so sharply with the kid-glove treatment industrial customers usually give to their suppliers that the oil industry must have been given orders by the Party leadership.)

But at the end of 1986 oil men still saw little improvement. G. P. Bogomiakov, first secretary of the Tiumen' obkom, observed that the volume of deliveries was up but that quality remained low and the most important items were still in short supply. He concluded:

> The machinery builders let the oil men down. For example, the gaslift equipment was not delivered on time, and we were forced to produce oil by using more manpower instead of technology. Year-end storming, improper operating methods, "extensive" development—all required adding more and more people.[35]

[29] See the minister's beginning-of-year policy statements in *Khimicheskoe i neftianoe mashinostroenie*, no. 1.

[30] However, the deputy minister of Minkhimmash for the oil and gas equipment sector, V. Reznichenko, has kept his job down to the present.

[31] *Sotsialisticheskaia industriia*, 4 Feb. 1986. This was a meeting devoted to oil and gas equipment, featuring a speech by Oil Minister V. A. Dinkov and an address by Politburo member L. N. Zaikov, the Central Committee secretary then in charge of the machinery sector.

[32] Four days after the meeting in Moscow, the first deputy chief of the Central Committee machine-building department, V. I. Pimenov, addressed a similar meeting at the Central Committee headquarters of the Azeri Communist Party. *Sotsialisticheskaia industriia*, 9 Feb. 1986. Local Azeri Party leaders were taken to task in the central press for having ignored Glavneftemash's problems.

[33] *Sotsialisticheskaia industriia*, 15 Oct. and 5 Nov. 1986.

[34] *Sotsialisticheskaia industriia*, 5 and 22 Feb. 1986.

[35] G. P. Bogomiakov, "Nadezhen li tyl?" *Pravda*, 10 Dec. 1986.

The response from the suppliers was mostly passive resistance. The Baku enterprises took to shipping their output by night to bypass the oil industry's representatives.[36] This was a foretaste of similar battles that erupted in Minkhimmash the following year over the state quality-control inspection system, *gospriemka*.[37]

Bureaucrats and reporters began pointing fingers in all directions. *Pravda* accused Azeri officials of "closing their eyes."[38] Construction companies in Baku were blamed for refusing to accept additional contracts to step up the modernization of Glavneftemash plants until they were given additional materials and manpower to match; this had caused Minkhimmash's paper plan for capital investment in Glavneftemash in 1981–1985 to be underfulfilled by half.[39] Glavneftemash's parent ministry, Minkhimmash, was accused of being uncooperative and of favoring its other activities.[40]

But clearly Glavneftemash's decrepitude could not be reversed overnight, because it resulted from a policy of neglect over decades. To account for the chronic weakness of industrial support for the oil and gas sector one must look to Brezhnev's investment priorities.

The Impact of Brezhnev's Investment Priorities

Charges that Brezhnev had allowed the civilian machinery sector to deteriorate were among the earliest to fly after his death. The accusa-

[36] *Sotsialisticheskaia industriia*, 22 and 29 Jan. 1986.

[37] According to the minister of Minkhimmash, V. M. Luk'ianenko, 95 enterprises of his ministry went over to the *gospriemka* system at the beginning of 1987, but I have not discovered whether any of the Glavneftemash enterprises were among them. See "Prevratit' plany v deistvitel'nost'," *Khimicheskoe i neftianoe mashinostroenie*, no. 1 (1987), pp. 1–4.

[38] Kuz'mishchev et al., "Partnery." From 1983 to 1985, according to another source, no district Party committee in Baku had ever discussed the problems of Glavneftemash. Melikov, "Spros strogii, spravedlivyi."

[39] Belanov et al., "Tekhnika dlia neftianikov."

[40] In addition to oil and gas service equipment, Minkhimmash makes machinery for oil and gas refining, chemistry, plastics and wood fiber processing, agriculture, and pollution control. It makes pumps, compressors, refrigerators, cryogenics, vacuum equipment, and tires. To judge from the allocation of space in its journal and in its leaders' speeches, Minkhimmash continues to give less attention to oil and gas service than to the rest. Unfortunately, since disaggregated investment data are lacking, it is not possible to pin down this point.

tions related not so much to quantity of output[41] as to quality.[42] A major reason for the technological stagnation of the civilian machinery sector was the preferential channeling of resources to the ministries making military machinery, which continued at least through the mid-1980s.[43] In short, the stagnation of the civilian machinery sector was due above all to the leaders' own priorities.

Within the civilian machinery group the investment priority of Minkhimmash's oil and gas support group was especially low. For years, say Soviet critics, the practice in the energy sector was to channel investment preferentially to the extractive ministries, while the supporting machinery ministries got "whatever was left over."[44] According to a leading Soviet specialist on investment, Minkhimmash was given only one-forty-seventh of the investment resources allocated to the ministries it supplied.[45] At a rough guess, this would mean that investment in Minkhimmash's oil- and gas-field machinery plants totaled perhaps 2 billion rubles from 1975 to 1985, compared to 134 billion for the machinery sector as a whole during the same period[46] and over 96 billion for the oil and gas industries (not counting transmission).[47]

These priorities were further reflected in the behavior of Gosplan.

[41] In 1982 prices, the share of the the machinery complex (which in Soviet usage seems to include the nine civilian machine-building ministries only) in total industrial output rose from 16.3 percent in 1970 to 28 percent in 1986. *Narodnoe khoziaistvo SSSR za 70 let*, p. 132. Even allowing for substantial inflation in Soviet machinery prices, this appears to represent substantial growth in real relative volume.

[42] For a review of the situation by the late Academician A. I. Tselikov, see "Aspekty dolgovremennogo razvitiia mashinostroeniia SSSR," *Vestnik Akademii Nauk SSSR*, no. 11 (1983), pp. 23–31.

[43] Robert W. Campbell, "Resource Stringency and the Civilian-Military Resource Allocation," in Thane Gustafson and Timothy J. Colton, eds., *Soviet Soldiers and the State: Civil-Military Relations from Brezhnev to Gorbachev* (forthcoming, 1990). See also Jan Vanous and Bryan Roberts, "Time to Choose between Tanks and Tractors," *PlanEcon Report* 2, nos. 25–26 (June 1986), pp. 8–9.

[44] Ognev, "Kakie mashiny nuzhny promyslu." Within the West Siberian energy complex, according to Ognev, only 0.2 percent of total investment was allocated to the machine-building industry.

[45] T. Khachaturov, "Investitsionnaia politika," *Sotsialisticheskaia industriia*, 20 July 1985. Essentially the same proportions continued through 1988: according to a Goskomstat press bulletin issued in early 1989, central investment in Minkhimmash in 1988 was only 0.54 billion rubles, compared to 25.0 billion for the Oil and Gas Ministries together. However, under the new rules, Minkhimmash is supposed to generate a large share of its capital funds from its own profits.

[46] *Narodnoe khoziaistvo SSSR za 70 let*, p. 330.

[47] See table 2.4.

Within the civilian machinery sector, according to Minkhimmash officials, Gosplan systematically supported retooling in other ministries first, such as Mintiazhmash, which got preference in the allocation of numerically controlled machine tools, as did the automotive and electrical power ministries.[48] In short, this too was no bureaucratic failure of coordination but a systematic application of the leaders' priorities.

The results, however, were evidently so disruptive for the oil campaign that the Oil Ministry began supplying some of its own resources to relieve the worst bottlenecks; this helps to explain why the pattern of supply mirrors the industry's own priorities. Thus Uralmash's relative success in mass-producing rigs for cluster drilling, mentioned earlier, turns out to be due in part to direct assistance from the oil men.[49] But the ministry declined to provide similar help to Minkhimmash, although it made an exception to help modernize one Glavneftemash plant that produces electric submersibles.[50]

Why did the Brezhnev leadership throw resources into the oil and gas campaigns without corresponding investment in the necessary industrial support? It could not have been for lack of expert advice. Modeling exercises performed by Soviet energy specialists in the late 1970s warned planners of the obvious, that they would need large increases in industrial support if they accelerated investment in energy production. The modelers were particularly concerned about what their studies revealed about the impact of an overly sudden increase in the gas program, so much so that they appear to have spoken out against the 1980–1981 decisions to launch a crash gas campaign. The ferrous metallurgy industry, they said, would require four to seven years of advance preparation, and the machinery sector seven to ten years, before a major gas campaign could be supported efficiently. If the leaders chose to go ahead regardless, they should at least have had some inkling of what faced them.[51]

What changes have occurred since Brezhnev's death? By 1983, if not before, Brezhnev's successors had heard the experts' message. The new leadership that took shape in 1985, though by no means united in its approach to reform and to investment priorities, at least appeared to be

[48] Belanov et al., "Tekhnika dlia neftianikov."

[49] Ibid.

[50] Ibid. The plant in question is the Dzerzhinskii Zavod. The modernization evidently took a long time to show results: in early 1986 the Dzerzhinskii plant was reported to have delivered only 150 electric submersibles out of a plan target of over 760. A. Petrov, "Ekho sryva," *Sotsialisticheskaia industriia*, 9 Feb. 1986.

[51] L. A. Melent'ev and A. A. Makarov, *Energeticheskii kompleks SSSR* (Moscow: Ekonomika, 1983), pp. 206–214.

of one mind on the need to slow down investment in extractive industries and to reallocate as many resources as possible to the task of modernizing the machine-building sector. But as we saw in Chapter 1, they were soon caught in the same trap that had snared their predecessors: to keep energy supplies growing and to avoid the danger of shortages, they were obliged from the start to invest in energy supply at an even faster rate than before.

As a result, the planned reallocation of investment resources from energy to civilian machine building has not yet taken place. In the first two years of the Twelfth Plan (1986 and 1987) energy investment raced ahead of the projected five-year pace, increasing by 21 percent in two years, while investment in civilian machine building, though it did rise by a rapid 25 percent in the same two years, nevertheless fell far short of the planned five-year growth rate.[52]

I have not been able to determine from the available data whether the low priority of Minkhimmash within the machinery sector, or that of the oil and gas service sector within Minkhimmash, is being raised. But in view of the leaders' stress on advanced forms of machinery, such as computers, automated manufacturing systems, and the like, my suspicion is that the relative priority of retooling and modernization for oil and gas service remains low.

As the oil and gas ministries read the Gorbachev reform decrees, they must have another concern. As we have seen, Minkhimmash and Mintiazhmash enjoy virtual monopolies in their fields. Consequently, if the Gorbachev reforms were fully implemented and enterprise managers were truly motivated to maximize profits, the most likely consequence would be large-scale price increases for oil and gas equipment. Moreover, associations like Glavneftemash are so decrepit that they are unlikely to be able to innovate through their own profits; and as monopolists they will not have much more incentive than they do today. Wholesale markets for producers goods will be of no help, again because of the lack of competition. Consequently, the oil and gas industries could end up paying much more for the same unsatisfactory equipment they are getting now.

[52] Data for 1986 are from *Narodnoe khoziaistvo SSSR za 70 let*, p. 330; 1987 data, from the statistical summary of economic performance for 1987 published in *Pravda*, 24 January 1988. The Twelfth Plan, as adopted in June 1986, projects a 35 percent increase in energy investment versus a 68 percent increase in machine building. The 68 percent figure for five-year investment growth in the machine-building complex is taken from Ed A. Hewett, Bryan Roberts, and Jan Vanous, "On the Feasibility of Key Targets in the Soviet Five-Year Plan," in U.S. Congress, Joint Economic Committee, *Gorbachev's Economic Plans* (Washington, D.C.: USGPO, 1987), vol. 1, p. 34.

What about imports as an alternative? During the Brezhnev years the Soviets made more use of foreign equipment than at any time since the First Five-Year Plan. Did imports manage to do what Soviet producers could not?

Imports to the Rescue? The Brezhnev Leadership's Choices

The most striking feature of foreign-trade policy under Brezhnev was the use of imported equipment and know-how to give a fast start to the government's highest-priority tasks, ranging from passenger automobiles to defense electronics. On the face of it, then, one would have expected that the sudden increase in attention to oil after 1977, followed by the crash gas campaign in 1981 and after, together with the two industries' importance as earners of foreign exchange, would have put their equipment needs at the top of the Soviets' shopping list. The result should have been a dramatic increase in imports of energy-related technology.

At first glance, that is exactly what happened. Between 1977 and 1983 Soviet imports of oil- and gas-related equipment from all sources jumped more than tenfold, from about 126 million rubles a year to nearly 1,300 million.[53] But then Soviet purchases receded sharply, sinking in 1985 to less than half the level of two years before, and the following two years brought only partial recovery. Most of the decline took place before the collapse of world oil prices in 1986; consequently, it was not caused primarily by hard-currency shortages (table 6.2).

Most of the rise, and then most of the subsequent fall, were due to imports for the gas industry. In contrast, imports for the oil industry have grown steadily if slowly throughout the same period; by the mid-1980s they had reached annual levels three to five times as great as ten years before and were still headed upward (see figure 6.1 and table 6.3), at least until 1988.

There are two inferences to be drawn about the policies underlying these trends. First, the priority of the gas campaign after 1981 was immediately reflected in increased purchases for the gas industry, mostly for gas transmission.[54] The sharp decline in gas-related imports after 1983–1984 resulted from the American embargo and the Soviet decision to halt further imports of compressors for gas transmission (see pp. 205–207 below).

[53] Category 127 is defined as "equipment for the oil-refining industry." Category 128 is "machinery, etc., for drilling, well development, and geological exploration." Category 266 is pipe, of which about two-thirds is destined for the energy sector.

[54] The numbers cited understate the dominance of the gas-related imports, since

TABLE 6.2
Soviet Imports of Machinery and Equipment for Drilling, Well Development, and Geological Exploration, 1970–1987
(Category 128; millions of rubles)

1970	20.7	1982	659.8
1975	133.1	1983	1,298.6
1976	198.5	1984	1,032.1
1977	126.3	1985	627.2
1978	251.2	1986	692.6
1979	136.3	1987	857.1
1980	249.0	1988	634.1
1981	199.4		

NOTE: Category 128 in the Soviet foreign-trade statistics does not include pipe or refinery equipment, although it evidently includes most nonpipe imports for gas transmission.

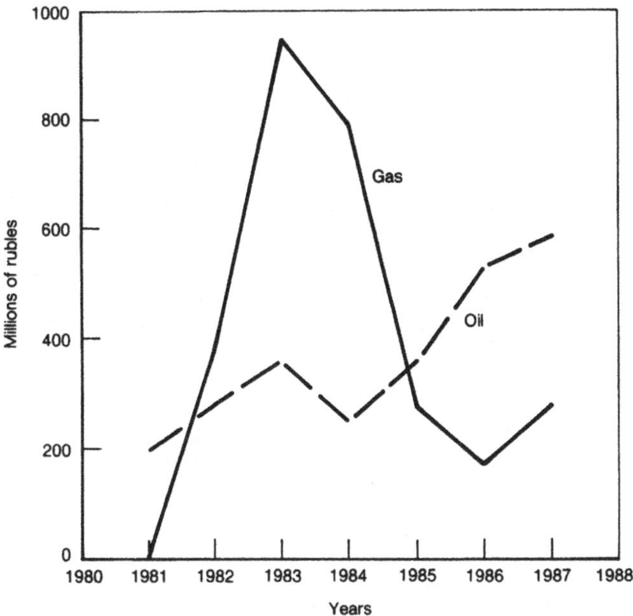

FIG. 6.1. Soviet Imports of Gas-Related versus Oil-Related Equipment. Source: *Vneshniaia torgovlia SSSR*. These figures exclude imports of pipe and refinery equipment.

TABLE 6.3
Soviet Imports of Gas Equipment versus Oil Equipment, 1981–1987 (Category 128, notably excluding pipe; millions of rubles)

	Gas	*Oil*
1981	4.8	194.6
1982	381.7	278.1
1983	942.4	356.2
1984	789.6	242.5
1985	273.2	354.0
1986	167.5	525.1
1987	277.2	579.9
1988	122.7	511.4

SOURCE: *Vneshniaia torgovlia SSSR,* relevant years. The gas figure is Category 128.75; the oil figure is derived by the difference between 128 and 128.75.

In contrast, the trends in oil-related imports suggest a rather different and unexpected pattern of decisionmaking: despite the sharp step-up of oil development and exploration and the clear disarray among domestic equipment suppliers, the oil industry did not make massive use of imports. Only after 1982 did its imports pass the 300 million ruble mark, but the growth rate of oil-related imports from 1982 to 1985 was not much faster than the growth rate of total oil investment itself (table 6.3).[55]

The year 1986 may have marked the beginning of a new phase: in 1986 and 1987, for the first time, oil-field equipment imports passed the half-billion ruble mark. Even so, investment in imported equipment

category 128 does not include pipe. One additional category, 155 ("Pumps and Compressors"), has not been used here. This category runs consistently between 200 and 250 million rubles a year and is thus too small and too steady to account for more than a small part of gas-related imports. A mystifying category is 167 ("Pipelines"), which rose briefly and spectacularly to 1.4 billion rubles in 1978, subsiding to minor levels in every year since.

[55] The rapid growth of oil-related imports for 1985 and 1986 suggests the possibility that policy has changed under Gorbachev, but at this writing (spring 1989) it is still too early to draw conclusions on the basis of the limited data available.

TABLE 6.4
Soviet Imports of Equipment Related to the Gas, Oil, and Oil-Refining Industries, 1970–1987
(millions of rubles)

	Category 127		*Category 128*		*Category 266*	
	CMEA	*West*	*CMEA*	*West*	*CMEA*	*West*
1970	15.8	5.8	12.6	7.6	34.3	148.8
1971	11.7	30.0	21.3	16.6	0.9	0.2
1972	6.6	37.2	12.7	20.7	1.0	0.2
1973	15.0	9.7	25.4	3.3	0.1	0.1
1974	5.3	34.0	25.7	4.7	0.1	0.2
1975	56.2	42.9	25.1	1.0	84.5	1,026.5
1976	33.5	0.9	30.7	159.6	84.6	862.7
1977	40.9	29.2	38.6	80.9	67.6	565.2
1978	93.8	197.0	51.9	185.8	82.2	842.3
1979	152.5	8.4	70.2	62.2	62.6	1,104.0
1980	154.5	11.5	78.1	132.7	71.9	964.0
1981	114.6	1.0	85.7	108.1	78.5	1,274.4
1982	48.2	5.7	213.7	401.9	232.8	1,414.4
1983	54.3	34.5	302.4	972.0	232.8	1,575.1
1984	52.4	6.3	267.9	738.1	233.0	1,556.3
1985	104.2	1.2	333.7	271.0	251.0	1,561.6
1986	97.7	2.3	427.3	221.6	270.1	1,657.9
1987	80.1	7.3	402.7	382.1	255.7	1,445.1*

SOURCE: *Vneshniaia torgovlia SSSR*, relevant years.

NOTES: Category 127 is defined as "equipment for the oil-refining industry." Category 128 is "machinery, etc., for drilling, well development, and geological exploration." Category 266 is pipe, of which about two-thirds is destined for the energy sector. The totals for West and CMEA do not fully add up to the total imports for each category, since they are drawn from *Vneshniaia torgovlia*'s partial listing of major originating countries. For the purposes of this table, Finland has been grouped with the West and Yugoslavia with the CMEA.

* In 1987 *Vneshniaia torgovlia* reported the countries of origin in Category 266 in physical quantities only. I have derived a rough ruble estimate by assuming that the average price per ton for each country's sales to the Soviet Union remained the same as in 1986.

still accounted for less than 4 percent of MNP's annual capital budget in those two years. In 1988, however, oil-field equipment imports fell back again.

The second major finding is that, while Western countries are the major suppliers of pipe and gas-related equipment, in oil-related imports it is Eastern Europe that has dominated the 1980s. (Table 6.4 shows the pattern for refinery equipment, oil- and gas-field equipment,

TABLE 6.5
Romanian Equipment as a Share of Total Soviet Oil Equipment Imports

	Total (10^6R)	*Romanian (10^6R)*	*Romanian Share (%)*
1981	194.6	85.7	44.0
1982	278.1	152.4	54.8
1983	356.2	198.0	55.6
1984	242.5	156.2	64.4
1985	354.0	253.0	71.5
1986	525.1	348.1	66.3
1987	579.9	346.3	59.7

SOURCES: For oil-related equipment, see table 6.3. Romanian equipment is Category 128 from *Vneshniaia torgovlia*, various years.

NOTE: Examination of the breakdown for Romania suggests that nearly all of Category 128 from that country is oil related.

and pipe.) One East European country alone, Romania, has accounted for well over half of the Soviets' total oil field-related imports each year since 1981 (table 6.5). Most of these imports have been low technology, chiefly Romanian rigs and drilling equipment. But Romania's dominant role may be slowly fading under Gorbachev, as the volume of Soviet oil-related imports grows: from a remarkable 71.5 percent of the Soviet market in 1985, Romania's share receded to 59.7 percent in 1987. The principal beneficiary was France.

What is most striking overall is that oil- and gas-related imports (and total energy-related imports, for that matter) have failed to make major or lasting gains as a share of the total Soviet import volume. In the early 1970s the oil and gas industries claimed under 3 percent of total Soviet imports; by the mid-1980s their share had grown to around 5 percent—a minor increase when one recalls the gigantic spurt of these two industries in Soviet domestic investment during the same interval—and in 1985–1987 their share sank back to the 4 percent mark (table 6.6).

Finally, oil- and gas-related imports as a share of fixed oil and gas investment, compared to total fixed investment in oil and gas, grew modestly if steadily from the early 1970s to the early 1980s (table 6.7). But if one reckons in the abrupt decline of gas-related imports after 1983, total gas- and oil-related imports relative to fixed domestic investment in oil and gas have now sunk back to the level of the early 1970s.

TABLE 6.6
Share of Energy-Related Imports in Total Soviet Imports, 1970–1987
(billions of rubles in current prices)

	Oil- and Gas-Related		*Total Energy*		*Total*
	Imports	*%*	*Imports*	*%*	*Imports*
1970	0.28	2.3	0.31	3.4	10.6
1971	0.32	2.9	0.46	4.1	11.2
1972	0.34	2.6	0.47	3.5	13.3
1973	0.44	2.8	0.57	3.7	15.5
1974	0.64	3.4	0.78	4.1	18.8
1975	1.46	5.5	1.69	6.3	26.7
1976	1.32	4.6	1.52	5.3	28.8
1977	0.93	3.1	1.20	4.0	30.1
1978	2.77	8.0	3.39	9.8	34.5
1979	2.08	5.5	2.68	7.1	37.9
1980	1.63	3.7	2.30	5.2	44.5
1981	1.77	3.5	2.56	4.9	52.6
1982	2.98	5.3	3.64	6.4	56.4
1983	3.31	5.5	4.26	7.1	59.6
1984	2.99	4.6	4.13	6.3	65.4
1985	2.64	3.8	3.82	5.5	69.4
1986	2.78	4.4	3.92	6.3	62.6
1987	2.93	4.8	4.05	6.7	60.7

SOURCE: *Vneshniaia torgovlia SSSR*, relevant years.

NOTE: Oil- and gas-related imports are taken as Categories 128, 266, and 167 (pipelines); total energy-related imports, as the above plus 127 (oil refining), 110 (equipment for the power sector), and 120 (mining equipment, primarily for the coal industry).

Overall, the Soviet oil and gas industries are nearly as autarkic today as they were before the Brezhnev energy campaign began.

How can one explain these patterns? What underlying policies do they reflect? What do they tell us about decisionmaking in foreign-trade policy and the ways internal priorities are connected to external ones? The pattern of imports is a mosaic, each piece resulting from a distinct set of aims and constraints. In the following section we look briefly at three specific cases and review a handful of others treated in previous chapters.

What might we expect to find? The general practice of the Brezhnev leadership, as we observed at the outset, was to turn to foreign equipment for "fast starts." But the Brezhnev years were also a time when the Soviets enjoyed an unprecedented hard-currency bonanza, chiefly from high oil and gas prices. In effect, Soviet decisionmakers enjoyed a soft-

TABLE 6.7
Oil- and Gas-Related Imports Compared to Total Soviet Oil and Gas Fixed Investment, 1971–1985 (Categories 128 and 266; including pipe; billions of rubles)

	Total Imports	*Total Investment*	*Imports versus Investment (%)*
1971–1975	3.21	27.8	11.5
1976–1980	6.60	48.4	13.6
1981–1985	13.25	79.0	16.8

SOURCES: import data: *Vneshniaia torgovlia SSSR*, relevant years; oil and gas investment: from Chapters 3 and 5.

NOTE: For this table I have used a looser definition of oil- and gas-related imports by including Category 266, even though only about half of it consists of energy-related pipe imports. The result is to exaggerate the size of oil- and gas-related imports relative to investment. For oil and gas exploration by the Ministry of Geology, all but about 20 percent of all exploration is financed on a "pass-through" basis from capital funds from the Ministries of Oil and Gas. The remainder goes directly to Mingeo from the state budget. For this table I have added 6 percent to the oil and gas investment totals to reflect exploration, on the assumption that total exploration is about 30 percent of total oil and gas investment and that the direct budgetary portion going separately to Mingeo is about 20 percent of that figure. I have not attempted to continue the exercise beyond 1985, since after that year Soviet statistical manuals began lumping all energy investment figures into a single total. However, the trend in 1985-1987 indicates a general decline in oil-and gas-related imports relative to fixed oil and gas investment.

This table is an admittedly crude pass through the problem, since the import and investment figures use different price bases.

ened hard-currency budget constraint, and one would expect to find that their import choices became more permissive, particularly in the Party leadership and in Gosplan. If, despite this permissive environment, we observe cases in which the Soviets did *not* turn to massive imports, then what were the reasons? In the following pages, we examine three specific cases.

Domestic Production versus Imports: Three Cases

CASE 1: COMPRESSORS FOR GAS TRANSMISSION

The sale of compressors for the Soviet gas pipelines in the first half of the 1980s is the most controversial case in the history of East-West trade. But what is chiefly of interest about it for this chapter is not the politics of the American embargo[56] but rather the insight the episode may give us into Soviet decisionmaking.

Transmission (as we saw in Chapter 4) had long been the chief constraint on the growth of the Soviet gas industry and particularly its expansion into West Siberia in the 1970s. The main reason was the unsatisfactory performance of domestically made turbine drives and compressors.[57] By the early 1970s, after much delay and difficulty, the principal Soviet manufacturer, the Neva Factory in Leningrad (in Russian, Nevskii Zavod),[58] had succeeded in putting a 10-megawatt gas-turbine drive into mass production. It proved so unreliable in the field, however, that complaints poured into Nevskii Zavod and led to a shake-up of its top ranks, conducted by the city committee of the Party, in about 1975.[59] The model was sufficiently improved so that during the second half of the 1970s it became the principal workhorse of the Soviet transmission network.[60]

But the gas industry's first major offensive into West Siberia in the second half of the 1970s required larger pipelines and more powerful compressors. Although Nevskii Zavod's designers had begun work on a 25-megawatt model in the 1960s, the project advanced slowly.[61] A first prototype was completed by 1977, but it took three more years for the second and third to appear, and the project bogged down while they awaited testing.[62]

In the meantime, because of Nevskii Zavod's chronic problems and delays, Soviet planners brought in another technology and another machine-building ministry. Nevskii Zavod belongs to the Ministry of

[56] The diplomatic aspects of the pipeline affair are ably told in Bruce W. Jentleson, *Pipeline Politics* (Ithaca, N.Y.: Cornell University Press, 1986), ch. 6.

[57] The history of the Soviet compressor program to the late 1970s is reviewed in Campbell, *Soviet Energy Technologies*, ch. 7. A technical note on the different components involved: The gas turbine (*gazoturbinnyi privod*) is the power source for the compressor proper (*nagnetatel'*). The combination of the two composes the compressor assembly (*gazoperekachivaiushchii agregat* or *ustanovka*), several of which make up the working core of the compressor station (*kompressornaia stantsiia*).

[58] Nevskii Zavod, whose machines are claimed to pump three-quarters of the gas piped in the Soviet Union, is subordinated to the Ministry of Power Machinery. The history of the Nevskii Zavod is described in a special issue of the ministry's house journal, *Energomashinostroenie*, no. 12 (1981).

[59] Ye. G. Gerasimov (then secretary of Nevskii Zavod's Party committee), "Nevskii variant," *Sovetskaia Rossiia*, 14 Nov. 1982. The article is an excerpt from Gerasimov's book by the same title, published by Lenizdat in 1983, which unfortunately I have not seen. For technical details on the 10–megawatt unit's troubled early history, see *Energomashinostroenie*, no. 12 (1981), pp. 11–12.

[60] Nevskii Zavod produced over 500 of the 10-megawatt units in the 1970s. *Energomashinostroenie*, no. 12 (1981).

[61] Campbell, *Soviet Energy Technologies*, p. 213.

[62] Gerasimov, "Nevskii variant."

Power-Generating Machinery (Minenergomash), and its heavy-duty gas-powered turbines were originally developed to generate electricity. But in the early 1970s the Ministry of Chemical and Petroleum Machine-building (Minkhimmash), whose role in oil- and gas-related machinery we have already discussed, was given the task of developing a 6.3-megawatt drive unit based on converted military jet engines.[63] Series production began in 1974, principally at Minkhimmash's Frunze plant in Sumy (Ukraine), and by the early 1980s there were several hundred units in operation. But the aviation-derived compressor drives initially went through many of the same problems as Nevskii Zavod's 10-megawatt model.[64]

As a result of the weaknesses in both programs, there was a continuous shortage of domestic capacity to support the Soviet gas pipeline program throughout the 1970s. To power their new large Siberian lines, the Soviets turned to Western equipment. From 1973 to 1976 they ordered 3,000 megawatts of large gas-powered turbines and compressors from Western firms,[65] which represented about 30 percent of the total net growth in compressor capacity for the Soviet gas transmission network in the second half of the 1970s[66] and virtually all of the power supply for the new large-diameter lines.

This brings us to 1980 and the beginning of Brezhnev's gas campaign. As we have already seen (Chapter 4), the decision to launch a massive gas campaign in 1981–1985 was taken suddenly, most likely without careful consideration of the industrial requirements involved. The five-year plan adopted in 1981 called for 20,000 megawatts of new compressor capacity for the six new West Siberian lines alone, far beyond anything Soviet industry had supported before. Puzzled Western analysts pointed to the gap between the plans and the capabilities and concluded that the Soviets were contemplating massive imports, of

[63] For background on the Minkhimmash program, see A. Aver'iakonov, "Effektivnost' ukrupneniia edinichnykh moshchnostei gazoperekachivaiushchikh agregatov," *Planovoe khoziaistvo*, no. 4 (1983), pp. 107–109. A similar pair of technologies was developed in parallel in the West: the so-called heavy-duty gas-turbine drives produced by General Electric and its licensees, and an airplane-derived, jet-engine model developed by Rolls Royce. The competition between these two types figured prominently in the bidding among Western manufacturers over the export pipeline contract.

[64] Aver'iakonov, "Effektivnost' ukrupneniia."

[65] Campbell, *Soviet Energy Technologies*, p. 218.

[66] A. D. Sedykh and B. A. Kuchin, *Upravlenie nauchno-tekhnicheskim progressom v gazovoi promyshlennosti* (Moscow: Nedra, 1983), p. 10, gives the net increase in Soviet compressor capacity from 1975 to 1980 as just short of 10,000 megawatts. But a more recent source gives only 8,200 megawatts, from 9,400 in 1975 to 17,600 in 1980. VNIIEgazprom, "Sovremennoe sostoianie gazovoi promyshlennosti SSSR" (Moscow, 1988), p. 19.

which the initial orders for the Urengoy-Uzhgorod export pipeline were probably only the beginning.

In fact, the disarray at the top during Brezhnev's last two years was so severe, and his last five-year plan so poorly constructed, that Soviet planners may have been improvising as they went along. One symptom of this is that development of Nevskii Zavod's 25-megawatt compressor drive continued to inch along, even though it was supposed to play the star role in the new campaign. Testing by the Ministry of the Gas Industry began only in 1979 and lasted well into 1982, prompting accusations from Minenergomash that the gas industry was dragging its feet because it preferred foreign equipment and that Gosplan indulged it with overly generous allocations of hard currency.[67] At Nevskii Zavod, the five-year plan called for a doubling of the capital budget to tool up for the new 25-megawatt model, which was supposed to account for 80 percent of all the plant's gas-turbine output by 1985.[68] But the plant had also been told to continue manufacturing the older 10-megawatt model and to satisfy all other orders without any slowdown, which of course hampered retooling.[69] On the eve of the American embargo, the minister of Minenergomash predicted that the new model would not be in series production before the second half of the 1980s.[70]

This, then, was the confused situation into which the American embargo intruded. Its immediate effect was to galvanize Soviet decisionmakers and raise sharply the political priority of both compressor programs. Boris Shcherbina, then head of the Ministry for Construction of Oil and Gas Enterprises (MNGS), vowed to "free the Soviet Union from compressor imports."[71] In Leningrad, Party leaders declared the 25-megawatt compressor their highest industrial priority,[72] and they organized a citywide campaign under the direct supervision of the Leningrad obkom (province committee of the Party).[73] Additional plants and workers were thrown into the front line, including ones drawn from the better-equipped nuclear power and aviation indus-

[67] V. V. Krotov (then minister of Minenergomash), "Energomashinostroenie i nauchno-tekhnicheskii progress," *Planovoe khoziaistvo*, no. 5 (1981), pp. 3–11.

[68] *Energomashinostroenie*, no. 12 (1981), p. 6.

[69] Gerasimov, "Nevskii variant."

[70] Krotov, "Energomashinostroenie."

[71] Boris Shcherbina, "Glavnye magistrali toplivnoi energetiki," *Stroitel'stvo truboprovodov*, no. 12 (1982), p. 7.

[72] Interview with S. Petrov, then head of the heavy industry department of the Leningrad obkom, "Trudovoe sodruzhestvo," *Izvestiia*, 4 July 1982.

[73] One could gauge the project's sudden high priority from the rank of the officials involved. In early July 1982 a conference was convened at obkom headquarters, chaired by then Politburo member and Leningrad obkom First Secretary G. V. Romanov and

tries.[74] In the Ukraine, Minkhimmash's Frunze plant in Sumy also accelerated its program. A new 16-megawatt jet-derived compressor drive, based on retired Tupolev-154 and Il'iushin-62 engines, went into series production in 1982,[75] soon joined by other Minkhimmash plants in the Urals cities of Sverdlovsk[76] and Perm'.[77]

The added political priority soon produced results. The 25-megawatt drive was rushed into series production by early 1983,[78] and similar reports came from the 16-megawatt producers in Sumy[79] and Sverdlovsk.[80] All told, well over one hundred of the two large units were claimed as completed by the end of 1983.[81] Meanwhile, production of the older 10-megawatt and 6.3-megawatt models was accelerated too.[82]

By late 1983 the Soviet press was hailing the crash response to the embargo as an immense victory, and rewards soon showered on the successful managers.[83] Interestingly enough, however, while the Frunze plant in Sumy became the hero of the day and has been a star in the Soviet industrial reform program ever since, Nevskii Zavod and

---

attended by the then president of the USSR Academy of Sciences, A. P. Aleksandrov, to examine the "urgent tasks connected with completing, testing, and speeding up mass production" of the 25-megawatt drives. Radio Moscow Domestic Service, reported in Foreign Broadcast Information Service, *Soviet Union Daily Report*, 13 July 1982.

[74] All told, some 40 Leningrad enterprises and institutes were mobilized to contribute to the 25-megawatt program, including Izhorskii Zavod, the Soviets' leading manufacturer of nuclear reactors and power plants. The latter plant's participation gives the measure of the Soviet leaders' determination, since the Soviet nuclear program was then badly behind schedule and could ill afford any distractions. "GTN-25: seriia nachinaetsia," *Leningradskaia pravda*, 9 July 1982.

[75] "Shagai bystree, trassa!" *Sotsialisticheskaia industriia*, 21 Nov. 1982; "Stantsiia v upakovke," *Pravda*, 9 Feb. 1983; "Agregat dlia gazoprovodov," *Sotsialisticheskaia industriia*, 10 July 1982.

[76] "Uskorim postavki sovremennoi tekhniki," *Ekonomicheskaia gazeta*, no. 29 (1982), p. 3. This was the Turbomotornyi Zavod in Sverdlovsk, which is also mentioned as a developer of the earlier 6.3-megawatt aero-derived model. *Energomashinostroenie*, no. 12 (1981), p. 13. See also "Turbiny magistral' poluchit," *Sotsialisticheskaia industriia*, 7 Aug. 1982.

[77] "Proshel ispytaniia," *Pravda*, 10 Oct. 1982.

[78] *Izvestiia*, 3 Oct. 1983.

[79] *Sotsialisticheskaia industriia*, 19 Aug. 1983.

[80] "Ural'tsy ne podvedut," *Sotsialisticheskaia industriia*, 25 Sept. 1982; "Ural—gazovoi magistrali," *Izvestiia*, 25 Aug. 1982.

[81] This estimate comes from adding the claims in the sources previously cited.

[82] "Trudovoe sodruzhestvo," *Izvestiia*, 4 July 1982; "Nash pervenets—GTN-25," *Leningradskaia pravda*, 24 Oct. 1982; Aver'iakonov, "Effektivnost' ukrupneniia," p. 109.

[83] Deputy Gas Minister S. S. Kashirov was awarded the Order of the October Revolution (*Pravda*, 22 Sept. 1983); Boris Shcherbina (then minister of MNGS) was given the

Minenergomash did not share in the laurels.[84] This was an early sign that Minkhimmash's aero-derived compressors had performed more successfully than Minenergomash's conventional heavy-duty units.

In hindsight it has become clear that Soviet industry did quite not pull off the miracle initially advertised. The 25-megawatt compressor of Minenergomash has proved an embarrassing failure and has resisted all attempts by its manufacturers and the gas industry to improve it.[85] The aero-derived alternatives produced by Minkhimmash have performed better, although they too experience frequent breakdowns and must be pulled out of the line for capital repairs at the factory. But now a new problem has arisen: since the passing of the emergency, the Ministry of the Aviation Industry has cut back its support.[86] As a result, growing numbers of compressors are standing idle (fully one-quarter of the 6.3-megawatt jet-derived units were out of commission in the fall of 1988), threatening gas deliveries to the European part of the USSR during peak periods of winter demand, and delays in deliveries of new compressors could slow the growth of the transmission network in the future.[87]

Nevertheless, there is no public talk of turning to the West. The Soviets may still be relying on Western manufacturers for compressor

---

Order of Lenin and made deputy chairman of the Council of Ministers; his deputy, Iu. P. Batalin, was promoted to chairman of the State Committee for Labor and Social Problems (he has since been promoted again, to chairman of the State Construction Committee and deputy chairman of the Council of Ministers); V. A. Dinkov, then minister of gas, was awarded the Order of Lenin (*Pravda*, 7 Oct. 1983).

[84] V. M. Luk'ianenko, then general director of the Frunze NPO to which the Sumy plant belongs, was promoted to minister of Minkhimmash under Gorbachev. In contrast, V. Krotov, former minister of Minenergomash, was retired in late December, even though earlier in his career he had served in Sverdlovsk under A. P. Kirilenko and might therefore have been expected to prosper as part of the "Sverdlovsk mafia" that did so spectacularly well under Andropov and Gorbachev in 1983 and after.

[85] V. T. Fadeev, "Effektivnost' gazotransportnoi sistemy: sovremennaia taktika tekhnicheskogo obnovleniia," *Gazovaia promyshlennost'*, no. 11 (1987), pp. 26–29. See also Ye. N. Yakovlev, "Tiumengazprom: At a Critical Turning Point," *Gazovaia promyshlennost'*, no. 4 (1988), pp. 5–6; translated in Foreign Broadcast Information Service, JPRS Report, "Soviet Union: Economic Affairs," JPRS-UEA-88-026, 5 July 1988, p. 52.

[86] The necessary airplane engines must come from the Aviation Ministry, but in 1986–1987 shipments were running between 50 and 75 percent of planned rates. The Aviation Ministry is also falling short on repairs.

[87] V. Tikhonov, "Postavkam gaza—vysokuiu nadezhnost'!" *Ekonomicheskaia gazeta*, no. 44 (1988). In particular, the gas industry was counting on a 70 percent increase in the number of aero-derived units during the second half of the 1980s, but at this writing that now looks unlikely.

parts and components for existing lines,[88] and they have continued to import large quantities of auxiliary equipment for pipe laying and pipeline operation,[89] but there has been no further sign of Soviet interest in large compressor orders.

The compressor episode suggests some interesting points about Soviet priorities and decisionmaking. First, if there had been no embargo by the United States, Soviet leaders and planners most probably would have continued to rely heavily on imported equipment for at least another five years, because under normal circumstances Soviet capacity would clearly have been inadequate. Second, the chronic problems at Nevskii Zavod (and the lesser but substantial difficulties at the Frunze plant in Sumy) had little to do with high technology;[90] rather, the case illustrates the debilitating effects of competition from military priorities on civilian programs, even high-priority ones. This problem continues today, despite Gorbachev's exhortation to the defense industries to support civilian programs. Third, and most important, the compressor case throws into sharp relief the improvisation and lack of coordination of Brezhnevian policymaking, which worsened from the mid-1970s on. Only the most extreme affront to national pride and economic autonomy finally forced the leadership to come to grips with the problem of neglected industrial support for the gas transmission program; but even the highest political priority could not reverse overnight the effects of years of neglect. Soviet industry met the political challenge, but at a high cost and with after-effects that will be felt for a long time.

CASE 2: LARGE-DIAMETER PIPE FOR GAS TRANSMISSION

With the rapid expansion of the gas transmission network after 1975 and its further acceleration after 1980, Soviet needs for high-quality, large-diameter pipe increased in proportion. Here too Soviet leaders found their domestic industry ill-prepared, and as a result they again

[88] In March 1983 the Soviets signed a $100 million contract with the West German firms MAN-GHH Sterkrade and AEG/Kanis to build 25 sets of rotor components for the Soviet 25-megawatt machines. *Financial Times*, 15 Mar. 1983; *Business Week*, 18 Apr. 1983.

[89] These include pipe layers, bulldozers, and tractors for gas pipeline construction, pipeline control systems, pipeline valves, and pipe coating and wrapping materials. Central Intelligence Agency, Intelligence Directorate, "Soviet Needs for Western Petroleum Technology and Equipment," xeroxed report, April 1986, p. 9 (I am grateful to the office of Senator Lloyd Bentsen for providing me with a copy of this document).

[90] It is true that, as the size of gas-turbine drives increases, they must operate at higher temperatures, speeds, and pressures, which in turn requires better materials and closer tolerances. The turbine blades of the 25-megawatt model require electron-beam welding; the combustion chamber uses heat-resistant alloys; and much of the fabrication calls for

faced a trade-off between crash modernization at home and massive imports from abroad.

The Soviet energy sector uses 65 percent of the country's output of steel pipe.[91] Although the Soviet Union is far and away the world's largest producer of this commodity (at nearly 21 million tons in 1988),[92] output has grown by only about 10 percent since 1980, while requirements have been growing rapidly. The difference has come from imports. Steel pipe is the largest single item, and the fastest-growing one, among all Soviet industrial imports (table 6.8).

About half of all Soviet imports of steel pipe are linked to the gas campaign. In particular, nearly all of the pipe used on the large-diameter trunk lines has been imported. This point is difficult to document conclusively, because Soviet sources are discrete and Western press reports are spotty. Nevertheless, the reasoning runs as follows. If one assumes that 1,420-millimeter gas pipe weighs about 600 tons per kilometer,[93] then the Soviet target of about 21,000 kilometers of trunk line scheduled for 1981–1985 required between 12 and 13 million tons. If one adds up the scattered reports in the Western press,[94] they suggest that Soviet imports increased steadily from 1980 to 1984, from about 1.5 million tons per year to between 2.7 and 2.8 million. This yields a total of about 11.5 million tons for 1980–1984, which indicates that the Soviets imported all but about 1 million tons of their total requirements for the 1,420-millimeter trunk lines. Robert Campbell, through a similar exercise, arrives at the same conclusion for the 1970s.[95] Soviet press items, which are far spottier, do not contradict this conclusion. As the Eleventh Five-Year Plan began, the Soviet ferrous metallurgy industry was producing large-diameter pipe at two locations: Khartsyzsk in Donetsk Province and Volzhsk in the southern

---

numerically controlled machine tools and automated process controls. Nevertheless, these are well-established techniques in the leading Soviet industries, and the heavy-duty turbine drives were a twenty-year-old technology in the West. A French manager of Creusot-Loire, a French licensee of General Electric, once described the U.S.-licensed machines to me as "une épouvantable charrue" (an awful plow).

91 M. I. Kamenitskii et al., eds., *Ekonomika neftegazovogo stroitel'stva: Spravochnoe posobie* (Moscow: Nedra, 1988), p. 7.

92 *Pravda*, 22 Jan. 1989.

93 Soviet estimates vary, but this appears to be the most common figure. See *Stroitel'naia gazeta*, 5 Feb. 1982; *Stroitel'stvo truboprovodov*, no. 1 (1983), p. 2.

94 For the details of this exercise, see Thane Gustafson, "Soviet Adaptation to Technological Pressures: The Case of the Oil and Gas Sector, 1975–1985," in Philip Joseph, ed., *Adaptability to New Technologies of the USSR and East European Countries*, Proceedings of the NATO Colloquium on the Soviet-bloc Economies (Brussels: NATO Economics Directorate, 1985), appendix, pp. 193–197.

95 Campbell, *Soviet Energy Technologies*, pp. 209–212.

TABLE 6.8
Soviet Imports of Pipe
(Category 266; billions of rubles)

1970	0.25	1979	1.37
1971	0.28	1980	1.24
1972	0.30	1981	1.58
1973	0.41	1982	2.17
1974	0.60	1983	1.93
1975	1.32	1984	1.85
1976	1.12	1985	1.89
1977	0.81	1986	2.00
1978	1.10	1987	1.73

SOURCE: *Vneshniaia torgovlia SSSR*, relevant years.

Volga Basin.[96] This was single-walled pipe, either spiral- or straight-welded, and not terribly satisfactory to Soviet policymakers because it was heavy and required alloying with "very scarce" (*ostrodefitsitnye*) metals such as niobium, molybdenum, and nickel.[97]

These are meager data, but they all point in the same direction: for the large-diameter trunk lines of the 1980s, as in the past, Soviet reliance on imports has been virtually total, and there has been little evidence of a trend toward greater independence.

But what of the next generation of trunk lines, scheduled for construction in the 1990s? A few years ago Soviet planners spoke confidently of moving up from the current 75 atmospheres to 100 or even 120 before the end of the Eleventh Plan (that is, 1985). But Soviet economic studies showed that moving up to 100 atmospheres would not be cost-effective unless lighter, cheaper pipe became available,[98] and there have been steady hints of opposition to the higher pressures.[99] Two different, multilayered designs have been under development, both using ordinary rolled steel. The first model, a five-layered

[96] *Stroitel'stvo truboprovodov*, no. 1 (1983), p. 18. The Khartsyszk plant was reported to have produced 500,000 tons of pipe in the first 8 months of 1982 (*Sotsialisticheskaia industriia*, 25 July 1982), at least some of it destined for the Urengoy-Uzhgorod export line.

[97] V. Cherkasov, "Truby dlia severa," *Pravda*, 16 June 1984.

[98] N. Kurbatov, head of the main pipe-laying administration in Siberia (Glavsibtruboprovodstroi), quoted in "Ratsional'noe ispol'zovanie material'nykh i trudovykh resursov na stroitel'stve magistral'nykh nefte- i gazotruboprovodov," *Planovoe khoziaistvo*, no. 4 (1981), p. 55.

[99] Gennadii Pisarevskii, an economic commentator writing in *Soviet Life* in July 1983, dwelled on the complexities of moving up to higher pressures. Cited in *Oil and Gas Journal*, 4 July 1983, p. 49.

design from the well-known Paton Electro-Welding Institute in Kiev, has been under development since the late 1970s. It was supposed to have entered production at the end of 1981, at the Vyksa Metallurgical plant in Gor'kii Province. The first production line was supposed to yield 250,000 tons a year (hardly enough, incidentally, for more than about 400 kilometers of trunk line),[100] with eventual capacity to reach 1 million tons a year.[101] As the Eleventh Plan neared its end, however, the Vyksa project was evidently at least three years behind schedule. Only "experimental batches" of the new pipe had been produced, and a planned 300-kilometer test line was still under construction.[102]

A competing design, the work of a team under the late Academician A. Tselikov, is a double-walled pipe that also requires no special alloys. In 1978 the Ministry of Ferrous Metallurgy authorized construction of two special lines for the new pipe at the Novomoskovsk pipe plant in the Ukrainian province of Dnepropetrovsk. After extensive field tests a Gosplan review commission (*ekspertnaia kommissiia*) recommended that the program at the Novomoskovsk plant be approved, with a design capacity of 650,000 tons a year. But by the mid-1980s the project had still gone nowhere. Minchermet started inauspiciously by canceling all funding for it in the Eleventh Plan. After the Central Committee's Party Control Committee intervened, the ministry revived the project in early 1982 but demanded new field tests. Though the new pipe reportedly performed well, the tests and subsequent interagency reviews took until mid-1983. At that point, Gosplan became locked in an internal dispute over whether there was enough rolled steel available to support the new project.[103]

The timing is significant: Minchermet's demand for new tests came only two months after the Reagan embargo was declared, and the project was allowed to drag along throughout the time the embargo was in force. In contrast to what was happening at the same moment at Soviet compressor plants, there was no sign of special priority, extraordinary meetings, or mobilization of additional workers or engineers. The Soviets evidently felt their sources of imported pipe were secure.

By the mid-1980s, development of the new generation of high-

[100] See details in Thane Gustafson, *The Soviet Gas Campaign: Politics and Policy in Soviet Decision-Making*, R-3036-AF (Santa Monica, Calif.: Rand Corporation, June 1983), pp. 90–91. The new pipe is described as being "slightly heavier" than the traditional sort.

[101] TASS report, reprinted in Foreign Broadcast Information Service, *Soviet Union/Daily Report*, 24 Aug. 1982.

[102] *Stroitel'stvo truboprovodov*, no. 9 (1984), centerfold. The initial reports of the test line said that the first lengths of pipe had been welded into place in 1982. *Izvestiia*, 31 July 1982.

[103] This account comes from V. Cherkassov, "Truby dlia Severa," *Pravda*, 16 June 1984.

pressure pipes had been so severely delayed that Soviet planners decided to contract with foreign firms to build a turnkey plant for conventional 75-atmosphere pipe. In 1985 they invited bids from Mannesmann, Italimpianti, and Finsider for a $1 billion metallurgical complex at Volzhsk.[104] In 1986 the contract was awarded to Italimpianti and construction began,[105] but it will be several years before the new plant makes a significant dent in Soviet pipe imports.

The outlook for the second half of the 1980s, consequently, is for continued reliance on imports for the expansion of the gas trunk-line network, and it is unlikely that the gas industry will attempt to move up to 100 atmospheres, especially in view of the mounting reliability problems in the existing network.

The Soviet decision to rely on imported pipe for the bulk of the large-diameter gas transmission system suggests what the compressor case might have looked like without the American embargo. In both cases, what is remarkable is the chronic inability of the civilian machine-building and metallurgical sectors to respond to the heightened requirements of the gas industry, even though the main trends in the gas industry had been clear since at least the mid-1970s. In metals as in machinery, the underlying reasons for failure have been abysmal civilian innovation and competition for the best people and the best output from the military-industrial sector (the former obviously aggravated by the latter). Nowhere is the Brezhnevian policy of using Western suppliers as a buffer against internal inadequacies clearer than in the case of steel pipe: domestic industry was so weak in this department that it is doubtful whether the gas campaign could have been conducted at all without Western imports.

CASE 3: OFFSHORE OIL AND GAS

The next generation of Soviet oil and gas could lie offshore, in the Caspian Sea and the Arctic Ocean. Since the mid-1970s the Soviets have been operating two separate programs, each with distinct priority,

[104] *Washington Post*, 27 Feb. 1985, p. A1. Since Volzhsk has hitherto produced conventional pipe and has not been involved in either of the newer models, I infer that the proposed turnkey plant would produce conventional pipe as well.

[105] "Dlia novykh promyslov," *Sotsialisticheskaia industriia*, 16 Sept. 1986. The decision to commission a turnkey plant represents a return to a strategy the Soviets used on a broad scale in the early 1970s, when they imported large quantities of equipment for the ferrous metallurgy sector. See Elizabeth Ann Goldstein, "The Impact of Technology Transfer on Production and Productivity in the USSR: The Case of the Ferrous Metals Industry," in Gordon B. Smith, ed., *The Politics of East-West Trade* (Boulder, Colo.: Westview Press, 1984), pp. 63–94.

prospects, and needs. Each has represented a different decisionmaking problem. The offshore program in the western Caspian Sea required relatively undemanding technology, carried low risks, and offered near-term returns but promised no bonanzas. (The eastern Caspian is a different story, as we shall see.) The arctic programs in the Barents Sea and off Sakhalin Island in the Pacific Ocean required the latest technology and skills, carried heavy risks, and looked to long horizons—but offered the chance of a spectacular return.

A betting man familiar with the behavior of Soviet planners and managers might have predicted that they would deal with offshore prospects in the following way. First, since they were more concerned to find new oil than new gas, both offshore programs would be concentrated in the hands of the oil industry. Next, because of the pressure for near-term results, the Soviets would give top priority to the Caspian and would import Western equipment for the purpose—but only after initially trying, and failing, to develop their own equipment. Arctic offshore programs, because of uncertain prospects and long-term payoff, would receive only secondary attention.

In fact, this would not have been a bad prediction, but it has taken a decade to come true. The Soviets initially behaved quite differently. In 1978 overall jurisdiction for all offshore exploration and development, both oil and gas, was given to the Ministry of the Gas Industry, and it was only at the beginning of 1988 that offshore was reassigned to the Oil Ministry.[106] The Caspian did indeed receive high priority; but the Soviets used little Western technology there, except as a "starter," and appeared at first to be succeeding in developing their own facilities for building domestic equipment. Finally, the arctic programs, far from

[106] I have been unable to discover an account of the reasons for this decision. One clue may be that the minister of gas at the time, S. A. Orudzhev, had been one of the pioneers and principal boosters of offshore oil in the Caspian earlier in his career, in the 1940s. N. Paniev, "Stroitel' neftianogo Kaspiia," *Izvestiia*, 20 July 1982. One should also recall that 1978 was the year when the Siberian oil campaign, launched by Brezhnev the previous fall, began gathering momentum. Advocates like Orudzhev may have wished to free the offshore program from a ministry that would necessarily be absorbed elsewhere, while the new minister of oil (N. A. Mal'tsev, appointed the previous year) may have been only too glad to get rid of a distraction.

Until 1983 MGP's offshore program was run by the then first deputy minister of gas, Iu. V. Zaitsev. Since Zaitsev's dismissal in that year, the program appears to have been under First Deputy Gas Minister V. I. Timonin, while responsibility for MGP's shipping and offshore equipment rested with Deputy Minister N. M. Nemchinov. Offshore exploration was conducted by Soiuzmorgeo, an office of MGP. The Arctic offshore fleet, which also belonged to MGP, was operated by Arktikneftegazflot, while the Caspian fleet was operated by another agency of MGP, Kaspmorneftegaz. In January 1988 responsibility for offshore operations was transferred to the oil industry.

being neglected, were pursued energetically, with heavy reliance on Western imports.

Part of the explanation for these unexpected initial responses may be that the Soviet offshore program grew out of decisions taken in the mid-1970s—that is, before the beginning of the Brezhnev oil offensive—when the Soviets first invited bids for Arctic drill ships and developed their first mobile drilling rig for the Caspian Sea. Geological exploration of the Barents Sea also began at that time, primarily by the USSR Academy of Sciences. But to explain why the various offshore programs then evolved as they did requires a closer look at each one.

The Caspian Sea. Off the coast of Azerbaijan the Soviets had been operating fixed platforms in the shallow waters of the Caspian Sea for years, with most of the rigs connected to land via long trestles.[107] But the program was not pursued vigorously, and offshore oil production began declining from 1970 on.[108] This provoked more concern than the modest numbers might suggest, because Azeri oil is a light, "sweet" crude (that is, low in sulphur) that supplies local refineries. The Eleventh Five-Year Plan (1981–1985) called for a rapid expansion of offshore operations, aimed at halting the Azeri decline,[109] and by 1984 the drop in Caspian production had been reversed.[110]

Beginning in the mid-1970s, the Soviets bought a handful of key foreign items, which they then used as models as they built their own. The original Soviet semisubmersible platform, the *Kaspmorneft'*, was based on a purchase from an American firm, Armco, and was at least partly assembled in Finland before being launched from Astrakhan' in 1981.[111] From this foreign ancestor Soviet designers derived in 1982 a

[107] In recent years about 70 percent of the output of Azerbaijan, once the center of the Soviet oil industry, has come from offshore. Interview with the first deputy chairman of the Azerbaijani Council of Ministers, S. Tatliev, "Neftianye Kamni prodolzhaiutsia," *Pravda*, 9 Dec. 1983.

[108] *Soviet Geography* 26, no. 4 (April 1985), p. 300.

[109] Isabel Gorst, "Big Boost to Offshore Oil Search," *Petroleum Economist*, April 1984, pp. 145–147.

[110] *Soviet Geography* 28, no. 4 (April 1987), p. 265.

[111] *Soviet Business and Trade*, 17 Jan. 1979, p. 2. According to news accounts at the time, the original Armco contract in 1976 also provided that Armco would license production of similar rigs in the USSR. *Soviet Business and Trade*, 4 Aug. 1976, p. 1; *New York Times*, 17 July 1976. But this arrangement did not materialize. In 1977 and 1978 the Soviets signed a series of equipment contracts with American firms that were related to the *Kaspmorneft'* project, but these too died away in 1979 and 1980. (I am indebted to Lawrence R. Hedges, Jr., for the opportunity to read his valuable paper, "US-USSR Petroleum Technology Transfer: An Assessment," unpublished, American University, 15 July 1980.)

homegrown rig, the *Shel'f*, now appearing in multiple copies from a new shipyard in Vyborg, which was completed during the first half of the 1980s.[112] Similarly, the first jack-up rig to operate in the Caspian (starting in 1968) was the Dutch-built *Khazar*. The Astrakhan' yard has since produced a number of Soviet-made jack-ups derived from it, the *Kaspii* series.

The relative speed with which these new shipyard facilities were built contrasts strongly with the anemic modernization program we have already observed for conventional oil and gas service equipment. (A new facility in Baku for deep-water fixed platforms, for example, was the largest construction program in the Caucasian republics in the first half of the 1980s.[113]) One might have thought that the planners were looking ahead, not just to the western but also to the much more promising eastern shore, off the coast of Kazakhstan. But this region has been much more technically demanding than the western Caspian, and the Gas Ministry proved reluctant to explore it vigorously.[114]

One suspects that the key reason for the rapid construction was the personal interest of Gosplan chairman N. K. Baibakov. Himself the son of a Baku oil man, Baibakov had spent his entire career in petroleum before he took over the leadership of Soviet planning, rising to the top of the industry as early as World War II and holding leading positions in it until the early 1960s. He had been associated with its pre-Siberian phases, however, and as chairman of Gosplan he remained interested in enhanced recovery in the older oil regions and in offshore development in the Caspian Sea.

The Barents Sea and Sakhalin Island. The pattern of Soviet offshore policy in arctic regions has been quite different from that in the Caspian region. Offshore work in the far north is much more demanding of men and equipment, and the prospects for major oil finds, if tempting, are more remote and far more uncertain. The arctic program that has received the greatest attention in the West is in the Barents Sea, east of Norway. Like its Caspian counterpart, it arose out of decisions made in

[112] *Shel'f-1* was built at Astrakhan', but all subsequent units of the Shel'f series have come from Vyborg. The drilling equipment, which was supplied for *Kaspmorneft'* by Armco, has been provided for subsequent semis by Uralmash, which as we have already seen also plays an important role in onshore rig production for West Siberia. *Oil and Gas Journal*, 5 Apr. 1982, p. 117.

[113] *Soviet Geography* 25, no. 12 (December 1984), p. 780. See also V. Goncharov and L. Tairov, "More zovet," *Pravda*, 21 Dec. 1984. The contractor is part of Minmontazhspetsstroi.

[114] E. Turkebaev and S. Shalabaev (energy officials in the Kazakh Republic Gosplan), "Put' k shel'fu," *Sotsialisticheskaia industriia*, 10 June 1984.

the mid-1970s;[115] but so far there have been no major oil finds, although there is evidence of abundant gas.[116]

In contrast to the policy pursued in the Caspian, Soviet exploration in the Barents Sea has relied heavily and continuously on Western equipment and on cooperation with Western firms, chiefly Finnish and Norwegian ones. The Soviets began with two Finnish-built drill ships equipped with computer equipment supplied by Norwegian manufacturers,[117] followed by two arctic jack-up drilling platforms and a number of service vessels, primarily from Finland.[118]

Even before the new Soviet leadership endorsed joint ventures with Western firms, Soviet gas men had been exploring more elaborate forms of collaboration in the Barents Sea. At the Soviets' request a Norwegian firm, Norwegian Petroleum Consultants, developed cost estimates for the development of several small fields in the Barents Sea. In 1983 it joined six other Norwegian companies in a consortium, called Boconor, that contracted with the Soviet Union to develop a master plan for a Barents Sea project.[119] At this writing, since no major

[115] Soviet exploratory drilling activity, which began in the Barents Sea in 1982, was preceded by extensive seismic surveys starting in 1978. Preliminary geological surveying had begun in the early 1970s, conducted not by the ministries of gas or geology but by the Institute of Oceanography of the USSR Academy of Sciences. A. Monin, "Arkticheskii poisk," *Pravda*, 3 Oct. 1983.

[116] For an excellent analysis of the Soviet arctic exploration program, see Helge Ole Bergesen, Arild Moe, and Willy Ostreng, *Soviet Oil and Security Interests in the Barents Sea* (New York: St. Martin's Press, 1987). The only oil find to date has been on Kolguev Island in the Pechora Sea. But the Kolguev deposit, first reported in 1983 (*Oil and Gas Journal*, 14 Feb. 1983, p. 72), is not an offshore find and had been under investigation since 1972. See also *Oil and Gas Journal*, 20 Aug. 1984, p. 72.

[117] A third Finnish-built ship operates in the Sea of Okhotsk and off Vietnam. These ships are described as the world's most advanced drilling units for arctic offshore work. They are equipped with computer-controlled dynamic positioning systems, and they are capable of doing advanced seismic work. Egil Bergsager, "Oil and Gas in the USSR," *Noroil*, August 1984.

The decision to order these ships dates back to 1976, when Kosygin's son-in-law, Dzherman Gvishiani, told the Western press that the Ministry of Geology was negotiating with Finnish and American firms for assistance in developing an arctic offshore exploration program. *Soviet Business and Trade* 5, no. 2 (23 June 1976), p. 5. When the contracts for the Finnish drill ships were first let in 1979, American firms were prominently involved as subcontractors. Hedges, "US-USSR Petroleum Technology Transfer," p. 39. I have no information on the subsequent fate of those deals, but they presumably came under the ban imposed on oil- and gas-related equipment by the Carter administration in the wake of the Afghan intervention.

[118] The *Kol'skaia* and the *Sakhalinskaia* were built by Rauma-Repola. "V moria—za kladami," *Komsomol'skaia pravda*, 2 Dec. 1984.

[119] Author's interviews with representatives of Boconor, Oslo, April 1985. The Soviets have evidently kept their options open, since they have negotiated at various times

oil prospects have been discovered, the Soviets appear to have postponed development efforts in the area, but their strategy clearly includes major Western participation.

Soviet policy in the Barents Sea reflected many of the same objectives and practices apparent in an earlier venture in offshore development off Sakhalin Island, at the other end of the country, where since 1975 the Soviets and the Japanese jointly explored and developed oil and gas deposits.[120] The Sakhalin Oil Development Company (SODECO) was not a jointly owned company; at the time it was created, the Soviets had not entered into any joint ventures with Western firms since the 1930s. Rather, the owners of SODECO were a consortium of Japanese companies (joined at one time by Gulf Oil).[121] It provided supplier credits to support exploration and development, in exchange for which it received half the oil and gas produced. The Soviets used the credits to buy Western equipment, and the risks were thus shared between SODECO and the Soviets.[122] On the whole, both sides were disappointed by the oil discoveries made, although the gas prospects proved more interesting.

Though they used foreign equipment, the Soviets resisted the presence of foreign operators and consultants, even when costly mistakes resulted. The initial agreement for SODECO, signed in 1975, allowed foreign experts to work on site, but almost immediately the Soviet side declared that only Soviet engineers would be acceptable.[123] Over the years, they stuck to the same position. Similarly, although the initial geophysical surveys were conducted by Japanese vessels, soon the Soviets were contracting to equip a Soviet ship with advanced French equipment and to train Soviet technicians to use it.[124] The Soviets were more flexible on this point in the Barents Sea,[125] but their insistence on making their own mistakes there showed the same basic objective of assuring ultimate independence from outside assistance.

---

with British and French firms for possible financing and technical assistance, and they have approached other Norwegian companies (*Financial Times*, 20 May 1985), as well as German ones.

[120] Peter Egyed, "Western Participation in the Development of Siberian Energy Resources: Case Studies," Carleton University (Ottawa, Canada), Institute of Soviet and East European Studies, East-West Commercial Relations Series, report no. 22 (December 1983).

[121] Ibid. p. 48, documents the dwindling participation of Gulf Oil.

[122] See ibid. for the detailed arrangements.

[123] Ibid., p. 49.

[124] Ibid., p. 51.

[125] According to Norwegian observers, the Soviets have signed annual maintenance

Two features of the overall Soviet approach to offshore development over the last decade stand out. First, from the beginning the Soviets have used Western equipment, but they have tried to avoid extended dependence on Western suppliers and to limit the presence of Western personnel. Second, the fact that both offshore programs have been pursued relatively energetically throughout the decade, instead of being overwhelmed by the short-term pressures of the oil and gas campaigns, suggests that there has been consistent high-level support for them. Soviet leaders evidently intend to raise the priority of offshore operations further in the 1990s. In a visit to Murmansk in October 1987, Gorbachev strongly endorsed the Barents Sea program.[126] According to preliminary figures, while exploratory drilling for oil and gas will increase overall by 40 percent between 1986 and 1990, offshore drilling will double.[127] The level of Western sales and participation may rise also, but presumably along the same lines as before.[128]

Explaining the Decision to Import

In this chapter and in previous ones we have examined six major cases in which the oil and gas industries faced a decision to import Western equipment, rely on domestic producers, or devise some middle course combining the two.[129] From these cases and from related Western literature,[130] what broad patterns emerge and how can one explain them?

What stands out from the case-study material, as it does from the statistics, is the wave of equipment imports for gas transmission, which

---

agreements that allow Norwegian personnel on board Soviet drill ships for extended periods. But this happened only after the Soviets attempted to move personnel from the Caspian to the Barents Sea, hoping that their skills would be transferrable. Only when that failed did they accept the need for stable maintenance. Author's interviews, Oslo, April 1985.

126 *Pravda*, 3 Oct. 1987.

127 TASS interview with USSR Minister of Geology E. A. Kozlovskii, "Intensifikatsiia—velenie vremeni," *Ekonomicheskaia gazeta*, no. 21 (1985), p. 6. It is not clear, however, whether these figures apply to drilling meterage or to the volume of investment, or what the distribution of effort between the Arctic and the Caspian will be.

128 One possible sign of things to come was the announcement in early 1985 that the Soviet Union had purchased four drilling platforms from a Brazilian firm and an option for ten more, presumably for use in the Caspian Sea. *Financial Times*, 6 Mar. 1985.

129 Gaslift technology and electric centrifuge pumps were discussed in Chapter 3, seismic exploration in Chapter 4.

130 In addition to the sources mentioned elsewhere in this chapter, the most comprehensive Western review of Soviet imports in the energy sector through the end of the 1970s will be found in U.S. Congress, Office of Technology Assessment, *Technology and*

begins in the early 1970s, rises over the next decade, and then abruptly collapses after 1983. That cycle, as we have seen, is easily explained by the combination of gas campaign and embargo. But how to account for the low level of imports for the oil industry and for the rest of the gas industry, apart from transmission? Why have the oil and gas industries not imported larger amounts of low-technology equipment for the high-priority tasks of drilling and well operation? If one compares the figures in table 6.9 with the data in Chapters 3 and 4 on the numbers of wells being drilled and developed, one can see how modest the share of imported equipment has been. At the same time, as we have seen, in a few categories and at various times imports have been sizable. What can one infer about the mix of objectives and decisionmaking processes that produced this pattern?

In Chapter 8 we will see evidence that the Soviets use a simple set of rules to decide oil export volumes in response to internal needs and world prices; so regular have exports been that one can visualize a group of high officials gathering around a table once or twice a year to apply the rules. But clearly there are no such straightforward rules or procedures governing imports. One might have imagined, for example, that ministries earning large amounts of hard currency would have a special voice in the use of it, that a ministry's high priority as an investment sector would give it a correspondingly high priority in import decisions, or that the more difficult field conditions facing the oil and gas industries would give them a special claim for emergency help. But that has been the case only sporadically in the oil and gas sectors.

Instead, the decision to import or not appears to have been shaped by a combination of the recent history of the sector and the institutional setting. Consider first the inheritance of the oil and gas industries as they entered the 1970s. The oil industry had been growing rapidly for two decades and was by most standards a phenomenal success. If it had not kept up with the latest technology, it had not really needed to, because the industry's move to West Siberia had brought (at least initially) easier drilling conditions and exceptionally productive wells.

Soviet Energy Availability (Washington, D.C.: USGPO, 1981). Mention should also be made of the refinery and gas treatment sector, which is analyzed in Matthew J. Sagers, "Refinery Throughput in the USSR," U.S. Department of Commerce, Bureau of the Census, Center for International Research, CIR Staff Paper no. 2 (Washington, D.C.: May 1984); and Matthew J. Sagers and Albina Tretyakova, "Restructuring the Soviet Petroleum Refining Industry," U.S. Department of Commerce, Bureau of the Census, Center for International Research, CIR Staff Paper no. 4 (Washington, D.C.: March 1985).

TABLE 6.9
Soviet Imports of Low-Technology Oil- and Gas-Field Equipment: Selected Items, 1975–1987

	Tool Joints (thous.)	*Blowout Preventers*	*Tricone Bits (thous.)*	*Pumping Jacks*	*Christmas Trees and Casing Heads (thous. tons)*
1975	104	169	15	170	2.8
1980	97	320	8	500	5.6
1981	105	420	13	124	7.4
1982	101	363	10	753	3.7
1983	108	440	16	723	6.2
1984	83	281	18	600	6.8
1985	102	260	23	950	4.4
1986	127	384	31	1,100	5.8
1987	145	360	31	1,810	6.2

SOURCE: *Vneshniaia torgovlia SSSR*, various years. All figures have been rounded.

Its traditions and pride were strong, and its leaders were confident that they could handle their own problems. Their careers had been made by meeting one challenge after another, first in the Caucasus, then the Volga, and then Siberia. They had known crises and conflict before and had survived them, and it is hard to imagine such men—at the beginning of the decade, at least—despairing of their own capabilities or of those of their supporting industries.[131]

The picture in the gas industry until the mid-1970s was not essentially different; the Gas Ministry had been part of the Oil Ministry until the mid-1960s, and most of its leaders had started out as oil men. Like the oil industry, the gas industry had grown by moving from region to region, surmounting hardship and skepticism and no small amount of rivalry from its former parent. Only in the early 1970s, as long-distance transmission emerged as the industry's key problem, did the situation of the gas industry begin to diverge significantly from that of oil.

Along the way both industries had developed a large network of research and development institutes, which, though poor innovators themselves, had an interest in defending their turf from Western encroachment. These institutes have frequently expressed hostility to im-

[131] Thus it is not surprising that when the Soviets considered a plan in the late 1960s to enlist Japanese equipment and cooperation in accelerating oil development in Tiumen', Oil Minister Valentin Shashin was said to be opposed. For a detailed account of the Soviet-Japanese negotiations over Tiumen', see Egyed, "Western Participation."

ports,[132] as have Soviet suppliers of machinery for the oil and gas industries. As an official of the Soviet compressor manufacturer, Soiuzkompressormash, put it,

> Several times more hard currency is spent every year for certain types of compressors and large centrifugal pumps than would be needed to produce them in Soviet plants. Machinery builders justifiably consider that if they are responsible for meeting the economy's needs, then it should be up to them to decide how to do it.[133]

In the 1970s several of the gas industry's own technical advisers held out for domestic solutions—Soviet compressors, Soviet pipe, and visionary technologies like pipeline capsules—and continued the fight even after the leaders' turn to a big gas policy had made Western equipment the only feasible course. In short, within both industries and their associated supplier ministries there are powerful groups with a broad bias against Western imports. The case against imports is further strengthened by evidence that imported equipment is frequently purchased in haste and then lies about unused.[134]

Standing against these, however, are program managers with pressing plan targets to fulfill and ministry leaders attracted by the prospect of quick solutions. As a result of these contending forces, each prospective import decision goes through a gauntlet of bureaucratic commissions and reviews, and the outcomes vary case by case.

This helps to explain some of the major features of the import pattern. First, Soviet import decisions often look like compromises. For example, it is agreed to import foreign gaslift devices but to use domestic compressors and pipe to run them. Second, large import packages may stand a better chance than small ones, because influential players outside the industry can be enlisted to support them; hence the prominent role of big turnkey projects. Third, buy-backs, gas-for-pipe, and similar "swap" arrangements may be easier to justify than straight purchases, particularly since they are confined to specific projects. And most important, Western imports may be concentrated in "new" programs for which no entrenched research institute or supplier bureaucracy yet exists. Finally, since each case is debated separately, imports

[132] Robert W. Campbell, "Issues in Soviet R&D: The Energy Case," in U.S. Congress, Joint Economic Committee, *Soviet Economy in a New Perspective* (Washington, D.C.: USGPO, 1976), pp. 96–112.

[133] Ognev, "Kakie mashiny nuzhny promyslu."

[134] For a case study involving control equipment for the export pipeline in the early 1980s, see Ye. Gaidar and V. Iaroshenko, "Nulevoi tsikl," *Kommunist*, no. 8 (May 1988), pp. 80–81. Goskomstat has taken to publishing regular bulletins listing the value of uninstalled imports for all the industrial ministries.

come in clusters, and imports of any one item swing sharply from year to year.

This picture is essentially one of bureaucratic struggle, with little systematic leadership from above. Oil and gas ministers, if convinced of the need for massive imports in the mid-to-late 1970s, could undoubtedly have acted against biases within their own bureaucracies and won out against their suppliers in lobbying with Gosplan. In the chemical industry L. A. Kostandov successfully played such a role, both in his long years as minister and then as deputy prime minister. (Even Kostandov, however, did not try to use imports to modernize the entire chemical industry but concentrated his efforts on "modern" chemistry, chiefly polymers and synthetic fibers, where there was little domestic institutional structure to oppose him and the leaders wanted new materials for consumer and defense goods.) In the oil and gas industries, in contrast, there has been no such committed hand. The oil industry changed leaders in 1977 and 1985, the gas industry in 1981 and 1985. The veterans who led the oil and gas industries in the 1960s and 1970s—Valentin Shashin in oil and Sabit Orudzhev in gas—were redoubtable enough, but as the architects of their industries' early growth they presumably saw little need for massive outside help. Of the younger leaders—Dinkov, Chernomyrdin, Chirskov—none has been in place long enough to develop similar power, and in any case the clout and prestige of ministers has diminished since 1985.

The most intriguing figure is that of former Gosplan chairman N. K. Baibakov. Gosplan is the place where hard currency is allocated among competing claimants, and in the 1970s Gosplan was regularly accused by Soviet technologists of being "soft on imports." We have seen Baibakov's role in the initial Soviet enthusiasm for tertiary recovery, and it is possible that he was responsible for the initial Soviet resort to imports for offshore work. But there is no evidence that Baibakov consistently favored imports. In most respects, he probably shared the pride of older oil men in what domestic industry had been able to achieve on its own.[135]

This picture of bureaucratic pushing and pulling at lower levels, combined with occasional intervention by leaders in specific cases, would account for the changeable, ad hoc quality of the import pattern

[135] In contrast, the most enigmatic figure among the Soviet policymakers was V. I. Dolgikh, who was responsible for Soviet heavy industry, including oil and gas, from 1972 to 1988. However, his public statements give little indication of his position on imports.

under Brezhnev. For the most part, it seems, there was no policy, only a series of improvised short-term responses as needs arose and priorities shifted. Even the Soviets' traditionally obsessive concern with autonomy was inconsistently applied: in the early 1970s the Brezhnev leadership was uncharacteristically relaxed about the danger of foreign leverage; by the early 1980s it had become exaggeratedly cautious. In sum, the Brezhnev leadership lacked a coherent strategy for combining foreign technology with domestic efforts to strengthen industrial support or to assist exploration and development.

It is too soon to say whether Gorbachev's dramatic reforms in the foreign-trade sector will change this pattern. It would seem that the case for massive imports of Western equipment for the oil and gas sector is now overwhelming and that the political atmosphere in Moscow is more receptive than ever before. But Gorbachev inherits many of his predecessors' conflicting pressures and ambivalent goals, and the very sweep of the reforms he has begun in the foreign-trade sector ensures that it will be several years before settled structures, procedures, and policies emerge. It is quite possible that the combination of hard-currency shortage, rejection of Brezhnevian precedents, heavy emphasis on the domestic machinery sector, doubts about the efficiency of imported equipment in Soviet settings, and lingering resentments over political pressures from the West in the last decade will add up to a continued bias against imports in the oil and gas sectors, punctuated as before by ad hoc exceptions.

Despite the publicity given recently in the West to the prospects for joint ventures and large turnkey contracts, most of the deals actually concluded in the petroleum area during Gorbachev's first four years have involved petrochemicals, gas treatment, and petroleum refining rather than exploration and development or industrial support for oil- and gas-field equipment.[136] The exceptions so far are mainly "problem" fields, those with especially complex geology, heavy oils with heavy paraffin content, or corrosive environments. A special case in point is the Tengiz field, located near the northeast shore of the Caspian Sea in Kazakhstan. Despite its potential as one of the world's largest giants, Tengiz poses unique problems because its main deposits are located in fissured limestone 4,500–5,500 meters deep, reservoir pressures are

[136] Only a handful of the joint ventures officially signed by the fall of 1988 had to do with oil and gas equipment, and only one concerned petroleum refining. For listings of joint ventures, see *Ekonomicheskaia gazeta*, nos. 44–46, 48, 49 (1988).

exceptionally high, and sulphur content ranges up to 25 percent. After trying and failing to develop special-purpose equipment on their own, in 1987 the Soviets turned to foreign companies for help.[137]

But the main Soviet objective in promoting joint ventures is to escape from narrow dependence on oil and gas for hard-currency revenue and to upgrade exports by selling value-added commodities rather than raw materials. Thus the largest group of joint ventures negotiated to date is a collection of five giant petrochemical centers in West Siberia.[138] This project has aroused tremendous controversy and opposition, partly on environmental grounds and partly because of fears that it amounts to "another sell-out" to the West.[139] This is ironic, because the plan was conceived precisely to defuse growing domestic resistance to oil and gas exports and to satisfy advocates of industrial diversification in West Siberia. The uproar shows what a sensitive issue the participation of foreign partners can easily become.

[137] The story is briefly told in "Resheno i podpisano," *Sotsialisticheskaia industriia*, 14 May 1988. A high-level interagency agreement signed in 1981 produced no response from the two major contractors, Minkhimmash and Minpribor, and degenerated into the usual finger-pointing. In 1986 and 1987 the Soviets turned to firms from France, West Germany, and Canada for a 3-million-ton-per-year "first phase," scheduled to begin producing in 1989. More recently, the Soviets have entered into a joint venture with Enichem, Occidental Petroleum, Montedison, and Marubeni to use associated gas from Tengiz to produced petrochemicals. B. Rachkov, "Vtoroe dykhanie Emby," *Ekonomicheskaia gazeta*, no. 15 (1988), p. 20. Two ancillary turnkey oil and gas processing plants will be built by Litwin and Lurgi of France. *Business Eastern Europe*, 6 June 1988. Still other Western firms are discussing participation at Tengiz, such as Jeumont Schneider of France. *Business Eastern Europe*, 22 Aug. 1988.

[138] According to Prime Minister N. I. Ryzhkov, the new West Siberian "petrochemical belt" will be based on the five cities of Surgut, Nizhnevartovsk, Tobol'sk, Novyi Urengoy, and Iarkovo (the latter still only a village). N. I. Ryzhkov, "Razvitiiu Zapadnoi Sibiri—sozidatel'nuiu energiiu perestroiki," *Pravda*, 15 May 1988. The new joint ventures announced in 1988 follow this pattern. Thus Combustion Engineering and McDermott International have signed letters of intent with Minneftekhimprom for petrochemical complexes at Surgut and Tobol'sk, while Occidental Petroleum will collaborate with Minkhimprom in a joint venture at Nizhnevartovsk. *Oil and Gas Journal*, 6 June 1988.

[139] The controversy was kicked off by an article by a group of prestigious scientists that sharply criticized the project as "another gas deal." (B. Laskorin et al., "Eshche odna 'stroika veka,'" *Izvestiia*, 3 Apr. 1989.) This drew an angry reaction from the oil and gas ministers (R. Lynev, "O sibirskoi stroike i glasnosti," *Izvestiia*, 6 Apr. 1989) and from the first obkom secretary of Tiumen', G. P. Bogomiakov (R. Lynev and Iu. Perepletkin, "'Stroika veka' na perekrestke mnenii," *Izvestiia*, 15 Apr. 1989), followed by renewed attacks (Otto Latsis, "Pochemu my bedno zhivem," *Izvestiia*, 19 Apr. 1989) and further defenses (A. Panferov et al., "Za kem poslednee slovo," *Izvestiia*, 29 Apr. 1989). The attacks grew so sharp that at the opening session of the USSR Supreme Soviet, on 10 June 1989, Prime Minister N. I. Ryzhkov was forced to defend the project in strong terms.

In short, despite signs in 1988 and 1989 pointing toward a change in Moscow's traditional autarky in industrial support for oil and gas, at this writing (spring 1989) no fundamental shift has yet occurred in the Soviets' volume of purchases from the West, and there has been only a tentative widening of the range of situations in which they are seeking Western help. Change is in the air, but it is slow to arrive.

CONCLUSIONS

The lack of sound industrial support is the greatest single problem of the Soviet oil and gas industries. The threat it poses is not that it slows down energy production[140] (although the gas industry will face severe problems with its pipeline network in coming years) but rather that it has raised costs and worsened the imbalances described in earlier chapters.

In particular, the oil and gas industries have been obliged to substitute scarce labor for missing equipment. "Managers cover themselves," says one reporter. "Knowing that they have little hope of getting new machines, they put in two men where they could get by with one."[141] Personnel in the oil and gas fields is now increasing "geometrically" in relation to output.[142] And it is not just the oil industry that is affected. All the ministries working in the West Siberian oil and gas region are using a labor-intensive strategy.[143]

The second consequence of the support problem is that the biases present in both industries have become fixed in the support system and in the existing equipment stock and are thus doubly difficult to correct. In the last two years, faced with a new crisis in the Siberian oil fields, planners have concluded that a crash effort must be devoted to well completion, mechanization, and maintenance. But since these are precisely the departments that had been neglected previously, it is unlikely that the support ministries—particularly Minkhimmash—will be able

[140] The oil industry claims that there has been little actual loss of oil output so far. The poor quality of Minkhimmash's output in the plants surveyed may have cost the Nefteiugansk and Nizhnevartovsk associations (two of the largest in West Siberia) about 250,000 tons a year in lost output. Nikolaev, "Burovye zhdut sovremennuiu tekhniku." But such claims should be viewed with skepticism.

[141] Ognev, "Kakie mashiny nuzhny promyslu."

[142] Ibid. The phenomenon is not confined to West Siberia. For the oil and gas industries nationwide, manpower has increased from 113,000 and 28,000, respectively, in 1975 to 164,000 and 36,000—substantial growth when contrasted with an increase from 34 million to 38 million in the total Soviet industrial labor force over the same period (Goskomstat, *Trud v SSSR* [Moscow, 1988], p. 49).

[143] Ibid.

to respond quickly or smoothly. Such imbalances, in turn, lead to still higher costs in the future, especially in view of the more difficult environments in which both industries must now work.

Consequently, to explain the problems of industrial support is one of the most important tasks in interpreting the Soviet energy crisis as a whole. At first glance, the main culprit is the system. The problems of industrial supply, quality, and innovation in the Soviet economy have been abundantly studied by two generations of economists and are by now well known.[144] But the crisis of industrial support in the oil and gas industries, while it presents all the classic symptoms of civilian industry, owes its special severity to the behavior of the Brezhnev leadership. If the leadership had promoted a coherent and stable import policy, if it had not overreacted to the American embargo, if it had matched its energy spending with corresponding attention to industrial support, if it had acted more decisively to curb competition from military industry—any of these modifications would have alleviated the worst failings.

In principle, it should be possible to produce rapid improvement, because few of the oil and gas industries' equipment needs call for high technology. But the monopoly position of the supporting industries virtually guarantees that, even if the Gorbachev reforms were fully implemented and wholesale markets in producers' goods became widespread, the oil and gas industries would not benefit quickly; indeed, they would be likely to face massive price increases for domestic equipment without significant improvements in quality.

The only way to produce rapid improvement in the oil and gas service sector is to subject Minkhimmash, Mintiazhmash, and the other support ministries to both internal and foreign competition. The Soviet gas industry should resume importing compressors. The oil industry should make large purchases of standard field equipment; it should buy turnkey plants to produce oil- and gas-field equipment and locate them in West Siberia; and above all, it should contract with Western teams to perform essential services, such as well-logging. Such a program would pay for itself immediately, both in added hard-currency income from oil exports and in reduced needs for domestic investment and manpower. It would buy time for a systematic modernization of domestic industry at little cost to the Soviets' own independence and initiative.

[144] See in particular Joseph Berliner, *Factory and Manager in the USSR* (Cambridge, Mass.: Harvard University Press, 1957), and same, *The Innovation Decision in Soviet Industry* (Cambridge, Mass.: MIT Press, 1976).

SEVEN

THE SLOW MOVE TO CONSERVATION

A High-Stakes, High-Risk Issue

The fundamental issue in Soviet energy policy is the same one facing the economy as a whole: Is it possible for a centrally planned system, originally built to manage forced-draft heavy industrialization, to operate efficiently? By the middle of the 1980s the traditional supply-oriented approach to energy had reached a dead end. To continue meeting Soviet energy needs solely by boosting production while ignoring inefficient consumption, despite the rapid growth of natural gas production after 1980, meant climbing ever-steeper cost curves, with no end in sight. The task of conservation, surely, could no longer be ducked.

Under Brezhnev, energy conservation had remained largely rhetoric. But as we saw in Chapter 2, Andropov appeared resolved to confront the issue head on, and Gorbachev, since becoming General Secretary in 1985, has continued to speak in the same vein. We have seen why: the reformers will not be able to transfer resources to manufacturing, consumer goods, and food unless they can displace capital from the extractive industries. But the only way to do that is to make a fundamental shift in energy policy from the supply side to the demand side, in order to curb energy consumption.

The potential benefits of energy conservation have been part of official Soviet prose since the mid-1970s. But as the costs of energy production rose and as Soviet energy experts came to perceive them more accurately, their estimates of the benefits of conservation became more concrete and more compelling. A standard ton of energy derived through conservation, reported one influential group of experts at the beginning of the 1980s, should cost only 60–90 rubles at the point of consumption, two to three times less than it would cost to develop and deliver the same amount from new sources.[1] And the advantages of conservation could only increase with time.

But to make good on this potential is another matter. Conservation

[1] L. A. Melent'ev and A. A. Makarov, *Energeticheskii kompleks SSSR* (Moscow: Ekonomika, 1983), pp. 116–118.

in the Soviet system faces three major obstacles: inertia, uncertainty, and expense. Inertia, not only of attitudes and institutions but also of a capital stock built up over half a century, almost inevitably means a lag between the launching of a conservation policy and its first results. Uncertainty about the response of the system to the new policy, particularly in view of the system's ingrained bias toward gross output, makes it impossible to plan the pace and scale of savings; indeed, it is entirely possible that in the early years there could be no response at all. Finally, energy savings require capital investment, even if ultimately less than energy production. But conservation requires an even scarcer resource: political attention and priority.

As a result, energy conservation is a high-risk strategy. Because of the problem of lag, the Kremlin cannot allow energy production to slacken before conservation gains offset reduced output. So it must keep spending money on production even as it begins investing in conservation. For an inevitable but undefinable period, therefore, Soviet leaders will have the worst of both worlds: high-cost energy production *and* high-cost energy conservation. And if they are unlucky, they could end up in a vicious circle, in which the expense of maintaining the "supply bridge" delays their plans for industrial reconstruction, which in turn delays the further energy savings that such a reconstruction is counted on to produce.

Faced with these possibilities, Brezhnev and Chernenko flinched. They continued a production-oriented policy for which their successors are now paying dearly, and by their preference for the safer course they worsened the policy dilemma for their successors.

Nevertheless, the decade was not entirely wasted, because two important changes took place. By boosting natural gas and nuclear power, Brezhnev prepared a bridge to carry energy policy through the next decade—an essential prerequisite for managing the uncomfortable interim period. Second, between 1975 and 1985 a process of fact-finding and consensus-building took place. By the time Andropov became General Secretary, planners, experts, and decisionmakers had reached agreement that conservation was both necessary and feasible, and they had mapped the outlines of a policy to achieve it. In other words, during the decade 1975–1985, underneath the conservative official policy, a major change in thinking was taking place within the Soviet elite.

The principal contribution of the new thinking was to suggest a combination of strategies to reduce the risk of the transition from a production-oriented to a consumption-oriented energy policy. Its essence was to divide the problem into two stages over fifteen years, the first one preparing the way and the second yielding the payoff. It is interesting to observe that the rest of the Gorbachev economic program, as it was first unveiled in 1985, was also a two-stage policy; in this respect the new thinking about energy reflected, and may have shaped, the new leaders' initial approach to economic policy as a whole.

But has Gorbachev used the map that was prepared for him? On past form, a pessimist would have predicted that the scarcity of investment resources and the pressure for near-term results would tempt leaders and planners to exploit the gas bridge, to displace oil where possible, and to postpone conservation. As we shall see, despite the remarkable reform program that Gorbachev and the reformers have launched, that is essentially what has happened so far.

This chapter has three major purposes. The first is to show how the demand-oriented approach evolved, as an example of how new ideas made their way into the Soviet leadership underneath the surface of conservative policy, preparing the way for new programs as soon as a succession made them possible. Second, an analysis of the energy program and the Gorbachev reforms will demonstrate both the potential for conservation and the obstacles it faces. Finally, we will examine the progress made in implementing conservation and in rationalizing the structure of consumption, chiefly by displacing oil with gas.

The Context of Soviet Energy Conservation

Trends in Energy Efficiency

Western and Soviet statistics disagree over whether the Soviet economy has grown more energy efficient since 1970 or less. The issue turns on what measure is used for economic growth and who does the measuring. If one uses GNP surrogates, as developed by the CIA, then Soviet energy efficiency has been declining (table 7.1).[2] But if one uses national income, as in the Soviet Union, then energy efficiency has improved. The difference stems partly from the fact that the Soviet measure of national income has been growing more quickly than the

[2] In 1987 Soviet statisticians first began reporting economic growth in GNP as well as by the traditional net material product. The Soviet measure is billed as conforming to United Nations methodologies, but exactly how it is calculated or how it differs from the CIA's measure is not yet known. The only thing that is clear is that they are different. Thus *Pravda* reported Soviet GNP growth in 1987 as 3.3 percent, while the CIA estimated 0.5 percent; in 1988 the two estimates were 5 and 1.5 percent, respectively. The CIA's methodology is described in detail in U.S. Congress, Joint Economic Committee, *USSR: Measures of Economic Growth and Development, 1950–1980* (Washington, D.C.: USGPO, 1982).

TABLE 7.1
Soviet Energy Intensity, as Measured against GNP
(tons of coal equivalent required to produce $1,000 of GNP)

	1960	*1970*	*1980*	*1985*	*1986*	*1987*	*1988 (est.)*
Energy Consumption (billions of tce)	0.67	1.12	1.67	1.88	1.91	1.97	2.01
GNP (trillions of $)	0.95	1.57	2.11	2.29	2.36	2.3	2.40
Energy Intensity (tce/$1,000 GNP)	0.71	0.71	0.79	0.82	0.81	0.83	0.84

SOURCES: for GNP: CIA, *Handbook of Economic Statistics, 1988* (Washington, D.C.: September 1988); for energy consumption: *Narodnoe khoziaistvo SSSR v 1987g.*

Western GNP surrogate, since the latter includes the slower-growing "non-productive sectors" such as social spending and services.

What is nevertheless quite clear from both Western and Soviet measures is that, despite an approximate trebling in marginal energy costs since 1970, the Soviet economy has failed to respond with major energy savings. Indeed, several alarming trends since the beginning of the 1970s bely the appearance of progress in the Soviet numbers, and serious Soviet energy experts take no comfort from the claimed improvements.

To follow their analysis, it will be helpful to invoke here a distinction that energy specialists make between the efficiency of final energy use (that is, products or services actually generated per unit of energy in final form) and the transformation efficiency (that is, the efficiency with which energy is converted from primary to final forms). For example, the latter measures the efficiency with which coal is transformed into electricity; the former measures how efficiently the resulting electricity is used to produce economic results.

As the Soviet experts see it, their problem can be summed up as follows. Since the beginning of the 1960s, such gains as there have been in overall energy efficiency have come from improved transformation, chiefly from improvements in heat rates in power plants, cogeneration, electrification of railroads, and shifts from coal to oil and gas, which together accounted for three-quarters of all energy savings from 1960 to 1980.[3] But gains in the efficiency of final use have been virtually nil; and for the so-called material production sector (that is, excluding resi-

[3] Melent'ev and Makarov, *Energeticheskii kompleks SSSR*, p. 121.

TABLE 7.2
Final Consumption per Unit of National Income
(gigacalories consumed per thousand rubles of national income)

	1960	*1965*	*1970*	*1975*	*1980*	*1985*
Total economy	11.7	12.6	11.5	11.5	11.4	11.4
Material production sphere	8.0	8.8	8.2	8.5	8.5	8.5

SOURCE: Melent'ev and Makarov, *Energeticheskii kompleks SSSR*, p. 74.
NOTE: The 1985 figure is a projection made at the beginning of the 1980s. I do not know the reason for the spike in 1965.

dential and municipal uses), efficiency has actually deteriorated, even by Soviet measures (table 7.2). To Soviet experts this is an ominous trend, because opportunities for further gains in transformation efficiency are likely to grow scarcer in the future. The battle for energy conservation, in the long run, depends on the system's ability to improve final consumption, and this is where recent performance has been least satisfactory.

What explains the stagnation in efficiency of final use? Soviet analysts call it a failure in policy, blaming the euphoria that accompanied the rapid growth of Siberian oil production and the first Siberian gas discoveries in the early 1970s. "Unjustifiably extrapolating into the future the very favorable conditions of the 1960s," as one expert put it, planners kept energy prices low and removed the rationing system in effect in earlier years.[4] As a result, the energy component fell to 5–7 percent of total production costs.[5] Consumption-related research and development slowed, and old equipment was not replaced. Demand policy, for all practical purposes, went to sleep.

At the beginning of the 1970s, the Soviet analysis continues, Soviet industry had just finished a major switch from coal to oil. But the switch itself had been badly handled: instead of building modern, large-scale oil-fired equipment, most ministries had simply converted what they had. The low oil prices then prevailing made such a move seem cost-effective; but as a result, by the end of the 1970s Soviet industry and municipalities found themselves with an obsolete stock of inefficient boilers and furnaces that required more than 5 million workers for maintenance and repair.[6]

[4] Ibid., p. 50.
[5] Ibid.
[6] Ibid., pp. 51–52. This source mentions (p. 51) a survey of 350 heavy industrial

In short, because of the fifteen lost years from the late 1960s to the early 1980s, during which planners failed to respond to the rapid rise in energy costs, Brezhnev's successors inherited an energy consumption structure that they themselves acknowledged to be both inefficient and seriously unbalanced. As they began calling, with increasing urgency, for renovation of the country's obsolete capital stock, the energy-consuming sector was one of the examples most prominent in their minds.

The Future Evolution of the Soviet Economy: Consequences for Energy Consumption

Earlier we mentioned inertia as one of the principal obstacles to conservation policy. The term should be understood both in its popular sense, something hard to move, and in its strict scientific sense, something hard to deflect from its course. The best example of inertia in the first sense is the dominance of industry in the Soviet consumption structure; the most striking manifestation of the second sense is the stability of the present trends in energy use.[7]

DOMINANCE OF INDUSTRY IN THE SOVIET ENERGY BALANCE

Industry accounts for a far larger share of total energy consumption in the Soviet Union than in other major industrial countries, and industry must therefore be the main target of Soviet conservation policy (table 7.3). This is unfortunate from the point of view of Soviet planners because industrial consumption is more difficult, expensive, and time-consuming to alter than transportation or residential consumption. In view of the relatively smaller importance of the latter in the Soviet energy balance, the USSR is denied the opportunities for quick energy savings that were such a striking feature of the Western response to the two oil shocks of the 1970s.

Moreover, Soviet industry is an inefficient energy consumer, when

---

enterprises, presumably conducted in the late 1970s, which showed that energy-related equipment had served on the average twice as long and had received only one-third as much capital investment as the average for the industry.

[7] A detailed picture of Soviet energy consumption trends, by sector and by fuel, can be found in a series of reports published by the U.S. Census Bureau's Center for International Research. The summary volume, which contains a listing of the more detailed studies, is Matthew J. Sagers and Albina Tretyakova, "USSR: Trends in Fuel and Energy Consumption by Sector and Fuel, 1970–1980," U.S. Department of Commerce, Bureau of the Census, Center for International Research, CIR Staff Paper no. 36 (Washington, D.C.: March 1988).

TABLE 7.3
Energy-Consumption Shares in the Soviet Economy, 1960–1985
(final use; percentages)

	1960	*1965*	*1970*	*1975*	*1980*	*1985*
Industry	51.1	52.8	53.6	53.4	53.0	52
Residential and municipal	31.6	30.1	28.2	26.1	25.0	25
Construction	3.2	2.7	2.6	2.4	2.2	2
Transportation	5.8	6.3	7.2	7.9	8.9	10
Agriculture	3.7	4.0	4.5	6.0	7.9	8
Other	4.6	4.1	3.9	4.2	3.1	3

SOURCE: Melent'ev and Makarov, *Energeticheskii kompleks SSSR*, p. 65.
NOTE: The 1985 column is a projection made in the early 1980s.

compared to Western counterparts.[8] This is partly because of the dominance of energy-intensive sectors in Soviet industry, especially metallurgy, and partly because of the wasteful use the economy makes of those sectors' products (with metallurgy again the prime example). A third major source of inefficiency is the energy waste built into Soviet industrial processes: thus refining a ton of copper requires more than three times as much electricity in the Soviet Union as in West Germany; a ton of Soviet cement requires twice as much heat energy to make as a Japanese one.[9] Hence the chances for success in conservation depend heavily on one direct factor and two indirect ones: how much energy Soviet industry can be induced to save, how quickly it follows the worldwide trend toward less energy-intensive sectors, and whether Soviet conservation policy can be aimed at saving energy-intensive materials as well as energy itself.

LIKELY FUTURE TRENDS

How is the Soviet economy likely to evolve in the remainder of this century, and what will be the consequences for energy consumption?

In the broadest terms, the Soviet economy is following the same

[8] Ed Hewett has calculated that Soviet industry in 1980 consumed 56 percent more energy per unit of value added than U.S. industry, while the Soviet economy as a whole consumed 32 percent more energy per unit of GNP than the American economy. Hewett, *Energy, Economics, and Foreign Policy in the Soviet Union* (Washington, D.C.: Brookings Institution, 1984), p. 108.

[9] V. I. Dolgikh, "Otnoshenie k resursam—vazhneishii kriterii perestroiki v ekonomike," *Pravda* 11 July 1988.

long-term path the Western ones have. The share of industry and construction in Soviet energy consumption, though high by Western standards, is slowly declining, while that of transportation is rising. Within industry, heavy industry is giving way to high-technology fields such as electronics and synthetic materials. For example, ferrous metallurgy is expected to decline in relative importance, while chemistry and machine building will increase.

The Soviet economy differs sharply from Western ones, however, in four respects that are likely to last well into the next century. First, the share of heavy industry in total energy consumption will probably decline more slowly. Second, much of the rising transportation burden is due to the growing need to ship energy from points of production in the east to centers of consumption in the west. Transmission accounts for about one-third of own use of energy by energy-producing ministries and is likely to increase its share in the future.[10] Moreover, insofar as new generations of industry are now growing up along the western borders of the USSR (Belorussia, Lithuania, and Western Ukraine) and in the Transcaucasus,[11] energy transportation lines will become even longer.

Third, whereas agriculture and food processing in the West have reached a stable plateau as energy consumers, in the Soviet Union they will continue to grow in relative importance, particularly as consumers of high-quality refined fuels. Finally, the energy share of the residential and communal sector of the Soviet economy has steadily declined and may stagnate in years to come instead of increasing as it has in the West.

This anticipated pattern of growth has implications for both halves of the conservation problem, that is, for efficiency of transformation and of final use. First, concerning transformation efficiency, the expected pattern should be good news to Soviet planners, because much of the increased demand of the future could be met with electricity generated from low-cost coal, which the Soviet Union, again in principle, possesses in abundance. Soviet experts believe that by the year 2000 the share of electricity in total final consumption will grow by 20 to 25

[10] Total direct own use by the energy sector amounted to about 16 percent of primary energy production in 1980. Iu. D. Kononov, *Vliianie energeticheskikh strategii na energopotreblenie* (Irkutsk: Sibirskii Energeticheskii Institut, 1985), p. 7. Dr. Kononov, in a presentation in Washington, D.C., in March 1988, estimated that this share will grow to 17 percent by 1990 and 19–21 percent by 2010.

[11] See Leslie Dienes, "Regional Development," in Abram Bergson and Herbert S. Levine, *The Soviet Economy: Toward the Year 2000* (London: George Allen and Unwin, 1983), pp. 232–244.

percent and that of steam and hot water (which could also be met with coal) by 15 to 20 percent, while that of fuels used directly will fall by 25 to 30 percent.[12] The lower transformation efficiency of coal to electricity would be offset by the advantages of electricity as an efficient energy source in final use.

Unfortunately, in reality, little of this scenario is likely to be realized—unless leaders and planners try very hard to make it happen. Because most of the growth in the share of electrical consumption is expected to come from agriculture, transportation, and services, which have highly variable patterns of demand, a policy of pushing electricity use will require heavy investment in peak-coverage generators, which in turn will call for high-quality fuels. Second, the coal industry is unlikely to be able to improve soon the quality of coal it delivers to power plants; consequently, coal-fired electricity will continue to pose severe problems (described in the last section of this chapter). Third, it is most unlikely that the growing geographical split between energy supply (centered in the east) and energy demand (concentrated in the west) will be alleviated in this century. Consequently, the use of coal for power plants will require high-technology processing and transmission in the form of slurries, high-voltage transmission lines, enrichment, and/or liquefaction, thus turning coal from a low-cost fuel into a high-cost one. In short, the coal-and-nuclear future will be expensive.

Obviously, then, if there is to be progress in overall energy conservation, it must come from gains in the efficiency of final use. There are two ways these can be achieved: first, through *direct* efficiency gains (that is, substitution of labor or capital to improve the efficiency with which energy is used to produce a given mix of commodities and services); second, through *indirect* energy-efficiency gains (that is, a shift in the economy's output toward less-energy-intensive goods and services).[13] Soviet energy experts know that both types of gains will be slow to realize and will depend above all on how successfully old capital stock can be retired, industry modernized, and consumption of energy-intensive materials controlled. The outlook is for a long and expensive program.

What are the chances that such a program will actually be implemented and, more important, adhered to for the length of time required? That, of course, is the great unknown. What can be gauged right now, however, is whether the necessary preparations have been

[12] Melent'ev and Makarov, *Energeticheskii kompleks SSSR*, pp. 85–89.

[13] Hewett, *Energy, Economics, and Foreign Policy*, pp. 110–111.

made. If the proper institutions, strategies, norms, and information have not been assembled, if minds have not been prepared and consensus reached, then the shift to a demand-centered policy will remain rhetoric. In the next section we examine whether these prerequisites now exist or are taking shape.

The Evolution of Soviet Conservation Strategy

Any major policy change requires preparation. Whatever the fate of the Soviet conservation policy in the second half of the 1980s and beyond, it is significant for our understanding of the Brezhnev period and the transition to the next generation of leaders to observe that the setting for policy changed substantially between 1975 and 1985. In the mid-1970s none of the prerequisites for a demand-oriented program existed; by 1985 a basis had been laid, much of it as a result of evolving views within the Brezhnev government itself. The further impetus given to conservation under Andropov and Gorbachev was thus an invigoration rather than an innovation.

But the question remains: Have the changes been sufficient to begin to overcome the obstacles we have reviewed? Do they provide enough of a basis to start—for Gorbachev to dare to start—a real shift of investment and priorities toward conservation?

Development of the Prerequisites for a New Policy, 1973–1982

At the beginning of the 1970s the basis for a systematic demand-oriented energy policy did not exist. The leaders had not yet focused on the problem of energy consumption; conservation had not been incorporated into the planning system; there was no enforcement mechanism; energy prices did not adequately reflect costs; consumption norms, where they existed, were crude; and for some fuels (notably gas) most consumers could not, for lack of meters, even measure their own energy use. Energy experts and planners could not have provided competent advice to the leadership because they had done little modeling or systematic data gathering; consequently, they had no detailed grasp of what conservation would entail.

Between 1976 and 1983, however, the perceptions of policymakers gradually changed, and the necessary ingredients for a new policy started to come together. Through speeches and official decrees one can observe a rise in the leaders' awareness of the need for conservation. Starting with a Central Committee decree in 1973 (largely devoted to the problem of capturing waste heat), the initial trickle of official directives quickened toward the end of the decade. Brezhnev devoted steadily more space in his speeches to energy conservation. By the time of the November 1979 and October 1980 plenums of the Central Committee and the Twenty-sixth Party Congress he had put the subject at the top of his list,[14] though not at the head of his investment priorities. Lesser officials followed in the same vein.[15]

Conservation was gradually incorporated into the planning and administrative system. To coordinate the overall effort, an Interdepartmental Commission on Savings and Rational Utilization of Material Resources was established under the State Committee for Supply, endowed with the power (at least on paper) to cut the fuel allocations of wasteful users.[16] Agencies for monitoring and enforcing energy conservation sprang up within the energy-producing ministries during the second half of the 1970s,[17] initially to supervise consumption within their own ministries, then after 1980 to monitor all energy users and to pass on prospective new ones.[18] In 1981 all ministries and state agencies, including republic-level councils of ministers, were ordered to establish energy conservation offices.[19] Gosplan was instructed to prepare tighter norms for energy consumption and to use them as the basis for targets to be sent to ministries and enterprises.[20] Enterprises were

[14] L. I. Brezhnev, *Leninskim kursom*, vol. 8, pp. 200 and 473.

[15] V. I. Dolgikh, the Central Committee secretary in charge of heavy industry and energy and the man most closely associated with the production-oriented approach to energy policy, echoed Brezhnev's new stress on conservation in one of his very few bylined articles, signed to press in late 1979. Significantly enough, however, Dolgikh's discussion of conservation consisted of a perfunctory page and a half tacked to the end of an article largely devoted to fuel production problems. Dolgikh showed reluctance, incidentally, to burn natural gas in power plants. Gas as a feedstock or in direct uses, he argued, brings ten times the return that it does when burned under boilers—an interesting point in view of the later evolution of policy. Dolgikh, "Povyshat' uroven' rukovodstva predpriiatiiami toplivno-energeticheskogo kompleksa," *Partiinaia zhizn'*, no. 1 (1980), pp. 15–23.

[16] N. Maliev, "Ekonomicheskie sanktsii za beskhoziaistvennost'," *Ekonomicheskaia gazeta*, no. 3 (1985), p. 16.

[17] In addition, previously existing bodies, such as the Main State Inspectorate of the State Supply Committee, began conducting energy-consumption inspections of their own.

[18] A decree on this subject appears in *Sobranie postanovlenii pravitel'stva SSSR*, no. 14 (1980), pp. 339–348.

[19] USSR Council of Ministers, "O merakh po usileniiu ekonomii toplivno-energeticheskikh resursov v 1981 godu," reported in *Sotsialisticheskaia industriia*, 4 Jan. 1981.

[20] A joint decree of the USSR Council of Ministers and CPSU Central Committee to this effect was issued in June 1981 (Melent'ev and Makarov, *Energeticheskii kompleks*

ordered to prepare energy-saving counterplans. Finally, and most important, energy prices were raised sharply.

Despite this evolution, by the time of Brezhnev's death in November 1982 Soviet energy conservation was still largely a paper policy. Few enterprises bothered at first to prepare even the pro forma savings plans required of them;[21] subsequently their compliance consisted largely of submitting inflated norms, in which their parent ministries conspired by giving their support. The planners could hardly challenge them, since they themselves had only the vaguest idea how much consumption was appropriate for each enterprise, process, or product.[22] The energy inspectorates dutifully reported awe-inspiring numbers of inspections, fines levied, and energy saved,[23] but Soviet critics charged the claims were largely empty.

The basis for enforcement was weak in any case, because many managers and consumers could not tell how much energy they were using. Their enterprises, farms, and residences lacked meters, especially for gas. In late 1983 one-half of all gas-consuming enterprises still could not measure their consumption.[24] Most central-heating systems had no regulators.[25] The principal agency in charge of making measurement devices, the Ministry of Instrument-making and Automatic Systems, dragged its heels throughout the first half of the 1980s. Only in 1985 did it finally respond with new investment plans that may meet demand by the end of the decade.[26]

PRICES

Energy prices in the early 1980s still did not fully reflect the opportunity costs of energy or impose adequate discipline on decisionmakers.

SSSR, p. 100) and described in "V Tsentral'nom Komitete KPSS i Sovete Ministrov SSSR," *Pravda*, 4 July 1981.

[21] S. Veselov, "Ratsional'no raskhodovat' toplivno-energeticheskie resursy," *Planovoe khoziaistvo*, no. 2 (1979), pp. 33–34.

[22] For a sampling of the numerous press items dealing with this subject, see V. A. Zhmurko, "Ekonomiia elektroenergii—zabota obshchaia," *Ekonomicheskaia gazeta*, no. 4 (1981), p. 9; S. Bogatko, "Kilovatt rabotaiushchii," *Pravda*, 8 Jan. 1980; D. Evdokimov, "Normativnaia baza ekonomii," *Ekonomicheskaia gazeta*, no. 20 (1984). Hewett, *Energy, Economics, and Foreign Policy*, pp. 123–126, gives an excellent analysis of the problems involved in using norms as the basis of policy.

[23] For example, the Ministry of Power's energy inspectorate reported that in 1980 it had made over 60,000 plant inspections, imposed over 100 million rubles in fines, and saved 1.5 billion kilowatt-hours. "Kilovattu rabotat'," *Pravda*, 15 Dec. 1980.

[24] "Tsena kilovatta-chasa," *Pravda*, 7 Mar. 1981; N. Fedorov, "Ekonomnoe plamia," *Pravda*, 2 Feb. 1981; S. Orudzhev, "Berech' prirodnyi gaz," *Pravda*, 18 Nov. 1979; Melent'ev and Makarov, *Energeticheskii kompleks SSSR*, p. 127.

[25] A. Makukhin, "Teplo dlia goroda," *Sotsialisticheskaia industriia*, 14 Oct. 1984.

[26] Statement by Deputy Minister N. Bezus, *Sotsialisticheskaia industriia*, 19 May 1985.

To follow the evolution of Soviet pricing policy, it will help to keep in mind the distinction in Soviet practice between planners' prices and wholesale prices.[27] Industrial wholesale prices, or the prices at which enterprises buy energy, were substantially increased in 1967 and again in 1982. By the end of the first round of increases they were in line with world levels, but they changed little for the next fifteen years. The two world oil shocks, in other words, hardly caused a ripple in the perceived costs of energy to Soviet consuming enterprises and their ministries. Only in 1982 were wholesale prices raised again, coal and gas by an average of 42 and 45 percent, respectively, and oil by 230 percent.[28]

Planners use a different set of energy prices, which govern investment decisions. Planners' prices are changed much more frequently and were never allowed to slip as far behind the world level as transaction prices did. Moreover, the basis on which planners' prices were calculated grew steadily more sophisticated. In 1974, after nearly a decade of debate, Soviet planners switched to a system of shadow prices (in Russian, *zamykaiushchie zatraty*, or closing prices) that more closely reflected marginal energy costs.[29] At that time planners' prices doubled,[30] and over the next five years they continued to rise, doubling again for coal and gas and tripling for oil.[31]

Planners' prices have also become more comprehensive. They now incorporate several previously excluded classes of costs (notably for exploration), and there is growing official acceptance of concepts previously rejected as alien. Charges for capital were incorporated as early as the 1960s and a form of rent charges by the early 1980s;[32] and Soviet economists (if not yet the planners) are edging toward the idea that the world price is the correct benchmark for Soviet pricing. The planners' growing use of computer modeling has contributed to the realism of pricing.[33]

Despite these major improvements, everyone agrees that Soviet energy prices do not come close to reflecting costs.[34] Wholesale prices, in

[27] I will not attempt to duplicate here the excellent discussions of energy pricing available elsewhere. See especially Hewett, *Energy, Economics, and Foreign Policy*, pp. 134–139; Robert W. Campbell, "Energy Prices and Decisions on Energy Use in the USSR," in Padma Desai, ed., *Marxism, Central Planning, and the Soviet Economy: Economic Essays in Honor of Alexander Erlich* (Cambridge, Mass.: MIT Press, 1983), pp. 249–274; and Bella Feygin, *Economics and Prices in the Soviet Fuel and Energy Industry* (Falls Church, Va.: Delphic Associates, January 1984).

[28] Feygin, *Economics and Prices*, p. 26.

[29] See Campbell, "Energy Prices."

[30] Melent'ev and Makarov, *Energeticheskii kompleks SSSR*, p. 51.

[31] Ibid., pp. 122–123.

[32] Feygin, *Economics and Prices*, pp. 11, 27.

[33] Ibid., pp. 106, 27.

[34] Campbell, "Energy Prices."

particular, lag behind planners' prices; and since they are adjusted infrequently, the lag worsens with time. This might have no importance if the pricing system had no influence on consumers' or planners' decisions, but the evidence is that ministries and enterprises did respond somewhat to the 1967 increases in transaction prices,[35] and investment decisions appear to have been shaped by the evolution of planners' prices over the last decade.[36] Consequently, one of the most important issues for Soviet conservation policy in the future (and one of the most important tests for the outside observer) is continued progress in energy pricing policy under the new leadership.

NORMS

Considerable effort has been devoted since 1982 to improving the system of norms regulating consumption of energy and energy-intensive resources, especially metals. The first attempt, begun in 1976 and accelerated in 1981, incorporated energy-saving targets into the annual planning process. But since in most cases no one knew how much energy each enterprise should consume, the targets were arrived at through bargaining, surrounded by all the usual tactics familiar to students of command economies. The predictable result was bogus energy savings.

Since 1982 an interagency program has been under way to provide a more scientific basis for energy-efficiency norms by establishing how much major processes and energy-using equipment should consume and then incorporating these "normatives" into state standards that can be used as the basis for planning. If the exercise is done correctly, it gives the planners at least a rough idea of the aggregate consumption targets for energy and metals that should be assigned to ministries.

This is of course a herculean task, and the standards writers have sensibly focused on a handful of high-priority targets, emphasizing processes over products and producer goods over consumer goods. The real priority of the effort is hard to judge; but for what it may be worth, the ministries in which most of the standards writing has been concentrated were prominently involved in the "economic experiments" begun in 1983, and in several of them the top leadership has been newly appointed since Brezhnev's death, in some instances from previous

[35] Ibid.

[36] Hewett, *Energy, Economics, and Foreign Policy*, pp. 137–138. There is evidence that the 1982 increases in wholesale prices were offset by corresponding cuts in turnover tax; the net effect was that the price increase was not actually passed on. See Morris Bornstein, "Soviet Price Policies," *Soviet Economy* 3, no. 2 (1987), pp. 96–134.

careers in military-industrial administration.[37] On the other hand, these are machine-building ministries, not among the heaviest energy consumers.

A second feature of the standards program that indicates serious intent is that energy efficiency is being included in the product-quality rating system. The idea is that only a product or process that is energy efficient (in addition to meeting the other technological criteria) can be assigned to the "Highest Category" group, qualifying its enterprise for bonuses and price advantages.[38] In view of the increased importance that this rating system is receiving under Gorbachev, it is possible that energy efficiency may get real consideration in the design process for new plant and equipment.

Using norms as an instrument of conservation has several serious drawbacks, however. First, there are soon so many norms that enforcement becomes impossibly cumbersome; thus in the Ministry of Construction Materials there are more than one hundred energy-saving norms in effect, and that is probably one of the easier cases. Second, once a manager meets his norms, he may have no further incentive to save energy. Conservation experts are now urging planners to replace the myriad energy-saving norms with a single ministrywide target for reducing energy intensity.[39] That would alleviate the first problem but not the second; and because such highly aggregated targets could not possibly be established scientifically, such a move would reopen the whole process to manipulation and bargaining. Norms, if soundly based, are useful for the guidance of designers and managers; when turned into plan targets, they become a classic "administrative" instrument and as such point in the wrong direction.

To sum up the situation at the time of Andropov's accession in 1983: Despite improvement in the previous few years, the available mechanisms for implementation of a conservation policy still had a long way to go. A consumption system with inadequate meterage, prices that did not reflect costs, and manipulated consumption norms produced a vicious circle: the deficiencies of the price system made the norms necessary; but the shortage of measurement apparatus and the planners' poor

[37] The four ministries most prominently mentioned are the Ministry of Heavy, Power, and Transport Machine-building (Mintiazhmash), the Ministry of the Electrical Equipment Industry (Minelektrotekhprom), the Ministry of Machine-building, Roads, Construction, and Municipal Systems (Minstroidormash), and the Ministry of Instrument-making, Automation Equipment, and Control Systems (Minpribor).

[38] G. D. Kolmogorov, "Standartizatsiia i ekonomiia toplivno-energeticheskikh resursov," *Ekonomicheskaia gazeta*, no. 23 (1985), p. 7.

[39] S. Iatrov, "Energoemkost' proizvodstva," *Ekonomicheskaia gazeta*, no. 6 (1986), p. 2.

picture of what consumption in each plant should look like made it difficult to know whether the norms matched reality; in the absence of such a check there was little to prevent the ministries and the enterprises from setting norms as they pleased; and finally, since these arrangements suited everybody's concern to maximize output, there was little incentive to improve measurement or to tighten enforcement. How would the new leaders break out of the circle?

The Andropov Accession and the Energy Program of 1983

Chapter 1 described how, within a few months of his accession, Andropov approved an energy program heavily oriented toward conservation. It was one of the first concrete measures to be considered by the Politburo and presented to the Central Committee in the spring of 1983.[40]

Unlike the other measures proposed by Andropov at the same time, which were vague and tentative, the energy program was a reasonably coherent package of measures, backed up by detailed studies. What made such a quick start possible was the work of a high-level commission of experts, summoned by Brezhnev in 1979 and chaired by the president of the USSR Academy of Sciences, A. P. Aleksandrov.[41] The commission's main contribution to policy was to offer a practical strategy for handling the dangerous transition to a consumption-oriented approach.[42] In essence, it proposed to divide the turn to conservation into two stages, one of preparation (1983–1990) and one of active execution (1990–2000).

For the first, preparation phase the experts recommended on the supply side that oil output be stabilized while gas and nuclear power be vigorously developed to serve as bridging fuels to the next century. On the demand side, the commission stressed measures that would not require massive investment but would create the preconditions for the second stage: improvements in measurement of consumption, oversight, accountability, and incentives (including price increases); retire-

[40] "V Politbiuro TsK KPSS," *Pravda*, 9 Apr. 1983.

[41] The work of the Aleksandrov Commission was itself the outgrowth of research and analysis of the economics of energy problems spanning more than two decades. Its leading technical experts were well known: L. A. Melent'ev had been a prominent specialist on energy balances and economics for the last quarter-century; A. A. Makarov and A. G. Vigdorchik had written extensively on modeling the fuel and energy complex.

[42] A summary of the group's data and recommendations was published in book form in 1983. See Melent'ev and Makarov, *Energeticheskii kompleks SSSR*, pp. 5–6. For a shorter exposition, see D. B. Vol'fberg and A. A. Makarov, "Ratsional'noe ispol'zovanie i ekonomiia toplivno-energeticheskikh resursov," in D. G. Zhimerin, ed., *Sovremennye problemy energetiki* (Moscow: Energoatomizdat, 1984), pp. 59–83.

ment of obsolete equipment, capture of waste heat, and improvement of coal quality. Finally, as a short-term tactical aim, the commission urged rapid fuel switching, especially displacement of oil by gas in power plants.[43]

The second stage, to begin in 1990, was to be the business end of the program. If the first stage were properly carried out, energy investment could then be shifted to the consumption side. The inevitable lag before conservation results were realized would be covered by the abundant gas and nuclear power developed in the first phase. Direct gains in final consumption would come from modernization of technological processes and further electrification of industry. Indirect gains would result from reductions in the use of energy-intensive materials. Further transformation gains would be achieved by accelerating cogeneration, centralizing heat supply, relocating energy-intensive industry, and rationalizing the country's transportation system.

The commission's strategy, as we have already observed, was not cheap. Energy investment would have to be increased to 20–22 percent of the country's total investment budget for the last fifteen years of the century. But this was essential to the basic logic of the plan, which was to launch the transition to energy conservation while simultaneously protecting the economy's energy supply.

If anything, the commission was too optimistic: its program and its estimates understated the investments likely to be required in stage one on both the supply and the consumption sides. The riskiest unknown in the equation was oil: What would it cost to maintain production? Could one afford to let oil output drop, or could one afford not to? On these questions the Aleksandrov Commission appeared to be divided. The published supporting papers dwelled on the high cost and uncertainty of oil and appeared to hint that there could be worse choices than allowing its output to fall.[44] Aleksandrov himself, however, called publicly for further increases in oil output. Other senior experts appeared similarly divided.[45]

The danger, in view of the leaders' past record, was that they would

[43] Melent'ev and Makarov, *Energeticheskii kompleks SSSR*, pp. 164–173 and 99–100; Vol'fberg and Makarov, "Ratsional'noe ispol'zovanie," p. 64.

[44] Melent'ev and Makarov, *Energeticheskii kompleks SSSR*, pp. 160, 165, 176–177.

[45] "Problemy i perspektivy otechestvennoi energetiki," *Vestnik Akademii Nauk SSSR*, no. 7 (1984), p. 59. Academician V. Kirillin used even stronger words, calling the idea of a drop in oil output "mythical" (although the word was supposedly addressed to "Western commentators"). "Aktual'nye problemy sovetskoi energetiki," *Sovetskaia Kirgiziia*, 10 Aug. 1984. But S. Iatrov, then head of Gosplan's energy-planning institute, appeared to line up with the commission's stress on the high cost of oil. "Problemy snizheniia energoemkosti," *Ekonomicheskaia gazeta*, no. 2 (1985), p. 10.

postpone the necessary preparation for conservation. Andropov had appeared determined to hold the line; but as his health weakened and as new clouds appeared over the energy sector in 1983–1984 (as described in Chapter 2), the energy program evidently ran into controversy. It was not finally published until March 1984, one month after Andropov's death and nine months after the program had been officially adopted. When the text appeared, its energy conservation measures for stage one were weaker than those recommended by the Aleksandrov Commission. Whereas the experts had spelled out in detail the urgent preparatory steps required, the official program called only for "creating the preconditions" for conservation. On the supply side, the experts' concern over the high cost and uncertainty of oil were missing; instead, the published program's language stressed the crucial importance of keeping up oil output. The caution of lower-ranking officials and budgetary constraints had apparently prevailed.

Conservation in Gorbachev's First Five-Year Plan

A similar ambivalence has marked the approach of the Gorbachev administration since it came to power in 1985. On the supply side, as we have seen, the new leaders have continued to push for increased oil output, and, so far at least, they have paid the investment costs entailed. On the demand side, conservation has been prominent in the rhetoric of the new leaders and in the targets of the Twelfth Five-Year Plan. The energy intensity of national income is targeted to drop by 8.5 percent in 1986–1890 (compared with a 5.4 percent decline in 1980–1985), which implies that energy consumption will grow by only 12.4 percent (table 7.4). More ambitious targets are projected for the year 2000, and these are still the official targets today, even though they were adopted a year before the 1987 package of economic reforms. It is clear, however, that the prospects for conservation will depend above all on how fast and how far Gorbachev's reform program continues to evolve in the near future.[46]

Gorbachev's economic reforms have potentially vast consequences for energy conservation. They consist of two main parts. The first, announced in 1985, called for an overhaul of the country's technological structure, the centerpiece of which was to be a massive modernization of the machine-building sector. "Revolutionary advances" were needed, he told his audiences. The country must replace its aging capital stock, and every sector of the economy must be re-equipped with

[46] The best and fullest account of economic reform, which contrasts Gorbachev's strategy with previous attempts and shows the gradual evolution of the present program, is Ed A. Hewett's *Reforming the Soviet Economy* (Washington, D.C.: Brookings Institution, 1988).

TABLE 7.4
Projected Decline in Energy Intensity of National Income, 1986–1990 and 1986–2000

	1986–1990 (%)	*1986–2000 (%)*
Growth of national income	22.1	100
Decline of energy intensity	8.5	40
Implied increase in energy consumption	12.4	43

SOURCES: for 1986–1990: N. Ryzhkov, "O gosudarstvennom plane ekonomicheskogo i sotsial'nogo razvitiia SSSR na 1986–90 gody," *Pravda*, 19 June 1986; for 1986–2000: "Ob osnovnykh napravleniiakh ekonomicheskogo i sotsial'nogo razvitiia SSSR na 1986–90 gody i na period do 2000 goda," *Ekonomicheskaia gazeta*, no. 12 (1986), centerfold.

up-to-date machinery. The prestige of the engineering profession must be restored.[47] The main implication of this part of the program was that capital would be reallocated from extractive industries (and also from defense, although the reformers were discreet on this point until 1988) to civilian machine building and manufacturing, particularly to advanced sectors such as computers, electronics, robotics, and modern chemistry.

The second part of the strategy was to transform the economic mechanism. This part of the program has undergone the most spectacular revision since 1986, as Gorbachev's views of the changes needed have grown steadily more radical. Yet Gorbachev's first words showed the same essential concerns that have characterized his approach ever since: not to do away with central planning but to find a more effective balance between central planning and local autonomy by shifting toward the latter, by stimulating managers to make more efficient decisions by using economic signals and levers instead of administrative ones,[48] and by giving individuals and cooperatives new freedoms and incentives to provide services and small consumer goods.[49]

[47] "O sozyve ocherednogo XXVII s"ezda KPSS i zadachakh, sviazannykh s ego podgotovkoi i provedeniem," *Pravda*, 24 Apr. 1985. See also "Korennoi vopros ekonomicheskoi politiki Partii" (address to a conference on scientific and technological progress, convened at Central Committee headquarters), *Pravda*, 12 June 1985, p. 1.

[48] See the joint decree of the CPSU Central Committee and the USSR Council of Ministers, no. 669 (12 July 1985), "O shirokom rasprostranenii novykh metodov khoziaistvovaniia i usilenii ikh vozdeistviia na uskorenie nauchno-tekhnicheskogo progressa." *Ekonomicheskaia gazeta*, no. 32 (1985), centerfold.

[49] "Ob individual'noi trudovoi deiatel'nosti," *Pravda*, 21 Nov. 1986.

By mid-1987 the economic reform had evolved into a comprehensive program covering every aspect of the Soviet economy.[50] But it is riddled with inconsistencies, partly because of divisions within the leadership and opposition from the bureaucracy, and partly because the reformers' own thinking has been evolving continuously since 1985. Thus, while the program stresses improvements in efficiency and innovation, it also aims to accelerate growth; and in the short run, these two objectives are incompatible, as Soviet critics are increasingly pointing out.[51] Similarly, though the reform program calls for local autonomy and economic incentives, it also relies heavily on administrative pressure and calls for discipline. And most important, while the reform aims to increase the importance of money instruments and price signals, the leadership has shrunk from price reform and has failed to control the budget and the money supply, thus opening the way to inflation.[52] These contradictory elements have contradictory implications for energy policy.

LONG-TERM IMPLICATIONS OF THE GORBACHEV PROGRAM

The planned reallocation of investment priorities will shift the overall structure of Soviet industry away from energy-intensive sectors and toward less use of energy-intensive materials. However, major indirect energy savings will come about only if energy conservation becomes an integral part of the processes of design and innovation. A first step in this direction was taken in the Twelfth Five-Year Plan, which provides that only machines that use 8 to 12 percent less energy than their predecessors can be inscribed in the science and technology section of the plan.[53] This guideline, however, is still observed mainly in the breach.

In contrast, Gorbachev's policy of limiting new starts in industrial investment and favoring in-plant modernization (*rekonstruktsiia*) will aggravate the geographic split between energy supply and consumption by keeping energy consumption centered in the traditional industrial

[50] The basic document summarizing the reform package was approved by the CPSU Central Committee and formally adopted by the Supreme Soviet in late June 1987. "Osnovnye polozheniia korennoi perestroiki upravleniia ekonomikoi," *Pravda*, 27 June 1987. These basic provisions are amplified in a series of ten decrees covering specific subjects and institutions, published as *O korennoi perestroike upravleniia ekonomikoi: sbornik dokumentov* (Moscow: Politizdat, 1987).

[51] See notably the speech of L. I Abalkin at the Nineteenth Party Conference (*Pravda*, 30 June 1988) and Nikolai Shmelev, "Novye trevogi," *Novyi Mir*, no. 4 (1988), pp. 160–175.

[52] Central Intelligence Agency, Directorate of Intelligence, *USSR: Sharply Higher Budget Deficits Threaten Perestroika*, SOV 88-10043U (Washington, D.C.: September 1988).

[53] "Otvechat' dukhu vremeni," *Sotsialisticheskaia industriia*, 2 Oct. 1985.

areas west of the Urals. Here is a further obvious inconsistency in Gorbachev's policies, for he has also strongly endorsed the concept of rationalizing the regional structure of Soviet industry by shifting energy-intensive consumers closer to the sources of energy supply, chiefly by moving them east of the Urals. But that will be possible only if he allows new starts.[54]

As for the impact of changes in the economic mechanism, the most important question is whether demand for raw materials will be curbed and, in particular, whether energy consumption can be separated from economic growth. So far, price reform is the main element missing from the package.[55] It is clear that higher prices for energy are on the way, but probably not before 1990, and their magnitude is still under discussion. The more important issues are how, and how frequently, energy prices will be adjusted thereafter, how they will affect the supply and allocation of energy supplies, and how they will influence the behavior of managers and consumers. As we have seen, wholesale energy prices remained essentially unchanged from the late 1960s to the early 1980s and thus failed to reflect the rapid rise in costs. If the price reform of 1990 were to consist of a similar one-time adjustment, energy prices would soon be out of line with costs again. And it is likely that changes will be infrequent, because energy prices will continue to be centrally fixed, unlike some manufactured goods, whose prices will be set by negotiation between buyer and seller. Thus energy prices will probably remain sticky and continue to lag behind rapidly rising costs, especially marginal costs.

For many manufactured goods wholesale markets will be created to take the burden off the supply system, but most energy will continue to be centrally allocated,[56] just as most energy production will be governed by "state orders"—in effect, by centrally mandated output targets. There may be market allocation of refined oil products, however,

[54] The cluster of joint ventures in the petrochemicals industry, described in Chapters 6 and 8, is a centerpiece of this policy.

[55] A comprehensive review of the price system is under way; it will produce revised wholesale prices by 1 January 1990 for implementation in the Thirteenth Five-Year Plan, beginning in 1991. The July 1987 decree on changes in the price system is briefer than the others and hews on the whole to the traditional cost-plus philosophy of Soviet price formation. One interesting departure, however, is that it acknowledges as desirable the general principle that Soviet prices should be brought into line with world price levels. Postanovlenie TsK KPSS i Soveta Ministrov SSSR, 17 July 1987, no. 820, "Ob osnovnykh napravleniiakh perestroiki sistemy tsenoobrazovaniia v usloviiakh novogo khoziaistvennogo mekhanizma," in *O korennoi perestroike*, pp. 150–164.

[56] Interview with the first deputy chairman of the State Committee for Supply (Gossnab), Iu. P. Boev, "Mekhanizm optovoi torgovli," *Ekonomicheskaia gazeta*, no. 32 (1987), p. 6.

with the possibility of negotiated retail prices, which would encourage savings of gasoline and lighter oil fractions. But on the whole, energy supply and distribution will remain highly centralized and controlled, and energy prices will continue to be centrally determined on the basis of costs, not demand. In particular, there will be little possibility of price competition among fuels.[57]

Increased energy prices will cut energy consumption only if managers have an incentive to respond. The single most crucial feature of the Gorbachev reform is the requirement that enterprises must pay their own way and be judged by their profits. If fully implemented, this would give managers a powerful incentive to economize on all inputs. The extent of the resulting energy savings would then depend on the relative prices set for raw materials, capital, and labor and the rates at which substitutions could be made among them. Unfortunately, managers are more likely to take advantage of their new freedoms to pass on higher energy prices to their customers; and in view of the general lack of competition among domestic producers, customers will have little choice but to accept higher-priced goods. In that case, the consequence of higher energy prices would be inflation but no major decline in energy use.[58]

Another reform-related issue is the speed with which energy experts themselves switch from a focus on supply to more detailed studies of demand. Most energy research institutes have been slow to adjust to the implications of the new policies and to reorient their studies toward conservation. Their modeling remains generally based on exogenously given demand levels and "rational" consumption norms and shows little understanding of the proper function of prices or their possible impact on economic behavior. At this point, leaders and planners lack the necessary research findings to implement conservation policy or to predict its results.[59]

[57] There has been some discussion of demand-related pricing to discourage consumption at peak seasons and times of day. Thus gas prices in mid-winter could be raised to limit consumption by power plants, the additional income to be used to finance gas storage facilities.

[58] This has been the experience of Hungarian reformers. See Janos Kornai, "The Hungarian Reform Process: Visions, Hopes, and Reality," *Journal of Economic Literature* 24 (December 1986), p. 1698.

[59] I am grateful to Robert Campbell for sharing with me his trip notes and the observations of an American delegation of experts on energy demand that visited Soviet institutes in the summer of 1987. See Diana B. Bielauskas, "US-Soviet Discussions on Energy Conservation," *Newsletter of the American Association for the Advancement of Slavic Studies* 27, no. 5 (November 1987), pp. 1 and 3. One important development is that Gosplan's own Institute for the Integrated Study of Fuel and Energy Problems, long

Of the two main sources of energy savings we have just discussed, reallocation of investment priorities will clearly take a long time to realize results under any circumstances, but savings via price reforms depend very much on how fast and vigorously the reforms are implemented. Meanwhile, what of the prospects of nearer-term measures?

NEAR-TERM IMPLICATIONS OF THE GORBACHEV PROGRAM

If the Gorbachev program succeeds in accelerating growth, then, in the near term energy demand will rise correspondingly. The measures available to contain demand while longer-range reforms take hold are to varying degrees unsatisfactory. Consider first the problem of curbing residential and municipal demand. Most residential use is still unmetered and highly subsidized; raising the price of energy to individuals would require a large investment in meters and would risk arousing popular discontent. In other words, curbing residential energy demand is part of the much larger problem of curbing the vast consumer subsidies to which Soviet citizens have grown accustomed. So far, the leaders have approached this issue in a gingerly way.[60] Consequently, even large increases in wholesale energy prices may have little effect on the consumption of energy for residential uses, particularly heating.

As for industrial demand, the only available near-term measure is tougher norms and quotas, amounting to rationing. Under the new reforms the central planners will set allocation levels (called *limity*) of principal inputs to enterprises; these will include energy and other raw materials. In the meantime, even before the new decrees were formulated, the new leadership began tightening conservation targets for energy and other raw materials and set stiffer penalties for enterprises violating the targets.[61] These are classic "administrative" measures, of

---

criticized for its neglect of conservation, has changed its leadership and its research profile. (In 1987 the founding director, S. N. Iatrov, was replaced by N. K. Pravodnikov.) An important exception to the general neglect of energy demand has been the work of specialists at the Siberian Energy Institute in Irkutsk, especially M. A. Gershenzon and Iu. D. Kononov. Even this work, however, does not study responses to price changes.

[60] Gorbachev and other Soviet leaders have called for an end to subsidized retail prices for foodstuffs, rents, and the like; but no timetable for the implementation of these increases has been set, and the leadership is evidently reluctant to grapple with this issue now. In a conference in Moscow in December 1987, in which this author was a participant, several economists known to be close to the general secretary told the American group that there were no concrete plans to raise consumer prices. See the comment of Academician Abel Aganbegian at this conference, as summarized in *Soviet Economy* 3, no. 4 (1987), p. 291.

[61] "O korennom uluchshenii ispol'zovaniia syr'evykh, toplivno-energeticheskikh i

course, and as such they illustrate the continued traditional strand in Gorbachev's reforms. The question is: Are they likely to work better than similar previous efforts? If energy quotas threaten plan fulfillment, one may predict that planners and ministers will conspire to bail out their enterprises as they have in the past, by easing allocation quotas or softening penalties.

In sum, the Gorbachev reforms, even if implemented on schedule, will not begin saving energy until the early 1990s, if then, while any near-term acceleration in economic output, especially industrial output, will nullify any near-term gains from tighter enforcement. The only way the leadership can save energy quickly is through rationing, but to make that stick they would have to send a clear signal throughout the bureaucracy that they are willing to sacrifice growth rates and gross output targets to economize on resources. Such a measure would be unpalatable on every count. Indeed, there is already a tacit rationing policy in effect for such scarce energy sources as kerosene, gasoline, and peak-demand electricity. Ministries react by canceling airline flights, cutting back ambulance service, and shedding their least influential customers. Clearly, rationing amounts to taking a meat cleaver to the demand problem.

Yet the leadership must find a way to lessen the effects of rising energy costs and mounting investment in energy supply, lest their industrial modernization program end up being sacrificed to it. Recent studies by Siberian economists put a dramatic new light on the problem. What would it take, they ask, to keep energy investment from expanding beyond 20 percent of total Soviet investment? At GNP growth rates of 1–2 percent, energy investment could be kept within its present bounds without major conservation gains. But at growth rates of 4–5 percent, the energy intensity of GNP would have to drop from its present level of about 0.8 to 0.5–0.6.[62]

Confronted with such stark trade-offs, yet constrained by the difficulty of realizing energy savings quickly, the leaders may flinch yet again. They may prefer to believe that the gas bridge will carry them for a few more years and that natural gas will remain about half as expensive as oil for some time to come. In that case, they will be tempted to

drugikh material'nykh resursov v usloviiakh intensivnogo razvitiia ekonomiki SSSR v 1986–90 godakh i na period do 2000." To my knowledge this decree has not been published, but it was mentioned as having been discussed by the Politburo at its meeting of 15 May 1986. *Pravda*, 16 May 1986.

[62] Presentation by Iu. D. Kononov of the Siberian Energy Institute at the National Academy of Sciences, Washington, D.C., 15 March 1988.

concentrate on fuel switching more than conservation. As we shall see in the next section, that may be precisely what is happening now.

Fuel Switching and Oil Displacement

If the Gorbachev leadership has so far only flirted with conservation, by contrast it has moved more vigorously to change the fuel mix, chiefly by replacing oil with natural gas. Right now, this is clearly the most rational strategy to follow. Delivered natural gas is still half as costly at the margin as oil. Above all, natural gas is the only energy source that can provide reliable growth in supply over the next decade.

But there are two potential sources of trouble here, to which the past history of Soviet energy policy should make us especially alert. The first is that switching to natural gas may paralyze progress toward use of other fuels, chiefly the brown coals of Kazakhstan and Siberia, that will eventually be needed once the marginal costs of natural gas begin to rise, as they inevitably will. The other potential problem is that switching to natural gas could become a substitute for conservation itself, because planners find it easier and safer. In that case, they could discover in another decade or two that they are just as far from the secure and energy-efficient future of Brezhnev's energy program as they are today.

Complicating the planners' calculations is the fact that to absorb natural gas into the economy at the rapid rate of the last decade is neither automatic nor cost free. Here, as elsewhere in the Soviet system, the crucial scarce resource is political attention and priority. As we shall see later, fuel switching lagged until the program was given top political priority and the necessary investments began to be made, which did not happen until Andropov's accession. The program has remained vigorous under his successors, but they have been disappointed to find that it has displaced less oil than they had hoped. Indeed, if the economy revives under Gorbachev, oil consumption (in absolute terms) will probably rise again, as it did in 1986.

Penetration of Gas into the Soviet Economy

Immense new quantities of natural gas are being delivered to the Soviet economy from West Siberia by the expanding pipeline network, and the share of natural gas in the fuel mix is growing rapidly. We should bear in mind that this is not an entirely new development: the economy has already been absorbing gas for some years. Hence the issues involved should not surprise Soviet planners. From 19 percent in 1970, the share of natural gas in total energy output grew to 26 percent in

1980 and to nearly 33 percent in 1985.[63] The growth of gas consumption, which has been slightly faster than the planners' initial schedule, makes it the dominant Soviet fuel today.

As rapid as the penetration of gas has been, there have been no radical changes in the allocation of it—with the one crucial exception of the power industry, examined in more detail below. Large quantities of new gas have been absorbed by all sectors, including agriculture, which is rapidly becoming a major consumer of high-grade fuels (table 7.5). What changes there have been reflect larger trends in the Soviet economy: municipal-residential consumption and demand by the chemical industry (most of the latter for feedstock) have grown fastest, while ferrous metallurgy and building materials have lost ground. But there is some evidence that in these sectors the planners had expected more gas use than actually occurred.[64] The one seeming anomaly was the declining share of the machine-building sector, despite very rapid penetration of gas into it during the 1970s;[65] this was presumably a reflection of the sector's slow growth in the Brezhnev period (discussed in Chapter 6). If Gorbachev's ambitious plans for accelerated growth in machine building become reality, that sector will presumably emerge as one of the major growth points for gas demand in the future.

Most natural gas is still consumed west of the Urals (table 7.6), and although the eastern zone has been gradually gaining, the west is unlikely to slacken its use quickly in the future, especially if the industrial ministries heed Gorbachev's orders to modernize existing plants instead of making new starts. This means that penetration of gas into the economy will require continued heavy investment in gas transmission (amounting, as we saw in Chapter 5, to about 70 percent of total gas investment). It also means heavy losses of gas to drive the system; by 1985 these accounted for about 8 percent of total gas production (table 7.7), but the share can be expected to continue growing in the future. Large-diameter trunk lines are faster and cheaper to build (per unit of work performed) than small-diameter local distribution systems. Hence the planners are interested in focusing on large-unit consumers, preferably located close to the sources of gas, if not in West Siberia itself then

[63] *Narodnoe khoziaistvo SSSR*, relevant years.

[64] The construction materials industry, for example, was slated for a 20 percent increase in gas consumption during the Eleventh Plan. V. Filanovskii, "Effektivnee ispol'zovat' prirodnyi gaz," *Ekonomicheskaia gazeta*, no. 13 (1984), p. 9. But actual consumption rose only about 15 percent.

[65] The share of natural gas in total fuel consumption by the machine-building and metal-working sectors grew from 13 percent in 1970 to 65 percent in 1980. N. A. Fedorov, *Tekhnika i effektivnost' ispol'zovaniia gaza*, 2d ed. (Moscow: Nedra, 1983), p. 27.

TABLE 7.5

Distribution of Primary Consumption of Natural Gas, 1965–1987
(in billions of cubic meters)

Sector	*1965*	*1970*	*1975*	*1980*	*1984*	*1985*	*1986*	*1987*
USSR Total	125.3	190.7	261.9	346.7	462.8	500.1	533.4	568.0
Housing and municipal sector	15.3	25.2	35.3	52.1	64.3	68.0	69.9	74.4
Industry	71.1	108.6	148.4	190.6	223.0	234.5	243.8	256.2
Ferrous metallurgy	17.6	28.2	34.4	40.4	45.1	46.0	46.4	47.7
Nonferrous metallurgy	0.8	2.6	5.9	7.0	8.4	9.0	9.1	9.7
Oil and gas*	8.4	12.8	21.3	26.7	29.4	32.0	35.2	36.9
Machine building and metal working	12.8	18.8	23.4	29.1	34.3	36.5	37.3	39.8
Chemical	6.1	12.9	21.0	36.4	47.9	51.5	53.9	57.4
Construction materials	13.6	18.3	23.2	26.6	30.9	31.5	32.5	34.1
Other branches	11.8	15.0	19.2	24.4	27.0	28.0	29.3	30.7
Electric Power**	35.7	51.1	68.7	91.1	156.7	176.5	199.0	214.7
Others	3.2	5.8	6.4	12.9	18.8	21.0	20.8	22.7
Losses	2.3	3.2	3.7	NA	NA	NA	NA	NA

SOURCES: *Soviet Geography* 29, no. 10 (December 1988), p. 889.

* Not counting gas used for transmission.

** Minenergo only.

TABLE 7.6
Regional Distribution of Gas Consumption, 1970–1986

	European USSR		*East of Urals*	
	bcm	*%*	*bcm*	*%*
1970	173.2	90.8	17.4	9.2
1975	224.9	85.8	37.0	14.2
1980	289.4	83.5	57.3	16.5
1986	440.1	82.5	93.3	17.5

SOURCE: M. V. Sidorenko et al., "Regional'nye i mezhotraslevye problemy osvoeniia gazovykh mestorozhdenii i razvitiia sistem dal'nego transporta gaza," *Ekonomika, organizatsiia i upravlenie v gazovoi promyshlennosti*, no. 7 (1983), p. 31. For 1986 see *Soviet Geography* 29, no. 10 (December 1988), p. 890.

as far "upstream" as possible and near the major trunk lines. This explains much of the recent Soviet interest in petrochemicals development in West Siberia.

This brings us to the single most important development in the fuel-switching program in 1981–1985: the massive increase in the use of natural gas by large power plants.

Gas Absorption and Oil Displacement in Power Plants

The most attractive target for the absorption of new gas is large electric power plants: they are large-scale single users, and many are already equipped to burn gas.[66] In the first half of the 1980s they accounted for well over half of the total increment of new gas supplied to domestic consumers.[67] Gas absorption in power plants accounts for most of the Soviet progress in displacing oil in recent years.

The planners' focus on power plants is not new; indeed, a major

[66] For much valuable material in this section I am indebted to the collaboration of Ms. Caron Cooper, whose work under the auspices of the Soviet Studies Program at the Center for Strategic and International Studies appears in her article, "Petroleum Displacement in the Soviet Economy: The Case of Electric Power Plants," *Soviet Geography* 27, no. 6 (June 1986), pp. 377–397.

[67] The increment in annual deliveries to users between 1980 and 1984 was 115.5 bcm; of that, 61.0 bcm went to power plants belonging to Minenergo. See Matthew J. Sagers, "How Has the Soviet Economy Absorbed All That Gas?" *PlanEcon Report* 3, no. 2 (14 Jan. 1987), p. 3.

TABLE 7.7
Natural Gas Consumed by the Pipeline System and Other Internal Uses, 1970–1987

	Bcm	*%*
1970	7.2	3.6
1975	16.4	5.6
1980	31.2	7.7
1985	57.9	9.0
1987	72.7	10.0

SOURCE: *Soviet Geography* 29, no. 10 (December 1988), p. 887.

strategic goal of the Tenth Plan (1976–1980) had been to displace fuel oil (*mazut*) with coal. The plan called for the Ministry of Power (Minenergo), which operates over 90 percent of the generating capacity of the Soviet Union, to cut the share of mazut in its fuel structure from 29.5 to 28 percent by 1980 by increasing coal usage (the share of gas was to remain at 22 percent).[68] Instead, the share of oil jumped to 35.7 percent. None of the envisioned avenues for oil displacement worked. Production of steam coal in the Donbas dropped both in quantity and in quality. Congestion on the railroad system hampered delivery of Kuzbas coal from Siberia to the Urals, while delays in pipeline construction prevented gas from reaching the Volga Basin as planned. Nuclear power development lagged. All these problems came together most spectacularly in the Ukraine, where power plants actually doubled their oil consumption between 1976 and 1980.[69] Another region where the strategy also miscarried badly was the Volga Basin, where the share of oil was to drop from 55.6 to 47.5 percent.[70] Instead, it rose to 62.7 percent.[71] In retrospect, the planners' coal program in

[68] A. M. Nekrasov and M. G. Pervukhin, *Energetika SSSR v 1976–80 godakh* (Moscow: Energiia, 1977), p. 151.

[69] A. M. Nekrasov and A. A. Troitskii, *Energetika SSSR v 1981–1985 godakh* (Moscow: Energoizdat, 1981), ch. 9. The share of oil in the fuel consumed by Ukrainian Minenergo soared from 6.2 percent in 1970 to 19.4 percent in 1975, and then to 34.4 percent in 1980. See A. P. Reshetniak, V. A. Zhmurko, N. S. Semeshko, and A. A. Tuzman, "Toplivno-energeticheskii balans Donbassa," *Energetika i Elektrifikatsiia* (Kiev), no. 1 (1984), p. 50.

[70] Nekrasov and Pervukhin, *Energetika SSSR v 1976–80 godakh*, p. 151.

[71] Nekrasov and Troitskii, *Energetika SSSR v 1981–1985 godakh*, p. 232.

the second half of the 1970s looms as one of the most colossal blunders of a bad decade.

By 1978, when it was clear that the five-year targets for coal were hopeless, Gosplan decided on an accelerated schedule of conversions to gas during the last three years of the Tenth Plan. Two hundred sixty-seven power plants and enterprises, the latter mostly in the ferrous metallurgy sector, were chosen as targets. But the plan remained a dead letter. By the beginning of 1980, Minenergo and Minchermet had not even submitted proposals for the conversion program.[72] Most of the reported progress in using gas came as an unintended by-product in the Urals, where delays in pipeline construction to the west of the region produced a temporary local gas glut, which helped to offset shortages of coal caused by overloading of the railroad system.

In 1980–1981 Gosplan was induced to try again. The Eleventh Plan target adopted in 1981 called for Minenergo to reduce mazut consumption from 114.8 million tons to 90 million, or from 35.7 to 25.9 percent of Minenergo fuel demand. This time the planners were more cautious and forecast only a slight increase in the share of coal. The emphasis instead was almost entirely on natural gas, which was slated for a 40 percent increase. Here the planners were more successful: the share of fuel oil in Minenergo power plants declined exactly as planned, dropping in volume to 94 million tons in 1985 (table 7.8).[73] The share of gas, in contrast, increased sharply, and its volume nearly doubled in five years.[74] The most recent data indicate that gas consumption by Minenergo continues to grow rapidly. Indeed, whereas the five-year plan calls for an increase of 34 bcm per year between 1985 and 1990, in 1986 alone Minenergo's gas consumption grew by 22.5 bcm.[75] Minenergo's power plants are clearly the fastest growth point for Soviet gas consumption: in 1985 they absorbed 52.9 percent of the total increment in gas consumption, and in 1986, 67.3 percent.[76]

Minenergo's initial difficulties in absorbing gas were due to two problems, which could still constrain the growth of gas consumption

[72] S. Iatrov, "Otrasl' bazovaia, kliuchevaia." *Krasnaia zvezda*, 4 Jan. 1980.

[73] A. A. Troitskii, ed., *Energetika SSSR v 1986–1990* (Moscow: Energoatomizdat, 1987), p. 78. There is a slight mystery about these fuel oil numbers. Until 1988 Minenergo journals made no claims of major victories, giving the impression instead that oil displacement was progressing poorly. In 1986 an industry exhibit in Moscow, observed by Matthew Sagers, reported an *increase* in oil consumption by 1985 to 116.5 million tons. The discrepancy (if such it is) is about 22 million tons.

[74] Troitskii, ed., *Energetika SSSR v 1986–1990*.

[75] *Podgotovka, pererabotka i ispol'zovanie gaza*, no. 11 (1987), p. 18. I am grateful to Matthew Sagers for calling my attention to this source.

[76] Ibid.

TABLE 7.8
Fuel Shares in Minenergo Power Plant Consumption, 1970–1990 (percentages)

	1970	*1975*	*1980*	*1985*	*1990 (plan)*
Oil	23.5	29.5	35.7	25.9	19.3
Gas	23.8	22.0	24.2	40.3	45.2
Coal	47.5	48.5	40.1	33.8	35.5

SOURCES: for 1970–1980: Cooper, "Petroleum Displacement" (citing Nekrasov and Troitskii, *Energetika SSSR v 1981–1985 godakh*, p. 32, and Nekrasov and Pervukhin, *Energetika SSSR v 1976–80 godakh*, p. 151); for 1985 and 1990: Troitskii, ed., *Energetika SSSR v 1986–1990*, p. 90.

before the end of the 1980s. On the one hand, a shortage of gas storage capacity prevents the power industry from meeting winter peaks in demand with gas, and many of its power plants, even those listed as "converted," continue to burn oil during the coldest parts of the winter. Second, the quality of coal delivered to power plants has deteriorated sharply, forcing the operators to supplement coal with gas and oil.

THE GAS STORAGE ISSUE

The Soviet gas distribution system suffers from an astonishing lack of gas storage capacity, which in large gas distribution systems plays the role of a buffer, enabling the system to absorb seasonal variations in demand. In contrast to the United States, where up to one-third of winter gas use comes from underground storage, in the Soviet Union the share is hardly more than 10 percent.[77] Instead, in the Soviet system it is the power plants themselves that play the role of buffer: many of them have long been equipped to burn both oil and gas; and indeed, in Soviet practice such power plants are referred to as "buffer stations." In the summer they burn gas; in the winter, when gas is needed elsewhere for residential systems, they burn oil. But the lack of gas storage limits oil displacement: additional mazut use by power plants for this one reason alone was 42 million tons in 1980, or 37 percent of total consumption by the Ministry of Power.[78] Much of that oil could be dis-

[77] Matthew J. Sagers and Albina Tretyakova, "Constraints in Gas for Oil Substitution in the USSR: The Oil Refining Industry and Gas Storage," *Soviet Economy* 2, no. 1 (January-March 1986), pp. 72–94.

[78] Melent'ev and Makarov, *Energeticheskii kompleks SSSR*, p. 167.

placed immediately for export if adequate gas storage capacity were available.

But to achieve that, the Soviets would have to triple the volume of gas storage. In 1980 the Soviet gas industry had only 22 bcm of capacity (in contrast to more than 90 bcm in the United States).[79] But despite initial plans to increase capacity to 40 bcm by 1985 (later amended to 1990),[80] there was little evidence of new construction until the mid-1980s. In 1986 and 1987 the rate of additions to gas storage capacity accelerated substantially (6 bcm in 1986; 7.6 bcm in 1987),[81] but even at the current pace of construction the Soviets will not have adequate capacity until the late 1990s.

The lack of progress in expanding gas storage capacity is a perfect example of the interaction of policy and system that results in a bottleneck. Building gas storage facilities does not require high technology, but good sites located near consumption points are hard to find and expensive to develop. Both the Ministry of the Gas Industry and its associated construction ministry have been preoccupied with developing the Siberian gas fields and the major trunk lines; gas storage has been at the bottom of the list of priorities (table 7.9). In addition, the Gas Ministry appeared reluctant until recently to fill up what little capacity it had, possibly because storing gas requires injecting a "cushion" that cannot subsequently be recovered. At any rate, it was not until 1983 that high-level pressure caused the ministry to devote more attention to the storage issue. Recent news reports that East European workers are helping to build storage facilities suggest that progress is finally being made.

DECLINING COAL QUALITY

The effort to displace oil is seriously hampered by declining coal quality. To compensate for rising ash and deteriorating heat content, Minenergo has been obliged to use increasing amounts of hydrocarbons to spike bad coal. Annual mazut consumption for this purpose has risen from 6 or 7 million tons in 1979[82] to about 20 million in the early 1980s.[83] Soviet energy policy in the last decade, by neglecting coal

[79] Cooper, "Petroleum Displacement," p. 384. These quantities are "working gas."

[80] "Razvitie gazovoi promyshlennosti," *Ekonomicheskaia gazeta*, no. 13 (1981), p. 2. Sagers and Tretyakova, "Constraints in Gas for Oil Substitution," have 22 bcm.

[81] V. Tikhonov, "Postavkam gaza—vysokuiu nadezhnost'!" *Ekonomicheskaia gazeta*, no. 44 (1988).

[82] K. F. Roddatis and V. S. Vdovchenko, "Kachestvo tverdogo topliva teplovykh elektrostantsii i ego vliianie na pokazateli parovykh kotlov," *Elektricheskie stantsii*, no. 5 (1982), p. 24.

[83] K. F. Roddatis and K. V. Shakhsuvarov, "O poteriakh v narodnom khoziaistve iz-za

TABLE 7.9
Investment in Underground Gas Storage by MGP, 1966–1980

	Rubles (millions)	*Percentage of Total*
1966–1970	44.6	1.1
1971–1975	91.5	0.9
1976–1980	277.7	1.4

SOURCE: Sedykh and Kuchin, *Upravlenie nauchno-tekhnicheskim progressom*, p. 8. I have not yet found information for 1981–1985.

investment (particularly in coal enrichment), has contributed to the problem; but even if the policy is reversed in the second half of the 1980s, the decline of the coal quality cannot be arrested in this decade. Therefore the issue facing the power industry is how fast it can substitute gas for mazut as a spiking fuel.

The coal-quality problem affects a large part of the Ministry of Power's operations. Nationwide, Minenergo power plants designed for coal use accounted in the early 1980s for about 36 percent of Soviet electrical output. Between 1965 and 1982 the average ash content of the coal burned in them rose from 28.7 to 33.2 percent, while calorific content dropped from 4,180 kilocalories per kilogram to 3,840.[84] The decline in quality has been particularly steep since 1977 and continues to this day.[85]

This has many negative effects on power plants (increased transportation and waste-disposal burden, wear and damage of boilers, and so on), but the two most serious are poor combustion and a consequent deterioration in the quality of electrical supply: lowered voltage and frequency, and recurring power outages. To maintain electricity supply, the ministry is obliged to bring reserve capacity into service, consisting of older, inefficient, mostly oil-burning plants.

The coal-quality problem is especially serious in three locations: the region served by Donbas hard coal around the eastern Ukraine, the area

ponizheniia kachestva uglei dlia teplovykh elektrostantsii," *Elektricheskie stantsii*, no. 2 (1985), p. 9.

[84] Roddatis and Shakhsuvarov, "O poteriakh v narodnom khoziaistve," p. 6.

[85] Soviet statistical manuals began reflecting the overall decline in coal quality in 1987. Compare the coal entries in *Narodnoe khoziaistvo SSSR za 70 let*, p. 163, with the series given the year before in *Narodnoe khoziaistvo v 1986g.*, p. 157.

south of Moscow supplied by Podmoskov'e brown coal, and plants in the Urals that burn brown coal from the Ekibastuz open-pit mines in Kazakhstan. These three "hot spots" account for two-thirds of the power reductions in the Minenergo system.[86]

The deterioration of Donbas hard coals has been the most serious of all. Quality trends for the leading category of Donbas steam coal are shown in table 7.10. Donbas hard coals supply twenty-six Minenergo power plants in the region around the eastern Ukraine and the North Caucasus, of which the six largest account for 75 percent of total consumption. The Donbas-supplied power plants are responsible for 42 percent of the power reductions in the Minenergo system, making them the worst trouble spots in the country. One reason is that coal washings and slag are added to the raw coal allocated to these power plants, so that the real coal quality available to them is even worse than the table suggests. The deterioration has continued to the present, and Minenergo has been forced to burn mazut and gas in boilers designed for coal. Indeed, the existing incentive structure encourages utilities to burn oil instead of coal, because they are rewarded for showing higher steady heat rates each year. As a result, in the first half of the 1980s unused coal stocks grew steadily even as oil was overconsumed.[87]

If the decline in coal quality is to be offset with gas instead of oil, further investment in gas transmission and storage will be required. Until that is done, the additional oil required for spiking in coal-fired plants will continue to offset many of the gains from displacing oil in dual-fired plants, as it did in 1983–1985. The implication is clear but undoubtedly unwelcome to the leaders and planners: there are steady gains to be made in displacing oil from power plants over the next decade, but only if substantial investment takes place.

The Outlook for Fuel Switching and Oil Displacement

The vigorous effort to absorb gas into the economy, especially since 1983, led to a dramatic 50 percent increase in gas consumption in the first half of the 1980s. Half of the increase went to power plants alone. Can this process continue, or will the rate of absorption of natural gas itself become a bottleneck in the energy sector? Three questions must be preoccupying the planners at this point. First, how much additional investment in gas transmission and storage will be required, now that the easiest conversion opportunities have been exploited? Second, how much treatment of coal will be needed to arrest the decline in the

[86] Roddatis and Shakhsuvarov, "O poteriakh v narodnom khoziaistve," p. 8.

[87] A. Troitskii, "O mekhanizme khoziaistvovaniia v elektroenergetike," *Planovoe khoziaistvo*, no. 7 (1982), p. 82.

TABLE 7.10
Quality Trends for Donbas Hard Coal

	Donetsk T Coal	
	Ash Content (%)	*Heat Content (gigacalories)*
1960	18.8	6,360
1965	20.6	6,180
1970	24.6	5,730
1975	24.4	5,670
1980	30.9	5,015
1983	31.5	4,947

SOURCE: Roddatis and Shakhsuvarov, "O poteriakh v narodnom khoziaistve," p. 8.

quality of steam coal delivered to power plants? Finally, will the modernization of industrial plants in other sectors provide sufficient opportunities for consuming large increments of natural gas?

The answer to all three questions depends on the resources the leaders are willing to invest and the administrative priority they will give. On past form, it is likely that the absorption of gas will displace as much coal as oil. In the long run, that amounts to displacement of a low-value fuel by a high-value one. But to realize coal's long-range potential as a cheap fuel, as envisioned by the authors of the energy program, will require major investment in coal utilization. The path of least resistance may be to use gas instead.

Conclusion: The Vital Importance of Conservation

What drives the Soviet energy crisis is uncontrolled consumption. The longer the Soviet leaders hesitate before beginning the transition to a policy based on curbing demand, the more they will be forced to disrupt their investment priorities to pay for ever more expensive energy supplies. The importance of conservation for sound energy policy can hardly be exaggerated.

Its importance as a test of Gorbachev's overall strategy and politics is equally great. If Gorbachev cannot succeed in saving energy, he is unlikely to succeed anywhere, because energy conservation should be thought of as the acid test of three essential propositions of Gorbachevian reform: that economic reform can be conducted in stages and parts; that increased reliance on economic methods can be combined successfully with central planning; and that long-term goals can be sufficiently defended from short-term urgencies to yield real progress.

Energy conservation lends itself well to a two-stage approach, as we have seen. Unlike more elusive quantities, such as "technological progress," energy savings are easily measured and rewarded. The Soviets currently do such a bad job of both that even a minimally resolute campaign of administrative sanctions and economic rewards, combined with a program to improve monitoring and measurement of energy use (using imported electrical and gas meters, if necessary), should produce large improvements, thus lessening the problem of lags described earlier. If the Gorbachev leadership is incapable of hitting so fat a target, what can it possibly achieve elsewhere?

In the longer term, energy conservation is once again the acid test of the Gorbachev program. If Gorbachev is able to reallocate investment toward new industries and stimulate modernization of existing facilities, then energy savings should be an almost automatic by-product. Similarly, any progress at all in forcing local decisionmakers to bear the costs of their decisions should produce energy savings almost automatically, even without elaborate price reforms; unlike new technology or consumer goods, energy comes in a small number of standard and stable forms, and it is one commodity for which input-output analysis, industry by industry, should provide enough information to keep supply and demand in balance by central allocations. Hence central price setting should not be an insuperable obstacle to improvements in energy consumption, provided planners keep raising energy prices at frequent intervals and managers actually feel the bite.

To Gorbachev's great good luck, the bountifulness of natural gas should preserve the Soviet economy over the next ten years from the jolts and shocks in energy supply of recent years, thus making it possible to concentrate on longer-range goals without alarms or distractions. If Gorbachev and his colleagues make any headway with their machine-building program, one of the beneficial results will be improvements in nuclear engineering and coal technology, essential prerequisites for the coal-and-nuclear future lying beyond the gas bridge. In sum, energy conservation and fuel switching should be less difficult, long, and expensive than some of the other tasks the Gorbachev leadership has set itself. That is why the initial returns are disturbing. They suggest that supply still dominates demand in the new leaders' thinking, that near-term urgency is still overriding long-term purpose, and that the reformers still shrink before the tough choices they face. The learning that has taken place over the last decade is not yet being translated into effective day-to-day policy. So far, the new leadership is not passing the acid test.

EIGHT

SOVIET ENERGY EXPORTS: FROM FREE RIDE TO RUDE AWAKENING

As future historians look back on Soviet Russia in the last half of this century and describe the slow settling of the Bolshevik upheaval, they will undoubtedly stress as one of its principal features the country's gradual return to the world economy. Its most extreme period of isolation ended soon after Stalin's death in 1953, but it took another two decades for foreign trade to become a significant factor again in the Soviet economy. A symbolic threshold was crossed in the first half of the 1970s, when foreign-trade turnover (that is, imports plus exports) reached one-tenth the size of the Soviet national income for the first time in forty years.[1] In the decade after 1975 foreign trade grew at over eight times the pace of national income, and by the first half of the 1980s its size relative to national income had ballooned to 27 percent.[2] As a result, for the first time in a half-century the world economy began to play a major role in Russia's internal, civilian affairs. Under Brezhnev foreign issues began to affect domestic decisionmaking, and vice versa, in key sectors such as agriculture, machinery, and, above all, energy.

Energy exports played the major role in this evolution, and energy policy became the prime example of this growing interaction. Energy exports as a share of total Soviet energy produced have grown steadily, interrupted only by the Soviet's difficulties with oil production after 1977 (figure 8.1 and table 8.1).[3] By 1983 the share had reached 16

[1] National income consumed in 1971–1975 was 1,647 billion rubles (measured in post-1982 prices). Foreign-trade turnover in the same period was 171 billion (measured in current prices). Since the price bases for the two measures are quite different, this is a rough estimate, but it indicates the general point. See *Narodnoe khoziaistvo SSSR v 1985g.* (Moscow: Finansy i statistika, 1986) and *Vneshniaia torgovlia SSSR v 1985g.* (Moscow: Finansy i statistika, 1986), respectively.

[2] Foreign-trade turnover in the Eleventh Plan was 639 billion rubles; national income consumed was 2,398 billion rubles (same price bases and sources as in note 1 above).

[3] Another dip in the share exported came in 1970–1973, but it was due to a sharp increase in oil imports (from 52.1 million barrels a day [mbd] in 1969 to 294.0 mbd in

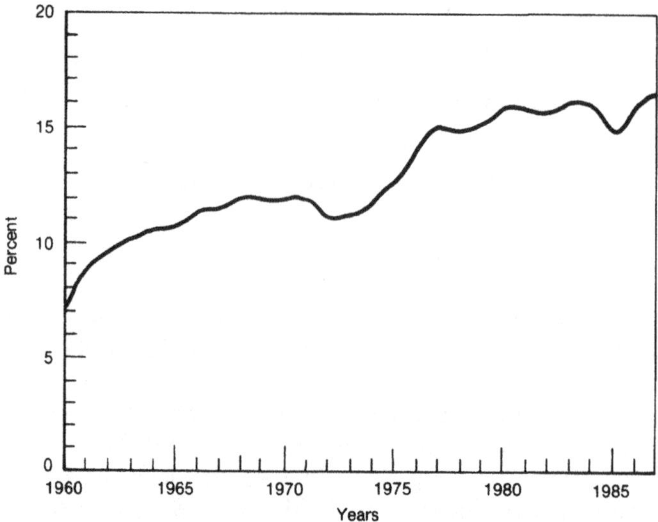

FIG. 8.1. Net Energy Exports as a Share of Total Soviet Primary Energy Production (percentages). Source: PlanEcon, *East European Energy Databank.*

percent, before renewed oil trouble inside the Soviet Union brought a second pause in 1985. This growth was stimulated by the twentyfold rise of world energy prices over the decade of the 1970s, which, combined with growing physical volumes exported, made energy the Soviets' leading hard-currency earner. As recently as 1970, energy had accounted for less than 30 percent of Soviet hard-currency income, but by the mid-1980s its share had risen to 80 percent.[4]

So long as world energy prices were rising, the Soviets enjoyed a bonanza. But in the early and mid-1980s, as energy prices declined, the country suffered a series of reverses that brought a rude awakening, which coincided with the political succession that began in late 1982 and the continued malperformance of the economy, particularly the energy crisis described in this book. As a result, the Soviets are today in the unenviable position of relying for the bulk of their hard-currency

1973, presumably representing Arab payment for weapons shipped during the War of Attrition) rather than a decline in gross energy exports.

[4] Data on hard-currency income are defined as "total exports to OECD (Organization for Economic Cooperation and Development) countries less Finland." Margaret Chadwick, David Long, and Machiko Nissanke, *Soviet Oil Exports: Trade Adjustments, Refining Constraints, and Market Behavior* (Oxford: Oxford University Press, 1987), p. 83.

TABLE 8.1

Soviet Energy Exports as a Share of Total Primary Energy Production, 1960–1987
(thousands of barrels per day)

Year	*Total Primary*	*Net Exports*	*Share (%)*	*Year*	*Total Primary*	*Net Exports*	*Share (%)*
1960	9,962.9	707.3	7.1	1975	22,772.2	2,883.7	12.7
1961	10,569.0	925.5	8.8	1976	23,885.2	3,388.6	14.2
1962	11,275.6	1,083.1	9.6	1977	24,979.2	3,744.0	15.0
1963	12,247.8	1,235.4	10.1	1978	25,963.9	3,849.2	14.8
1964	13,153.0	1,390.5	10.6	1979	26,808.8	4,037.1	15.1
1965	13,934.5	1,511.3	10.8	1980	27,544.7	4,340.6	15.8
1966	14,896.1	1,698.5	11.4	1981	28,064.0	4,395.2	15.7
1967	15,632.0	1,814.0	11.6	1982	28,669.4	4,481.4	15.6
1968	16,254.5	1,950.2	12.0	1983	29,259.4	4,687.0	16.0
1969	16,994.6	2,051.6	12.1	1984	30,087.4	4,764.1	15.8
1970	17,893.1	2,123.7	11.9	1985	30,841.8	4,520.8	14.7
1971	18,728.1	2,209.1	11.8	1986	32,208.0	5,108.2	15.9
1972	19,524.5	2,134.6	10.9	1987	33,255.5	5,460.9	16.4
1973	20,431.6	2,285.2	11.2	1988	34,067.5	5,675.1	16.7
1974	21,534.9	2,569.8	11.9				

SOURCE: PlanEcon, Inc., *East European Energy Databank.*

revenue on a commodity that may even now cost more, on the margin, to produce and deliver than it will fetch on the market.[5] Over the coming decade, world oil prices are likely to rise again; but, as we have seen, the marginal production costs of Soviet oil are likely to rise much faster.

The Soviets' re-entry into the world market, then, adds a major new dimension to their domestic policymaking, making them increasingly vulnerable to external economic changes and political pressures. This amounts to a reversal of a longstanding division of roles: whereas since the 1930s Soviet planners had used the world economy as a buffer against unforeseen variations in the internal plan, they now have to provide internal buffers against fluctuations from the outside.[6]

This raises several basic questions about Soviet policymaking. Has there been a coherent strategy behind the Soviets' expanding foreign trade and, in particular, behind its energy trade? Can one discern clear purposes and choices in Soviet behavior? To what extent were Soviet foreign-trade objectives connected to domestic ones? Is there evidence of learning, of debate or conflict, of adjustments in policy? In short, were the rude awakenings of the 1980s inevitable, or did they result from some of the same deficiencies in policymaking that produced the domestic energy crisis?

One cannot but be struck by the parallels between the domestic

[5] Such a statement, of course, rests on heroic assumptions: first, that we know even approximately the marginal cost of producing and delivering Soviet oil (especially if reckoned in terms of opportunity cost); second, that we can define a meaningful exchange rate (which must logically take into account such subtleties as the relative productivity of imported machinery versus domestic); and third, that we can identify an appropriate world price. Matthew J. Sagers estimates the cost of producing a new barrel of Soviet oil in the mid-1980s at about $14.00 per barrel, compared to a world price of about $15.00 at this writing. Sagers, "Oil Production Costs in the USSR," in *PlanEcon Long-Term Energy Outlook* (Washington, D.C.: PlanEcon, Inc., Fall 1987), p. 50. In July 1988 an article by V. I. Dolgikh estimated that the "capital cost of developing 1 ton/year of new capacity" had passed from 46 rubles in the early 1970s to 88 rubles in 1985 and would reach 129 rubles in 1990. At a conversion rate of $1.00 to the ruble and 7.3 barrels per ton, that would suggest that the marginal capital cost of new oil at this writing is between $15 and $16 a barrel. See Dolgikh, "Otnoshenie k resursam—vazhneishii kriterii perestroiki v ekonomike," *Pravda*, 11 July 1988. However, everything depends on the exchange rate. If one uses instead a rate of $0.60 to the ruble, Soviet oil would remain economic to export (at present world prices) through the first half of the 1990s.

[6] This implies, incidentally, that the Soviet Union can no longer be ignored as an anomalous case by international political economists. Soviet foreign economic policy must wrestle with the "antinomies of interdependence" just as other countries do, and the Soviet Union now takes its place along the continuum of nations seeking a stable balance between participation and autonomy.

energy crisis and the crisis in energy trade that took place at about the same time, by the same combination of extraordinary successes and severe reverses. Indeed, this chapter will argue that they *are* the same crisis, not simply in the obvious sense that energy trade is tied to domestic energy balances, but in the same failure of leadership to adapt in a measured way to changing circumstances and to combat the biases built into the inherited system.

Patterns of Decision in Soviet Energy Trade

Foreign trade grew under Brezhnev, but the institutions that conducted it did not, any more than did the basic assumptions and practices that had shaped foreign economic policy for a half-century. The Ministry of Foreign Trade continued to preside over a state monopoly that was older than the command economy itself.[7] In Stalin's generation this monopoly was used to pursue a policy of import substitution so rigorous that it could fairly be called trade-averse.[8] By the beginning of the 1970s Soviet foreign-trade policy, while certainly no longer trade-averse, remained distinctly antimercantilist: its main purpose, then as before, was to obtain the imports necessary to meet internal goals, while exports were viewed as a necessary evil and limited to the value required to pay for imports.[9] Despite a growing scholarly literature that praised the principles of economic interdependence and international specialization of production,[10] Soviet planners continued to treat foreign trade essentially as a residual. Domestic industry had little incentive to produce manufactured goods for export; the system worked best at exporting primary goods.[11] Domestic prices were determined by

[7] For a Soviet treatment of the origins of the foreign-trade monopoly, see the two-volume study by V. A. Shishkin, *V. I. Lenin i vneshneekonomicheskaia politika sovetskogo gosudarstva (1917–1923gg.)* (Leningrad: Nauka, 1977) and *"Polosa priznanii" i vneshneekonomicheskaia politika SSSR* (Leningrad: Nauka, 1983).

[8] The best summary description of Soviet policy during this period is that of Franklyn D. Holzman, "Foreign Trade," in Abram Bergson and Simon Kuznets, eds., *Economic Trends in the Soviet Union* (Cambridge, Mass.: Harvard University Press, 1963), pp. 283–332.

[9] This formula comes originally from Holzman, "Foreign Trade," p. 302. See also Holzman, *International Trade under Communism—Politics and Economics* (New York: Basic Books, 1976).

[10] For a useful analysis, see Erik P. Hoffmann and Robbin F. Laird, *The Politics of Economic Modernization in the Soviet Union* (Ithaca, N.Y.: Cornell University Press, 1982). A stimulating statement from a perennial Soviet radical is N. Shmelev, "Avtarkhichna li sotsialisticheskaia ekonomika?" *Voprosy ekonomiki*, no. 4 (1976), pp. 88–98.

[11] See the discussion by Ed A. Hewett in his chapter, "Foreign Economic Relations,"

internal policies and remained unaffected by world prices, even in the case of a major export commodity such as energy.[12] The foreign-trade system was administered by a specialized bureaucracy with its own incentives and interests, one of the most important of which was to separate Soviet firms from contact with foreign buyers and sellers.[13] It would be an exaggeration to say that this system had not changed at all since the early 1950s; for one thing, Soviet traders were already becoming sophisticated about Western commodities markets and banking (one thinks of the tactical skill shown in the "Great Grain Robbery" of 1972, when Soviet traders surreptitiously bought up a large share of the U.S. wheat crop at subsidized prices).[14] But the structures, procedures, objectives, and attitudes that the Soviets brought to foreign trade were essentially those of the past.

How much of that changed with the oil-price boom of the 1970s and the expansion of Soviet foreign trade to the mid-1980s? In particular, what objectives did the leadership pursue in its energy trade, and to what extent were these effectively coordinated with increasingly pressing issues in domestic energy policy? We look now at the ways the Soviets dealt with three specific decisions: How much energy to export? What kind of energy to export? To whom to sell it?

How Much Energy to Export?

The pattern of Soviet energy exports for hard currency between 1970 and 1985 appears to have been the result of a consistent decision rule. In the short run (that is, over periods of up to five years), whenever imports had surged ahead, producing a deficit in the balance of payments, energy exports were periodically adjusted to restore the hard-currency trade balance. This was particularly the case with crude oil. In an admirable study, a group at the Oxford Institute for Energy Studies has shown how Soviet planners used oil exports as the principal "swing

in Abram Bergson and Herbert S. Levine, eds., *The Soviet Economy: Toward the Year 2000* (London: George Allen and Unwin, 1983), pp. 291–298.

[12] See Robert W. Campbell, "Energy Prices and Decisions on Energy Use in the USSR," in Padma Desai, ed., *Marxism, Central Planning, and the Soviet Economy: Economic Essays in Honor of Alexander Erlich* (Cambridge, Mass.: MIT Press, 1983), pp. 249–274.

[13] Stephen Gardner, *Soviet Foreign Trade: The Decision Process* (Boston: Kluwer-Nijhoff, 1982).

[14] For another example, see the discussion of the evolution of Soviet international financial dealings in the 1960s and early 1970s in J. Wilczynski, "Financial Relations between the EEC and the CMEA," in Avi Schlaim and G. N. Yannopoulos, eds., *The EEC and Eastern Europe* (Cambridge: Cambridge University Press, 1982), pp. 189ff.

fuel" in adjusting the hard-currency trade balance.[15] The group presented three key findings. First, adjustments in oil export volumes were made ad hoc, in response to above-plan imports, especially of grain. Second, while other levers were available for adjusting the trade balance, principally gold sales and adjustments in levels of external borrowing, Soviet decisionmakers came to rely increasingly on the oil spigot as their principal instrument.[16] Third, Soviet behavior remained clearly antimercantilist: when world energy prices rose and the trade balance did not require adjustment, Soviet hard-currency oil exports either stagnated or dropped.

One important point to stress about this pattern is that, while it was not unaffected by domestic considerations—principally by the desire of the Brezhnev leadership to advance or protect its top domestic programs through imports—it was not driven by the internal costs of energy. Up to the end of the 1970s, when the marginal cost of new Soviet oil was still low compared with the world price, the Soviets would have been better off, from an economist's point of view, to export more energy to the West than they did. It was only very gradually that Soviet economists began to argue, beginning in the second half of the 1970s, that the world price should be taken as the basis of internal pricing and decisionmaking, but to this day planners continue to resist the idea.

This pattern of "underexporting" was particularly evident during the period 1978–1982, when the share of Soviet energy exported stagnated even though oil production was still growing, large new supplies of natural gas were coming on line, and world energy prices were still rising rapidly. But was that policy still due to antimercantilist self-restraint, or were there other causes? A glance at apparent oil consumption during the period 1977–1981 shows that it outstripped the growth of oil production;[17] in other words, increases in oil output and fuel switching from oil to gas were not yielding more oil for export. This means that by the late 1970s antimercantilist bias could well have ceased to be a restraining factor in Brezhnev's foreign-trade policy. Brezhnev might well have wished to export more oil if he had had it,

[15] Chadwick, Long, and Nissanke, *Soviet Oil Exports*. This is particularly the work of Nissanke, whose hypotheses and econometric tests of them make up Part II of the volume.

[16] Nissanke's analysis focuses on four occasions in which the Soviet Union experienced short-term deteriorations in its trade balance: 1972–1973, 1975–1976, 1978, and 1981.

[17] According to Chadwick's oil-balance calculations, apparent oil consumption rose by 58.1 million tons/year between 1977 and 1981, while crude oil production grew by only 54 million tons/year. Chadwick, Long, and Nissanke, *Soviet Oil Exports*, p. 29.

and the fact that he did not, one suspects, was one of the strong motives leading him toward the gas campaign.

Export Gas or Oil?

A second major issue in Soviet energy trade has been whether to export oil or gas. Other things being equal, oil is a more attractive export than gas: it usually fetches a better price for equal heat content, requires less capital investment, and gives the seller greater flexibility. At most times this is how the Soviets have reasoned. Only twice have they appeared to waver (at least where exports to the West are concerned; Eastern Europe is discussed in the next section). The first time was in the early 1970s, when the Soviets reacted with interest to overtures from a group of American corporations to develop West Siberian gas for export to the United States in the form of liquefied natural gas (LNG), the so-called North Star project.[18] Soviet interest is easily explained. As we saw in Chapter 5, the gas industry at this time was still reluctant to invest heavily in West Siberian development, and transmission capacity was the main constraint on the growth of gas production. LNG exports appeared to offer an attractive way of marketing supplies that might otherwise not be developed for some time. But by the mid-1970s the gas industry was finally committed to West Siberian development, and most of the Soviet interest in LNG faded.[19]

The second episode is the famous export pipeline of the early 1980s. This was not the first time the Soviets had sold gas to the West; between 1968 and 1977, they had signed eleven gas contracts with West European countries, and Western contractors had supplied pipe, compressors, and other equipment for a major export line from Orenbourg to Eastern Europe.[20] But the new project was far more ambitious. For

[18] Joseph T. Kosnik, *Natural Gas Imports from the Soviet Union: Financing the North Star Venture Project* (New York: Praeger Publishers, 1975). See also Jonathan P. Stern, *Soviet Natural Gas Development to 1990* (Lexington, Mass.: D. C. Heath/Lexington Books, 1980). A Soviet analysis will be found in I. S. Bagramian and A. F. Shakai, *Kontrakt veka* (Moscow: Politizdat, 1984).

[19] The last glimmers of North Star could still be seen as late as 1980, but one suspects that the mild show of Soviet interest by then was designed to demonstrate that, despite the U.S. sanctions of that year, Moscow was still willing to do business with American companies. See Bagramian and Shakai, *Kontrakt veka*, p. 26.

[20] A listing of these earlier contracts is given in Iu. Baranovskii, "V/O Soiuzgazeksport na rynke gaza," *Vneshniaia torgovlia*, no. 5 (1983), pp. 23–27. On the Orenbourg pipeline, see J. B. Hannigan and C. H. McMillan, "The Orenbourg Natural Gas Project and Fuel-Energy Balances in Eastern Europe," Carleton University (Ottawa, Canada), Institute of Soviet and East European Studies, East-West Commercial Relations Series, report no. 13 (July 1980). See also Bagramian and Shakai, *Kontrakt veka* pp. 19–22 and 40–47.

the first time, in the largest single deal in East-West trade to date, the Soviets proposed to build a gas pipeline serving the West European market directly.

There was some controversy on the Soviet side, initially over the project itself and subsequently over the role of gas exports. The West European businessmen who went to Moscow in early 1980 to discuss the pipeline found that the Soviet side was not ready to do business and that the leaders were divided. Only a few years before, gas had been considered far scarcer than oil, and it took some time for Soviet planners to adjust to the new prospect of abundance. (Gosplan chairman Baibakov, in particular, was one of those reported to have reservations over the pipeline.) Moreover, the long-term commitments required in gas trade caused some grumbling that such a valuable and nonrenewable resource as gas should not be "squandered" (*razbazareno*) by shipping it to the capitalists.[21]

But there were also voices on the other side of the issue. The energy experts of the Aleksandrov Commission, which drafted the energy program in the early 1980s, advocated a policy of switching gradually from oil exports to gas, to lessen pressure on the Soviet oil industry.[22] Such views may have been prompted by the fact that in the mid- to late 1970s the market share of natural gas in Western Europe had been growing rapidly, and by 1980–1981 the West Europeans were simultaneously very eager to buy more gas, sell more equipment, and supply credit on very attractive terms. But it is more likely that these experts had internal factors in mind: in 1980 they were acutely conscious of the rapidly rising cost of oil and probably also of the difficulty of quickly displacing oil with gas at home. In 1980–1981 the returns from the previous five-year plan were coming in, and they showed runaway growth in oil consumption and little progress in replacing it with gas.

As late as 1982, one energy expert described the question of oil versus gas exports as "complex and not fully decided,"[23] but it appears

[21] The existence of such sentiment is confirmed by West European businessmen and Soviet visitors, but it can also be sensed in Soviet sources in the care with which certain Soviet officials during this period went out of their way to defend gas exports to the West. See, for example, an account of a roundtable of Soviet gas experts, at which Iulii Bokserman, then vice-chairman of Gosplan's Projects Evaluation Commission (and himself a vigorous defender of the export pipeline), asked rhetorically, "Are we squandering our gas, or at any rate are we using it sufficiently rationally, by sending it to the capitalist countries?" "Gazovaia promyshlennost': itogi i perspektivy," *Planovoe khoziaistvo*, no. 6 (1982), p. 20.

[22] L. A. Melent'ev and A. A. Makarov, *Energeticheskii kompleks SSSR* (Moscow: Ekonomika, 1983), pp. 160, 164, and 169.

[23] A. A. Makarov, V. N. Khanaev, and A. P. Golovin, "Rol' nefti i gaza Zapadnoi

in retrospect that the issue was settled shortly afterward in favor of oil. Once again, a combination of foreign and domestic factors was at work. In 1983–1984 the Soviets, already somewhat disappointed by the commercial return from the export line, found their income drifting downward because the contracts' pricing formulas reflected the general decline in world energy prices. Internally, as described in Chapter 7, a more vigorous effort to displace oil with gas began about 1983 and soon showed results. In 1982 Soviet oil exports started rising again and have continued their growth to this day, interrupted only by the crisis year 1985. Meanwhile, there has been no mention of another gas pipeline to the West. This suggests that after some hesitation the Soviets reverted in 1882–1983 to their previous preference for oil as the hard-currency earner of choice, using gas to displace oil both at home and in Eastern Europe. This traditional bias was presumably reinforced still further in 1984–1985, when the 1982 contracts came up for renegotiation and the Soviets were obliged to cut both deliveries and prices.[24]

On the face of it, this is sound policy, since at the moment the marginal cost of delivered gas is about half that of the same amount of energy in the form of oil. If gas displaces oil in internal uses and the displaced oil is exported, then in effect the marginal cost of Soviet oil exports becomes that of the gas that backs it out. But as we have seen in previous chapters, there are several problems, real and potential, that threaten this displacement strategy. Displacement is not costless; it requires investment in gas storage and distribution. Moreover, once the Soviets run out of easy targets for conversion to gas, it is not inconceivable that they could find themselves with an awkward surplus of gas production capacity. In that case, they may wish to explore the possibility of another export pipeline to the West, again using Western equipment.

Export to the West or to Eastern Europe?

A third major issue for Soviet foreign-trade policy has been the priority to give to hard-currency revenue from exports to the West, weighed against exports to Eastern Europe. Trade among the centrally planned economies is conducted according to rules quite different from those

---

Sibiri v razvitii toplivno-energeticheskogo kompleksa strany," in S. N. Starovoitov, ed., *Problemy razvitiia Zapadno-Sibirskogo neftegazovogo kompleksa* (Novosibirsk: Nauka, 1983), p. 13.

[24] For an account of the negotiations with the French, see Véronique Poisson, "La renégociation du contrat gazier de 1982 entre la France et l'URSS," *Le Courrier des Pays de l'Est*, no. 304 (March 1986).

governing hard-currency trade with capitalist partners. Energy trade, in particular, is based on a complex combination of barter, deferred payments, negotiated price formulas, and subsidized credits, as well as some actual hard-currency transactions. Difficult as they may be to follow in detail, the pattern of prices and volumes adds up to a clear policy: from the first oil shock in 1973 to the oil price collapse of 1985–1986, the Soviets sought to soften the shock of higher energy prices to their vulnerable East European clients by guaranteeing them stable oil supplies at subsidized prices, and to some extent this preferential treatment continues today.

Beginning in 1975, the Soviets sold oil to Eastern Europe under the so-called Bucharest formula, a five-year moving average of the world price. In effect, the East Europeans received a substantial energy subsidy, which at its height in 1980 was on the order of $10 billion a year.[25] The sums involved were so large that they can only have been a deliberate policy by the Brezhnev leadership, even though they were not announced as such at the time.

Price arrangements since Brezhnev's death have become even more difficult to follow. A strict application of the Bucharest formula, after world oil prices began declining in 1981, would soon have forced the East Europeans to pay the Soviets *more* than the world price.[26] In practice, the Soviets have backed away from the formula. The persistence of delayed payments, settlements in soft currencies, and high prices for East European machinery exports to the Soviet Union amount to a continued policy by Moscow of providing favorable terms of trade.[27]

The record of oil exports since Brezhnev's death can be read in two

[25] The argument behind this conclusion is laid out in detail in Michael Marrese and Jan Vanous, *Soviet Subsidization of Trade with Eastern Europe: A Soviet Perspective* (Berkeley, Calif.: Institute of International Studies, 1983). For the best review of the energy issue in the context of overall Soviet–East European trade and relations, see Ed A. Hewett, *Energy, Economics, and Foreign Policy in the Soviet Union* (Washington, D.C.: Brookings Institution, 1984), pp. 193–223.

[26] Some analysts believe that the five-year moving average was changed to a three-year one as early as 1980, which would have brought the CMEA pricing formula into even more rapid alignment with world prices. See Jochen Bethkenhagen, "The Impact of Energy on East-West Trade: Retrospect and Prospects," in C. T. Saunders, ed., *East-West Trade and Finance in the World Economy: A New Look for the 1980s* (London: Macmillan, 1985), p. 186. In retrospect, this does not appear to be the case.

[27] It is striking, at any rate, that no East European countries have rejected Soviet oil. Some analysts, indeed, believe that Soviet oil is a bargain under current pricing arrangements. If one assumes the effective exchange rate to be $0.55 to the ruble (based on Hungarian commercial rates), then Soviet oil exports to Eastern Europe in early 1988 were priced at about $10.00 a barrel. See *PlanEcon Report* 4, no. 28 (15 July 1988), p. 5.

ways. On the one hand, the developed West has claimed all of the substantial increase in gross Soviet oil exports in recent years; thus its share has grown from 34 percent in 1981 to 43 percent in 1987. Clearly, hard currency has been the Soviets' principal objective. But the Soviets have also continued to reserve a fairly stable share of their oil exports for Eastern Europe (table 8.2). They have broken the pattern only once, in 1982, when they cut oil deliveries by 14 percent (reneging on an apparent pledge made by Kosygin in 1980). The new level of oil shipments remained stable for the next three years, even in 1985, when Soviet oil production dropped sharply and exports to the West plummeted by 0.35 million barrels per day. Then in 1986 and 1987, when Soviet production recovered, oil exports to Eastern Europe returned to roughly the 1981 level. In short, there is evidently still a Soviet commitment to Eastern Europe.

Nevertheless, the emphasis in Soviet policy has clearly shifted since Brezhnev's death. In contrast to his final years, when Eastern Europe's share of Soviet oil grew steadily, Eastern Europe now gets a fixed residual whose relative size has been dropping (table 8.3).

At the same time, however, the Soviets have been promoting exports of gas and electric power to Eastern Europe in an attempt to displace oil—a doubly attractive arrangement from their point of view, since the East Europeans pay competitive prices for Soviet gas, and the displaced oil is sold on the world market for hard currency. In effect, Eastern Europe is part of the Soviet domestic fuel-switching strategy. A second export pipeline to Eastern Europe has just been completed, and Soviet gas exports to Eastern Europe have grown steadily, reaching one-quarter of total Soviet energy deliveries to the region in 1986–1987.[28] But oil is not as easily displaced from the East European economies, where it is already used relatively efficiently, as it could be from the Soviet economy, where it is not.[29] Consequently, the Soviets will face continued strong demands for cheap oil from their East European clients for the foreseeable future.

Inferences about Soviet Objectives and Foreign-Trade Style

No single strategy could have guided Soviet decisions through the turbulent energy years from 1973 to 1986 or through the cycle from

[28] PlanEcon, Inc., *East European Energy Databank*.

[29] John P. Hardt, "Soviet Energy Policy in Eastern Europe," in Sarah M. Terry, ed., *Soviet Policy in Eastern Europe* (New Haven, Conn.: Yale University Press, 1984), pp. 189–220.

TABLE 8.2
Share of Eastern Europe in Gross Soviet Energy Exports, 1970–1987 (thousands of barrels per day of oil equivalent)

	Total Exports	*CMEA Six*	*E. Europe Share (%)*
1970	2,379.8	1,080.1	45.4
1971	2,604.3	1,215.2	46.7
1972	2,646.9	1,300.0	49.1
1973	2,919.6	1,459.8	50.0
1974	3,022.9	1,601.1	53.0
1975	3,391.8	1,745.8	51.5
1976	3,872.2	1,882.2	48.6
1977	4,215.9	2,026.3	48.1
1978	4,348.3	2,063.5	47.5
1979	4,436.5	2,241.1	50.5
1980	4,582.4	2,418.7	52.8
1981	4,614.4	2,396.9	51.9
1982	4,841.4	2,318.2	47.9
1983	5,142.6	2,305.9	44.8
1984	5,303.5	2,358.8	44.5
1985	5,007.0	2,409.3	46.4
1986	5,640.4	2,615.6	46.4
1987	5,956.3	2,631.5	44.2
1988	6,494.6	NA	NA

SOURCE: PlanEcon, Inc., *East European Energy Databank*.

détente to freeze, with its repercussions on East-West trade. In its basic features the external energy challenge to policymakers resembled the domestic one: a fast-moving and unpredictable environment, conflicting advice and information on highly technical issues, and a rapidly changing mix of competing objectives.

Yet the outcomes are also oddly parallel. After fifteen years of extraordinary expansion in energy trade, the Soviet leaders find themselves acutely dependent on a single export commodity, constrained in their alternatives, and discontent over how little they have to show for the years of abundance. This is the external face of the Soviet energy crisis. The question is: Were there similar failures of leadership?

In this section we attempt to draw out larger patterns from the decisions we have just analyzed. Was there learning? As the scale of energy trade grew, was there coordination with domestic policies? Were there consistent choices on risk or time horizon? In addition to

TABLE 8.3
Soviet Oil Exports to the
Developed West versus Eastern Europe
(gross exports; thousands of barrels per day)

	Production	*Exports to Developed West*	*Exports to Eastern Europe*
1977	10,934.8	1,320.8	1,473.6
1978	11,452.2	1,357.7	1,513.4
1979	11,736.3	1,144.6	1,581.8
1980	12,093.4	1,068.9	1,625.2
1981	12,209.3	1,101.5	1,610.0
1982	12,284.7	1,421.1	1,502.6
1983	12,360.9	1,681.3	1,465.3
1984	12,288.7	1,665.6	1,480.8
1985	11,943.4	1,316.4	1,507.6
1986	12,338.9	1,569.4	1,623.5
1987	12,528.6	1,687.1	1,599.5

SOURCE: PlanEcon, Inc., *East European Energy Databank.*

the material previously discussed, we draw on insights from Soviet negotiating strategies in gas trade.

Growing Technical Skill and Sophistication

Although the Soviets have been selling energy to the West since the revolution (as did the tsarist government before them), the growing size and importance of the energy trade since the beginning of the 1960s have required the development of more elaborate marketing and financial strategies. Two generations of Soviet foreign-trade experts have shown increasing technical skill and sophistication in every aspect of energy trade, including the negotiation of credit packages and the purchase of machinery for pipelines. An excellent British study describes the complex marketing arrangements for Soviet crude oil and products,[30] and the technical structure of the gas trade is similarly intricate.[31]

The way the Soviets negotiated the East-West gas pipeline in 1980–

[30] David Long, "Soviet Oil in the World Petroleum Market," in Chadwick, Long, and Nissanke, *Soviet Oil Exports*, pp. 176–238.

[31] Jonathan P. Stern, *International Gas Trade in Europe: The Policies of Exporting and Importing Countries* (London: Heinemann Educational Books, 1984), pp. 42–71.

1982 provided a particularly convincing demonstration of the Soviet traders' technical skill.[32] In previous gas-for-pipe deals they had worked through a single Western financial consortium and, for the most part, a single Western supplier or general contractor.[33] This time they did things differently. They negotiated separate credit packages with each of the major supplier countries, ending up with a total envelope considerably larger than their actual needs; and instead of dealing through a single general contractor, the Soviets chose all of their subcontractors themselves and negotiated every supply contract separately. These two tactics had a mutually reinforcing effect: the separate credit packages in each country stimulated fierce competition among equipment suppliers, whose eagerness, in turn, put pressure on banks and governments to sweeten terms. As a result, the Soviets gained major savings on both counts.

But whatever else might have been new in the Soviet pipeline strategy, it was not the top negotiators themselves. The overall leader of the Soviet side, the veteran deputy minister for foreign trade, Nikolai Osipov, had directed every Soviet gas export deal since the first one in 1967.[34] The man who led the Soviet gas contract talks, Iurii Baranovskii, director of Soiuzgazeksport, had likewise been directly in charge of Soviet gas exports since the earliest days. Equally long in service was Iurii Ivanov, head of the Bank for Foreign Trade (Vneshtorgbank, now renamed Vneshekonombank) since 1969 and its first deputy head for five years before that. Only Stanislav Volchkov, the head of Mashinoimport, the Soviet foreign-trade organization for machinery imports, seemed a newcomer by comparison, having been appointed in 1974.[35] All four of these men already held their current jobs

[32] The observations on the pipeline negotiations in this and the following sections are condensed from a longer study by the present author, *Soviet Negotiating Strategy: The East-West Gas Pipeline Deal, 1980–1984*, R-3220–FF (Santa Monica, Calif.: Rand Corporation, February 1985).

[33] Deutsche Bank in the 1970s formed five different consortia of German banks. See details in *Handelsblatt*, 7 July 1970, 14 June 1971, 10 Apr. 1972, 8 Oct. 1973, 6–7 Sept. 1974, 4 Nov. 1974, and 23 Dec. 1975.

[34] N. G. Osipov, born in 1918, was deputy minister of foreign trade from March 1965 to 1987.

[35] Brief biographies of Baranovskii, Ivanov, and Volchkov appear in *Vneshniaia torgovlia*, no. 10 (1973), p. 58; no. 3 (1983), p. 55; and no. 7 (1973), p. 59, respectively. Both Baranovskii and Volchkov were initially trained as engineers (Baranovskii in petroleum engineering and Volchkov in power engineering), and both served for several years abroad in Soviet foreign-trade offices. Ivanov worked in the State Bank and Vneshtorgbank since his graduation from the Moscow Institute of International Relations in 1951.

when the Orenbourg project, the first Soviet export pipeline, was negotiated and built in the mid-1970s.

Some of the novel elements of Soviet strategy in the pipeline talks may have come from newer people one level lower, suggesting a new generation on the way. Two of the main technical specialists on the Soviet side, who struck West European businessmen with their detailed knowledge of Western prices and trends, Karen Vardanian of Soiuzgazeksport[36] and Iurii M. Ter-Sarkisov of Mashinoimport, represented a slightly younger generation of officials, appointed since the mid-1970s. Both Mashinoimport and Soiuzgazeksport had had substantial turnover in their top ranks in the previous years. In Soiuzgazeksport, though the top leader, Baranovskii, had remained, four of the top eight positions below him had changed hands since 1980.[37] Mashinoimport had been extensively reorganized in 1979 as part of a ministrywide series of changes mandated by a decree the previous year; of the thirteen firms in existence in 1982, only four were still headed by the old office directors. The new men, mostly in their mid-forties, resembled Volchkov in their basic career background: a diploma in engineering, followed by the Academy of Foreign Trade and a tour or two in Soviet trade offices abroad. They had all risen through the ranks of Mashinoimport.[38] (In contrast, however, there had been little turnover at the next higher level, that of the deputy general directors of Mashinoimport.)

For West European businessmen, the most impressive new development on the Soviet side was Mashinoimport's command post in Cologne, where a large staff of younger specialists worked on the equipment contracts, supplying Volchkov and Ter-Sarkisov with a wealth of up-to-the-minute detail. Though the Soviets had set up other such temporary foreign field offices in the past (most notably to oversee engineering and design work under the Pullman contracts for the Ka-

[36] K. A. Vardanian's brief biography appears in *Vneshniaia torgovlia*, no. 2 (1981), p. 56. Like his chief, Baranovskii, Vardanian had an engineering background (he graduated from the Bauman Higher Engineering School in Moscow) and spent several years in Soviet foreign-trade posts abroad. He followed much the same path as Baranovskii and since 1978 had been head of Eksimgaz, the gas trade organization dealing with nonsocialist countries. Neither Vardanian nor Baranovskii appears to have been a graduate of the Academy of Foreign Trade.

[37] Compare the 1980 and 1983 editions of the Central Intelligence Agency, Directorate of Intelligence, *Directory of USSR Foreign Trade Organizations and Officials*, CR 80-10788 and CR 83-10599, respectively (Washington, D.C.).

[38] Brief biographical material on the new officials appeared in *Vneshniaia torgovlia*, August 1981, March 1983, September 1980, and April 1982. The author is indebted for this information to Scott Monje of Columbia University's Research Institute on International Change.

maz truck plant[39]), this was the first time the Soviets had deployed such a large back-up staff for a commercial negotiation, and one of its side benefits was to train the next generation of Mashinoimport's top specialists.

On the whole, though, despite the new faces, an equally important change on the Soviet side was the experience and sophistication in the older officials at the top. Commenting on the evolution of Soviet gas negotiators, a West European gas executive observed, "In the late 1960s and early 1970s international gas trade was a new field and we were all starting out together. The Soviets began with a handful of inexperienced people, mostly brought over from the oil-export business. In the last decade, as the contracts have grown larger, they have grown more sophisticated, as have we." The same point holds equally for the Foreign Trade Bank. The experience accumulated by the top four men—Osipov, Ivanov, Baranovskii, and Volchkov—was crucial in the pipeline deal, since every step on the Soviet side was centralized in their hands, with the veteran Osipov clearly in charge. From 1982 to 1987 the same foursome remained in position, despite the initial shake-up of the Soviet foreign-trade apparatus in 1985–1986.[40]

Such veterans may have gained in technical skill over decades of experience, but they also carried traditional attitudes about foreign trade. More important, there is no evidence that they had a role in larger policy. Consequently, one suspects that most of the learning that took place from the 1960s to the 1980s concerned tactical issues rather than overall strategy. Some indirect evidence on this point comes from the mix of objectives pursued in energy trade, to which we turn now.

Soviet Objectives in Hard-Currency Energy Trade

There has been a striking difference between the Soviets' approach to hard-currency trade, where their preoccupation has been almost entirely the bottom line, and their approach to trade within the socialist bloc, where their political aims have dominated their commercial ones. One might have thought that the Soviets would try to use energy trade with the West to serve their foreign policy, and indeed they have not been oblivious to the public-relations aspects of energy trade. But apart from a handful of minor cases—most of them, significantly enough,

[39] CIA, National Foreign Assessment Center, *The Role of Foreign Technology in the Development of the Motor Vehicle Industry* (Washington, D.C.: October 1979).

[40] With the next round of foreign-trade reforms in 1987–1988, all four lost their positions. Osipov appears to have retired. Baranovskii now heads an FTO in the petrochemicals industry. Ivanov is now a council member of the International Investment Bank of CMEA. Volchkov's new assignment is unknown.

involving other socialist countries—the Soviets have not used energy as a weapon, and they have consistently put hard-currency income ahead of diplomacy whenever the two were in conflict.[41]

Energy relations with Western Europe over the last decade are a prime example. At the end of the 1970s, with the fall of the Pahlavi monarchy and the American determination to shore up its shaken position by deploying new military power to the Persian Gulf area, Soviet commentators began to suggest to West European audiences that they should think twice about relying on the United States for their energy security. While not exactly offering itself as an alternative, the Soviet Union had been advocating for some time an expansion of energy ties between Eastern and Western Europe.[42] An all-European energy conference had been on Moscow's agenda since it was first proposed by Kosygin in 1971,[43] and in early 1980 a well-placed Soviet commentator, Nikolai Portugalov, suggested that the security of Persian Gulf oil supplies be one of its topics.[44] In short, energy had been a prominent item in the diplomacy of détente in Europe for some time. Yet it would be hard to show that Soviet strategists thought concretely about using energy to drive a wedge between Western Europe and the United States. There was a desultory quality to these proposals (matched by the Europeans' polite but lukewarm responses), which strongly suggested that the foreign-policy overtures were for show, as have been subsequent Soviet statements of solidarity with Third World gas exporters and offers of cooperation with OPEC.

During the negotiations over the East-West pipeline in 1981–1982, the Soviet side showed the same inclination to put income over foreign policy. To be sure, the timing of some of the Soviet moves showed the influence of diplomatic motives, such as key Soviet concessions on credit terms (following hard on the Western economic summit in Ot-

[41] See a review by Jonathan P. Stern, *Soviet Oil and Gas Exports to the West: Commercial Transaction or Security Threat?* (Aldershot: Gower, 1987), pp. 48–52.

[42] For example, at the 1980 World Energy Congress the Soviet Union outlined a plan to export 40–50 Bkw-hr of electricity to Europe by 1990, of which some 10 billion would go to Western Europe. Since then, the Soviet Union has submitted a variety of proposals to the European Economic Council of the United Nations, calling for the construction of long-distance transmission lines to Western Europe, including a 1,150-kilovolt AC line from Kursk and the Ukraine to West Germany and Switzerland. Iurii Savenko and Mikhail Samkov, "Tendentsii razvitiia obmena elektroenergii mezhdu elektrosistemami evropeiskikh stran," *Ekonomicheskoe sotrudnichestvo stran-chlenov SEV*, no. 3 (1982), pp. 68–72.

[43] See Angela E. Stent, *Soviet Energy and Western Europe*, The Washington Papers, no. 90 (Washington, D.C.: Praeger, 1982), pp. 54–59.

[44] Nikolai Portugalov, TASS International Service, 29 Feb. 1980, translated in *FBIS/Soviet Union*, 3 Mar. 1980, p. G1.

tawa in July 1981) and on gas prices (timed for Brezhnev's visit to Bonn in November 1981, perhaps with one eye on Poland). The Soviet trade negotiators, if they had had their way, might have held out a little longer than they did. But the real test of the Soviet leaders' priorities lies in those cases in which economic and diplomatic motives were in conflict. Here the Soviets' decisions consistently put hard-currency income ahead of other objectives, particularly diplomatic ones. They refused to form a common front with Algeria on crude oil parity (despite brief but costly hesitation in Moscow when Algiers appealed at the last minute for solidarity). Likewise, the Soviets did not shrink from offending West Europeans in awarding equipment contracts: the Dutch and the Belgians, who were initially willing to do business but attempted a "counter-linkage" to tie gas and credits to equipment sales, received no contracts at all. The Germans, with whom the Soviets had the greatest diplomatic stakes, were disappointed and offended at having received so few orders and at having had their margins so ruthlessly squeezed.[45]

Then, in mid-1982, when the Reagan administration attempted to block the delivery of compressors for the pipeline, one might have expected the Soviet Union to capitalize on the opportunity to build good feelings with West European manufacturers and their governments. Instead the Russians initially behaved as though they did not really believe the West Europeans would stand up to the United States. They summoned the equipment firms to Moscow and threatened to invoke the penalty clauses contained in the contracts if they did not stick to schedule. Not only were such actions diplomatically clumsy, but they appeared to reveal the absence of precisely that quality that opponents of the pipeline claimed was its greatest danger, namely, a strategic vision of the possible uses of energy exports to build good will and mutual dependence. Such a vision should logically have led the Soviets to tailor their approach so as to bring in all the potential West European customers and not just some, to make price concessions so as to increase their share of the European gas market, and to treat equipment suppliers as privileged partners. In short, in precisely the respects in which a diplomatic strategy might have been expected to show up, no evidence of one can be found.

Soviet behavior in the pipeline affair was typical of the relationship of East-West trade and foreign policy in the Brezhnev years. There was an opportunistic, episodic quality to Soviet trade initiatives that suggested decisions made by technicians without much regard for diplomatic

[45] Axel Lebahn, "Die 'Jamal-Erdgasleitung': UdSSR-Westeuropa im Ost-West Konflikt," *Aussenpolitik*, no. 3 (1983), p. 268.

consequences. Moscow seemed unaware, as its traders mapped out the Great Grain Robbery of 1972, of the hackles they would raise in Washington, just as it later failed to capitalize on the diplomatic potential of the pipeline affair. The sharp annual fluctuations in Soviet trade with Western Europe likewise made few friends. Even when trade and diplomacy briefly mixed, there was a narrow horse-trader's quality to the Soviet approach, as when they launched the explosive process of Jewish emigration in exchange for short-lived American promises over trade.

Interaction of Foreign-Trade Issues with Domestic Ones

Traditionally, the Soviets have tried to insulate their domestic economy wherever possible from the vagaries of the world market and to separate foreign-trade policy from domestic decisionmaking. But willy-nilly, the Soviet Union has now left the era of autarky; and as Soviet foreign trade has grown, its interaction with the domestic economy has also increased. Not only are major domestic institutions increasingly affected by foreign-trade policy (we have seen several cases in earlier chapters), but foreign trade in turn is influenced by domestic events. During the Brezhnev years, however, this interaction increased without much apparent effort on the leaders' part to regulate it, plan it, or think through what the expanded association with the world economy would mean.

One result of growing participation in foreign-trade decisions by domestic institutions may be to slow down decisionmaking and cause foreign-trade policy to resemble domestic policy. Consensus becomes harder to reach as the number of players grows, and more players mean more competing objectives that must be reconciled at higher political levels. As the monopoly of central foreign-trade institutions is broken, and as the role of the ultimate domestic users and suppliers of foreign-traded items keeps growing, the top leaders may find themselves called upon to resolve internal conflicts even more frequently than in the past, despite their efforts to give local enterprises more autonomy.

This kind of complex interaction was a prominent feature of the negotiations over the East-West pipeline, and the leadership was repeatedly forced to intervene. One such issue was the design of the pipeline itself. The initial concept proposed to the West Europeans was highly ambitious. Using special high-performance pipe recently developed by Mannesmann, the new pipeline would have operated at 100 or even 120 atmospheres, a higher pressure than any pipeline currently used in the world. (The current generation of large lines in the Soviet network is designed for 75 atmospheres.) In other words, one of the initial intentions on the Soviet side was to use the new pipeline as a demonstration project for the next generation of gas transmission technology.

The 100-atmosphere concept was backed by the technical department of the Ministry for the Construction of Oil and Gas Enterprises (MNGS) and by the Project Review Commission (Gosekspertiza) of Gosplan,[46] but it was opposed by then Gas Minister Sabit Orudzhev, who felt the move to higher pressures was premature. He was also opposed to another ambitious early concept, that of drawing the new gas for the export line from an as yet undeveloped field, Yamburg, located deep in the permafrost zone beyond the Arctic Circle, outside the zone of established communications and other infrastructure.[47] Orudzhev's views soon prevailed on both issues, but such internal conflicts delayed the Soviet side for some months. Sometime between the fall of 1980 and the early winter of 1981 the Ministry of the Gas Industry won its battle for a more conservative design that would operate at the 75 atmospheres to which the Soviet industry was already accustomed.[48]

The Soviets were also divided over which technology to use for the gas-turbine drives for the pipeline's compressor stations. The two main contenders were a heavy-duty model developed and licensed by General Electric and one derived from an airplane-engine design, manufactured by Rolls-Royce. The Soviets, having used both in the past, were familiar with the pluses and minuses of each. Once again, the issue boiled down to a disagreement between those who favored the most progressive and energy-efficient technology and those who wanted reliability of operation and ease of maintenance.[49] It was finally thrashed out in late August 1981 at a high-level meeting in Moscow, with several ministers in attendance. The conservative views of the Gas Ministry again prevailed, but the result was further delay in the negotiations.

[46] See Iulii Bokserman, "Stal'nye rusla gazovykh rek," *Izvestiia*, 11 Nov. 1981.

[47] Author's interviews with West European participants in the pipeline negotiations.

[48] *New York Times*, 5 July 1980; *Financial Times*, 30 Oct. 1981; *Wall Street Journal*, 23 Jan. 1981. According to the *Financial Times*, the Soviet decision to drop the 100-atmosphere concept was made in the fall of 1980. But according to the *Wall Street Journal*, as late as January 1981 the chief of the Technical Department of MNGS, Oleg Ivantsov, was quoted in favor of the higher parameters. One of the West European supplier representatives who was in Moscow at the time believes that the final Soviet decision on this point was not taken until February 1981.

[49] *Financial Times*, 30 Oct. 1981. According to the *Financial Times*, the main advocates of the Rolls-Royce model were inside Gosplan. But according to West European businessmen, Rolls-Royce had other advocates too. Inside the Gas Ministry, indeed, General Electric and Rolls-Royce drives were handled by separate offices, which acted as advocates for "their" technology.

The pipeline negotiations suggest weak coordination between trade policy and domestic policy. So does the evolution of Soviet oil trade. As domestic production approaches a ceiling, the future growth of Soviet oil exports depends, as we saw in Chapter 7, on the success of gas-for-oil substitution. Substitution has been official policy since 1976, but only after 1983 was it implemented seriously, and even now there has been a lag in the associated investment required to distribute and store gas.[50] Similarly, there has been little progress in developing the secondary refining capacity needed to "whiten the oil barrel" and thus enable the Soviets to export more high-value refined products instead of fuel oil. This suggests that decisionmaking on fuel exports, while presumably connected to internal energy strategy at the stage of five-year plans, proceeded independently in the year-by-year execution.

These patterns of decisionmaking suggest something about the attitudes of the Brezhnev leadership toward risk and the future, which turn out to be curiously parallel to those of other major energy exporters. Fen O. Hampson, in a detailed study of Canadian and Mexican energy policies, concludes that the main explanation for those countries' energy-pricing and export policies was the desire of their elites to avoid political risk to themselves and their domestic programs.[51] In the Soviet case, it has become the conventional wisdom to say that energy exports were Brezhnev's crutch, a means of feeding his key programs (particularly agriculture) and upgrading domestic technologies without risking domestic reform. But first, were his export policies themselves risk-averse? In some important respects, yes. By reserving half of their energy exports for Eastern Europe, the Soviets clearly aimed for political insurance; by favoring cash flow over diplomacy in hard-currency trade, they avoided possible complications in their income; by exporting oil instead of gas, they gained flexibility and avoided giving hostages to fortune; and by using oil sales as a regulator, they limited their foreign indebtedness.

But ironically, in a larger sense Brezhnev's energy-trade policy was not risk-averse at all. The very act of increasing the country's volume of foreign trade also increased its exposure, particularly that of the domes-

[50] The failure of gas-for-oil substitution from 1976 to 1983 is one of the very few points on which one might take issue with the fine study by Chadwick, Long, and Nissanke, *Soviet Oil Exports*. It is true, as the authors point out, that the share of oil in the total Soviet fuel mix has fallen sharply in recent years. But the relevant category is not the share of oil but the absolute quantity of oil consumed, and on this front there has been only limited progress. As of the beginning of 1988, apparent oil consumption had declined 1.8 percent from its peak in 1981. PlanEcon, Inc., ***East European Energy Databank***.

[51] Fen O. Hampson, "Fraught with Risk: the Political Economy of Petroleum Policies in Canada and Mexico" (Ph.D. diss., Harvard University, 1982).

tic energy sector. Soviet leaders at the beginning undoubtedly thought of energy exports as a "cash cow"—a low-cost generator of hard currency with which to finance a policy of import-led growth in other sectors. Their reluctance to give up this idea in the late 1970s and early 1980s contributed to the pressure on the domestic energy sector, helping to put the entire economy at risk. A further element of risk associated with increased exposure to the outside came from the Soviets' extreme sensitivity to economic threats or humiliation from the United States (themselves a reaction against the excessive optimism with which the Soviets initially ventured into détente); thus the overresponse of the Brezhnev leadership to the CIA's oil reports and to the compressor embargo added further to the imbalance of Soviet energy policy at home. Brezhnev's policy may have been risk-averse in intent, but it raised unintended and unforeseen risks instead.

These might have been alleviated if the Brezhnev leadership had developed a longer-range vision in its energy trade. The main immediate cause of trouble was the Soviets' drift into nearly exclusive reliance on oil as their primary source of hard-currency income and as the principal regulator of their foreign-trade balance.

Toward a New Foreign-Trade Policy under Gorbachev

In 1985 and 1986 Soviet energy trade was jolted in succession by the downturn in domestic production and the collapse in world oil prices. Soviet crude oil exports to the OECD dropped by 24 percent in 1985: since this was two-thirds of the total decrease in Soviet oil production, it was clear that the planners had little flexibility left.[52] In 1986 the collapse of world oil prices, combined with the sharp decline of the dollar, gutted Soviet hard-currency balances. Though domestic oil production recovered, apparent domestic consumption rose also, and as a result the Soviets were unable to increase net oil exports to the nonsocialist countries by more than about 14 percent. The risks of a one-crop export policy stood revealed.

As the news worsened, Gorbachev began paying more public attention to foreign trade policy. Three months after his election as General Secretary he called for a major change in the structure of Soviet exports. The country should export fewer raw materials, he said, and more manufactured goods.[53] In the fall of 1985 he spoke out against grain

[52] Chadwick, Long, and Nissanke, *Soviet Oil Exports*, pp. 146–147.

[53] M. S. Gorbachev, *Izbrannye rechi i stat'i*, 5 vols. to date (Moscow: Politizdat, 1987), vol. 2, pp. 263–264.

imports;[54] and by June 1986 he was addressing the problem of reform in the structure of the Ministry of Foreign Trade.[55] In scattered remarks Gorbachev indicated that he shared the widespread disillusionment in Moscow with the results of Brezhnev's import-led strategy and the resentment over the political pressures that followed. As he told an audience in Warsaw the same month, "We were late in understanding what traps are laid along the trade paths leading to the West." He went on to criticize the notion that "it is simpler to buy on the capitalist market than to produce ourselves," and he condemned "excesses" and "inadmissible dependence."[56]

But it was not until June 1987 that Gorbachev explicitly linked Brezhnev's foreign trade with his domestic policies in a sweeping indictment of Brezhnev's overall management of the economy. He accused him of masking the worsening economic situation with massive exports of energy and of wasting the hard-currency proceeds mainly on "current tasks" instead of economic modernization.[57] Brezhnev had squandered his oil income to import grain instead of using it to help modernize the engineering sector. Thus, for Gorbachev, Brezhnev's foreign-trade policy, and his energy trade in particular, were an integral part of the overall economic crisis.

After a brief recovery in 1987, in 1988 world oil prices headed down again, driving the Soviets' terms of trade with the West back to the abysmal levels of 1986. The purchasing power of a barrel of Soviet oil, reckoned in terms of West German machinery, fell to one-quarter of what it was in 1985.[58] But now, with the advent of *glasnost'*, new critics joined Gorbachev. An economist named A. A. Arbatov (seemingly a brother of the Americanist G. A. Arbatov) attacked oil and gas exports as a "narcotic,"[59] and others have argued that, were it not for exports, it would be unnecessary to push the northern oil and gas fields so hard.[60]

Even if he agreed with such extreme views (which is unlikely), Gorbachev has few alternatives to oil exports in the short run. To coun-

[54] Ibid., p. 405.

[55] Ibid., vol. 3, pp. 446–447.

[56] Ibid., p. 469.

[57] Speech to the Central Committee of the CPSU, "O zadachakh po korennoi perestroike ekonomikoi," *Pravda*, 26 June 1987.

[58] Estimate from *PlanEcon Report* 4, nos. 39–40 (14 October 1988), p. 2.

[59] A. A. Arbatov, "Chinovniki i kuptsy," *Komsomol'skaia pravda*, 15 July 1988. The economist, Aleksandr Arkad'evich Arbatov, has the same patronymic as the well-known director of the USA Institute, Georgii Arkad'evich Arbatov.

[60] The views of such critics are referred to in an interview with the general director of Urengoygazdobycha, Rim Suleimanov, "Chto ostavim potomkam," *Sotsialisticheskaia industriia* 9 July 1988.

teract the deterioration in terms of trade, the Soviets have increased foreign borrowing and have accepted a higher level of indebtedness than Brezhnev ever did;[61] they have curtailed hard-currency food imports[62] and increased exports of nonpetroleum commodities; and they have gradually increased exports of gas and electrical power. Even so, they have also been forced to limit Soviet imports of Western machinery and equipment.[63]

Will Soviet planners begin to take account of the rapidly rising marginal cost of oil and re-examine their energy-trade policy? If they do their sums properly, their decisions should depend not only on world oil prices and their own oil costs but also on how they perceive the marginal productivity of imported machinery. A Soviet source says that the planners do not take their calculations that far (or at least did not do so in the recent past).[64] But the leaders probably do, at least in some rough intuitive sense; for them the value of imported equipment is measured by much more than its price tag. Does it provide competition to monopolistic domestic producers, thus holding back inflation? Does it relieve bottlenecks in high-priority programs? Or does it sit in the rain and snow unused?[65] Considerations such as these make the whole subject more sensitive politically than pencil-and-paper calculations would suggest.

A second factor in the leaders' calculations is that, if they displace oil with gas and export the oil, then the effective marginal cost of exports becomes that of the gas. As we saw in Chapter 5, Western calculations suggest that the marginal production cost of Soviet gas at the wellhead is only one-eighth that of oil, and the gap is still widening.[66] Even after one allows for transmission, local storage, and distribution, which together nearly quadruple the cost of gas,[67] the marginal cost of gas

[61] For figures on Soviet indebtedness, see Chapter 2, note 103.

[62] Food imports from nonsocialist countries dropped sharply from the $2.4 billion range in 1984 to half that amount in 1986–1987. *PlanEcon Report* 4, nos. 39–40 (14 October 1988).

[63] Soviet imports of machinery and equipment from nonsocialist countries, measured in 1980 dollars, fell from nearly $11 billion in 1983 to less than $8 billion in 1987, although there was some recovery in 1988. *PlanEcon Report* 4, nos. 39–40 (14 October 1988), p. 11.

[64] Makarov and Melent'ev, *Energeticheskii kompleks SSSR*, pp. 255–257.

[65] As of the beginning of 1988, MNP had 295 million rubles and MGP 473 million rubles worth of foreign equipment stored in inventory, about the equivalent of a year's imports. *Ekonomicheskaia gazeta*, no. 10 (March 1988). By 1 January 1989, both ministries claimed substantial improvement, to 146 and 351 million, respectively.

[66] Sagers, "Oil Production Costs," p. 52.

[67] V. P. Mozhin, ed., *Planirovanie razmeshcheniia proizvoditel'nykh sil SSSR* (Moscow:

delivered to the Soviet border may still be only half of that of oil. But the marginal cost of Soviet gas is also rising rapidly, and some Soviet critics are now predicting that by the end of the century it too will have become a high-cost fuel. Nevertheless, in the interim gas-for-oil substitution gives the Soviets a breathing space, and therefore their chief concern for the present is to make sure such displacement goes fast and smoothly. For the longer term, only progress in curbing energy demand will enable the Soviets to maintain energy exports while cutting energy investment, thus finally taking themselves off the hook upon which Brezhnev left them.

The larger question about Soviet foreign trade, however, is whether the Gorbachev leadership will redefine its role in the Soviet economy, rethinking particularly the role of energy exports.[68] Imports have an essential part to play in economic reform, as a means of drying up savings, providing labor incentives, and putting competitive pressure on Soviet manufacturers to keep prices down.[69] But to ensure a steady flow of hard currency for these purposes, the Soviet reformers must cut their dependence on oil exports as the chief regulator of their hard-currency balance. More radical measures are now being implemented or are on the way, such as more liberal terms for joint ventures (partly intended to improve the competitiveness of Soviet manufactured goods abroad), higher domestic food prices (to curb demand for meat and grain), and more decentralization of the foreign-trade machinery.[70] But what is not yet clear is whether the old attitudes that created it in the first place, particularly the antimercantilist attitude toward foreign trade, are breaking up as well.

Ekonomika, 1986), vol. 2, pp. 341–342. Mozhin, the first deputy chief of the CPSU Central Committee's Economics Department (and listed as the author of the chapter in which this item appears), gives the average cost (*privedennye zatraty*) of a standard ton-equivalent of natural gas at the wellhead as 7 rubles (which is not much different from Sagers's estimate of 5.45 rubles), but as 26 rubles when delivered to customers in central European Russia.

[68] A thought-provoking recent essay is Jerry Hough, *Opening Up the Soviet Economy* (Washington, D.C.: Brookings Institution, 1987).

[69] Ed A. Hewett, *Reforming the Soviet Economy* (Washington, D.C.: Brookings Institution, 1988). This view of the role of imports is now widespread among Soviet reformers. See A. Aganbegian, "V gozu ili pod goru?" *Pravda*, 6 Feb. 1989.

[70] The latest dramatic liberalization in foreign-trade legislation allows all Soviet enterprises and cooperatives to conduct foreign trade and hold hard-currency bank accounts. See "Postanovlenie Soveta Ministrov SSSR," *Ekonomicheskaia gazeta*, no. 51 (December 1988), pp. 17–18. It is even possible that Soviet enterprises will be allowed to negotiate foreign credits with Western banks directly. See I. Aleksandrova, "Podaianie valiutoi," *Pravda*, 9 Feb. 1989.

NINE

EXPLAINING THE SOVIET ENERGY CRISIS: SYSTEM VERSUS LEADERSHIP

Two symbolic events, seemingly a world apart: in the spring of 1978 Brezhnev toured West Siberia to launch his emergency oil campaign; in the fall of 1985 Gorbachev toured the same region to announce *perestroika* in the oil and gas fields. But their main messages were not in fact so very different. More than a decade after Brezhnev's crash response to the first oil crisis of 1977, after three successions and the start of a new leadership under Gorbachev, Soviet energy policy has remained remarkably constant. Despite the new rhetorical stress on conservation and the beginnings of economic reform, it is still overwhelmingly oriented toward supply rather than demand. The obsession with keeping oil output growing is slowly abating, but it has been succeeded by a similar obsession about gas; and despite recent measures to improve housing, infrastructure, and supply in the field, both oil and gas policy remain shortsighted and unbalanced. The antiquated oil and gas service industries have yet to respond to the high priority now being assigned to the civilian machinery sector—indeed, after two years of overambitious reform efforts, they are now further hampered by the turmoil besetting the machine-building sector as a whole. Nuclear power and coal-utilization technologies continue to lag, the former still much affected by the complex repercussions of Chernobyl'. Foreign technology remains underused, and much of what is imported is ineffectively applied. The essential approach to energy supply is still the forced-draft campaign, backed by political pressure.

Driving the supply problem, today as yesterday, is the country's uncurbed demand for energy. Massive absorption of natural gas has prevented the oil squeeze from becoming a disaster, but it has had the perverse result of displacing nearly as much coal as oil. Above all, the virtual one-for-one connection between economic growth and energy consumption has not been broken.

Yet inside Soviet borders the world's largest flow of oil and gas moves day and night through the world's mightiest system of pipelines, guaranteeing the Soviet Union unchallenged first place in oil and gas production, and a strong position in energy exports, for many decades to come. But the issue is cost: Soviet oil will soon cost more at the margin than it will bring on the world market, and Soviet gas, though still half as expensive as oil at the point of use, is growing rapidly dearer. As a result, investment in energy supply remains the chief claimant to new investment resources in Soviet industry and the main obstacle to the leaders' plans for economic modernization. Energy policy is still today what it was a decade ago. Gorbachev's intentions are clearly different from Brezhnev's, but his energy decisions so far look the same.

How can one explain the constancy of these self-defeating features? In the introduction to this book we asked whether the cause was the leadership or the system, compounded by the inheritance of two generations of central planning. What are the implications for the future of reform? In this chapter we return to those initial questions.

First, to put the problem in proper context, we should remember that in 1970 the Soviet Union did not have an energy problem. Energy, for the first time in Soviet history, was abundant and cheap, thanks to the discovery of Siberian oil. The policies, technologies, and institutions employed to produce it were reasonably well suited to the circumstances, and a supply-oriented approach made sense. On the consumption side, advances in the previous two decades—the switch from coal to oil, electrification of the railroads, economies of scale in power generation—were still producing rapid gains in transformation efficiency.

Within a few years the Soviet leaders faced a sudden and unexpected problem. Energy costs skyrocketed, but the patterns of energy supply, processing, delivery, and consumption were anchored to the country's physical and economic structure and could not be changed quickly. In the short term, it was easier to try to outrun the threat by expanding energy production year after year, even though that meant racing up a slope of rising costs that loomed steeper and steeper. At first, that was a rational response: the problem was new, the stakes high, the alternatives unclear and unready. But fifteen years later the leaders are, in effect, still running.

Who deserves the blame? The first word belongs to the geologists, who remind us that fossil fuels are wasting assets and that the iron law of diminishing returns weighs equally on all regimes and economic systems. The floor goes next to the economists, who tell us why centrally planned systems are inevitably costly and supply-constrained. All that is true. But if energy supply is an uncertain and ultimately a losing game against nature, the uncertainty need not be so high and the diminishing returns need not set in so quickly as they have in the Soviet case. And if the system generates characteristic biases and faults, it is the leaders' job to offset them—if they can. Did the Brezhnev leadership attempt to do so and fail? Is farsighted, "intensive" policy beyond the ability of a system that can govern only with its thumbs? Or is the core of the explanation that the political elite, especially under Brezhnev but also under his successors, has lost the capacity to learn and the power to act on its learning? Can Gorbachev do better, or does the system put so severe a burden on its leaders that even the best of them will be overwhelmed? Must he await the uncertain outcome of systemic reforms that at best will take a decade to show results?

The following sections attempt to draw out the implications of the previous chapters for these questions, focusing first on the systemic factors in policy, then on the roles of the leaders. In the last section we return to the Gorbachev leadership and the potential for reform in energy policy.

The Role of the System

If we suppose for the sake of argument that the paradoxes of Soviet energy policy are entirely due to the system, we arrive at the following hypotheses. The characteristic imbalance of policy is caused by the power and inertia of the vast vertical hierarchies, only weakly offset by the available mechanisms for central oversight and horizontal coordination. The near term and the long term are represented by different institutions, as are the various fuels, the different aspects of field development, and the phases of each industry's activity. The prevailing system of prices, targets, norms, and reporting drives these organizations toward near-term goals, toward a focus on process instead of final results, and toward conflict instead of cooperation. As a result, most of the participants in the system tend to be conservative and risk-averse, preferring incremental solutions using familiar instruments. Thus conflict, imbalance, failure to adapt, and shortsightedness are all products of the system. Bad leadership can aggravate them; but good leadership can only moderate them.

This is a political scientist's list, of course; an economist would come up with a different one, stressing the lack of reliable information, the conflicting preferences, the many reasons for "softness" in the constraints bearing on decisionmakers in a centrally planned system, and so forth. But they are actually the same list; the features highlighted above are the institutional expression of the command economy, the organizational responses to its characteristic properties. As Peter Hauslohner puts it nicely, both the command economy and the command polity are the embodiment of the Stalinist strategy of economic growth, a theme to which we return later in this chapter.[1]

Overall Policymaking

A chronic problem of Soviet energy policy has been weak central management. The decisionmaking system for energy has traditionally been polycentric and remains so today.[2] Until quite recently there was no single ministry of energy or state committee with formal jurisdiction over the entire subject; neither was there a single person responsible for energy policy in all its aspects. Over the years there have been many calls in the Soviet press for a unified command, but only after Gorbachev's accession did the idea make headway.[3] In 1985 a Bureau for the Fuel and Energy Complex was created under the USSR Council of Ministers, one of several similar amalgamations announced in that year. At this writing, however, its functions and powers remain vague.

Until the oil emergency of 1977 Prime Minister Kosygin and his staff played the most visible policymaking role in energy matters; thereafter the Party side took the lead, beginning with Brezhnev himself. The leading players, until the fall of 1988, were the Party secretary for heavy industry and energy, V. I. Dolgikh, and his veteran department head, I. P. Iastrebov. Dolgikh chaired official meetings on fuels from the early 1970s to 1988; and after the retirement of Politburo Secretary A. P. Kirilenko in 1982, he presided over those on electricity and nuclear power as well.[4] But Dolgikh was not responsible for conservation, which is now handled as part of the overall program for conserving natural resources (see Chapter 7), or for industrial support for the energy industries, which is considered part of the machine-building sector.

[1] Peter Hauslohner, "Gorbachev's Social Contract," *Soviet Economy* 3, no. 1 (January-March 1987), pp. 54–89. Organizational changes that took place as this book was going to press are reviewed in the Epilogue.

[2] I have borrowed this term from Robert Campbell. See especially Campbell, *Soviet Energy Technologies: Planning, Policy, Research and Development* (Bloomington: Indiana University Press, 1980), pp. 18ff.

[3] The years from 1966 to 1975, on the contrary, witnessed a steady process of subdividing ministries and state committees into smaller and more specialized subunits. The movement then stabilized from the mid-1970s to Gorbachev's accession, when a process of amalgamation began, starting with the agricultural sector. For a valuable road map, see the chart published by the Central Intelligence Agency, *Evolution of the Central Administrative Structure of the USSR 1917–1979*, CR 79–10123 (Washington, D.C.: 1979).

[4] This expanded jurisdiction was formalized in 1984 when the word "Energy" was added to the name of the Central Committee Department of Heavy Industry, and Iastrebov became the formal head of it. In previous years Dolgikh had combined the positions of secretary and department head, while Iastrebov had been his first deputy.

Since Brezhnev's death, the successive general secretaries have continued to play the leading role in energy policy; but with the appointment in 1985 of a vigorous new prime minister, Nikolai I. Ryzhkov, the Council of Ministers has again come to the fore. Its Presidium, much rejuvenated since Kosygin's death in 1980, added two deputy chairmen who made their careers in Siberian oil and gas: Boris Shcherbina, heading the new Energy Bureau, and Iurii Batalin, in charge of all construction.[5] But for the first three and a half years under Gorbachev, Dolgikh on the Party side remained the dominant figure. As time went on, however, his position looked increasingly fragile. Though himself a Siberian, Dolgikh did not appear to be a member of the inner circle of the new leadership; and indeed, his continued political survival was remarkable, since one might have expected him to be a convenient scapegoat for the troubles of the oil, coal, and nuclear industries. By 1988 Dolgikh had apparently associated himself with the conservatives in the Politburo, and in the fall of that year he was dismissed.[6]

Dolgikh's departure was more than a simple changing of the guard; his position vanished with him, as Gorbachev simultaneously shut down the Central Committee departments that had traditionally overseen the command economy from the Party side. Gorbachev's aim is to remove the Party from the job of day-to-day economic management and to strengthen the authority of the government. While it is too soon to tell what precise forms this policy will take or how long it will last, the immediate effect is to leave the Council of Ministers' Energy Bureau as the principal central staff for energy policy.

But even before the latest changes there had been more unified oversight of the energy sector than the divided lines of responsibility suggested. As the urgency and expense of energy problems grew, so did the direct attention given to them by the top leadership. Yet neither the Party Central Committee nor the Council of Ministers has had the staff needed for detailed supervision of energy affairs,[7] and the creation of

[5] Iurii Batalin, a career construction expert in energy in the Urals and Siberia, was first deputy minister of MNGS, with special responsibility for pipeline construction, at the time of the East-West pipeline affair. In 1983 he was promoted to the Council of Ministers as chairman of the State Committee for Labor and Social Questions, and in December 1985 he was named deputy chairman of the Council of Ministers. *Izvestiia*, 22 Dec. 1985. In August 1986 he was named to head a reorganized and strengthened State Committee for Construction.

[6] *Pravda*, 1 Oct. 1988.

[7] An organization chart on energy affairs, published by the CIA in 1981, listed a consultative-advisory body to the Council of Ministers, called the "referentura." This body presumably included specialists on energy; however, to the author's knowledge no one from the referentura has played a prominent public role in energy politics during the

the new Energy Bureau is unlikely to change this. In practice, the only high-level body with the staff and the jurisdiction to cover the entire energy sector in all its aspects is Gosplan.

Gosplan is the place where political goals and scarce resources must be confronted and reconciled. Over the last decade Gosplan officials have been much in view on energy matters, beginning with the long-time chairman from 1965 to 1985, Nikolai K. Baibakov, himself a former minister of oil. The names of key Gosplan deputies and department heads have also been familiar bylines on energy policy.[8] In addition to its fuel departments, Gosplan also maintains two research institutes devoted to planning the use of natural resources, one of which specializes in energy problems.[9]

In some respects the greatest potential force for integrated policy, at least at the level of strategy, is the Soviet science establishment.[10] Through a large network of institutes, scientific councils, and special commissions, the Academy of Sciences, the State Committee for Science and Technology, and the individual energy ministries (especially the Ministry of Power) support research, present data, and recommend policy. Over the years, high-level ad hoc interagency commissions composed of members from these institutions have made reasonably successful efforts to integrate this work into unified positions for practical policy. Two such commissions, chaired by A. P. Aleksandrov, president of the Academy of Sciences and a prominent nuclear physicist, supplied the technical background and policy recommendations for the energy program of 1983–1984, and a third commission has been at work since 1985. The role of the energy experts over the last decade, particularly

---

period covered by this study, and it is possible that the body ceased to exist after Kosygin's retirement.

[8] Deputy Chairman A. M. Lalaiants has been in overall charge of energy matters at Gosplan since 1965. A. A. Troitskii has been responsible for power and electrification since 1980 but had previous experience in the same department. Gosplan's Department of Oil and Gas was headed for many years by V. I. Filanovskii-Zenkov, now first deputy minister of oil. Filanovskii-Zenkov began his career in the Kuibyshev oil industry, then went to Tiumen', where he was a protégé of the legendary first head of Glavtiumenneftegaz, V. I. Muravlenko. He rose to chief of construction for MNP before moving to Gosplan in the mid-1970s. After his return to the Oil Ministry in 1984, he was succeeded at Gosplan by E. Iudin.

[9] The first is the Institute for the Integrated Study of Fuel and Energy Problems, whose long-time director, S. Iatrov, also appeared with some frequency in the press (in 1985 he was replaced by N. K. Pravodnikov). The other Gosplan institute is the Council for the Evaluation of Productive Resources (SOPS), which has played an important role in comparative analyses of nuclear, gas, and coal options.

[10] For a valuable overview of the energy research and development system, see Campbell, *Soviet Energy Technologies*, ch. 2.

that of economists and systems analysts, has been one of the most striking illustrations of the growing participation, access, and visibility of the technical adviser in Soviet policymaking.

But the experts are not necessarily a force for integrated policy; it is not only the unified voice of the official commissions that the decision-makers hear. Every institute has its favorite technology and its own vigorous champions, and their access to policymakers is not limited to the integrated channels of commissions like Aleksandrov's. Through their own ministries and agencies, through innumerable "review commissions" (*ekspertnye komissii*) that pass on individual projects, the champions of "coal by wire" do battle with the defenders of coal liquefaction, nuclear power contends with coal, AC high-voltage transmission competes with DC, and partisans of magnetohydrodynamics, 120-atmosphere gas pipelines, tertiary oil recovery, and even dirigibles (proposed for transportation over Siberian wastes) all have their say. Thus the system's tendency toward polycentrism and suboptimization in policy implementation and execution is reinforced by polycentric and suboptimized technical advice. Under the pressure of actual decision-making, the fragile unified positions of the formal commissions can break; the Aleksandrov Commission, for example, was evidently divided over whether oil output should be allowed to peak and over whether nuclear power was really as cost-effective as its defenders claimed.

A more fundamental problem is that the experts' advice tends to be the voice of the long term, whereas the policymaker must balance the long term with the short. One of the reasons for the oil emergency of 1977 is that the experts in Moscow, whose long-range vision of the coal-and-nuclear future had been written into the Tenth Five-Year Plan two years before, ignored the oil problem in front of their noses and played down the prospects for natural gas. In the decade since, the experts' advice has become more realistically balanced but not necessarily more unified.

This profusion of views and roles among energy experts provides an interesting commentary on the relation of knowledge to power in Soviet policymaking. As Peter Hauslohner points out, there are broadly two views among Western scholars on this question.[11] The first stresses the dependence of specialists on political support, the second their growing freedom from political constraint. The energy case yields illustrations of both but suggests that they apply in different circumstances. Where energy *supply* was concerned, specialists worked from

[11] Peter A. Hauslohner, "Managing the Soviet Labor Market: Politics and Policymaking under Brezhnev" (Ph.D. diss., University of Michigan, 1984), pp. 28ff.

longstanding and secure bases, published through long-established journals, and enjoyed access to policymakers through familiar committees, task forces, and so on. But this network of research and advice gave almost no attention to energy ***demand***. So long as the political leadership showed little interest either, there was small encouragement for new institutes, departments, or individuals oriented toward conservation. Only at the very end of Brezhnev's life, as the leaders' interest moved toward demand management, did the the necessary processes of resource allocation, changes of leadership, and institutionalization begin, and the experts' focus shifted correspondingly. This suggests that in well-established fields and subjects the "supply-push" aspect of policy advice has become more prominent, while in newer ones "demand-pull" is still the rule.[12]

In sum, the system's capacity for unified overview and strategy is strongest at the top, where overall objectives and output targets are set and investment decisions are made. But implementation, reporting, and the details of planning are another matter. These are the province of the large, vertically organized ministries responsible for each fuel. Central decisionmakers must fit them together as well as they can and somehow cope with the ragged edges between them.

The same is true when it comes to coordinating the domestic aspects of Soviet energy policy with the foreign. While the major decisions, such as the volume of energy exports and the share to be reserved for Eastern Europe, appear to be decided at the highest levels and are closely tied to domestic policies, implementation is less closely integrated; there too the process is polycentic and suboptimized, dominated by vertical hierarchies. This is evident in the case of imports of oil- and gas-related equipment: the decision to rely or not to rely on the outside varies from case to case, depending on whether the need is urgent, whether there are alternative Soviet technologies, whether the West is perceived to have a decisive edge, and whether there are strong

[12] In a chapter of an earlier work of mine, devoted to the roles of technical specialists in bringing new ideas into Soviet politics, most of my examples were of the latter sort, drawn from the revival of fields such as genetics, agronomy, economics, and sociology. Now that those fields have gone through the initial stages of institutionalization and professionalization, I would expect more of a "supply-push" and less of a "demand-pull" pattern to the participation of those specialists in policymaking. This trend has been accentuated, but not caused, by ***glasnost'***. See Gustafson, ***Reform in Soviet Politics: Lessons of Recent Policies on Land and Water*** (New York: Cambridge University Press, 1981), ch. 6. A similar trend can be inferred from Peter Solomon's work on the growing influence of criminologists in Soviet legal reform, in contrast to the dominance of the "demand-pull" pattern twenty years ago. See his ***Soviet Criminologists and Criminal Policy: Specialists in Policy-Making*** (New York: Columbia University Press, 1977).

agencies and players involved on one side of the issue or the other. As Soviet foreign-trade policy becomes more decentralized, these traits will become even more prominent.

Vertical Hierarchies: The Ministries

The major sectors of the Soviet economy are organized into a hundred-odd ministries, vertically integrated giants that are typically weak at crossing their own boundaries to coordinate policy with other ministries. These ministries are frequently referred to in Russian as "branches" (*otrasli*) and this system of organization as the "branch principle." Despite Gorbachev's reforms so far, the ministries remain the major players, especially in the energy sector.

Four ministries occupy this vertical dimension of the organization chart in the oil and gas sectors, and other fuels and energy sources are similarly organized. They are the Ministry of the Oil Industry (MNP), the Ministry of the Gas Industry (MGP), the Ministry for Construction of Oil and Gas Enterprises (MNGS), and the Ministry of Geology (Mingeo). The two fuel ministries are responsible for the development, transmission, and wholesale distribution of oil and gas, as well as certain aspects of exploration. But for supporting operations they depend on other ministries: machinery, roads, powerlines, on-site construction, geological surveying—these are largely the domain of other vertical giants.[13]

The Oil Ministry is the ancestor of MGP, which was split away as an independent ministry in the mid-1960s, and of MNGS, which was created in 1972, mainly to accelerate Siberian pipeline construction. Many top officials in both bodies thus began their careers as oil men. The relationship of these three agencies is a complex mixture of cooperation and competition at all levels, from Moscow boardrooms to the fields. The oil industry, long the dominant partner, was accustomed until the beginning of the 1980s to having top priority, and in many places it still does. In Tiumen' Province, in particular, geology and climate join history in working to the oil industry's advantage, because oil in Tiumen' is concentrated in the more accessible southern half of the province, and most of the gas is located in the inhospitable north. Workers and their organizations prefer to operate in the south; and this enables the oil industry to bid workers away from the other agencies, hampering the gas industry's drilling and the geologists' exploration.

[13] More detailed discussion of the division of labor in exploration will be found in Chapter 3, in industrial support in Chapter 6, and in housing and infrastructure in Chapter 5.

MNP probably also enjoys better support from ancillary ministries for the same reason.

MNGS is the principal construction partner for both agencies. Its job starts after the oil and gas leave the ground: it builds field facilities for gathering and processing the raw fuel, then for transporting it to refineries (where begins the domain of yet another ministry in charge of petroleum refining and petrochemicals). In recent years MNGS has had the all-important assignment of building the large-diameter gas trunk lines from Siberia to the European USSR. Like other Soviet construction ministries, MNGS acts as the contractor (*podriadchik*), while MNP and MGP are the customers (*zakazchiki*). When MNGS completes a project, it turns it over to MNP or MGP, which then operates and maintains it.

Mingeo is responsible for the preliminary stages of exploration (geophysical mapping, prospecting, and the like) throughout most of the country, and in the newer oil and gas regions it is responsible for the later stages as well (delineating fields and proving up reserves). Thus Mingeo undertakes most of the oil exploration in Siberia. Once again, the result is an uneasy blend of collaboration and tension.

At several important points the history of each agency has strongly influenced its behavior. The oil and gas industries, as well as Mingeo, originated outside Siberia. The oil industry has its roots in the prerevolutionary Caucasus,[14] and then for a generation after World War II its center was the Volga Basin. The gas industry, before its formal independence from MNP, grew up in the Ukraine and Central Asia in the 1950s. The Ministry of Geology has a more varied history, since it is responsible for all mineral resources, not just oil and gas; where oil and gas are concerned, however, its antecedents lie outside Siberia too.

This helps to account for all three agencies' marked reluctance to take the plunge into Siberia. The geological establishment long resisted the idea that a major oil province would be found there; and even after it had been proven wrong, it was similarly skeptical about the prospects for gas. The gas industry itself was equally resistant. As late as the mid-1970s MGP leaders considered Siberian gas too expensive to gamble on, an "exotic commodity,"[15] and even in the Tenth Five Year Plan

[14] As late as the 1960s many of the senior oil men working in Siberia had started their careers in Azerbaijan. When the first commercial find in Siberia was made in 1960, the site chief, wishing to keep the size of the strike confidential, informed his superior in a telegram written in Azeri, though both men were Russians. F. Salmanov, "Optimizm i optimizatsiia," in *Tiumenskii meridian* (Moscow: Politizdat, 1983), p. 84.

[15] A. Aganbegian and Z. M. Ibragimova, *Sibir' na rubezhe vekov* (Moscow: Sovetskaia Rossiia, 1984), p. 26. The skepticism of the Soviet oil and gas industries about Siberian

(1976–1980) they continued to push investment in the older gas-producing regions faster than in Siberia.[16] When the idea of a crash gas campaign was being debated in 1980, MGP officials were distinctly cautious, particularly Minister S. A. Orudzhev, whose career spanned the entire early history of MGP. Only after Orudzhev's death in 1981 did a new generation of gas men with Siberian careers finally assume leadership, and MNP followed a few years later.[17] The traces of this long reluctance can still be felt today. As late as 1980 none of the top leaders of these agencies had made his career in Siberia, and most of their personnel and capital were still concentrated west of the Urals.

In contrast, Siberia was the main reason for MNGS's creation in the early 1970s, and thus the construction agency has always had a different attitude toward Siberian oil and gas development. The older leaders (presumably Baibakov as well as Orudzhev) had been reluctant to invest in Siberian pipelines.[18] But shortly after MNGS was created, it was placed under the leadership of one of the most vocal Siberian energy

---

prospects has a long history. In the early 1960s, relates the then second secretary of the Yamal-Nenetsk regional Party committee, V. N. Tiurin, there were more pessimists than optimists, and the former controlled the money and the resources needed for exploration and development. It was not until 1970–1971 that the first major gas development project was begun (at Medvezh'e). See "Iamal'skii potentsial," *Oktiabr'*, no. 4 (1976), pp. 134–135.

16 "Ekonomicheskaia effectivnost' kapital'nykh vlozhenii v gazovoi promyshlennosti za 1971–79 gg.," in VNIIEgazprom, *Ekonomika gazovoi promyshlennosti*, seriia ekonomika, organizatsiia i upravlenie v gazovoi promyshlennosti (obzornaia informatsiia), no. 10 (1980), p. 5.

17 V. A. Dinkov, lately minister of oil, rose up through the production side of the Gas Ministry, becoming deputy minister in 1970, first deputy in 1971, and minister of gas in 1981, then moving to the head of the Oil Ministry in 1985. His successor at the Gas Ministry, V. S. Chernomyrdin, had a distinctively different career path, serving in the Central Committee apparatus from 1973 to 1982, when he was put in charge of gas production in Tiumen' with the rank of deputy minister of the gas industry. He was promoted to deputy in 1985. *Sovetskii entsiklopedicheskii slovar'*, 4th ed. (Moscow: Sovetskaia entsiklopediia, 1987). In the process the more senior previous first deputy minister, Rantik Margulov, was bypassed, but he has since been appointed first deputy chairman of the Council of Ministers' Fuel and Energy Bureau under Boris Shcherbina. *Pravda*, 16 Sept. 1987.

18 Constraints on pipeline capacity and performance were the chief reason the gas industry frequently failed to meet its output targets during the first half of the 1970s. Campbell, *Soviet Energy Technologies*, documents the low efficiency of the Soviet trunk-line network, but another problem was insufficient investment. A Soviet source discreetly blames the industry (and presumably the planners) for their lack of foresight in failing to give higher priority to gas transmission. A. D. Sedykh and B. L. Kuchin, *Upravlenie nauchno-tekhnicheskim progressom v gazovoi promyshlennosti* (Moscow: Nedra, 1983), pp. 7–8.

boosters, the former first party secretary of Tiumen' Province (subsequently deputy prime minister), Boris Shcherbina. MNGS, in other words, has had a Siberian vocation from the start, whereas for MGP and MNP it is a late conversion.

The relationship between client and contractor is always a difficult one in Soviet administration, but it is especially so in Siberia. Even though MNGS is technically responsible to MGP and MNP, it receives its orders (as well as its resources and materials) from Gosplan and its related state committees (the state committees for construction, supply, and so on). Consequently, MGP and MNP are for all practical purposes hostages to MNGS. The ministry has every incentive to build fast but not necessarily to build well or to suit its customers' priorities. In allocating its scarce time and resources, MNGS is naturally encouraged to concentrate on the most central tasks of the moment (for example, in the first half of the 1980s, the export pipeline); as a result, more peripheral jobs are left undone (such as spur lines to power plants or gas lines to gaslift systems in the oil fields). MGP and MNP, the customers, have little recourse except to appeal to higher political authority and complain loudly to the press, neither of which necessarily does much good.

The same is true of most Soviet operating ministries in their relations with construction ministries. To free themselves somewhat, the operating ministries resort to developing their own construction firms (about 10 percent of all Soviet construction projects are now of that type). But such efforts are an inefficient second best. MGP and MNP can offset the worst consequences of MNGS's neglect of secondary tasks by building on their own; but if MNGS delivers badly welded pipeline or falls behind schedule in completing processing plants, the fuel ministries have to live with the consequences. These problems not only lessen the efficiency of the oil and gas campaign but can also distort its direction.

Tension and poor cooperation affect even ministries with complementary missions, but the problem grows worse as one turns to ministries with more remote central tasks. MNP and MGP depend on ancillary ministries to build roads and housing, to transport freight and workers, and to assemble power plants and powerlines. Even though these ministries are crucially important to the oil and gas campaigns, the reverse is not usually the case, and the job of wrestling the noncongruent priorities of such side players into even minimal alignment is one of the most difficult tasks of Soviet administration. For the Ministry of Power and Electrification (Minenergo), for example, building a 500-kilovolt powerline to the Urengoy gas field is a minor (and fairly unappealing) part of a countrywide construction program, some of which—such as nuclear power—is also under direct Kremlin scrutiny.

Consequently, although power supply to the oil and gas industries of Tiumen' Province has turned into one of the most highly publicized problems of the area, putting pressure on Minenergo does not necessarily produce results.

Industrial support for the oil and gas campaigns is a special case in point, because the usual problems of coordination have been aggravated by the investment policy pursued at the top. The oil and gas campaigns required a vast expansion in the flow of machinery and equipment to Siberia. But during the Brezhnev years the civilian machinery sector was neglected, and its output stagnated in both quality and quantity. The machine-building ministries, even with the best will (which was not always present), have been unable to respond to the field ministries' requirements for increased reliability, productivity, or even quantity. To make matters worse, they too embody their history: very few of the major machine-building enterprises supporting the oil and gas industries are located in Siberia; instead, most are in the original Soviet oil and gas province of Azerbaijan, thousands of miles away. Thus to the usual conflictual relations between supplier and client are added the problems of doing business at long distance through overloaded transportation and communications systems.

The problems of vertical organization account for much of the jurisdictional instability characteristic of the energy sector. Attempting to rescue neglected programs at the boundaries of the ministries, the leaders redraw the organization charts, creating new ministries or shifting functions from one to another. Thus since the early 1970s responsibility for oil- and gas-related construction has been vested in MNGS, but jurisdiction over coal machinery has been returned to the Coal Ministry. Offshore exploration was the province of the oil industry before 1978, when it was given to the gas industry; it then returned to the oil industry in 1988. Nuclear safety has been entrusted to a separate state committee; nuclear power has been split away from the Power Ministry; and the oil industry has been given increased responsibility for Siberian exploration. And when the process of shifting responsibilities does not occur officially, it sometimes happens unofficially. Thus the extractive ministries have developed construction and housing industries of their own and large shops to repair the numerous defects in the equipment they receive. These shifts remind one of the Russian story of Trishka's *kaftan*, which was too short to cover his whole body at once: when he hiked it up to cover his shoulders, it left his legs bare, and vice versa.

Soviet administrators have tried other ways of escaping from Trishka's dilemma. One of them, with which every Soviet leader has experimented, is stronger horizontal integration.

Devices to Provide Horizontal Integration

In one way or another, each of the methods by which Soviet leaders have tried to cope with the problems of vertical hierarchies has aimed at providing a measure of horizontal integration, whether applied from the top (functional state committees or special-purpose commissions) or at local levels (territorial complex, production association, local soviet, or local Party apparatus). As a general rule, such devices work well enough in integrating the highest priority tasks (for example, the institution of the general designer in military procurement), but for the common run of policy problems they are either too weak, in which case they have little effect, or (more rarely) too strong, in which case they produce side effects, such as "regionalism" or "localism," that not only threaten Moscow's control but are genuinely disruptive in a system so accustomed to central direction. The happy medium has never been found, and Soviet policy oscillates, though never venturing for long from the centralized, branch-based principle.

The oldest and most important of the horizontal coordinators are the state committees, which are organized by what American administrative parlance refers to as "cross-cutting functions," such as planning, prices, supply, state security, and so on. We have already looked briefly at Gosplan. But verticalism affects even Gosplan: its branch departments reproduce the broad lines of the ministries, are frequently staffed by officials drawn from them, and often defend the ministries' interests and viewpoints. As a counterweight to these, Gosplan has an array of "horizontal" departments that deal with fuel balances, capital investment, and territorial planning, but it is commonly charged in the Soviet press that the vertical departments rule the roost. In effect, Gosplan has reproduced inside itself the dilemmas of the administrative system as a whole.

Moreover, Gosplan is far away from the field, where the practical problems of integration arise. At the local level the vertically organized ministries have virtually total control over the allocation of resources. Investment is channeled predominantly through them, and they have traditionally been responsible not only for their own missions but also for most support functions. For example, in cities where a single ministry is the principal employer, it is typically responsible for building and administering housing, schools, utilities, and mass transit.[19] In extreme cases, such as regional development around a single major industry, one ministry or even one ministry office is responsible for everything, be-

[19] For a sample of the large Soviet literature on this subject, see A. G. Aganbegian, ed., *Territorial'no-proizvodstvennye kompleksy: planirovanie i upravlenie* (Novosibirsk: Nauka, 1984), esp. ch. 5.

coming, in effect, its own horizontal empire.[20] Frequently, though, the dominant ministry simply abdicates responsibility over all but its primary task, and so the "secondary" tasks are neglected.[21]

It is widely recognized by the Soviets themselves that such extreme vertical dominance is unsound, but periodic attempts to develop a regional approach have invariably foundered, the most spectacular instance being Khrushchev's regional "economic councils" (*sovnarkhozy*) of the late 1950s and early 1960s. The branches remain supreme, but the tension between branch and region is one of the perennial themes of Soviet debates over economic policy.[22]

The Siberian oil and gas industries are vivid cases in point. In the West Siberian region (more exactly, the entity known as the West Siberian "territorial-production complex"), three ministries—MNP, MGP, and the Ministry of Petroleum Refining and the Petrochemical Industry (Minneftekhimprom)—control over 70 percent of total investment.[23] Soviet analyses frequently cite this lopsided dominance as the main reason for the underdevelopment of housing and infrastructure in the oil and gas region.[24]

At the end of the 1970s the pendulum of Soviet administrative fashion, having swung back to total dominance by the branch principle after Khrushchev's fall in 1964, began to move back toward experimentation with regional notions, and the movement has since become more pronounced under Gorbachev. For West Siberia, two new bodies were created in 1980–1981: a special commission under the Council of Ministers to oversee the oil and gas complex, and a special local division of Gosplan for the same purpose. The West Siberian commission, under the veteran deputy chairman of the Council of Ministers, Veniamin

[20] The classic case was the development of the region around the giant hydropower station at Bratsk in the 1950s and 1960s. The builder of Bratsk, I. I. Naimushin, assembled an 80,000-man work force that was also in charge of building the aluminum-smelting and logging industries that consumed the plant's power. Naimushin, with the support of the Irkutsk Party apparatus, wielded enormous influence, to such a degree that even the Ministry of Power did not attempt to reassign his crews or otherwise trifle with him. G. Vol'deit and V. Gukov, "Uroki Bratska," *Sotsialisticheskaia industriia*, 10 Sept. 1986.

[21] A striking case is that of the textile city of Ivanovo, which in the words of one of its plant directors has remained essentially a village because of the systematic neglect of the Ministry of Light Industry.

[22] Boris Rumer gives a valuable review in *Investment and Reindustrialization in the Soviet Economy* (Boulder, Colo.: Westview Press, 1984), pp. 74–78.

[23] Aganbegian, ed., *Territorial'no-proizvodstvennye kompleksy*, p. 120.

[24] For example, see V. P. Kuramin et al., "Problemy planirovaniia i upravleniia razvitiem zapadno-sibirskogo neftegazovogo kompleksa," in S. N. Starovoitov, ed., *Problemy razvitiia Zapadno-Sibirskogo neftegazovogo kompleksa* (Novosibirsk: Nauka, 1983), pp. 33–47.

Dymshits, until his retirement in 1985, was never much more than an empty shell[25] and has since been incorporated into the new Energy Bureau.

The Gosplan office, however, was a novel experiment, and for a time it generated a flurry of publicity. It was located directly in Tiumen' City, the first time such a local base had been tried. Its head, Vladimir Kuramin, was not a career official of Gosplan but the former head of oil and gas construction in Tiumen' Province, a man with long experience of the area. Between 1981 and 1983 Kuramin, evidently a vigorous and colorful character, appeared frequently in the Soviet press as the gadfly of the ministries.[26]

But it was clear from the first that Kuramin's powers were weak. Major sectors, such as transportation and communications, were left out of the definition of the West Siberian oil and gas complex; in any case the Gosplan office was only a planning organization and controlled no resources. Its staff was small, and in practice it stuck (no doubt wisely) to a small handful of targets, principally the problems of supplying electricity to the oil and gas fields. Much of its time was taken up answering requests from the Council of Ministers commission in Moscow, which, having no staff of its own, used the Gosplan office as its fact finder, absorbing the latter's limited energies. Worst of all, the Gosplan office was given the cold shoulder by the Tiumen' Province Party committee. By 1984 Kuramin had been transferred to Moscow as deputy minister of MNGS, and the Gosplan office, though it continued to exist, ceased to attract much notice.

But that was not the end of the experiment. It was considered sufficiently encouraging that a similar local Gosplan office later opened in Murmansk to coordinate the development of the Kola Peninsula, and still others may turn up elsewhere. As for Kuramin himself, he reappeared in the media in 1986 as deputy head of the new Energy Bureau of the USSR Council of Ministers, working directly under Deputy Prime Minister Boris Shcherbina in Moscow, presumably with ex-

[25] For example, it was supposed to maintain a resident "plenipotentiary" (*upolnomochennyi*) in Tiumen', but it never did so. Aganbegian, ed., *Territorial'no-proizvodstvennye kompleksy*, p. 56.

[26] This discussion of the Gosplan commission is drawn from the following press accounts: V. P. Kuramin, "Kompleks problem," *Stroitel'naia gazeta*, 30 Aug. 1981; same, "Mezhvedomstvennaia territorial'naia," *Sotsialisticheskaia industriia*, 19 June 1981; same, "Povyshat' uroven' upravleniia truboprovodnym stroitel'stvom," *Planovoe khoziaistvo*, no. 12 (1981), pp. 74–79; same, "V goru semero vezut," *Sotsialisticheskaia industriia*, 28 Oct. 1982; same, "Planiruem kompleks," *Pravda*, 3 Mar. 1982. For further information about Kuramin, see V. Lisin, "Sbivshis' s shaga," *Pravda*, 21 Jan. 1983, and a chapter co-authored by Kuramin in Starovoitov, ed., *Problemy*.

panded authority for coordinating Siberian oil and gas operations—perhaps a harbinger of interesting new developments.[27]

At any rate, the fate of the Tiumen' Gosplan office in the early 1980s reminds us where the real local power lies—in the province committee (*obkom*) of the Party. Students of the local Party apparatus have always found it an intriguing mixture of power and weakness, and the Tiumen' obkom is no exception. On the one hand, the obkom first secretary is a provincial viceroy, acting as expediter, overseer, coordinator, and occasional knocker of heads of the local representatives of the ministries. He also defends the interests of his region and lobbies for favorable plan targets and allocations of resources.[28] Thus it is fitting that the obkom first secretaries are traditionally the pool from which Politburo members are drawn, and this is as true under Gorbachev so far as it was under his predecessors.

But, as Jerry Hough observed, the local Party apparatus depends on Central Committee headquarters for its power and looks to it for its orders; it cannot reassign resources or change the priorities set in Moscow, nor can it move ahead of them, except as an advocate. Peter Rutland, in a stimulating book, rightly points out that the power of the obkom is at best a palliative, relieving some of the worst consequences of verticalism but hardly overcoming them. In practice, Rutland observes, the local obkom "rushes from one crisis to another—with some of them being crises of their own making."[29] The power of the obkom, in sum, is greatest along the vertical grain, helping local directors to meet their targets, and weakest across it.

These descriptions fit exactly what we have seen of the Tiumen' obkom and its role in oil and gas policy. It is common for an obkom and its departments to specialize in the dominant activities of its jurisdiction, but the Tiumen' obkom goes further than most. Co-opted oil and gas men can be found on its staff at every level, beginning with the veteran first secretary, G. P. Bogomiakov, formerly an institute director in the oil industry. His long-time secretary for oil and gas, E. G. Al-

[27] In 1986 Gosplan Deputy Chairman Lalaiants stated in an interview that the powers of the Tiumen' office would be strengthened (*Sotsialisticheskaia industriia*, 24 Apr. 1986), but the following year the CIA's *Directory of Soviet Officials* still gave no new head for it.

[28] The best source is Jerry F. Hough's classic study, *The Soviet Prefects* (Cambridge, Mass.: Harvard University Press, 1969). The role of the obkom first secretaries as regional advocates is especially visible in their speeches at Party congresses.

[29] Rutland, *The Myth of the Plan* (La Salle, Ill.: Open Court, 1985), pp. 173–179. I have also benefited from the opportunity to read Peter Rutland's doctoral thesis, "The Role of the Soviet Communist Party in Economic Decision-Making" (University of York, Dept. of Sociology, 1987).

tunin, had previously headed the Tiumen' gas industry.[30] Even those officials who are "pure" Party apparatus men spend much of their time on oil and gas affairs, following the northward-moving wave of development.[31] As a result of such career-crossing and specialization, the traditional powers of the local Party apparatus are being exercised in Tiumen' by officials who have ample technical expertise and experience of the area—but who are therefore prone to share the industry's outlook and weaknesses.[32]

The Tiumen' obkom, despite its visibility and seeming power, has limited leverage over the ministries. As a former head of the industrial department of the Tiumen' obkom ruefully admitted, the Moscow offices of the ministries call the tune and the local Party organization does not have the weapons to enforce horizontal coordination over their resistance or their indifference.[33] The obkom has concentrated its attention on the oil and gas fields, pushing and shoving to try to ensure that the right equipment and people appear on the scene in the right sequence: roads and temporary housing first, then powerlines, then drillers. But it can hardly be said to have been successful. The roads and powerlines have seldom been in place by the time the drillers arrived, housing often takes the form of tents and primitive wagons, and the local Party has usually been helpless to do much about it, except to complain vigorously. The obkom has had even less success in improving life for the local towns: despite pressure and publicity, the Party authorities consistently failed to get MNP, MGP, and the other ministries to give higher priority to housing and basic urban services—at least, until the new General Secretary lent a hand in 1985.

Neither has the obkom been particularly effective in dealing with

[30] Altunin came in as secretary at the beginning of the Brezhnev campaign in 1978 but was dismissed in the spring of 1985, one of the many victims of a provincewide purge of the industry. *Sovetskaia Rossiia*, 20 Apr. 1985. He has since been replaced by V. Kitaev, whose background is unknown.

[31] A prominent example is E. F. Kozlov, currently the first secretary of the Novyi Urengoy city committee (*gorkom*), who headed the Nadym gorkom from 1972 to 1980 before being named to his present post in 1981. *Pravda*, 10 Feb. 1981 and 15 Oct. 1981.

[32] There are also prominent cases of movement in the other direction, such as Boris Shcherbina, the former Tiumen' obkom first secretary who rose to head MNGS and then to deputy chairman of the Council of Ministers, or the former obkom second secretary, Gennadii Shmal', who went on to become first deputy minister of MNGS. Shmal' worked in Tiumen' until 1982 (he is mentioned as second secretary in *Sovetskaia Rossiia*, 22 Dec. 1976, and *Sotsialisticheskaia industriia*, 3 Mar. 1978), when he was appointed deputy minister of MNGS (*Sotsialisticheskaia industriia*, 1 Sept. 1985).

[33] B. Trofimov, "Formirovanie tiumenskogo neftegazovogo kompleksa," *Planovoe khoziaistvo*, no. 9 (1981), and same, "Zadachi dal'neishego razvitiia neftegazovogo kompleksa v tiumenskoi oblasti," *Planovoe khoziaistvo*, no. 7 (1982), pp. 107–110.

problems arising outside the region, even though this is one area in which the cross-cutting Party structure is supposed to be able to help. For example, there has been little visible Party hand in alleviating the oil and gas industries' chronic problems with industrial support. The low priority given to the machine-building sector under Brezhnev was matched by the indifference of the Party authorities in areas like Baku and Sverdlovsk, where the oil and gas service industries are concentrated. (That may be changing, now that machine-building is once again a high-priority sector under Gorbachev.)

In the end, it is probably fair to say that the obkom did not try very hard. In the boom years of the early 1970s the local Party shared the oil industry's obsession with drilling and near-term output targets and did not appear to pay much more attention to infrastructural problems (let alone workers' housing and amenities) than the industry did; and in its personnel policy it rewarded or punished local oil men almost entirely for the oil they produced.[34] The obkom's own internal structure contributed to these lopsided priorities: as in most obkoms around the country, the Party's oversight functions are carried out by specialized secretaries and departments, who defend their assigned sectors jealously.[35] Thus the obkom secretary for oil and gas traditionally does not worry about housing, and the vertical structure of the ministries is reproduced inside the obkoms as well, just as it is in the Central Committee and in Gosplan in Moscow. Ultimately, of course, it is up to the first secretary to strike the balance, but Bogomiakov, taking his signals from Moscow, knew the oil output target came first.

Having shared in the credit for the Siberian miracle, then, the local Party has also shared in the blame for the bad times since. In 1984–1985 there was almost as substantial a purge of the obkom as of the local oil industry. How Bogomiakov himself managed to hang on to his job is a minor miracle, which may be explained by the presence of powerful former colleagues in the Council of Ministers, especially Boris Shcherbina, who was probably his patron from the beginning. It will be interesting to see how he handles the mixed signals now coming from Moscow to produce oil and gas but also to build housing, protect the environment, and promote democratization and *glasnost'*. These are not easy times for obkom secretaries.

There is one important exception to the obkom's general neglect of housing and infrastructure. As we have seen, there has been an ongoing battle over whether to bring in temporary workers or attempt to build a

[34] V. V. Kitaev, "Start posle finisha," *Ekonomicheskaia gazeta*, no. 2 (1987), p. 9.

[35] This phenomenon is described candidly in Anatolii Salutskii, "Svoi i chuzhie," *Pravda*, 21 Dec. 1986.

settled population. The Tiumen' Party apparatus has consistently been a strong advocate of the latter—a strange position, one might think, in view of its apparent inability to help the settlers. The explanation probably has to do with the obkom's other prominent role over the years, that of chief regional booster and tub-thumper for West Siberia. As we have seen, successive Tiumen' first secretaries have been promoting West Siberian oil and gas for nearly a quarter-century, initially in the face of skepticism and inertia from ministry officials, planners, and leaders in Moscow. More recently, when doubts began to spread about West Siberian oil reserves, the obkom never showed any uncertainty about the longer-term prospects. Arguing for a settled West Siberian population is consistent with this upbeat view of the region's future, and the Tiumen' Party apparatus made its points so loudly and consistently that it probably influenced the leaders' thinking in Moscow and led directly to Gorbachev's endorsement of the concept when he visited Tiumen' in 1985.

But we should note that the kind of Siberian development that men like Shcherbina and Bogomiakov advocate is not the balanced approach that the Siberian scientists in the Academy of Sciences in Novosibirsk would like. On the contrary, seen from Novosibirsk, the Tiumen' obkom is a threat to the real interests of the region, and it is clear in Moscow today that the alumni of Tiumen' have little in common with prominent Siberian reformers like Abel Aganbegian, Tat'iana Zaslavskaia, and the graduates of the Siberian Division of the Academy of Sciences at Akademgorodok.

In sum, the history of the Tiumen' obkom demonstrates how little power or inclination the local Party apparatus has to offset imbalances that originate in Moscow. Its most important roles in Brezhnev's energy policy were probably, first, as a loud member of the chorus that sang the West Siberian alternative throughout the 1960s and 1970s and, second, as the executor of Brezhnev's unbalanced policy priorities at the local level. In neither of these roles did the Party apparatus help to relieve the lack of horizontal integration, nor was it really expected to do so.

Targets, Incentives, and Plans

Overlapping the problems of systemic structure are those of process. The centrally managed economy generates far more targets than managers can meet. The incentive system encourages them to respond by giving priority to the targets that will preserve their jobs and their incomes, which usually means the gross output target or some functional equivalent to it. The result is imbalance, which must be reallocated through constant corrections at all levels of the system, which put still further pressure on managers. The system in theory is planned and predictable; in practice it is negotiated and fraught with risk and conflict for all the participants. In theory it concentrates control in the hands of the leaders and planners; in practice much of the control is dissipated, except for the handful of near-term targets that the leadership chooses to put first.

Ministers and managers have had fifty years of experience in working with the Soviet system of central management, and in many situations they have adjusted to its pathologies. An enterprise that has been in business for a long time, for example, is perfectly familiar to ministry officials, and its director will find it difficult to fool them, say, by understating output possibilities or overstating input requirements. By the same token, ministry officials may refrain from imposing plan increases that they know the enterprise cannot meet.[36]

But such mutual adjustment requires a stable and familiar setting. In the oil and gas fields of West Siberia, in contrast, production potential, performance, and costs have been unstable and uncertain, especially in the last decade. One would predict, therefore, that the classic dysfunctions of Soviet ministry-enterprise relations—unrealistic, changeable targets and administrative pressure from the ministry, distorted execution and fraudulent reporting in the field—would be present to an exceptional degree, and so they have been. One important result has been a flood of false, biased, and conflicting data. On two occasions—in 1975–1977 and in 1983–1985—such false reporting apparently caused Moscow to miss the signs of impending trouble, and when Gorbachev visited the Siberian oil region in the fall of 1985, he wagged his finger angrily at the oil men. But the temptation to cheat is built in to the system.

The atmosphere surrounding the machine-building enterprises that provide industrial support for the oil and gas campaigns has been similarly unclear and the demands on them equally unrealistic. They have been asked to double and triple gross output while simultaneously innovating and increasing productivity with obsolete plant and essentially unchanged resources. But here Moscow has only itself to blame for the results, because these old plants were only too well known. Machine-building managers have naturally responded with phony in-

[36] The classic work on managerial latitude is by Joseph Berliner, *Factory and Manager in the USSR* (Cambridge, Mass.: Harvard University Press, 1957). The possibility that managerial autonomy has been somewhat curtailed is raised by recent émigrés and is analyzed by Susan J. Linz, "Managerial Autonomy in Soviet Firms" (unpublished paper, February 1986).

novation, hidden price increases, and systematic misreporting. Manufacturers of Soviet producer goods enjoy a sellers' market, and the oil and gas industries, being especially desperate customers, are obliged to accept whatever the machine-building ministries give them. Here the Gorbachev reforms could make a difference: if new enterprises started manufacturing petroleum equipment and selling it through wholesale markets, as the reformers propose, and if the oil and gas ministries command their own hard-currency budgets to bring in competitive imports, they could improve their leverage. The balance of forces would then change sharply, but that is a long way away.

The net effect of these dysfunctions is to weaken further an already weak planning system. Soviet planners have come a long way since the fevered days of the First Five-Year Plan, when, as one of the founding fathers of Soviet central planning, the late economist S. G. Strumilin, acidly recalled, "The planners preferred to stand up for higher targets rather than sit for lower ones." (The Russian verb "to sit" means here "in prison or in a concentration camp.") In the energy sector, in particular, Soviet planners have made elaborate use of modeling, forecasting, and scenario building;[37] and in at least some instances these models have had direct influence as a basis for choosing among broad technological options (such as Siberian coal versus European nuclear power). But most plan targets are still arrived at through a combination of political directive, extrapolation "from the achieved level" (as the Soviet expression goes), and a large amount of plain horse trading. As five-year plans are translated into annual and monthly targets and assignments, the bargaining continues. Politicians change course, ministries plead poverty, unforeseen bottlenecks force readjustments—in short, as it goes along, the plan loses consistency and predictability. These faults are accentuated as political pressures rise.

In sum, the planning process, which is the command system's indispensable instrument of decisionmaking, fails to provide policymakers with a clear and integrated picture of the situations they face or to give them the means of making informed choices among competing objectives, strategies, and horizons. These faults are now widely acknowledged by Soviet economists and managers, together with their consequence: the targets are much influenced by whoever can shout the loudest. Hence the important role of conflict in decisionmaking, no less under Gorbachev than before him.

[37] For an elaboration of this point and some examples, see Leslie Dienes and Theodore Shabad, *The Soviet Energy System: Resource Use and Policies* (New York: Wiley and Sons, 1979); and Campbell, *Soviet Energy Technologies*, pp. 21–25.

The Role of Conflict among Institutions and Groups

In a system based on administrative rather than economic signaling, dominated by vertically organized giants only weakly coordinated in the field, conflict is bound to be the norm. In classic Stalinist administration, indeed, promoting conflict was a deliberate aim; whether consciously or not, Stalin exploited conflict to maximize the information flowing to him and hence his control. Multiplication of reporting agencies, proliferation of watchdogs, institutionalization of mutual suspicion, overlapping jurisdictions—these are characteristic features of Soviet administration to this day, no less under Gorbachev than under his predecessors.

Because there has been no top governing body for all energy matters, one would predict that in the energy sector the tendency toward conflict would be especially great. Moreover, since energy programs are expensive, risky, and uncertain,[38] interregional rather than local, and technical rather than ideological, the factors favoring conflict are many and those inhibiting it are few. Therefore, as a corollary to a systemic explanation of energy policy, one would predict that conflict is endemic in energy politics and strongly shapes the policy agenda and the subsequent execution of policy.

What we actually find in the energy sector is rather different. Conflict is indeed endemic, and interest groups and coalitions are strongly present, but their motives and interactions are more complex than a standard interest-group approach might predict. None of the main events in Soviet energy policy over the last fifteen years and none of its essential character can be explained as the result of battles among institutions determined to promote "their" fuel and to expand "their" turf and resources.

On the contrary, the energy ministries in our story behave like reluctant heroes, and expansion of their "market share" does not typically appear to interest them. While they defend their core missions, they are are not noticeably eager to enlarge them, and they typically lobby for lower targets, not higher ones. All the fuel ministries, for example, had to be prodded to move into Siberia. The main exception was the hydropower group within the Ministry of Power and Electrification, which expanded enthusiastically into Siberia in the 1960s because it was

[38] The conventional distinction between risk and uncertainty in decisionmaking literature is that there is risk where the odds are known or at least calculable, uncertainty where they are not. In the passage above, however, I mean uncertainty in the sense of uncertain information.

blocked in European Russia—in other words, to preserve its core mission.[39] Another exception was the gas industry in its early days, when it was striving to establish its independence from its former parent, MNP—in other words, also to establish its core mission.[40]

Thus ministries do fight, but their aims are typically negative and defensive, consisting of rear-guard actions to defend resources or bickering over who will bear the blame for shortcomings. The fuel ministries in West Siberia compete with one another in the field, stealing one another's manpower and maneuvering for preference from contractors. When the plan is not met, they point the finger at suppliers and support ministries, who point back. Even seemingly self-aggrandizing moves, when they occur, are usually defensive in essence, as when ministries develop their own construction or manufacturing operations to make up for other ministries' failure to provide them.

Where budgetary battles are concerned, the issue is more difficult to judge. One cannot doubt that ministries fight hard for their budgets, and their collective pressure makes centrally planned systems chronically unable to keep investment from running ahead of the plan. But such institutional and interest-group pressure fails to account for the main trends in energy investment during the period covered by this book. The big events in investment policy—the underspending on hydrocarbons before the mid-1970s, the acceleration in oil investment after 1977, the step-up in gas spending after 1980, the brief stabilization of oil investment after Brezhnev's death and its renewed acceleration in 1985—all of these are clearly traceable to the leaders' own priorities or to pressing policy needs, not to interest-group lobbying.

The real turf wars originate lower down. The aggressive policy entrepreneurs in the Soviet Union, vocal people with something to prove and careers to make, are to be found in the research institutes, the subunits of ministries, and the regions. Frequently their pet policies pit them against their own superiors. Thus we have seen the Siberian geologists enthusiastically defending oil prospects in north Tiumen' against a reluctant geological establishment, supporters of advanced oil-recovery techniques lobbying against a traditional ministerial preference for waterflooding, boosters of advanced gas pipeline concepts urging them on a risk-averse ministry leadership, and the promoters of rival gas-turbine-drive concepts doing battle. This combination of entrepreneurial enthusiasm and ministerial reluctance may account for the

[39] See Gustafson, *Reform in Soviet Politics*, ch. 7.

[40] Esfir Raykher, "Decision-Making in the Soviet Gas Industry" (Falls Church, Va.: Delphic Associates, 1988).

curious tendency, noted by Robert Campbell, for ministries to support a wide variety of research options but to make premature choices for scale-up and development, as though the ministries wished to end internal disputes and limit uncertainty by narrowing their options as quickly as possible.[41]

Policy entrepreneurs find allies outside their own ministries, in Gosplan, the State Committee for Science and Technology, the Academy of Sciences, regional authorities, or, if they are very successful, in the Central Committee and among the top leaders themselves. Thus, instead of battles among institutions, debates over energy policy more frequently involve coalitions that cut across institutional lines and whose main objective is to win the ear of influential leaders. The decision to break with the coal-and-nuclear strategy of the Tenth Five-Year Plan, for example, pitted a group consisting of Siberian economists and Party officials, the Oil and Gas Department of Gosplan, and the heavy industry staff of the Party Central Committee against the energy advisers to Prime Minister Kosygin, the energy research and development establishment in the Academy of Sciences, and the nuclear and coal promoters inside specialized institutes in the ministries of power and coal. The former group won the day when the oil and coal crisis of 1976–1977 discredited the policy of the latter and caused Brezhnev to listen to its recommendations.

One of the arts of courtier politics the world over is to win a sentence for one's pet project in a major speech by the top leader. Advocates for a high-voltage DC line from mine-mouth power plants in Kazakhstan to the center managed to win Brezhnev's endorsement in a speech to the Central Committee in 1979, while their competitors, backing coal liquefaction, made their way into Brezhnev's Party congress speech in 1981. More recently, the Siberian reformers did battle to win a line for their program in Gorbachev's 1985 energy speech in Tiumen'. But short of the General Secretary, lesser officials will do. Thus the campaign to plunge into tertiary oil recovery in the late 1970s drew support from the State Committee on Science and Technology and the leadership of Gosplan, even though sharply opposed by local oil men, with the leadership of the Oil Ministry appearing to take a neutral position. The advocates gained the support of Gosplan Chairman Baibakov in the mid-1970s, and more recently they appear to enjoy approval among higher leaders, notably Ligachev.

These examples may make it seem as though interest-group politics are crucial after all, but on closer examination it appears that what drove

[41] Campbell, *Soviet Energy Technologies*.

policy mainly was the perception of events in the field (for example, the Siberian reserves crisis and the poor performance of the coal industry) or the degree of "ripeness" of a proposed technology. Indeed, what DC transmission, coal liquefaction, and enhanced oil recovery all have in common is that, despite the leaders' endorsements, these technologies were not yet ready for implementation at the time their boosters were pushing them.

Conflict among regions illustrates the same point. The Siberian gas lobby shouted long and loud against reluctant planners, leaders, and ministers but to little avail until the middle and late 1970s. The reason was not opposition from other regions; one looks in vain for an anti-Siberian voice from other regions, even the Ukraine. In recent years only two leaders, Dolgikh and Ligachev, have made statements that could be interpreted as leaning toward the older oil regions and away from Siberia—and both had Siberian careers.

One reason policy advocates may command more media attention than policy influence is that they are usually divided among themselves, typically along several lines simultaneously. The Siberians are again the best example. There is no single "Siberian lobby"; instead, prominent Siberians are divided over competing priorities for the region—coal versus oil and gas, all-out energy development versus balanced development, permanent settlements versus fly-ins, and environmentalists versus advocates of maximum growth. If there has been a Siberian bias to Soviet energy policy in the last decade, it is certainly not because the Siberians are a united interest group.

It is possible that a more basic reason policy advocates are not more successful is that they have little incentive to develop coherent, unified positions, as they would have to do to win votes in a Western parliament. Instead, if the prize is to win the leader's ear, then we may have here a political equivalent of the "free rider" problem: policy courtiers have an incentive to break ranks with their fellows when they see an opportunity for influence.

The other striking feature of interest-group conflict in energy policy is that the issues at stake are not solely, or even primarily, the conventional ones of resources and turf. It is consistent with the defense-mindedness of the major agencies that they contend most over the issues of risk and horizon. In the next sections we shall see that the Soviet system speaks with two voices about these issues.

ATTITUDES TOWARD RISK AND UNCERTAINTY

Finding and developing energy is an inherently risky business. The only way to reduce this risk is through exploration, which buys information about potential future supplies; but exploration brings further risks, since it may fail or not yield enough information to pay for itself. That risk in turn can be reduced through technological innovation, but innovation is itself risky, since it too may fail or not pay for itself. This hierarchy of risks can be reduced by cutting the need for new supplies in the first place, that is, through conservation. But Soviet energy consumption patterns are deeply entrenched; to try to change them brings further risks.

Soviet attitudes and practices toward risk are worth a book in themselves. The general Western impression is that the Soviets are averse to taking risks, and Soviet writers themselves frequently agree. Leaders stick to standard approaches; managers resist innovation and bargain for easy targets; research and design institutes follow proven Western examples—the cumulative results of these familiar examples is a tendency toward risk-aversion in entire branches of industry and in the economy as a whole.

But the Soviet system also has more constructive ways of dealing with risk, of lessening its costs without paying the price of avoiding it altogether. As a general proposition, risk can be decoupled, displaced, or contained. The classic example of decoupling is the special laboratory for exploratory research, whose survival does not depend on near-term results. Imports of foreign technology are a way of displacing risks—make the foreign innovator bear the load. And finally, risk can be contained through temporizing strategies, such as fuel switching as a first stage of energy conservation, or through "end-run" solutions, such as the use of the turbodrill instead of the more demanding rotary-drill technique. Lastly, the Soviets have a time-honored, if costly, way of reducing risk: the mass campaign, which aims to overwhelm risk by sheer force of numbers.

The common feature of all these strategies is that one reduces risk by paying extra. The danger is always that one may pay too much (aptly enough, the Russian term for excessive risk-aversion, *perestrakhovka*, means exactly that: overinsurance). At the extreme, the risk-reducing strategy itself becomes a source of risk: the research laboratory can become divorced from reality; imports can make the country dependent and vulnerable; exploration can take resources away from development; fuel switching can become a substitute for conservation and the mass campaign a replacement for sound policy.

These risk-reducing strategies have agencies and constituencies to represent them, and consequently it is not correct to visualize the Soviet system as a whole as risk-averse. Rather, the choice of an appropriate policy on risk is itself a major policy issue, with forces arrayed on both sides. On balance, it is probably true that there is a net systemic bias in favor of caution, but not invariably, and the balance can be changed by the intervention of the leadership.

CONFLICT OVER COMPETING HORIZONS

Throughout this book we have seen two standards of rationality contend. The first is the voice of long-term wisdom; the other voice is that of short-term caution. Behind these two standards are competing views about the "right" horizon.

The choice of a horizon is always a fundamental issue in any system. Sometimes the issue is simply, "How far into the future should we look?" The more difficult political issue is, "How shall we weigh future costs and benefits against those of today?" This is what economists call the issue of the "social rate of time preference," that is, the rate at which a society or state discounts tomorrow's costs and benefits. In a market-based system, interest rates provide a rough yardstick of society's preferences, which governments must at least consider even if they then choose to depart from it. But Soviet decisionmakers are on their own, and the result is more nearly a bargained decision.

Different Soviet agencies have different built-in horizons, and the voice of the long term, as we have seen, is well represented. The USSR Academy of Sciences, the State Committee on Science and Technology, the major energy ministries, and Gosplan all have offices and research institutes specializing in long-term energy policy. This is the voice that shaped the Soviet response to the first world oil shock of the early 1970s, encouraging Kosygin to support a far-seeing program oriented toward coal and nuclear power in the Tenth Plan. The same voice caused Brezhnev, in the midst of the transition to a big gas policy at the end of the 1970s, to convene the conservation-oriented commission that produced the energy program of 1983. This voice had the ear of Andropov when it argued for a switch to conservation, and its influence over Gorbachev's thinking, if not yet over his allocation decisions, is obvious.

Over the last fifteen years the long-term voice has not only grown louder, but it has also become more articulate. A steady accumulation of facts and studies about energy, on such topics as energy cost trends, concrete policy options, and the results of past policies, has enabled the spokesmen for the long term to state their case more persuasively and in greater detail than they could a decade ago. Soviet energy experts have become more skilled in economic analysis and modeling, and the leaders are more aware of their own need for concrete policy advice. As a consequence, the overall long-term design of Soviet energy policy, as expressed in the energy program of 1984, is far superior to the unrealistic program of the mid-1970s, and the revisions introduced in 1988 and after represent still further improvement.

But in the month-to-month and year-to-year planning and decision-making that spell out actual policy, the voice of the near term is louder, and in annual target setting and funding decisions it has been overwhelming. The output targets are relentlessly ratcheted upward, and the ministerial machinery moves into gear to execute them. Moreover, the institutions that are supposed to represent the long horizon sometimes depend on financing from agencies geared toward the short. Thus it is widely charged (by Gorbachev himself among others) that the research and development apparatus inside the ministries of oil and gas has abdicated its job of looking out for long-range issues. But the clearest illustration is the Ministry of Geology, whose drilling program is largely financed out of the capital budgets of MNP and MGP. Thus Mingeo, which is supposed to represent the long-horizon, risk-taking end of the oil and gas business, is constrained by poor funding and support from Gosplan, by its dependence on MGP and MNP for capital for drilling, by the technological conservatism of the ministries that supply it, and by the prevailing system of incentives, all of which cause Mingeo, like other agencies, to emphasize near-term measures of performance, such as meters drilled, over more significant criteria. In West Siberia these factors combined to make the geologists complacent and unenterprising, a major factor in the crisis of 1977, and more recently they account for the geologists' continued emphasis on downstream exploration.

Different agencies and coalitions, in sum, represent different attitudes toward risk and different choices of horizon. These issues, rather than direct competition for turf and resources, have generated much of the conflict that has shaped Soviet energy policy over the last decade. Compared to Western systems that have at least a market yardstick by which to measure society's preferences for risk and horizon, the Soviet system appears divided between institutions that favor high-risk and long-horizon choices, frequently unrealistically so, and those that favor near-term, risk-averse strategies instead. One of the system's difficulties is that it lacks mechanisms for reconciling these two levels. Left to itself, the system tends toward one and then toward the other, oscillating for example between wish-list five-year plans and crash-campaign annual ones. The result is a special burden on the political leadership, which must attempt to balance between the two tendencies, but without any ready guide to help pick the right balance point.

The Case for a Systemic Explanation of the Energy Crisis

Many of the systemic features described in this section we think of as "characteristically Soviet," but they are not the only choices of which the system is capable. What appears to be systemic is often in fact the product of history, policy priorities, and the technological characteristics of the energy sector. Alternative designs are available to the leaders, even within the general framework of the command economy.

Consider first the organization of the fuel ministries. The Soviet system of large ministries organized around gas, oil, coal, and nuclear power reproduces a familiar Soviet pattern. But the fact that it endures reflects partly the continued dominance of supply over demand in Soviet energy policy. Soviet leaders could perfectly well create a Ministry of Energy if they chose to do so; indeed, as they gradually focus on problems of consumption, they are moving in that direction (the Russian Federation, for example, already has a Ministry of Energy, and the USSR Council of Ministers has its new Energy Bureau).

Similarly, Soviet energy production should lend itself easily to a more horizontally integrated, regional approach once the leaders seriously try to apply it. Until recently, new Soviet energy sources have tended to occur in large fields in virgin areas. This led to a kind of leapfrogging pattern of development in which the "energy now, housing and roads later" campaign approach, aimed at developing the fattest targets as fast as possible, was a natural and not necessarily irrational temptation. But if henceforth most new discoveries are located at the edges of established provinces, specialized construction agencies based on a regional principle are perfectly within Soviet capabilities; and indeed, the State Construction Committee has recently been reorganized on that basis.

The characteristic underpricing of energy in the Soviet system reflects not only a longstanding neglect of the full costs of natural resources but also the very rapid increase in fuel costs in the last fifteen years, to which the price system has been slow to adjust. Yet the traditional Soviet system is not entirely incapable of price discipline—witness the determined and successful efforts of the power industry over decades to reduce the cost of producing electricity.

The low technological level and poor industrial support characteristic of the Soviet oil, gas, and coal industries are likewise the product, at least in part, of a specific historical setting: until the beginning of the 1970s, the sector's requirements for advanced technology were low, and its needs for industrial support were straightforward. It is undoubtedly true that the Soviet system has special difficulties in improving innovation and interbranch supply, but one should bear in mind that these problems are also very largely due to the leaders' longstanding bias in favor of military programs. This bias is a core feature of the Stalinist strategy but not necessarily of the command economy per se.

These examples illustrate that, in fact, the features of energy policy that we think of as systemic represent policy choices among variants that the command system has available. There is a danger, then, of labeling every action or choice as "systemic," which produces the impression that any observed faults in policy are somehow foreordained. Even the Soviet system offers choices, and this is where the role of leadership comes in, as the next section will argue.

Nevertheless, beyond the features that can be adjusted are others that are more properly the core characteristics of the system. One of these is the tension between political control and the conditions required for economic efficiency, such as greater reliance on local decisionmakers and decentralized economic signals. The second is the lack of benchmarks, such as those provided automatically by a market system, for establishing smooth trade-offs between the present and the future and for dealing with risk and uncertainty. Ultimately, the systemic features we have described in this section are symptoms of problems such as these. But it is important to see how they interact with political choices. This brings us back to the question of leadership.

The Role of Leadership

The actual course of policy depends on how vigorously the leaders act to offset the system's biases and tendencies, or, if they cannot, to alter the system itself. Gorbachev's criticism of Brezhnev is that he did neither and that, as a result, the country drifted into crisis.

Just what was the role of Brezhnev's leadership? We are concerned specifically with the following questions: Why did the Soviet leaders appear unaware until late 1977 that the energy situation was deteriorating, despite what at least some of their own experts were telling them? Once they were confronted with the problem, why did they not design and implement a more balanced response? As the costs of their policy mounted, why did they not change course? Why was the rhetoric of their energy policy so far removed from reality? Why were the domestic and foreign sides of energy policy so poorly matched? If the system imparts the biases described in the first part of this chapter, why did the leaders fail to take stronger, sounder, and speedier steps to combat them?

There are several possible explanations: The leaders may have been divided, incompetent, unable to learn, or engaged by other priorities.

They may have perceived no clear or feasible alternatives. Or, finally, the burden imposed by the system may be so great that it overwhelms and exhausts its leaders.

A Divided Leadership?

One of the most familiar themes in Western writing about the Soviet system is that policymaking is dominated by power politics, because the bodies that make policy are the same ones through which politicians build power and because power in Soviet politics is fluid and shifting and must forever be guarded and displayed. As Zbigniew Brzezinski wrote in the early 1960s, "Policy-making in the Soviet Union . . . is one aspect of the struggle for power and is absorbed into it. . . . Policy proposals are forever involved in (if not always motivated by) the struggle for or the consolidation of personal power."[42] More recent writers have amended this picture by drawing a careful distinction between power and authority, but their analysis of the situation is not essentially different: a Soviet politician's authority, in the absence of electoral or constitutional mandate, rests mainly on his reputation as a problem solver and consensus builder.[43] Hence, although no politician makes policy without an eye to his power and authority, the concerns of Soviet politicians in policymaking remain uniquely dominated by their need to attend ceaselessly to their standing.

At first glance, energy policy should be the classic illustration of these propositions. Not only has energy been a crucial issue—the most disruptive factor, we have argued, in Soviet resource allocation over the last ten years—but it has been filled with conflict at every level. There has been plenty of malperformance to criticize, and there have been two major policy alternatives and a host of lesser ones for political rivals to quarrel over. Finally, since energy continues to be the single most important claimant of any increments in the leaders' resources, it is a policy issue that cannot be ducked. With Moscow's thoughts from the mid-1970s constantly focused on Brezhnev's decline and then on three successions in less than three years, how could energy have failed to be a political battleground?

For a brief period, it was. From the mid-1970s, as the performance of the economy deteriorated, Brezhnev faced mounting threats to his authority and his program. He reacted with new initiatives in a wide

[42] Zbigniew Brzezinski and Samuel P. Huntington, *Political Power: USA/USSR* (New York: Macmillan, 1963), pp. 191–192.

[43] George Breslauer, *Khrushchev and Brezhnev as Leaders: Building Authority in Soviet Politics* (London: Allen and Unwin, 1982).

range of policies—defense,[44] manpower,[45] agriculture, and, above all, energy. It was during this period, as we have seen, that Brezhnev took personal control of energy policy, setting aside the long-range coal-and-nuclear program adopted in 1975–1976 and launching an all-out oil offensive in West Siberia. Brezhnev remained on the offensive in energy policy to the end of his life, expanding the oil campaign in 1980–1981 to include gas as well. Contrary to a widespread view in the West at the time that the Kremlin was paralyzed and adrift, closer examination in retrospect shows clearly that the General Secretary—or at any rate, his staff—remained capable of making policy initiatives very nearly to the end, if mainly in speeches rather than actions. On issue after issue he co-opted the rhetoric of his critics, so much so that passages of Brezhnev's later speeches sound eerily like Gorbachev's.

This flurry of activity was directed in part at Kosygin, who re-emerged briefly as a critic of Brezhnev's policies in his last years. But as George Breslauer observes, Kosygin was not personally challenging Brezhnev's leadership. Brezhnev's precedence had been settled a decade before, and by the late 1970s Kosygin was a sick man with no political ambitions.[46] Rather, in a variety of ways Kosygin was questioning Brezhnev's effectiveness as a problem solver. In those circumstances, Brezhnev may have taken some comfort from the energy case, because there it was Kosygin's problem solving that had gone wrong. As coal production collapsed, nuclear construction stagnated, and oil consumption soared ahead of the plan, it was plain that Kosygin had listened to the wrong advice and had focused on the wrong problem. Brezhnev could argue that his own West Siberian oil program made much more short-term sense. Politically, it was effective because it was an eye-catching show of action, and for the time being it worked.[47] But the moderate revival of competition with Kosygin was only a minor spur to Brezhnev; his main concern was to insure himself and his authority against the much greater threat that an energy shortage would have represented. This was clear in 1980–1981. By that time Kosygin was dead, but Brezhnev embraced the West Siberian energy policy more enthusiastically than ever with the launching of the gas campaign.

[44] Bruce Parrott, "Political Change and Soviet Civil-Military Relations," in Timothy J. Colton and Thane Gustafson, eds., *Soviet Soldiers and the State: Civil-Military Relations from Brezhnev to Gorbachev* (forthcoming). See also Jeremy R. Azrael, *The Soviet Civilian Leadership and the Military High Command, 1976–1986*, R-3521-AF (Santa Monica, Calif.: Rand Corporation, 1987).

[45] Hauslohner, "Managing the Soviet Labor Market," esp. ch. 5.

[46] Breslauer, *Khrushchev and Brezhnev*, p. 229.

[47] Hauslohner makes the same point about Brezhnev's social policies in "Managing the Soviet Labor Market," pp. 452ff.

This last point, I think, is the main reason energy policy did not become a political issue in the three post-Brezhnev successions—at least, there is no evidence of direct disagreement over energy or energy investment among the various contenders for power, whereas on other issues the competition was fierce. Andropov does seem to have curbed the growth of oil investment in 1983–1984 and ordered the power industry to get down to business about switching from oil to gas. This major decision implied that Brezhnev's supply-side energy policy had aroused much criticism inside the elite in his final years (although Brezhnev, true to form, blunted it by including conservation in his speeches). Under Chernenko oil investment began to grow again, and we have noted the signs of disagreement in the handling of the publication of the energy program in 1983–1984, as well as indications that figures such as Dolgikh and Baibakov were reluctant to let oil output decline. But this hardly means that oil-eaters were arrayed against conservationists in the battle for the succession. Chernenko did not change Andropov's economic course (although, to be sure, Chernenko's hands never really grasped the wheel). His renewed spending on oil was mainly due to the sudden deterioration of output in the field in 1984; had Andropov lived, he might well have done the same, just as Gorbachev has since.

Similarly, there is no evidence that the role of energy exports in foreign economic policy became an issue of power or authority during the last Brezhnev years or that Soviet export policy was driven by conflict or competition among the leaders. Rather, this was another case in which Brezhnev tried to protect his authority at the end by making himself the spokesman of Soviet resentment (which he undoubtedly shared) against outside economic pressure and disappointment over the meager benefits of East-West trade, a stance that subsequent leaders have maintained. There have been disagreements over specifics, but that is something else. Thus the Soviet leaders hesitated over the East-West gas pipeline in 1980 and, subsequently, over the right mix and volume of gas and oil exports. We may also be sure that there were lively discussions at Politburo meetings of such issues as the import of Western equipment and machinery, the danger of dependence on the West, the proper response to the American pipeline embargo of 1981–1982, and oil export policy after oil prices collapsed in 1986. But these show no sign of having been politically divisive.

Why has so important a policy issue as energy not become a political issue? Part of the explanation is the exceptional nature of the three successions of 1982–1985. Unlike previous occasions, there were no clear-cut duumvirates or triumvirates of rivals looking for policy issues to exploit. The losers—Chernenko in 1982 and Romanov and Grishin in 1985—lost so quickly that there was barely a fight. If there were policy issues involved, they hardly came to the surface.

But the absence of political competition over energy may also be due in part to the existence of an ironic double consensus: a general agreement that the hydrocarbon-centered, supply-side policy must eventually change, combined with a lack of viable near-term alternatives over which political competition might spark. In the mid-1970s the advocates of the coal-and-nuclear future briefly succeeded in writing their positions into the official agenda. But events proved their advice so ill timed that from 1978 on there could be no basic disagreement among the leaders that oil and gas had to come first and that big coal was not ready. It was only in 1983–1984 that the energy program provided the beginnings of a practical policy map, but even now policymakers lack detailed data and guidelines to implement a sound conservation program. From day to day the hydrocarbon policy must appear to the leaders as indispensable as ever.

One is tempted to add to these points that the Soviet political system itself may have evolved somewhat toward a greater separation of policymaking from power politics. The roles of the General Secretary and the Central Committee staff have become more institutionalized and routinized than they were a generation ago, in practice and habit if not in formal writ. Policy debate on most economic and technical issues has become more open, more detailed, and more "secular" in recent decades, and on such questions as oil production and fuel switching one did not have to wait for the age of *glasnost'* to see printed views that disagreed openly with the leaders' policy without seeming to challenge their authority.

Might energy become a power issue under Gorbachev? It has long been apparent that there are two conflicting tendencies among the reformers. Overdrawing only slightly, one might label them the "machine builders" and the "economists." The former stress the modernization of Soviet industry, particularly the machine-building sector, as the main key to success; their model is the "Leningrad-90" program. The economists emphasize the importance of reform and consumer welfare as the only effective means of raising labor productivity. The first is essentially a painted-over supply-side approach, the second a demand-side approach.

But if this difference in approaches becomes a line of cleavage in a power struggle in the Politburo, the two groups would find little to disagree over in energy policy. The machine builders want capital for machinery; the only way to get it is through conservation. The economists want energy efficiency; the only way to get it is through industrial modernization. Both sides want safety, and therefore neither wants a collapse in energy production. One would predict that the same essential double consensus will continue to prevail—and this, indeed, may be one reason Soviet energy policy continues to evolve slowly.

The dismissal of V. I. Dolgikh in the fall of 1988 suggests that energy policy may have become entangled in a wider battle between reformers and conservatives after Gorbachev's first three years, but for indirect reasons. Dolgikh, as we have seen, stood for the Brezhnev energy policy, but as secretary for heavy industry he was probably also unenthusiastic about Gorbachev's plans to reallocate investment toward the consumer sector in the next five-year plan and to curtail the Secretariat's role in overseeing the economy. Thus on balance there is still no particular sign that energy has become a power issue dividing the Gorbachev Politburo, unlike, say, *glasnost'*.

To return now to Brezhnev and the role of leadership: in seizing upon the energy issue in the mid-1970s Brezhnev was trying to reassert his authority in response to the bad news from the oil fields but also in reaction to mounting criticism from Kosygin and elsewhere (including, it would seem, the CIA's famous oil reports). Given the circumstances, Brezhnev could only turn to the one main alternative available—the West Siberian option—and seek to make his response as eye-catching as possible. That dictated the broad strategy of the Brezhnevian policy. But to explain how that strategy was spelled out, one must look for answers in Brezhnev's character as a leader. Here we explore three aspects: competition among Brezhnev's own objectives; his attitudes toward risk and uncertainty; and finally, his capacity to seek and act on new information and alternatives.

The Character of the Brezhnev Leadership

The balance sheet of the Brezhnev era has been difficult for scholars to draw. His policies were an ambiguous, frequently incongruent mixture of innovation and conservatism, of plan and improvisation, and of farsightedness and myopia. Timothy Colton describes "the three faces of Brezhnevism"—simultaneously conservative, reactionary, and timidly reformist.[48] But the Brezhnev that Soviet posterity is likely to remember is the ineffectual figure Gorbachev describes in his speeches, the man under whom "burning issues were allowed to remain unresolved for decades."[49]

Gorbachev's criticism does not quite do Brezhnev justice. Brezhnev was more ambitious in his aims than we tend to remember now; in

[48] Timothy J. Colton, *The Dilemma of Reform in the Soviet Union*, 2nd ed. (New York: Council on Foreign Relations, 1986), p. 11.

[49] Speech in Krasnodar, *Pravda*, 20 Sept. 1986.

many ways, he was attempting to address the missing revolutions of the first Soviet half-century—in agriculture, consumer welfare, technology, and foreign trade—while simultaneously preserving the Stalinist approach and priorities essentially intact. During the first half of Brezhnev's rule, roughly from 1965 to 1975, the leadership appeared to make headway. The program to modernize agriculture by "industrializing the countryside" brought initially impressive results. Military spending grew steadily and Soviet forces were expanded and reequipped. Increasingly aware of deep-seated problems with technological innovation, the leadership experimented with new approaches (many of which, such as science and production complexes, are now being expanded under Gorbachev). Foreign trade grew as never before.

With such a program Brezhnev can hardly be faulted for timidity, risk-aversion, or shortsightedness. On the contrary, his agricultural policy can be criticized as excessively long-range and risky. His central strategy—to industrialize the countryside while retaining the traditional management system—denied him the quick gains in productivity that Kosygin hoped for by overhauling the incentive system and tied him to a technological transformation that was bound to take decades. He was undoubtedly overoptimistic; and in the final years he tried half-heartedly to combine technology with economic experimentation. But the point is that his policy did not lack vision or courage—even if it stayed within traditional lines.

Brezhnev's other major life work—his defense policy—was similarly long-range and ambitious. From the time he first supervised military-industrial affairs as a Party secretary in the mid-1950s to his death a quarter-century later, Brezhnev presided over a vast expansion in the missions of the Soviet military, aimed not only at attaining strategic parity with the United States but also at projecting conventional Soviet power across the globe. He led an impressive modernization of Soviet military-industrial design and management, matching American technological superiority with new generations of advanced weapons, although again using largely traditional approaches.[50] One may argue that behind these venturesome and visionary-seeming policies Brezhnev's approach to the modern world was ultimately shortsighted and fearful, based on a largely military conception of national security and diplomacy. Nevertheless, to implement it he was capable of looking far and taking chances.

After the mid-1970s the economy faltered and the leadership was

[50] Gustafson, "Responses of the Soviet Military and the Military-Industrial Sector to Technological Challenge in Weapons Design, Development, and Procurement, 1965–1985," in Colton and Gustafson, eds., *Soviet Soldiers and the State*.

thrown on the defensive; none of the major programs begun during the first half of Brezhnev's rule worked during the second. Yet Brezhnev stuck doggedly to his initial priorities, and this very persistence undoubtedly worsened the downturn of the second half, as Brezhnev fought to keep the initiative, to salvage his authority, and to respond to crisis. Agricultural investment retained its high priority; indeed, after the launching of the food program in May 1982 it was higher than ever. The share of resources flowing to the military and the military-industrial sector did not decline.[51] To pay for these programs, Brezhnev allowed the growth of industrial investment to slacken, as he had consistently since the mid-1960s, a strategy that prepared further trouble. Lastly, as we have seen, the unexpected energy crisis absorbed most of the capital going to industry.

Brezhnev must have died a disappointed but also a deeply puzzled man. Why had things gone so badly wrong? His whole experience up to the mid-1970s gave him no reason to doubt that the Stalinist system would continue to be the immense success that it had been for a half-century, provided only that one attend to its imbalances and excesses. He stuck to traditional structures and procedures, not out of inertia or fear, but out of what he would have regarded as a responsible conservatism.[52] The model he defended so stubbornly was not a failure in his eyes but a lifelong success, and his approach to the programs he pursued must have seemed to him so obviously the right one—he had, after all, Khrushchev's counterexample to prove it—that its failure must have baffled him.

The result was a string of ironies. Striving to redress the principal imbalances in the Stalinist legacy while simultaneously maintaining Stalin's unconditional priority for the military, Brezhnev threw the industrial system into disarray. Trying to protect long-range programs of modernization in weaponry and agriculture, Brezhnev forced major sectors such as transportation, energy, machine building, and construction into a pattern of short-focus expedients. Attempting to assure national security through armed strength and to protect his programs through a limited opening to the world economy, Brezhnev saw both objectives miscarry, producing insecurity instead. And above all, aiming to fill in the missing revolutions of the past, Brezhnev neglected the new industrial revolution that was upon him.

Against this background some of the likely reasons for the style of the Brezhnev energy program become clearer. For Brezhnev the oil emer-

[51] Robert W. Campbell, "Resource Stringency and the Civilian-Military Resource Allocation," in Colton and Gustafson, eds., *Soviet Soldiers and the State*.

[52] Hauslohner "Managing the Soviet Labor Market," reaches similar conclusions about Brezhnev's social policies.

gency of 1977 must have been an especially unwelcome intruder. From 1977 to 1982 he had no choice but to take emergency action to head off a severe hydrocarbon shortage, both to save the plan and to save his authority. But the character of the oil and gas campaigns—unbalanced, shortsighted, and risk-averse—was at least partly due to Brezhnev's determination to prevent the oil emergency from wrecking his two top programs. Likewise, the modest use of foreign technology in the oil and gas sectors, though the product of a complex mix of motives, was at least partly associated with Brezhnev's determination to use his limited supplies of hard currency for his higher priorities.

The Brezhnev leadership faced risk and horizon in energy policy with ambivalence and inconsistency. In some instances, the approach was that of conservative, near-term risk reduction—the prime cases being the steps taken to ensure the success of the pipeline-building campaign in the early 1980s and the sharp increase in development drilling in West Siberia in 1977–1980. On the other hand, Soviet decisionmakers under Brezhnev consistently "underpurchased" risk-reducing options such as oil exploration and Western oil technology. In some cases they needlessly increased their exposure to risk by committing themselves prematurely to insufficiently proven technological choices, such as enhanced oil recovery and coal by wire. But the most important example of a flawed approach to risk can be seen in the leaders' overall policy design: they consistently ducked the risks of a demand-oriented strategy while simultaneously attempting to smother the risks of a supply-side strategy by the campaign method. Only since 1983, as we have seen, have the Soviets begun tackling the lower-risk end of the demand side by focusing on fuel switching.

One may object that Brezhnev could have served his larger goals more effectively through a policy of conservation. But here Brezhnev appeared to doubt the capacities of his system. No matter how strongly he praised conservation in his speeches, he never appeared to believe the system could be trusted to produce it. His policies continually stressed expansion of supply over rationalization of demand, whether of crops, steel, water, or energy. Ambitious in his aims, Brezhnev had learned from Khrushchev's misadventures to be cautious in his means. The net result was a policy of avoiding risk in the near term at the cost of increasing longer-term dangers.

Capacity for Learning and Adaptation

Faced with mounting troubles, was the Brezhnev leadership able to learn and adapt? The first prerequisites for learning are adequate information and advice. These improved greatly during Brezhnev's two decades. Many new fields of knowledge, previously neglected or despised under Stalin and Khrushchev, gained recognition and official standing, particularly in the life and social sciences.[53] The quantity and quality of information mobilized and exchanged improved steadily, and economic analysis and research gained strength. Restraints on public discussion of many technical policy issues relaxed, while the range of subjects that could be treated as safely "technical" (as opposed to "political" or "ideological") broadened. The result was a striking improvement in the sophistication of published policy analysis, and it is safe to surmise that the quality of unpublished, "inside" analysis improved correspondingly.

Faced with more complex policy problems, more diverse objectives, and more subtle and yet intractable constraints than its predecessors, the Brezhnev leadership encouraged the growth of advisory institutions and mechanisms. The quality of participation by technical experts in policymaking, as measured by the apparent timeliness of their advice and their level of access to leaders, rose sharply.[54] All this was true in the energy field in particular.

Did the leaders listen? On the most general level of broad concepts, they clearly did. Brezhnevian rhetoric over the years incorporated one fashionable notion after another—cybernetics, the computer revolution, the latest management schemes, "intensification" and energy conservation, environmentalism, the international division of labor, and many more.

But when it came to designing policies, the Brezhnev generation stuck close to its Stalinist experience. Most of the major initiatives of the Brezhnev period—whether in energy, agriculture, technology policy, or computerization of planning and management—took the form of Bolshevik campaigns, hastily conceived and prepared, relying heavily on massive funding and administrative pressure, inadequately supported by facts or analysis. New ideas were usually incorporated in their most conservative form, that is, centralizing and technocratic, while potentially radical elements were removed. When resistance was encountered, new ideas were quietly confined to minor experiments and isolated cases; or, if the leaders adopted them, the new ideas soon came to resemble the old. Finally, implementation came in extremes—either timid experimentation in one or two places or mass campaigns with inadequate preparation.

[53] For illustrations from sociology, economics, agricultural science, genetics and biology, management sciences, and others, see Gustafson, *Reform in Soviet Politics*, ch. 6. The best case studies are Peter H. Solomon, Jr., *Soviet Criminologists and Criminal Policy*, and Peter Hauslohner's study of manpower policy, "Managing the Soviet Labor Market."

[54] The most systematic discussion of this process is in Solomon, *Soviet Criminologists*.

What was new under Brezhnev, however, was that, when the disappointing returns from these policies started to roll in, journalists, academic specialists, and even officials criticized them far more freely than would have been imaginable under Stalin or even Khrushchev. In some cases, these criticisms clearly influenced the further development of policy.

Agriculture is a case in point. Brezhnev's agricultural policy was itself the product of collective learning under Khrushchev, which eventually (if slowly) led to a consensus that only massive investment in the countryside could produce a strong agricultural sector.[55] As initially designed, Brezhnev's agricultural policy focused on modernizing the fields, chiefly through reclamation, mechanization, and expanded production of fertilizers and agricultural chemicals. As the 1970s went on, the leaders realized that they had to look beyond the fields to the farm as a whole (storage, electrification, buildings) and finally beyond the farm itself to the entire chain of agricultural production (rural transportation, food processing and preservation, marketing). The scope of the agricultural program steadily broadened until finally, at the end of Brezhnev's life, the leaders had been brought to consider the whole food complex. Gorbachev's food policy, as so much else in his program, is the culmination of a twenty-year evolution.

In energy policy, likewise, we have witnessed the process of "central probing" by which advisers, planners, and leaders first confronted the long-term problems of energy supply, then moved gradually toward a more sophisticated, demand-oriented view of the energy problem, and then finally to the incorporation of energy conservation in an overall strategy of resource use and a restructuring of the country's resource-using base. But in these as in other Brezhnev policies, the evolution can best be described as schizophrenic. Technical advisors learned and adapted faster than planners or leaders, and the programs evolved much slower than the advice. On the whole, it is fair to say that the essence of the Brezhnevian approach to policy did not change anywhere.

There are two ways to enhance the speed of a learning process. First, learning can take place quickly when objectives do not conflict or compete, thus sparing the decisionmakers painful review or reranking of their goals. Second, learning proceeds most rapidly when coalitions inside an organization or group are fluid, more slowly when they are stable or frozen. Each of these points leads to a hypothesis about learning during the Brezhnev period: the major objectives of Brezhnevian

[55] See Werner G. Hahn, *The Politics of Soviet Agriculture, 1960–1970* (Baltimore: Johns Hopkins University Press, 1972).

economic policy could be summed up in three clusters: "efficiency," "safety," and "control." The Brezhnevian pattern of adaptation and learning can be explained, therefore, by the degree to which these objectives were in conflict or in harmony within a given policy. When a proposed policy idea appeared to serve all three objectives, it was likely to be embraced with enthusiasm. Hence the extraordinary receptiveness of the Soviet leadership to cybernetics, systems theories, and schemes for centralized computerization in the decade from 1965 to 1975.[56] In such cases, one can speak of "overlearning" among the Soviet elite, a paradoxical behavior that, in the past, has been just as characteristic of Soviet decisionmaking as resistance to learning, producing familiar fads and campaigns.

The hypothesis suggested by the second point above is that learning among the Soviet elite proceeds fastest not at the beginning or the height of a General Secretary's reign but at the end, when his health or power are ebbing. That is when would-be successors begin forming coalitions, ambitious advisers and managers jockey for patrons, competing policy options are debated, and the lessons of the closing period are drawn. Even as official policy innovation slows down or stops, elite learning behind the scenes accelerates. Thus one can speak of "*perestroika* before *perestroika*."

This process of *fin-de-regne* elite learning could be clearly seen in Khrushchev's last years, when the main lines of post-1965 agricultural and defense policy were formed. George Breslauer observes that, by the time they overthrew Khrushchev, his successors had already undergone a kind of negative learning as a result of Khrushchev's "hare-brained schemes," which produced a sharp improvement in the elite's state of knowledge about its own system, about what would work and what would not: "This enabled many of them to rationalize the rejection of decentralization in favor of a period of experimentation with efforts to improve the command economy by reducing the level of pressure, rationalizing jurisdictions and information flows within the bureaucracy, allowing for a period of administrative stability."[57]

The same pattern was apparent during Brezhnev's decline and the following successions. The entire panoply of Gorbachev's ideas can be found in embryo in Soviet newspapers and articles, *samizdat* publications, and even Brezhnev's speeches. Key policy decisions, ranging

[56] See William K. McHenry, "The Absorption of Computerized Management Information Systems in Soviet Enterprises" (Ph.D. diss., University of Arizona, 1985).

[57] Breslauer, *Khrushchev and Brezhnev*, pp. 273–274.

from the cancellation of the river-diversion projects[58] and the slowdown of the Baikal-Amur Railroad to Gorbachev's cautious policies toward the Third World and naval power projection, can be traced as they evolved in Soviet discussions from the mid-1970s on. In energy policy, in particular, we have seen the gradual turning of attention to conservation. What Brezhnev's learning seemed to conclude was that the goals of safety, efficiency, and control could not be served simultaneously, and therefore one should stay with safety and control. The single most striking characteristic of the Gorbachev leadership, in contrast, is its apparent willingness to trade a measure of safety and control in exchange for gains in efficiency.

Conclusion

The broad answer suggested by this section is that the Brezhnev leadership, rather than offsetting the biases and tendencies imparted by the system, aggravated them instead, not because of conflict within the leadership but because of the character of Brezhnev as a leader. There are three periods to consider. The case is least clear for the initial period, from 1970 to 1977. The energy crisis in the West focused Soviet attention on energy issues; advisory groups formulated plans for a long-term, coal-and-nuclear future; and by 1975–1976 the leaders must have thought they had done their job of setting policy. If there was a failure of policy, they might have argued, it was due to the highly complex and technical nature of the issues, the uncertainty of the data, and conflicting signals from the experts.

Yet it is hard to resist the conclusion that during this critical initial period the leadership was complacent, for they would have seen strong signs of danger if they had cared to look. The older oil-producing regions had weakened dramatically during the first half of the 1970s; Siberian oil output depended on a handful of fields that were already being pushed beyond their original planned maximums; and oil consumption was growing fast. The problems of the coal industry were well known, as were the constraints on gas transmission. These facts were familiar to the leaders: they were being published, discussed at meetings that leaders attended, and examined in high-level reports to them.

If the bad news had little impact until 1977, it was probably for several reasons. After 1973–1974 the high optimism of the first half of the Brezhnev period was already beginning to disappear. Problems

[58] See Gustafson, *Reform in Soviet Politics*, ch. 5.

were looming all around, in agriculture, in technology, in consumer welfare, and in foreign policy. Energy must have seemed a blessed exception, one of the few sectors in which the main news—continued rapid growth of oil output—still seemed good. Meanwhile, Brezhnev was already beginning to rely on oil exports to cover mounting needs for imported grain, consumer goods, and technology. The temptation must have been strong to continue thinking of the oil industry as a cash cow that would provide hard currency indefinitely to support Brezhnev's other goals.

The failure to prepare the way during the first period defined the emergency reponse of the second period, from 1977 to 1980–1981. At this point it was not merely the five-year oil target that was in danger but Brezhnev's authority as well. We have argued that Brezhnev's extreme response in 1977 became itself one of the chief sources of trouble later; but there were strong political reasons for the course he chose. Alarmed by the urgent signals from Siberia, stung by growing domestic and foreign criticism, Brezhnev needed a response that would look strong and decisive. At the same time, he attempted to safeguard his previous priorities and thus favored short-term measures designed to stave off the worst until the next supergiant could be found.

During the third period, 1980–1981, Brezhnev embraced energy even more strongly as a means of safeguarding his authority and his program. The gas bridge seemed a godsend, and Brezhnev reached for it enthusiastically; but he had no solutions to the underlying problem, which was not that of finding new supplies but of containing costs. The basis for improved industrial support and technology had not been laid, and, above all, the shift to a demand-oriented policy would have required taking risks that were beyond the experience or character of the Brezhnev leadership. Knowing that information was frequently false or biased, the leaders tended to discount it. Aware that radical new initiatives—such as a switch to conservation—were likely to be resisted in execution, the leaders hesitated to gamble on them. Understanding that the only way to get sure results quickly was to lean on the system with might and main, the leaders resorted to campaigns, which generated a pathology of their own. "The economy," Gorbachev told the Twenty-seventh Party Congress in early 1986, "out of inertia, continued to grow on an extensive basis." Not exactly: partly out of inertia, but partly also (at least where energy was concerned) out of the leaders' apparent fear that the oil situation was too urgent to tamper with. Thus they persevered in a policy whose very conception was risk-averse.

If the rhetoric of energy policy was frequently ahead of the reality, it is because learning and adaptation in the Soviet system proceed at different levels and at different speeds. The Brezhnev leadership was exposed to new ideas (some of them, indeed, not so new) and adapted its language accordingly. But to act on them required new instruments, new priorities, a new atmosphere—in a word, a new leadership.

If in the end the Brezhnev leadership quailed before the new tasks, that is not to say that it achieved nothing. On the contrary, Gorbachev's program would not stand a chance today if it were not for the contributions—both positive and negative—of the Brezhnev period. Brezhnev's policy of industrializing the countryside, however wasteful and inefficient it proved to be, has created a material basis for agricultural reform that Grobachev can now maneuver with as Kosygin could not. Gorbachev's attempts to use arms-control diplomacy to free himself to concentrate on domestic issues would not be politically feasible were it not for the strategic parity with the United States that Brezhnev bequeathed to him. Brezhnev's very mistakes, like Khrushchev's, have demonstrated the limits of the traditional command system and have gone a long way toward creating a consensus for change that did not—could not—exist in the mid-1960s. The same is true in energy policy: Brezhnev's gas bridge has provided Gorbachev with the crucial margin needed to begin a demand-oriented policy, and ten years of learning have produced a consensus in the leadership that no other course is possible. Can Gorbachev now do better?

Energy as a Reform Issue

Does fundamental improvement in Soviet policymaking, and in the energy sector in particular, require radical, systemic reform? On this point the economists are most persuasive: the command economy's distorted information, conflicting preferences, and soft constraints lead ineluctably to artificially induced scarcities. That is precisely what we have witnessed in the energy sector. If bad leadership turned scarcity into crisis during the decade from 1975 to 1985, the scarcity was built-in, both in the system as it operates today and in the physical structure it has erected over the last two generations. Therefore, in the long run, there is no alternative to systemic reform.

But this brings us back to the reformer's dilemma with which this book began. In the long run, systemic reform is essential, but it cannot be realized quickly. Therefore, the crucial question is whether there exist middle-range strategies that will ease the "crisis of effectiveness" while systemic reforms are being implemented. Specifically, the reformer must do three things: buy time, split the reform problem into manageable pieces, and simultaneously continue to build support for more radical measures. Can these conditions be met in the energy sector?

In several respects the energy sector is actually less daunting in its requirements for middle-range reform than many of the other issues the Soviet leaders are wrestling with. It does not require, on the whole, high technology. There are exceptions, to be sure, such as geophysical exploration and high-voltage transmission. But most of the energy sector's technological requirements are more humble, consisting of things like better steel for drill pipe and bits, common chemicals for drilling muds, and engines and lubricants adapted to extreme cold. Gorbachev and his colleagues vow to put Soviet industry "on the world level," but in the energy sector it would take only modest advances to bring about a world of improvement.

The energy sector's technological needs are old-fashioned in one more respect: they are not especially fast-moving, variable, or exacting. Contemporary technology can now custom-design new chemicals, materials, genetic codes, and softwares on demand and produce them quickly in limited runs for detailed local applications. This kind of "custom tech," even more than "high tech," puts the traditional Soviet system at a disadvantage. But the energy sector needs little of that; it mainly requires sturdy equipment of reliable quality, produced in large, uniform runs. Mass manufacture, not custom design, is the main key to improvement.

The same is largely true of the energy sector's products. Unlike consumer industries, which must respond to the shifting tastes of increasingly affluent and choosy Soviet buyers, the energy sector produces a relatively straightforward and stable array of wares—in fact, the more stable, the better, as far as the customers are concerned. This in turn makes progress relatively easy to monitor and price discipline simpler to apply.[59]

The energy sector's relatively modest technological requirements make it easy to turn to a wide array of international suppliers, especially in Eastern Europe. The lesson of the gas pipeline affair in the early 1980s was precisely that compressor technology was so widely available that even American control over key licenses was not enough to deny deliveries to the Soviet Union, and careful Western studies have shown that there is little energy technology for which the same cannot be said. The Soviets' worst enemy in foreign trade is their own decisionmaking

[59] One hundred percent of the output of the oil and coal industries is marketed under state contracts; the gas industry may sell up to 10 percent of its output independently.

procedures; but, as Gorbachev is already demonstrating, a "systemic" reform of the monopoly of the Ministry of Foreign Trade can proceed ahead of systemic reform of the command economy as a whole.

Economic reform becomes potentially explosive when it touches on the accursed issues of inequalities and sources of income, the organization and rights of local enterprises, and the roles of established institutions (especially the Party). But reform in the energy sector, unlike agriculture or urban services, hardly raises these questions. There are undoubtedly improvements to be made in the incentive system (such as rewarding drillers for successful finds instead of meters drilled), but the large, capital-intensive organizations that make up the energy sector have less to gain from local decisionmaking autonomy than others; moreover, there is little room for local initiative because of the high capital intensity and large unit scale of most energy investments, whether for supply or consumption. Energy distribution and marketing raise few problems of discipline. Only gasoline poses a significant black-market problem; for electricity and gas, the question hardly arises.

Reform in the energy sector is further aided by the fact that it is compatible with the major elements of the Gorbachev reform program. The leaders' modernization programs for the machinery sector, metallurgy, electronics, and automatic control systems, if even minimally successful, will ease longstanding constraints on efficiency in the energy sector. The policy of revitalizing old plants has mixed effects, since it limits the prospects for relocating energy-intensive industries closer to energy sources, but on the whole it is one of the most important keys to long-term improvement in the energy efficiency of Soviet industry.

Lastly, in the energy sector time is on Gorbachev's side. The steady evolution of the Soviet economy, slow though it may be, leads gradually to energy-saving structural changes: less metallurgy and materials processing, for example, and more manufacturing and construction; less heavy industry and more light; more services; and a slow migration of energy-intensive industries closer to their sources of supply. The inexorable rise of energy-supply costs produces a steeper and steeper gradient in favor of energy efficiency, if only the leaders will allow the signals of scarcity to be felt by consumers and give them an incentive to respond.

In sum, the energy sector suggests that in some cases reform, even substantial systemic reform, could be implemented stepwise and piecemeal, with less upheaval and less political disruption than is usually considered possible by Western analysts. To be sure, offsetting these features are the high costs, long lead times, and uncertainty characteristic of energy investments and the inertia of the existing energy structure on both the supply and the consumption sides. If Brezhnev's bad leadership turned a problem into a crisis, Gorbachev's leadership has yet to prove it can make a difference. Nevertheless, if Gorbachev can show even modest gains in energy-consumption efficiency while gradually rebalancing and modernizing the energy-extracting industries, he will succeed in avoiding the recurrent squeezes and panics of the last fifteen years, and that in turn would make it possible to start shifting investment resources.

In these respects the energy sector is representative of a broad group of basic industries, such as transportation, metallurgy, and traditional chemistry—the ones that we are quick to shrug off as smokestack industries but that are still vital to any country's industrial power. Weaknesses in precisely these industries were at the core of the Soviet economic downturn of the late 1970s and early 1980s. But they should also be the easiest to begin turning around, although the dead weight of the existing capital structure will make overall progress slow. Recent improvements in ferrous metallurgy, transportation, and oil production show that even substantial changes can come quickly.

Above all, Gorbachev must buy time. The easy answer is that the gas bridge gives him a decade. But if that remains Gorbachev's only answer, he will have a worse energy crisis in the year 2000 than any witnessed to date. There are other middle-range moves available. On the supply side, he can use joint ventures to build up the Soviet oil and gas equipment and service sectors and to improve exploration capacity (in particular by allowing Western exploration and logging teams on location). On the demand side, he must raise energy prices quickly, especially for residential heating and transportation, without waiting for expert commissions to make their reports. The big industrial enterprises will not respond to price signals in the early stages of the reform; to deal with these, he must lay aside economic principles and impose an administrative freeze on fuel allocations at their present levels, with mandatory annual reductions to follow.

Second, Gorbachev must build support for progressively more radical measures. In the energy sector, the runaway growth of investment speaks for itself. It should not be difficult to muster a consensus for any program that promises to free tens of billions of rubles for everybody else. There should be an easy constituency for raising energy prices as there is not for raising bread prices. If price reform is to bite, let it bite first in the energy sector. The leadership as a whole must be prepared to pay a price in the near term, however, as the economy adjusts to higher energy prices. Are the leaders prepared to sacrifice economic growth in the near term as the price for initial success in conservation?

The elements required for a major improvement in energy policy are now present: a new leadership, a decade of experience and learning, an arsenal of facts and options, and an ample store of negative examples. Most important, the leaders are fully aware that it is not possible to continue the traditional supply-side approach to energy and that they have no choice but to take risks to bring about change. The energy sector is a fertile and comparatively easy field for middle-range reform. But if they do not act decisively, the Soviet leaders will find that the energy sector will continue to generate crises, diverting their resources and attention from the more difficult and fundamental tasks of reform elsewhere in the economy. In that case, the most reformable sector of the system will continue to block reform elsewhere, and the country with the world's largest energy supplies will continue to be the only industrial nation still locked in an energy crisis.

EPILOGUE

Any book about Soviet politics and policy written during the Gorbachev years is out of date before it reaches the printer, and this book is no exception. On 10 June 1989, at the opening session of the new USSR Supreme Soviet, Prime Minister Nikolai I. Ryzhkov announced a drastic reorganization of the government's executive branch. He cut the number of ministries and state committees by more than half, while weakening the powers of the ones that remained. At the same time, he fired a multitude of high-level officials.

Ryzhkov's shake-up hit the energy-producing sector especially hard, sweeping off the stage many of the key players of the last two decades. The deputy prime minister in charge of the Energy Bureau, Boris Ie. Shcherbina, who was one of the earliest boosters of Siberian gas and subsequently distinguished himself as the overseer of the pipeline construction program, was abruptly retired in favor of a newcomer to the energy sector, Lev D. Riabev, formerly the minister of "medium machine-building," the wondrously named agency that makes nuclear warheads.[1] The oil and gas ministries were reunited into a single ministry for petroleum, and the former ministers for oil and gas, Vasilii A. Dinkov and Viktor S. Chernomyrdin, were likewise retired.[2] To head the new combined petroleum ministry, Ryzhkov nominated the veteran obkom first secretary for Tiumen', Gennadii P. Bogomiakov.

But in an unprecedented move, the Supreme Soviet rejected Bogomiakov, on the grounds that in his single-minded pursuit of oil and gas he had neglected the Siberian environment. This extraordinary event may or may not herald the rise of a strong and assertive legislature—the battle over that question is only beginning—but what it does show, at the very least, is the rapidly growing emotional force of the environmental issue in the minds of Soviet citizens. The environ-

[1]The Ministry of Medium Machine-building does have an indirect connection with energy, however, since it oversees the management of nuclear fuel-cycle operations for Minenergo.

[2]According to rumors in Moscow that had been circulating for months, Dinkov was in disfavor because of the recent downturn in oil production and because of the continued inefficiency of the oil industry, while Chernomyrdin was in poor health.

ment is transforming energy politics: nuclear power, oil and gas development, open-pit coal mining, and joint ventures in petrochemicals all face mounting public opposition, which is actually influencing leaders' decisions.

Industrial support for the oil and gas ministries was also affected by the shake-up. Yuri P. Batalin, the deputy prime minister for construction, who like Shcherbina had led the Soviet pipeline campaign of the early 1980s, was also dismissed. The seven ministries of the construction sector were collapsed into two. In the civilian machine-building industry, the eight former ministries were combined into four. It is not obvious that this will raise the status of the makers of oil- and gas-field equipment, but help may be on the way from another quarter: it appears that the defense industry is being enlisted to manufacture more equipment for the oil and gas industries.[3]

The reorganization of the ministry structure in the energy sector coincides with a major review of Soviet energy policy, based on the findings of an expert commission that has been at work since 1985. The experts have recommended the following changes.[4]

a major new commitment to energy conservation, beginning with sharp price increases for energy;

a reduced (though still substantial) commitment to nuclear power;

a stabilization of oil and condensate output;

a continued rapid expansion of gas output and displacement of oil by gas throughout the economy;

a radical modernization and expansion of the equipment and construction industries serving the energy sector;

a continued commitment to energy exports.

This amounts to an admission that the shift to a demand-centered policy has not yet begun and that, in effect, the last five years have been lost. Thus the latest recommendations amount to a new energy program (although its authors refer to it only as a new *redaktsiia*), with the clock reset at zero and the horizon moved back ten years to 2010. It is not known for certain how many of the expert recommendations the

[3]A possible harbinger is a recent news item that a former military plant in Nikolaev (under the new name of the Zaria Production Association) has been reassigned to manufacture 16-megawatt turbine drives for gas transmission. BBC Monitoring Service, *Summary of World Broadcasts*, Weekly Economic Report on the Soviet Union, 14 April 1989, p. 21.

[4]The supporting studies and recommendations are summarized in a special issue of *Izvestiia Akademii nauk SSR, seriia Energetika i Transport*, no. 4 (1988).

leadership has actually approved, but there is one it undoubtedly does not like at all: the price tag for this program would run to 800 billion rubles by the year 2000. The leaders want to spend less on energy, not more: they have already announced that they will cut back nonfood investment in 1989 and 1990,[5] which—taken together with environmental opposition—augurs downward pressure on energy investment in the 1990s as well.

Getting the energy program restarted while cutting back energy spending will require much more than redrawing the organization chart, and it is not clear how the latest shake-up will contribute to coping with the problems described in this book. Merging the oil and gas ministries will undoubtedly relieve some coordination problems in West Siberia, and it may help programs that have long fallen through administrative cracks, particularly the failure to recover associated gas, most of which at present is still flared off. But reorganization alone will make little difference.

The main aim of the June 1989 reorganization is to break the ministries' power to dictate to local managers, thus freeing the latter to pursue profits, to redirect investment resources, and to enter new lines of business. This is indeed one of the essential steps on the way to making managers sensitive to price signals and profit opportunities, without which energy conservation stands no chance. In the oil and gas sector, such decentralization, combined with the recent liberalization of foreign-trade policy, could also enable local oil and gas producers to make their own import decisions.[6]

In sum, depending on how it is implemented, the June reorganization could be simply another substitute for action; or, if combined with price reform and decentralization of supply, it could provide an impetus to greater efficiency on both the production and consumption sides of the energy equation. Similarly, the rise of popular environmental sentiment, depending on how the leadership chooses to respond to it, could be a valuable opportunity. In a country in which everyone complains about waste but no one has incentive to do anything about it, popular outrage over the environment could provide the extra political energy to get real conservation started. Is the Soviet energy system finally about to take a turn?

[5]Interview with former finance minister Boris I. Gostev, *Izvestiia*, 31 Mar. 1989.

[6]Starting in 1989, Glavtiumenneftegaz has been given authority to sell 20 percent of any above-plan output for hard currency, mainly to finance purchases of foreign equipment (*Summary of World Broadcasts*, 16 September 1988, p. 8.) Since at the moment the association is producing below plan, this dispensation remains theoretical, but it is at least a step in the right direction.

APPENDIX

DRILLING STATISTICS

Key to Sources

Journals

Burenie [Drilling]
Ekonomicheskaia gazeta [The economic newspaper]
Ekonomika neftianoi promyshlennosti [Economics of the oil industry]
Gazovaia promyshlennost' [The gas industry]
Geologiia nefti i gaza [The geology of oil and gas]
Neftianoe khoziaistvo SSSR [The oil industry]
Razvedka i okhrana nedr [The prospecting and conservation of minerals]

Books

Brenner	M. M. Brenner, *Ekonomika geologorazvedochnykh rabot na neft' i gaz v SSSR* [The economics of geological exploratory work on oil and gas in the USSR] [Moscow, Nedra, 1979]
Campbell	Robert W. Campbell, *Trends in the Soviet Oil and Gas Industry* (Baltimore, Johns Hopkins University Press, 1976)
Dinkov	V. A. Dinkov, *Neft' SSSR, 1917–1987* (Moscow: Nedra, 1987)
Kozorezov and Posrednikov	A. A. Kozorezov and V. K. Posrednikov, *Ekonomika poiskovo-razvedochnogo bureniia na neft' i gaz* [Economics of prospecting-exploratory drilling for oil and gas] (Moscow: Nedra, 1985)
Lee and Lecky	J. Richard Lee and James R. Lecky, "Soviet Oil Developments," in U.S. Congress, Joint Economic Committe, *Soviet Economy in a Time of Change* (Washington, D.C.: USGPO, 1979), vol. 1, pp. 581–585.
Tekhnicheshkii progress	*Tekhnicheskii progress v neftianoi promyshlennosti v desiatoi piatiletke* [Technical progress in the oil industry in the Tenth Five-Year Plan] (Moscow: Nedra, 1981)

I am grateful to Ms. Caron Cooper of the University of California, Berkeley, for her collaboration in compiling the tables in this appendix.

TABLE A.1

Oil and Gas Drilling, Exploratory and Developmental
(all performers; countrywide; millions of meters)

	Exploration	*Development*	*Total*
1970	5.15[a]	6.74[b]	11.89[b]
1971	5.25[b]	6.88[b]	12.13[b]
1972	5.14[b]	7.58[b]	12.72[b]
1973	5.22[b]	8.41[b]	13.63[b]
1974	5.36	8.89	14.25
1975	5.42[a]	9.44	14.86
1976	5.20[f]	10.63	15.83
1977	5.20[f]	11.48	16.68
1978	5.20[f]	12.52	17.72
1979	NA	14.08	NA
1980	5.89[a]	16.70	22.59
1981	6.17[a]	20.35	26.52
1982	6.17[a]	22.04	28.21
1983	6.48[a]	25.05[c]	31.53
1984	6.46[a]	26.65	33.11[d]
1985	6.77[a]	29.23	36.00[e]
1986	7.19[a]	NA	NA
1987	7.81[a]	NA	NA
1961–1965	24.7[f]	NA	NA
1966–1970	26.2[f]	30.4[f]	56.6[f]
1971–1975	26.1[f]	41.8[f]	67.9[f]
1976–1980	26.7[g]	66.0[h]	92.7
1981–1985	32.1[a]	132.3[h]	161.5[h]

NOTE: Where no source is given, the figure is derived by addition from other tables in this appendix.

[a] *Narodnoe khoziaistvo SSSR*, various years. Dinkov, p. 148, gives 29.2.

[b] Campbell, p. 17.

[c] Derived from *Geologiia nefti i gaza*, no. 4 (1985), p. 3.

[d] Review of *Soviet Oil*, no. 4 (1985), p. 43.

[e] Estimated in *Oil and Gas Journal*, 25 August 1986, p. 20.

[f] Brenner, pp. 86–89.

[g] *Ekonomicheskaia gazeta*, no. 5 (1983), p. 1.

[h] Dinkov, p. 148. The discrepancy in the totals arises from the fact that Dinkov gives only 29.2 for exploratory in 1981–1985.

TABLE A.2
Total Developmental and Exploratory Drilling for Oil and Gas by Ministry
(millions of meters)

	MNP	*MGP*	*Mingeo*	*Total Drilling*
1970	9.03	0.82	2.06	11.89
1971	9.25	NA	NA	12.13
1972	9.90	NA	NA	12.70
1973	10.55	NA	NA	13.63
1974	10.98	NA	NA	14.26
1975	11.66	1.15	2.37	14.84
1976	12.07	1.55	2.30	15.92
1977	12.80	1.63	2.65	16.68
1978	13.68	NA	NA	NA
1979	15.17	NA	NA	NA
1980	18.00	1.55	3.12	22.63
1981	21.60	1.73	3.25	26.52
1982	23.32	1.59	3.30	28.21
1983	25.70	2.25	3.58	31.53
1984	27.40	2.05	3.66	33.11
1985	29.7	NA	3.98	36.58
1986	34	NA	4.29	NA
1987	38.0	NA	4.78	NA
1988	41.6			
1971–1975	52.30	NA	10.70	67.90
1976–1980	71.00	8.12	NA	NA
1981–1985	143.8	NA	17.8	NA

SOURCES: See tables A.3 and A.5.

TABLE A.3

Oil and Gas Drilling by MNP

(millions of meters)

	Exploration	*Development*	*Total*
1970	2.83[a]	6.20[b]	9.03[a]
1971	2.95[a]	6.30[a]	9.25[a]
1972	2.90[a]	7.00[a]	9.90[a]
1973	2.87[a]	7.68[a]	10.55[a]
1974	2.92[a]	8.06[a]	10.98[a]
1975	2.73[a]	8.93[c]	11.66[a]
1976	2.55[a]	9.52[a]	12.07[a]
1977	2.40[s]	10.40[d]	12.80
1978	2.23[e]	11.45[e]	13.68[e]
1979	2.17[e]	13.00[e]	15.17[e]
1980	2.32[f]	15.80[p]	18.00[h]
1981	2.46[f]	19.14[h]	21.60[h]
1982	2.44[f]	20.88	23.32[i]
1983	NA	NA	25.70[k]
1984	NA	NA	27.40[k]
1985	NA	NA	29.7[r]
1986	NA	NA	34[l]
1987	NA		38.0[m]
1988			41.6[r]
1961–1965	16.30[n]	NA	NA
1966–1970	15.40[n]	29.56[a]	44.71[a]
1971–1975	14.50[n]	37.8	52.3
1976–1980	11.27	65[p]	71.0[o]
1981–1985	13.7[p]	130.1[p]	143.8[p]

[a] *Burenie*, no. 9 (1977), p. 4.
[b] *Burenie*, no. 9 (1977), p. 4; but Dinkov says 6.70.
[c] *Burenie*, no. 9 (1977), p. 4; but Dinkov says 8.80.
[d] Derived from *Neftianoe khoziaistvo*, no. 3 (1979), p. 3.
[e] *Tekhnicheskii progress*, p. 25.
[f] Kozorezov and Posrednikov, p. 8.
[g] Dinkov says 15.80.
[h] *Neftianoe khoziaistvo*, no. 3 (1982), p. 3.
[i] *Neftianoe khoziaistvo*, no. 3 (1983), p. 3.
[j] *Neftianoe khoziaistvo*, no. 4 (1981), p. 4.
[k] *Neftianoe khoziaistvo*, no. 2 (1985), p. 11.
[l] *PlanEcon Long-Term Energy Outlook*, p. 67.
[m] *Neftianoe khoziaistvo*, no. 3 (1988), p. 2.
[n] Brenner, p. 93.
[o] *Neftianoe khoziaistvo*, no. 12 (1981), p. 3.
[p] Dinkov, p. 148.
[r] *Neftianik*, no. 3 (1989), p. 4.
[s] Lee and Lecky.

TABLE A.4
Oil and Gas Drilling by MGP
(millions of meters)

	Exploration	*Development*	*Total*
1970	0.28[a]	0.54	0.82
1971	NA	0.58	NA
1972	NA	0.58	NA
1973	NA	0.73	NA
1974	NA	0.83	NA
1975	0.33[a]	0.82[a]	1.15[a]
1976	0.52[a]	1.03[a]	1.55[a]
1977	0.55[a]	1.08[a]	1.63[a]
1978	0.62[a]	1.07[a]	1.69[a]
1979	0.6[a]	1.08[a]	1.68[a]
1980	0.53[a]	1.02[a]	1.55[a]
1981	0.52[a]	1.21[a]	1.73[a]
1982	0.50	1.09	1.59
1983	NA	NA	2.25
1984	NA	NA	2.05[b]
1985	NA	NA	NA
1986	NA	NA	NA
1961–1965	0.04[c]	NA	NA
1966–1970	0.14[c]	NA	NA
1971–1975	0.88[c]	NA	NA
1976–1980	2.83[d]	5.29[d]	8.12[d]
1981–1985	3.15[e]	7.25[e]	10.40[e]

[a] *Ekonomika neftianoi promyshlennosti*, no. 4 (1983), and *Gazovaia promyshlennost'*, no. 10 (1981), p. 3.

[b] Derived from *Gazovaia promyshlennost'*, no. 7 (1985).

[c] Brenner, p. 93.

[d] *Gazovaia promyshlennost'*, no. 10 (1981), p. 3.

[e] Plan figures.

TABLE A.5

Exploratory Drilling for Oil and Gas by Ministry
(millions of meters)

	MNP	*MGP*	*Mingeo*	*Total Exploration*
1970	2.83	0.28	2.06[a]	5.15
1971	2.95	NA	NA	5.25
1972	2.90	NA	NA	5.14
1973	2.87	NA	NA	5.22
1974	2.92	NA	NA	5.36
1975	2.73[a]	0.33	2.37	5.42
1976	2.55	0.52	2.30[b]	5.29
1977	2.00	0.55	2.65	5.20
1978	2.23	NA	NA	NA
1979	2.17	NA	NA	NA
1980	2.32	0.53	3.12[a]	5.89
1981	2.46	0.52	3.25[a]	6.17
1982	2.44	0.50	3.30[a]	6.17
1983	NA	NA	3.58[a]	6.48
1984	NA	NA	3.66[a]	6.46
1985	NA	NA	3.98[a]	6.77
1986	NA	NA	4.29[a]	7.19
1987			4.78[a]	7.81
1961–1965	16.34	0.04	8.26[c]	24.70
1966–1970	15.40	0.14	10.70[c]	26.20
1971–1975	14.50	0.88	10.70[c]	26.20
1976–1980	11.27	2.83	NA	26.70
1981–1985	13.7	NA	17.8[d]	32.1

SOURCES: For total exploration, see table A.1.

[a] *Narodnoe khoziastvo SSSR*, various years.

[b] Derived from *Razvedka i okhrana nedr*, no. 4 (1979), p. 1.

[c] Brenner, p. 93.

[d] Dinkov, p. 148, says 14.2.

INDEX

Made in the USA
Columbia, SC
18 March 2022

57837844R00212